BOSNIA'S PARALYSE

D1458399

CHRISTOPHER BENNETT

Bosnia's Paralysed Peace

HURST & COMPANY, LONDON

First published in the United Kingdom in 2016 by
C. Hurst & Co. (Publishers) Ltd.,
41 Great Russell Street, London, WC1B 3PL
© Christopher Bennett, 2016
All rights reserved.
Printed in India

A Cataloguing-in-Publication data record for this book
is available from the British Library.

978-1-84904-054-9 *paperback*

978-1-84904-053-2 *hardback*

This book is printed using paper from registered sustainable
and managed sources.

www.hurstpublishers.com

In memory of David Bennett, scholar, gentleman and loving father

CONTENTS

CONTENTS

ACKNOWLEDGEMENTS

I wish my father were alive today to see this book in print. I returned to England from Bosnia when he unexpectedly fell ill, hoping he would recover and that the two of us would be able to work side by side on our respective book projects. Sadly, he did not recover. Before his untimely death, he had commented faithfully on everything I had written, as he always did, helping make the book a better and easier read. He died on the day he had been scheduled to give a lecture at a conference of the Linguistic Association of Canada and the United States in New York. I completed this book on his computer and had the impression that he was helping along the way.

My mother is the reason for my interest in Bosnia. She was born and brought up in Slovenia when Slovenia and Bosnia were both part of Yugoslavia. As a child, I visited Yugoslavia with my family most years. We generally spent our vacations in Slovenia and on the Croatian coast. In 1981, however, my parents took my brothers and me on the journey that my mother had taken with her class the year she finished school. This brought in many places of significance to the partisans' struggle in the Second World War. In this way, we travelled across Bosnia and visited places such as Jajce, the town in which the Socialist Federal Republic of Yugoslavia was created in 1943, and Tjentište, site of the 1943 Battle of Sutjeska, as well as Sarajevo. I do not remember quenching my thirst at the Sebilj fountain, but presume I must have, as, according to local legend, anyone who drinks this water will return.

ACKNOWLEDGEMENTS

The US Institute of Peace and the Wilson Center believed in the project sufficiently to award me fellowships to carry out research, for which I am grateful, even though I was unable to avail myself of either as a result of other commitments. I am also grateful to Dubioza kolektiv, a talented group of musicians, commentators and activists, for allowing me to use the design of their *Apsurdistan* album sleeve on my front cover.

Many people have helped me to a better understanding of the former Yugoslavia in general and Bosnia in particular—too many to acknowledge individually. The book could not, however, have been written in the way it has without the input of certain individuals, above all colleagues, who merit special acknowledgement. At the International Crisis Group, Hrair Balian, Sandy Coliver and John Fawcett all helped improve my understanding of complex issues related to Bosnia, human rights and peace-building. At both the International Crisis Group and the European Stability Initiative, Gerald Knaus was an inspiring counterfoil with whom I was able to work and rework issues. Ben Reilly, now dean of the Sir Walter Murdoch School of Public Policy and International Affairs at Murdoch University in Western Australia, helped me to understand the power of electoral systems in divided societies. Daniel Lindvall, then of Södertörn University, Sweden, provided me with relevant and extremely informative sections of his 2009 doctoral thesis on police reform. And Roland Kostić of Uppsala University, Sweden, shared with me the results of in-depth opinion polling contained in his 2007 doctoral thesis.

I have benefitted greatly from the expertise and institutional memory of many colleagues at the Office of the High Representative (OHR) over many years. Kevin Sullivan, a former OHR colleague and gifted writer, read the book chapter by chapter and greatly improved both style and content. Mark Wheeler, both a former OHR colleague and the professor who nearly thirty years ago taught me Yugoslav history at London University, helped with advice on both style and content, as well as access to his remarkable library of books on both Bosnia and the former Yugoslavia. James Lyon, another former OHR colleague, was supportive throughout the writing process, as well as a fountain of insight, and provided detailed comments on the first

ACKNOWLEDGEMENTS

three chapters. Bob Donia, one of the finest historians of Bosnia, provided extremely insightful feedback on the first seven chapters. Liam Hunt, a retired professor from St. Lawrence University in New York, cast his critical eye over the final manuscript. Sebastian Ballard, a cartographer from Hampshire, drew the map. Kathryne Bomberger, director-general of the International Commission on Missing Persons, enabled me to finish the book by providing flexible employment. Kenneth Morrison of De Montfort University, Leicester, helped me over the finishing line. Michael Dwyer, my publisher, stuck with me. And my wife Sandrine Bardouil, my daughter Manon and my son Pierre have shared the entire writing experience, proofreading text, providing constructive suggestions, and keeping me going throughout.

In attempting to synthesise a vast amount of material in a relatively small number of words, there may be errors of omission, interpretation or fact. For this, I alone am responsible.

ABBREVIATIONS

BiH	Bosna i Hercegovina (Bosnia and Herzegovina)
Bosnia	Bosnia and Herzegovina
CAFAO	Customs and Fiscal Assistance Office
CEC	Central Election Commission
CRA	Communications Regulatory Agency
CSCE	Conference on Security and Co-operation in Europe
DAP	Demokratska alijansa za promjene (Democratic Alliance for Change)
DF	Demokratska fronta (Democratic Front)
DNS	Demokratski narodni savez (Democratic People's Alliance)
EC	European Commission
EC	European Community
ECHR	European Convention on Human Rights
ECtHR	European Court of Human Rights
ECMM	European Community Monitoring Mission
EU	European Union
EUAM	European Union Administration of Mostar
EUFOR	European Union Force
EUPM	European Union Police Mission
EUSR	European Union Special Representative
HDZ	Hrvatska demokratska zajednica (Croat Democratic Union)
HDZ 1990	Hrvatska demokratska zajednica 1990 (Croat Democratic Union 1990)

ABBREVIATIONS

HDZ BiH	Hrvatska demokratska zajednica Bosne i Hercegovine (Croat Democratic Union Bosnia and Herzegovina)
HJPC	High Judicial and Prosecutorial Council
HNS	Hrvatski narodni sabor (Croat People's Assembly)
HNZ	Hrvatska narodna zajednica (Croat National Union)
HSP	Hrvatska stranka prava (Croat Party of Rights)
HSS	Hrvatska seljačka stranka (Croatian Peasant Party)
HVO	Hrvatsko vijeće obrane (Croat Defence Council)
ICFY	International Conference on the Former Yugoslavia
ICG	International Crisis Group
ICJ	International Court of Justice
ICMP	International Commission on Missing Persons
ICTY	International Criminal Tribunal for the former Yugoslavia
IFOR	Implementation Force
IMC	Independent Media Commission
IMF	International Monetary Fund
IPA	Instrument for Pre-Accession Assistance
IPTF	International Police Task Force
ITA	Indirect Taxation Authority
JMO	Jugoslovenska muslimanska organizacija (Yugoslav Muslim Organization)
JNA	Jugoslovenska narodna armija (Yugoslav National Army)
JRZ	Jugoslovenska radikalna zajednica (Yugoslav Radical Union)
KNS	Koalicija narodnog sporazuma (Coalition of National Agreement)
MIP	Mission Implementation Plan
MNO	Muslimanska narodna organizacija (Muslim National Organisation)
NATO	North Atlantic Treaty Organisation
NDH	Nezavisna država Hrvatska (Independent State of Croatia)
NSRzB	Narodna stranka Radom za boljitak (People's Party for Work and Betterment)
OHR	Office of the High Representative

ABBREVIATIONS

OIC	Organisation of Islamic Cooperation
OSA-OBA	Obavještajna i sigurnosna agencija/Obavještajna i bezbjednosna agencija (Intelligence-Security Agency)
OSCE	Organization for Security and Co-operation in Europe
PBS	Public broadcasting system
PDP	Partija demokratskog progresa (Party of Democratic Progress)
PEC	Provisional Election Commission
PIC	Peace Implementation Council
R2P	Responsibility to Protect
RDC	Research and Documentation Centre
RRF	Rapid Reaction Force
RRTF	Return and Reconstruction Task Force
RSK	Republika Srpska Krajina (Republic of Serb Krajina)
RTV	Radio-Televizija
SAA	Stabilisation and Association Agreement
SBB	Savez za bolju budučnost (Union for a Better Future)
SBiH	Stranka za Bosnu i Hercegovinu (Party for Bosnia)
SBP	State Border Police
SBS	State Border Service
SDA	Stranka demokratske akcije (Party of Democratic Action)
SDP	Socijaldemokratska partija (Social Democratic Party)
SDP	Stranka demokratskih promjena (Party of Democratic Change)
SDS	Srpska demokratska stranka (Serb Democratic Party)
SFOR	Stabilisation Force
SGV	Srpsko građansko vijeće (Serb Civic Council)
SIPA	State Information/Investigation and Protection Agency
SK-SDP	Savez komunista-Socijalistička demokratska partija (League of Communists-Social Democratic Party)
SNSD	Stranka/Savez nezavisnih socijaldemokrata (Party/Alliance of Independent Social Democrats)

ABBREVIATIONS

SNO	Srpska narodna organizacija (Serb National Organisation)
SP	Socijalistička partija (Socialist Party)
SPS	Socijalistička partija Srbije (Socialist Party of Serbia)
SRS	Srpska radikalna stranka (Serb Radical Party)
SRSJ	Savez reformskih snaga Jugoslavije (League of Reform Forces of Yugoslavia)
SRT	Srpska Radio-Televizija (Srpska Radio-Television)
UBSD	Unija Bosansko-Hercegovačkih socijaldemokrata (Union of Bosnian and Herzegovinian Social Democrats)
UJDI	Udruženje za jugoslovensku demokratsku inicijativu (Association for a Yugoslav Democratic Initiative)
UK	United Kingdom
UN	United Nations
UNDP	United Nations Development Programme
UNHCR	United Nations High Commissioner for Refugees
UNPROFOR	United Nations Protection Force
UNTAES	United Nations Transitional Administration of Eastern Slavonia
US	United States
VRS	Vojska Republike Srpske (Army of Republika Srpska)
ZL	Združena lista (Joint List)

GUIDE TO PRONUNCIATION

In Serbo-Bosno-Croat,

c is pronounced 'ts' as in 'mats'
č is 'ch' as in 'chore'
ć is 'tj' or 'tu' as in the British-English pronunciation of 'tune'
dž is 'dg' as in 'edge'
d is 'g' as in 'germ'
j is 'y' as in 'yes'
lj is 'liyuh' like the middle sound of 'million'
nj is 'ny' as in 'canyon'
š is 'sh' as in 'shore'
ž is like the 's' sound in 'pleasure'

All vowels are short. Other letters are pronounced much as in English. Short words are stressed on the first syllable and longer words are generally stressed on the third syllable from the end.

PREFACE

'If you always do what you've always done, you'll always get what you've always got.'

Henry Ford

Probably the best commentaries on life in Bosnia over the past decade can be found in the songs of Dubioza kolektiv (DK), the country's most popular contemporary band with a committed following throughout the former Yugoslavia. DK, who formed in 2004, sing with bitter irony and caustic humour of the problems of Bosnian society, of corruption, of injustice and of the scourge of nationalism. In an attempt to reach out to a wider audience, the band perform not only in their mother tongue, but also in deliberately and heavily accented English. The two latest albums, aptly entitled *Wild Wild East* and *Apsurdistan*, give musical expression to the frustrations, struggles and aspirations of ordinary Bosnians, two decades after the peace accord negotiated in Dayton, Ohio, ended Europe's bloodiest conflict since the Second World War.

Apsurdistan is, sadly, a fitting name for Bosnia in 2016. The formula of one country, two entities and three constituent peoples at the heart of the Dayton Peace Agreement was not a blueprint for resolving or even managing conflict. It was simply the compromise the presidents of Bosnia, Croatia and Serbia—Alija Izetbegović, Franjo Tuđman and Slobodan Milošević—and their negotiating teams could agree on in November 1995 at the Wright-Patterson Air Force Base, after more than three-and-a-half years of fighting. It achieved what its principal architect, US Assistant Secretary of State Richard Holbrooke, set out to do, namely 'to end a war' (the title of his subsequent book on Bosnia). But it was never meant to be a long-term solution. It was a temporary settlement that would need to be reformed and revised. Yet it remains in place—even as Bosnia decays.

On many levels, the peace process resembles *Groundhog Day*, the 1993 comedy starring Bill Murray and Andie MacDowell, in which Murray's character, Phil Connors, is forced to relive the same twenty-four hours over and over again. During a hedonistic phase early in the film, Connors, a shallow and arrogant misogynist, appears to enjoy himself greatly. But as time drags on and he realises he is trapped in a time loop, he becomes increasingly depressed and seeks relief in suicide—to no avail. Bosnia, too, is unable to move on. The issue of relations among Bosniaks, Croats and Serbs crowds out all others. Many of the same politicians continue to use the same provocative, insensitive and irresponsible rhetoric. Political processes are deadlocked. And the country is in a state of political, social and economic paralysis.

As Bosnians went to the polls in October 2014 in their country's seventh post-war general elections, the sense of despair was palpable. According to the 'Global States of Mind 2014' study published by Gallup the same month, Bosnia's government was the least popular in the world, with an approval rating of just 8 per cent. Nevertheless, most Bosnians opted to re-elect the same ethno-national parties and politicians who had presided over their country's decay. While most would have preferred to see change, few believed they had the luxury to vote for a non-nationalist alternative. The logic was the same as in every preceding election, serving to perpetuate the cycle of fear, insecurity and loathing the country had been stuck in since the first multi-party elections in 1990 heralded the onset of zero-sum politics.

Peace processes are invariably complex and fraught with pitfalls. Indeed, many unravel within just a few years. The fighting that erupted in Bosnia in April 1992 rapidly degenerated into a war of attrition for ethno-national survival. In the wake of such a conflict, ethno-national identity is far more salient than it would have been in other circumstances. Moreover, it will remain the key mobilising factor as long as group members and elites continue to feel that their identities are threatened. The war had not run its course when it ended. Without external intervention, it would almost certainly have continued for some time, generating further casualties and refugees with the risk of regional contagion and other, unforeseen consequences.

No matter how grim today's situation may appear, it is incomparably better than it would have been had the war not been brought to an end. International intervention changed the course of Bosnia's future and, although belated, was sufficiently robust to create the preconditions for a process that held out the prospect of lasting peace. Moreover, the peace process has been well resourced by a broad coalition of countries and international organisations and guaranteed by an international peacekeeping force. However, time and money have failed to heal Bosnia's wounds. Despite unprecedented international investment and attention, the country has failed to evolve into a self-sustaining and stable democracy. Moreover, the situation is deteriorating at an accelerating pace, a fatalistic cynicism appears to have taken root, and much of what was achieved earlier in the peace process now appears to be at risk.

The peace process can be divided into two phases. The first, which lasted for roughly the first decade, was when the Office of the High Representative (OHR) drove peace implementation forward and oversaw reform processes designed to turn Bosnia into a functioning state. Vast resources were pumped in and the peace process appeared to be going well. The second phase began with the downsizing of the OHR at the end of 2005 and is ongoing. The OHR stepped back in favour of a transition to local ownership, in the expectation that the domestic authorities could take the peace process forward with support from the European Union. This has not happened. Instead, as the international community has reduced its presence and involvement in the country, conditions have deteriorated, irredentist agendas have resurfaced and the outlook has become increasingly negative.

Bosnia's trajectory since 2006 has been consistently downwards, with the pace of descent accelerating every year. The international community has operated on the premise that the prospect of European integration is sufficient to transform Bosnia into a self-sustaining and stable democracy. International officials repeat the mantra that there is no alternative to Bosnia's European path, as if this will become a self-fulfilling prophecy, despite nearly a decade of evidence to the contrary. Meanwhile, Bosnia's ethno-national elites continue to pursue the same goals they did in the war, albeit using different tactics.

The discrepancy between international policy-making and Bosnia's reality is not new. It has plagued peace-building efforts since before the outbreak of fighting. The repeated refusal to deal with the conflict on its merits has contributed to policies that treat the symptoms, rather than addressing the underlying causes. During the war, humanitarian aid helped keep people alive, but this was no substitute for the decisive military intervention that eventually came in 1995, and which was required to end the fighting. Similarly, in the course of the peace process, the international community has been extremely busy overseeing implementation of a vast number of projects, but it has not dared open up the settlement so as to address the causes of instability. International decision-makers appear to prefer avoiding difficult courses of action and the risks associated with them until all other options have been exhausted.

Having reported on the first fourteen months of the Wars of Yugoslav Dissolution and then written a book on Yugoslavia's disintegration, I returned to Bosnia shortly after the Dayton Peace Agreement came into force to help set up the first field mission of the International Crisis Group. In this way, I was one of the first people to travel the length and breadth of Bosnia as soon as this became possible, analysing the situation on the ground and focussing in particular on the construction of a political system. It rapidly became clear that organising elections so soon after the end of hostilities was detrimental to the longer-term prospects of peace. Although my colleagues and I campaigned against holding premature elections, these polls, nevertheless, took place. And although we catalogued the many abuses involved and even managed to prove a turnout of more than 100 per cent, the results were recognised, effectively cementing a system of zero-sum politics.

The ruling ethno-national parties had not needed to resort to fraud to win the elections, but probably decided it was not worth running even the smallest risk of an upset. They were doubtless also confident that there would be no negative consequences (for them at least), given the apparently overwhelming desire in key capitals for a poll to take place. And they were correct in their assessment. There were no consequences, just a certain amount of embarrassment among those international officials determined to declare the elections a triumph of democracy, irrespective of evidence to the contrary. However, the real problem was not fraud but the electoral system, and the incentives contained within it. While elections and democracy were being presented as a panacea for Bosnia's many ills, the electoral system appeared to be exacerbating conflict, rather than mitigating it. At the time, large numbers of academics and graduate students were carrying out field research in Bosnia, many of whom came by my office. One visitor lent me a copy of *Ethnic Groups in Conflict* (Berkley: University of California Press, 1985) by Donald L. Horowitz, a renowned US political scientist specialising in ethno-national conflict. Finding important insights that seemed to apply to the situation in Bosnia, I began systematically reading the political science literature on democracy in divided societies.

Having determined that the existing electoral system was flawed and that it would only lead to paralysis or worse, I set about designing a more appropriate system, tailoring academic theory and electoral practice in other multi-ethnic states to Bosnia's circumstances. This led, among other things, to the publication in March 1998 of a discussion paper on electoral reform. I naïvely hoped that it might influence the Organization for Security and Co-operation in Europe (OSCE) in the run-up to the September 1998 elections. It did not. Most OSCE officials appeared to believe that Bosnians just needed to 'learn democracy', that this was a single, linear process and that even flawed elections were better than no elections. My proposals, nevertheless, generated interest among Bosnians. The paper was widely distributed in the local language in urban centres throughout the country via an association of non-governmental organisations eager to stimulate discussion on the matter; and a steady stream of Bosnians visited my office to discuss the possibilities.

PREFACE

I left Bosnia at the end of 1998 and returned seven-and-a-half years later as communications director of the Office of the High Representative (OHR) and EU Special Representative (EUSR). I found a country that looked physically much better, but that had failed to move on politically. Indeed, the political atmosphere appeared to me worse in June 2006 than it had been at the end of 1998. Some people like to believe that time heals. In reality, however, open wounds fester. Despite the enormous efforts and best intentions of large numbers of internationals who had come to work on Bosnia's reconstruction, the country had not broken decisively with its past. Although the international community had been able to give the impression that progress was being made—by intervening on a regular basis, imposing legislation and removing recalcitrant individuals—the shift to local ownership in 2006 laid bare the reality. International policy had been akin to pushing a square peg into a round hole.

Had international strategy been successful, the 'pull of Brussels' was supposed to replace the 'push of Dayton'. This was to be manifested in closure of the OHR, including the relinquishment of the high representative's executive powers, and its replacement with an operation headed by an EU special representative, equipped with an advisory mandate. I drafted the June 2006 Peace Implementation Council communiqué heralding OHR closure at the end of June 2007 after a review in early 2007 'taking into account the overall situation in Bosnia and the region'. And then in February 2007 I drafted the communiqué reversing the provisional decision to close the OHR. The decision was reversed because transition had failed in the course of 2006. The risks of proceeding were too great, given the deterioration in the political climate. And yet there was no revision of international strategy. Instead, the issue became one of the timing of the transition, not of the policy itself. The consequence has been an obsession with the structure of the international presence in Bosnia, not the situation on the ground. While the peace process has been unravelling, the international community has debated how to cut its own capabilities.

Giving up executive powers and closing the OHR has been the strategic priority of the European Commission and a handful of EU member states for many years. The rationale behind this goal has been the desire to shift responsibility for the peace process from the international community to the domestic authorities. Only once the international community has given up executive powers, it has been argued, will local leaders take responsibility for the future of their country. This might be a solution if Bosnia had a functioning political system and if the obstacle to its development were the international presence. However, the problem is and always has been Bosnia's dysfunctional politics. The OHR is certainly part of Bosnia's dysfunctional political scene, but Bosnia's domestic political system has already disintegrated into violence once and could do so again in the absence of the mandate of the high representative. No other mechanism obliges the entities to participate in the state institutions holding the country together. While the regional situation is not as toxic today as it was in 1992 or up until 2000, the possibility of renewed hostilities cannot be ruled out.

Even if things were going well in Bosnia, I believe that the international community should retain executive powers, as it did in Germany following the Second World War, as a long-term insurance policy against the possibility of a resurgence of extremist politics. Indeed, it was only in March 1991, more than five months after German reunification, that the Allies finally relinquished executive powers established over forty-five years earlier. The fact that West Germany was not fully sovereign did not prevent the country from joining first NATO and then the European Economic Community, or from serving terms on the UN Security Council. Although the Bosnian War is not comparable to the Second World War in scale, it was, nevertheless, of sufficient magnitude to merit the long-term retention of whatever safeguards might help prevent its repetition.

As the inconsistencies in the peace accord and mistakes of peace implementation come back to haunt the peace process, pressure will increase to change the Dayton settlement. Indeed, domestic actors have been marking out diametrically opposed positions for the past few years in preparation for that day. But in the absence of consensus on an alternative model, the country will remain trapped in an unworkable framework and the political environment, which

PREFACE

has been disintegrating ever since the international community
began loosening its control, will continue to get worse.

Bosnia must move beyond zero-sum politics if it is to make
progress. There is an alternative to paralysis, but getting there
requires a paradigm shift. This requires examining how democracy
works in a multi-ethnic state, designing a system tailored to Bosnia's
circumstances and then overseeing its adoption and implementation. It also requires re-examining Bosnia's relationship with its
neighbours and developing mechanisms for them to forge positive-
sum relations and come to terms with their collective past.
Moreover, it requires developing new international approaches and
mechanisms to support Bosnia's evolution. The starting point is to
recognise the failure of international strategy to date.

Discussion of the complexity of democratic governance in
divided societies is almost as old as liberal political thinking.
Writing in the nineteenth century, John Stuart Mill was extremely
pessimistic about the capacity of what he called 'pluralistic societies'
for representative government, a pessimism that has frequently
proven justified. To be sure, the debate has evolved greatly in the
intervening period. Political scientists have developed a series of
models for democratic co-operation in divided societies, based on
empirical evidence that was not available to Mill. But while it may
in theory be possible to construct systems to balance the interests of
different peoples sharing the same territory, all too often the system
that is chosen fails to provide ethno-national security.

If the peace process is examined through the prism of ethno-
national security, it is possible to rationalise political behaviour that
has often perplexed the international community, as well as to
predict attitudes, likely reactions and trends. While international
officials wish to see all Bosnians join together in a common
European cause, Croats and Serbs are, above all, fearful of the
prospect of domination by or assimilation among Bosniaks. In
Bosnia's ethno-democracy, ethno-national security is achieved via
the ethno-national rule of one constituent people over specific
territory at the expense of the country's two other constituent
peoples, as well as over Bosnians who are not Bosniaks, Croats or
Serbs. The consequence is a system of institutionalised discrimination
at the local level throughout the country.

PREFACE

The current settlement—requiring grand coalitions involving representatives of all peoples, the need for consensus in decision-making and proportional representation—corresponds to what political scientists call 'consociationalism'. Even advocates of this approach recognise that it will not work in the absence of over-arching loyalties to the state and a tradition of elite accommodation, both of which are missing in Bosnia.

It is, of course, easy to say that Bosnia is dysfunctional and that the peace process has failed. It is far more difficult to propose an alternative. That is what I explore in the penultimate chapter, 'Changing the logic of Bosnian politics'. My approach has been inspired by the political philosophy of John Rawls, as set out in his *Theory of Justice* (Cambridge, MA: Belknap Press, 1971). I have aimed to devise a system that is fair to every Bosnian, irrespective of ethno-national origin. I have also drawn on the writing of political scientists such as Donald L. Horowitz who seek to shift the focus of politics away from ethno-national identity towards less volatile issues, by using institutions and, in particular, the electoral system to foster inter-ethnic co-operation. This is often referred to as 'centripetalism', since the objective is to draw the electorate towards shared interests in the political centre-ground. I have pieced the elements of such a system together from electoral practice in various countries and adapted them to the Bosnian context. These proposals are designed to ensure ethno-national security for all Bosnians; provide incentives for conciliation by obliging politicians and political parties to seek support from peoples other than their own; give Bosnians a chance to vote on issues, not simply according to their ethno-national identity; facilitate stable and efficient government; and, with time, build a pluralistic party system.

My aim in writing the book has been to draw attention to the problems in Bosnia, including the danger of further hostilities; to present an analysis of the Bosnian Question over the centuries; to examine Bosnia's disintegration and war; to present a comprehensive analysis of the peace process, including successes as well as failures; to highlight the potential dangers of democracy in multi-ethnic states, including questioning the legitimacy of elected leaders who rule exclusively in the interest of one of the country's

PREFACE

communities as opposed to the entire electorate; to weave into the narrative political science theory on managing deep-rooted conflict; and to demonstrate that there are alternative and better ways to balance the interests of Bosnia's communities and citizens.

The proposals in this book have been formulated, above all, to generate discussion on how to reform the Dayton settlement, since there has been a dearth of ideas on this issue. Even if policy-makers reject every proposal, they could and should use the analysis of the past twenty-five years to develop fresh approaches, rather than sticking with policies that already failed a decade ago. I hope, therefore, that the book can mark the beginning of a third, 'self-improvement' phase to the peace process, as in *Groundhog Day*, so that eventually it is possible for Bosnia to cease being *Apsurdistan* and to begin to offer a promising future to all its citizens.

Having lived in Mostar for two years, I am very aware that the name of the country is Bosnia and Herzegovina and not just Bosnia. I have, nevertheless, used the journalistic shorthand for the sake of simplicity. When I write Bosnia, I mean Bosnia and Herzegovina and when I write Bosnians, I mean Bosnians and Herzegovinians. I apologise to my Herzegovinian friends for this usage, which is geographically inaccurate, but more convenient for readers. I write of 'Muslims' up until September 1993 and 'Bosniaks' after that point. This is because the Second Bosniak Congress decided to reintroduce the term 'Bosniak' in that month to describe this community.

Sarajevo   Christopher Bennett
April 2016

Post-Dayton Bosnia

1

INTRODUCTION

'Consolidating democracy is never easy. It requires skilled leadership, an active civil society, functioning political institutions, and—most importantly—a significant degree of time. These are scarce commodities in even the most benevolent transition to democracy. In a post-conflict scenario, however, the challenges are multiplied many times over. Deep-rooted conflicts impact negatively on almost every area of political and social relations. Civil society is often weak or highly partisanized or both; leaders and local elites are usually the very people who have until recently been engaged in the conflict itself; the economy will have been severely damaged; and the basic institutions of government have either ceased to function or face severe crises of legitimacy. Under such conditions, attempts to reconstruct a sustainable democracy face huge obstacles. It is not surprising, therefore, that the record of promoting democracy in such cases includes many failures and relatively few unambiguous successes.'

Peter Harris and Ben Reilly[1]

Deep-rooted conflict

Because of their complexity, peace processes often unravel within a few years. The greatest problem is usually the absence of longer-term investment to maintain momentum and overcome obstacles that inevitably arise. This has not been the case in Bosnia, where the peace process that began at the end of 1995 has been well resourced by a broad coalition of interested countries and international organisations and effectively policed by an international peacekeeping force. As a result, the country rarely features in news bulletins or newspaper articles in international media today, in contrast to the saturation coverage it received during the 1992–95 war. This does not mean that Bosnia has succeeded in leaving the past behind. Despite international investment and attention on an unprecedented scale, including the carrot of eventual membership in the European Union and NATO, the country has failed to evolve into a self-sustaining and stable democracy. While neighbouring countries appear to have embraced Euro-Atlantic integration as a means to reform, modernise and move forward, Bosnia remains mired in zero-sum politics, often described as 'the continuation of war by other means', which manifests itself in provocative rhetoric, institutional paralysis and stagnation. Moreover, the situation is deteriorating at an ever-accelerating pace; a fatalistic cynicism appears to have taken root; and much of what may have been achieved earlier in the peace process today seems to be at risk.

The Bosnian conflict, which erupted in war in April 1992 and lasted for the best part of four years, is clearly deep-rooted. In the wake of extensive reporting, terms such as *etničko čišćenje* (ethnic cleansing) passed from the local language into English and other languages to encapsulate the brutality of a war in which the principal aim appeared to be to clear territory of rival communities and erase all trace of their culture. The campaign of atrocities to 'cleanse' territory that so shocked international opinion in the 1990s is not, however, unique to Bosnia but a characteristic of identity-related conflict. It is this feature that makes the Bosnian conflict and identity-related conflicts in general so emotionally charged and difficult to manage. Indeed, the issues involved go to the heart of what gives people a sense of themselves.

The Bosnian Question is about relations among three peoples—Bosniaks, Croats and Serbs—with three distinct ethno-national identities emanating from allegiance to three different faiths, who have lived together in Bosnia and the wider region for centuries. The nature of the relationship among the three peoples has changed over the years and has depended on the political systems in which they lived. Each has, at one time or another, been privileged over the other two. The key determinant in this relationship has usually been external, namely the dominant force in the political entity to which they belonged at the time. In addition to the internal and regional dynamics of the Bosnian Question, there has also been a significant international dimension. That dimension remains to this day, manifested in the presence and mandates of a multitude of international organisations in the country.

Under both Ottoman and Habsburg rule, Bosnia enjoyed prolonged periods of stability, during which inter-communal violence was rare. Traditionally, Bosnians of all ethno-national origins lived together in peace, albeit leading parallel lives with limited contact. Modernisation and urbanisation in the late nineteenth and twentieth centuries, as well as the creation of a South Slav state, changed the dynamic of relations among communities, increasing the level of interaction and placing it within a wider regional context. Bosnia's experience in the interwar period within Royal Yugoslavia was sobering, as the new country's nascent democratic institutions struggled to balance the interests of the many peoples living within it. Much of the most savage killing of the Second World War in Yugoslavia took place in Bosnia. Nevertheless, it was also in Bosnia that a multi-ethnic partisan movement emerged that eventually took control of the entire country. Under communism, Bosnians of all ethno-national origins began genuinely to live together in increasingly integrated towns and cities. The exceptions to peaceful coexistence, therefore, were the periods of extreme change when empires and countries disintegrated and political authority broke down. These periods, and especially the Second World War, were marred by brutal sectarian violence. Accordingly, it was the disintegration of the Socialist Federal Republic of Yugoslavia and the demise of the political authority of the League of Communists that presaged the descent into war in the 1990s.

For almost forty-five years, communism had been the glue holding Yugoslav society together. In its absence, the country remained intact, but required major structural reform. The interwar debate as to the best form of government for a common state had been reopened. While the experience of the interwar period was not a good omen for the prospects of a third Yugoslav incarnation, the country had come a long way in the intervening period. In a climate of goodwill it might have been possible to build a new Yugoslavia. The country was still a mosaic of nationalities whose destinies could not be separated without bloodshed. And a single Yugoslav state both enabled the vast majority of Slavs to live within the same country and provided a framework within which to reconcile rival claims to ethno-nationally mixed territories. Goodwill was, however, in short supply. The timing of Bosnia's move from authoritarian to democratic forms of government could hardly have been worse. In the key months leading to multi-party elections, as well as in their aftermath, when the new multi-party system should have been embedded, events elsewhere in the Yugoslav Federation had a momentum of their own. Though Bosnians were to bear the brunt of the fall-out from Yugoslavia's break-up, the key decisions leading to it were taken elsewhere: in Belgrade, Ljubljana and Zagreb.

In theory, Bosnia's three-way divide, in which no single people forms an absolute majority, presents one of the more stable frameworks for co-existence and democratic government in a multi-national state. It would certainly be possible to devise power-sharing models to encourage inter-group consensus, thereby making the settlement durable. In practice, however, insufficient thought was given to system design.

The holding of multi-party elections transformed relations among peoples throughout Yugoslavia and especially in those republics where the population was most mixed. The new political parties that emerged to contest Bosnia's November and December 1990 elections were predominantly ethno-nationally based, with the dominant Croat and Serb parties the same ones that had already contested the Croatian elections in April and May. Moreover, the Croatian precedent was extremely worrying. The communist system had bent over backwards to make Serbs feel secure in Croatia, but in the wake of elections political power was transferred to a political party that represented exclusively Croat interests. By August, a Serb revolt had begun in a part of Croatia with a predominantly Serb population, which would escalate into war within a year.

INTRODUCTION

With more than 80 per cent of voters opting for the three main ethno-national parties, Bosnia's poll appeared more of a census than a contested election. Despite dividing along ethno-national lines, Bosnians were not voting for conflict. Rather, they were seeking security at a time when the demise of communism and the emergence of Serb and more recently Croat nationalism in Serbia and Croatia made ethno-national security an issue. Fear was one of the most important motivating factors, since anyone not voting for his or her own ethno-national representatives would effectively only be increasing the ethno-national representation of the other communities.

In theory, it is possible for representatives of different communities to govern together in the common interest. Given Bosnia's ethno-national mix, such an approach would certainly have been in the interests of the vast majority of the population. Indeed, having joined forces to defeat the former communists, the three ethno-national parties agreed to form a coalition to govern together. In practice, however, apart from agreeing on the need to purge the former communist administration, the three ruling ethno-national parties found it virtually impossible to co-operate. Instead of working together, the three ethno-national ruling parties developed their own parallel power structures, reproducing the communist *nomenklatura* system but drawn up on ethno-national lines. The centralised administrative structure bequeathed by the communists was bypassed. Serb autonomous authorities became the effective government across much of the republic. Croat administrative bodies took charge in Western Herzegovina and some other Croat enclaves. Moreover, the centralised system of tax collection and disbursement disintegrated in such a way that tax revenues were appropriated by ethno-national administrations at the local level, thus leaving the central government increasingly short of resources. In the wake of elections, Bosnia was both polarised and paralysed.

Discussions on reform of the Yugoslav Federation—which evolved into weekly summits of the six republican presidents at the end of March 1991—failed to generate results. A central element of disagreement was conflicting definitions of 'nation': whether all people living within the territorial boundaries of a political community or all members of a particular ethno-national group. Rival leaders held incompatible views as to where sovereignty lay, depending on the geographic distribution and status of the community on whose behalf they claimed to speak. The Serb position was clear. Sovereignty lay in the ethno-national group, and if other nations sought self-determination and wished to secede from the common Yugoslav state, they were entitled to do so, but they would not be able to take territory with them on which Serbs lived. In the event that nations did, nevertheless, seek to secede from the internationally recognised state and to take territory with them on which Serbs lived, Serbs, too, had the right to self-determination and would seek to remain part of Yugoslavia. If Croats in Croatia or Croats and Muslims in Bosnia had the right to secede from Yugoslavia, then Serbs had the right to secede from Croatia and Bosnia and to remain part of Yugoslavia.

While the international community stayed out of these discussions in the hope that Yugoslavs would resolve their own differences, the outbreak of war on 27 June 1991 in the wake of independence declarations in Slovenia and Croatia, and the prospect of refugees fleeing into Western Europe, obliged the European Community (EC) to become engaged. Two days after the start of hostilities, the *troika* of foreign ministers co-ordinating the European Community's foreign policy arrived hoping to help mediate a solution.

Though poorly equipped to deal with the complexity and urgency of the Yugoslav crisis, the European Community appeared to get off to a good start, negotiating an end to hostilities in Slovenia, including a three-month moratorium on independence declarations, and establishing a Peace Conference on Yugoslavia. Moreover, to provide the Conference with legal advice, a five-member Arbitration Commission was created, made up of the heads of the constitutional courts of five EC countries. This Commission was to issue a series of opinions to assist the European Community in its decision-making in relation to the Yugoslav conflict, determining firstly that the Socialist Federal Republic of Yugoslavia was in the process of disintegration, and subsequently the criteria by which republics applying to it for recognition would be recognised as independent states. While Slovenia and Croatia were recognised in January

1992, Bosnia, which applied despite Bosnian Serb opposition, was not. Instead, the Commission decided that evidence of the state of public opinion should be gathered, 'possibly by means of a referendum', before it could consider the matter further. Meanwhile, a separate conference was set up within the EC Peace Conference on Yugoslavia to mediate between increasingly hostile rival ethno-national elites in Bosnia.

A referendum took place in Bosnia on 29 February and 1 March 1992 with EC financial support despite a Serb boycott. The result was 99.7 per cent support for independence. Turnout was 64.4 per cent, which roughly corresponded to the proportion of Croats and Muslims in the population. Before the results came through, a Serb attending a wedding in Sarajevo was shot dead and within the hour masked Serb gunmen had erected barricades around the city. Amid escalating violence, EC mediators sought to find a structure for Bosnia that would be acceptable to all and might also head off catastrophe. The proposed solution was 'cantonisation', the division of Bosnia into 'three constituent units, based on national principles and taking into account economic, geographic and other criteria'. The flaw was that there was no clear way to divide Bosnia. The country did not fragment neatly along ethno-national lines. Croat negotiators were the first to reject the agreement, as it became clear that close to two thirds of Croats would be living in Muslim or Serb constituent units. It was then rejected by the Muslim-led Bosnian government, in part because of the implications of a territorial carve-up, and in part because of expectations that the European Community and, in particular, the United States would recognise Bosnia's independence.

The European Community and the United States did, indeed, recognise Bosnia on 6 and 7 April 1992 respectively, but only after hostilities had already broken out and without providing the assistance that might have helped the new state survive. From the European Community's perspective, recognition appeared to have held out hope for a quick-fix solution. But when the policy failed to halt the fighting, there was no international will to deploy the military force necessary to oblige the combatants to make peace, until the summer of 1995. In the intervening three-and-a-half years, more than half of Bosnia's 4.3 million population were driven from their homes and some 100,000 lost their lives.

Peace-building challenge

The war ended after a NATO air campaign helped transform the military situation on the ground and a sustained US diplomatic offensive gave the parties little choice but to agree to a peace accord. The settlement was reached after three weeks of negotiations between 1 and 21 November 1995 on an airbase outside Dayton, Ohio, and the peace accord was formally signed in Paris on 14 December 1995. The Bosnian War had not, however, run its course. In the absence of outside intervention, it would almost certainly have continued either until a genuine stalemate had been reached and the parties were forced to recognise the front lines as borders or until one or even two peoples had been defeated and definitively 'cleansed'. The Dayton Peace Agreement satisfied none of the belligerents, but all sides could take something from it. The peace accord ensured that no people was defeated, and was sufficiently flexible to set in motion a process that held out the prospect of a better future, without specifying the kind of country Bosnia should ultimately become. The settlement was, nevertheless, based on a balance of terror in the country and the wider region, and littered with unrealistic deadlines aimed at providing an exit strategy for the international military presence. It risked amounting to a long ceasefire rather than a lasting peace.

At the end of 1995, the Bosnian Question was far more complex than it had been in 1991 on the eve of war. The already multifaceted issue of how to reconcile the interests of Bosniaks, Croats and Serbs in a democratic framework was exacerbated by the legacy of armed conflict. The new country and the international community now also had to address the consequences of nearly four years of warfare, ethnic cleansing and genocide, as well as a peace accord that included internal territorial divisions, cumbersome decision-making structures and mechanisms for power-sharing that might have been necessary to end the war but further complicated the prospects for effective governance. In addition, Bosnia would belatedly have to make the transition from a socialist to a capitalist economy.

INTRODUCTION

When the Dayton Peace Agreement came into force, some 1.2 million Bosnians were living as refugees abroad, with another 1.2 million internally displaced within Bosnia. Of the 3 million people remaining in the country, some 2.4 million or 80 per cent were dependent on humanitarian aid. The precise number of dead was unknown, but at least 30,000 were missing. Religious buildings had been desecrated, infrastructure shattered and just under a third of the housing stock damaged or destroyed. More than half a million landmines remained in the ground. GDP per capita had slumped to less than $500 or about 20 per cent of the pre-war level. And the heavy industry that had formed the backbone of Bosnia's pre-war economy was now dated, looted or destroyed.

The physical challenge of reconstruction was great but surmountable given the level of international aid. The transition from a socialist to a capitalist economy was more complex, but again it could be achieved with a combination of aid, training and expertise. By contrast, the political challenge involved in piecing Bosnia back together, if only in the limited form of the Dayton Peace Agreement, was of another order of magnitude.

Although the focus of the Dayton talks had been on the internal territorial division and on the military aspects of the settlement, the bulk of the accord covered civilian issues. Indeed, military matters only featured in the first and second annexes. The remaining nine addressed civilian implementation, providing a blueprint for post-war reconstruction, including a constitution for the state of Bosnia. Given how comparatively little time was devoted to drafting civilian aspects of the accord and how irreconcilable the differences, the final text was a remarkable document. In addition to an end to hostilities, it appeared to hold out the promise of return for people who had been expelled from their homes, of political regeneration and justice in terms of elections and war-crimes trials, and of international assistance to get the country back on its feet. As such, it provided a starting point for a process that in theory had the potential to lead to a functioning and self-sustaining arrangement.

The drafters of the Dayton Peace Agreement were under no illusions about the settlement. It was a means to end a war, not the basis of a permanent solution to the Bosnian Question. After all, the peace accord and the constitution contained within it were prepared, agreed and officially published in English and not in any of the languages of the country; the status of Brčko, the most strategically important municipality in the country, remained open; and the governing structures bequeathed to Bosnia—in addition to being extremely complex—were so expensive to maintain that servicing the settlement alone risked undermining the country's longer-term prospects.

Although the parties to the peace accord were expected to implement it, the chances of them doing so voluntarily were minimal. Given the animosity and absence of trust, and the fact that both Croat and Serb political leaders continued to aspire to union with Croatia and Serbia respectively, the necessary consensus did not exist. Power was concentrated in the hands of individuals with a vested interest in maintaining the ethno-national divisions institutionalised in the war, since they themselves had created them and were the principal beneficiaries. If the accord were implemented to the letter, if refugees and the displaced were able to return to their homes, if war-crimes suspects were brought to trial, and if Bosnia were to become a functioning democracy governed by the rule of law, their power bases would evaporate.

The reality in Bosnia was three ethno-national mini-states, each with its own armed forces, police, media, administration, official documentation and vehicle licence plates. Separate currencies circulated: the Yugoslav dinar in Republika Srpska, the Croatian kuna in Croat-held Federation territory, the Bosnian mark in government-controlled Federation territory, with the German mark accepted everywhere. There were no telephone lines between the entities, let alone bus routes, postal services or other means of communication. In addition, both Croatia and the Federal Republic of Yugoslavia retained a large capacity to influence events and undermine the settlement. Indeed, both Zagreb and Belgrade continued to finance critical elements of their respective communities' power structures.

To address the many likely obstacles, provision for international involvement in all aspects of the peace process was built into the peace accord with overall co-ordination entrusted to a high representative, an ad hoc position specifically created to oversee civilian implementation. In addition to the co-ordinating role of the high representative, the Organization for Security and Co-operation in Europe (OSCE) was mandated to monitor the human rights situation, to oversee arms reduction and to supervise elections. The Office of the UN High Commissioner for Refugees (UNHCR) was to prepare a repatriation plan to enable refugees and displaced persons to return to their homes. And a UN International Police Task Force was to 'assist, advise, monitor and observe the work of local police'. An international presence was also embedded in a host of ostensibly domestic institutions, including the Central Bank, the Human Rights Ombudsman, the Human Rights Chamber, the Constitutional Court, the Commission on Real Property Claims of Displaced Persons and Refugees, the Commission to Preserve National Monuments and the Commission on Public Corporations.

Measuring success

The fifty-five countries and organisations with a stake in the peace process came together as the Peace Implementation Council (PIC) at a conference in London on 8 and 9 December 1995. This ad hoc group aimed to manage the peace process, setting its direction and mobilising resources. The PIC was not answerable to the United Nations, which was largely bypassed because it was perceived to have failed during the war, but invited the UN Security Council to endorse its decisions. At the London meeting, an agenda was set aiming, among other things, to create a climate of stability and security; to establish new political and constitutional arrangements in a framework of democracy and the rule of law; to protect and promote human rights and the prompt return of refugees and displaced persons; to establish an open, free-market economy; to kick-start economic reconstruction; and to create 'a direct and dynamic contractual relationship between Bosnia and the European Union within the framework of a regional approach'. On 20 and 21 December 1995, the European Commission and World Bank hosted a first donors' meeting in Brussels to begin putting in place what became in March a $5.1 billion, five-year reconstruction programme.

The scale and ambition of international mobilisation behind the peace process were seemingly unprecedented. Attitudes to the international engagement in Bosnia were, however, divided. The bulwark underpinning the settlement was the international military presence. And early debates over the aims and ambitions of that mission highlighted these differences. Should the Dayton Peace Agreement serve as a window of opportunity to provide the country's leaders some breathing space to resolve their differences? Or was a more proactive and longer-term approach required to enable peace to take root?

In contrast to the United Nations Protection Force (UNPROFOR), the peacekeeping force deployed during the war, the 60,000-strong NATO-led Implementation Force (IFOR) was equipped with a peace-enforcement mandate. This enabled it to do whatever necessary to create and maintain a safe and secure environment. Moreover, IFOR, which deployed in December 1995, rapidly succeeded in overseeing key elements of the peace accord's military annexes, including, in particular, the cessation of hostilities. However, the deployment was initially limited to one year and the mandate was interpreted in restrictive terms. The overriding concern of policy-makers was not the cost of the international military presence, though this was by far the greatest expense of peace implementation, but the prospect of casualties. Given the absence of a clearly defined national interest, policy-makers in troop-contributing countries were concerned that public opinion at home would turn against the deployment in the event of fatalities. While setting a one-year deadline on IFOR's presence may have been politically necessary to secure its deployment, it also served to preserve wartime mindsets and attitudes.

The holding of elections nine months after the signing of the Dayton Peace Agreement failed to revitalise Bosnia's political landscape. Instead, it entrenched ethno-national divisions. Had the NATO-led peacekeeping force withdrawn from Bosnia one year after its deployment as scheduled, the outlook would have been bleak. Implementation of the peace accord's military annexes alone was not sufficient to prevent a return to war. In the absence of a long-term, open-ended military commitment, there was no prospect of getting to a durable settlement. This reality was reluctantly recognised by decision-makers who, in November 1996, agreed to extend the military presence for an additional eighteen months, and eventually—after two ,years of the peace process—for as long as would be required to secure lasting peace.

Extending the international military presence and removing artificial deadlines for its withdrawal were important steps towards bringing peace to Bosnia. Moreover, in the course of 1997 and 1998, the focus of IFOR's successor, the Stabilisation Force (SFOR), shifted from preventing a resumption of hostilities and force protection to creating the conditions in Bosnia for civilian implementation of the peace accord. The change reflected a broader shift in international strategy, including, in particular, a reinterpretation of the authority of the high representative at the Peace Implementation Conference in Bonn, Germany, in December 1997. To break the political deadlock, the PIC conferred executive powers, which became known as the 'Bonn Powers', on the high representative, including the ability to impose legislation and dismiss office-holders.

The conclusions of the Bonn Peace Implementation Conference also referred to 'two multi-ethnic entities'. This was the first such reference in any official document, including the Dayton Peace Agreement itself. In effect, the PIC had decided after two years of systematic obstructionism that it would not be possible to build peace in collaboration with the ethno-national parties. Rather, it would be necessary to take them on, dismantle their power structures and seek to build multi-ethnic solutions. This meant overruling or bypassing the democratic institutions whose creation had been the reason for the 1996 elections.

The problems inherent in such a strategy were immediately evident. How could the high representative and international civil servants make decisions on matters of importance to Bosnians when they were not answerable to them and would not live with the consequences? How would decisions be implemented without local buy-in? To what extent was it possible to build democracy by undemocratic means? And how far could this process go without embedding a culture of dependency?

In the months following the Bonn Peace Implementation Conference, the high representative began cautiously to impose decisions. The aim was to help form the basic institutions envisaged in the Dayton Peace Agreement in the hope that implementation of the peace accord's key principles would follow. When this did not happen, the international community set about overcoming obstructionism and, with ever more frequent recourse to the Bonn Powers, forcing through implementation in spite of the positions of the domestic authorities. By 2000, this had evolved into a coordinated institution-building strategy, covering all spheres of life, not just those institutions specifically listed in the Dayton Peace Agreement.

Institution-building appeared to offer both a practical and a philosophical justification for the need to override Bosnia's democratic institutions. In essence, Bosnia's democracy was immature, it was argued, because the country's institutions were weak. The international community needed to nurture domestic institutions until they were sufficiently robust for peace to become self-sustaining, at which point it would be possible to hand 'ownership' of the process to them. Institution-building also dovetailed with reforms required to prepare Bosnia for membership of the European Union, an aspiration shared by the vast majority of Bosnians, irrespective of their ethno-national origins, since it appeared to offer the prospect of prosperity, stability and long-term security.

In this way, the ambition of the peace process had grown from halting the fighting to embedding peace via European integration, with the benchmark for gauging success moving accordingly. The most difficult decision that the PIC would have to make was how and when to bring the Dayton process to an end. That decision required a comprehensive assessment of the peace accord's implementation as well as of Bosnia's ability to move forward on its own. If Bosnia's elected leaders were not capable of governing the country without the massive international support mechanism that had surrounded it since the end of the war, the failure would bring into question the entire Dayton project.

2

THE BOSNIAN QUESTION

'Bosnia, which existed as a state or administrative entity in one form or another from the tenth century or earlier to 1929, acted as a mould that produced three nationalities that were at once very different from and similar to each other, alternately antagonistic and co-operative and at once Bosnian and extra-Bosnian in their orientation—the Bosnian Serbs both Bosnian and Serbian, the Bosnian Croats both Bosnian and Croatian and the Bosnian Muslims both Bosnian and Ottoman or Islamic.'

Marko Attila Hoare[1]

Balancing act

At its simplest, the Bosnian Question boils down to two issues: how some 2.2 million Bosniaks can live amid 4.5 million Croats and 8.5 million Serbs in the former Yugoslavia; and how some 750,000 Croats and 1.3 million Serbs can live together with 1.9 million Bosniaks within Bosnia itself. Depending on where borders are drawn and whether or not they are respected, Bosniaks either form a minority squeezed between two more powerful ethno-national groups, or they comprise a relative majority in a territory shared with two large minority communities, both of whom generally consider the neighbouring states of Croatia and Serbia their mother countries.

15

In addition to the internal and regional dynamics of the Bosnian Question, there is also an international dimension. This includes the international presence in Bosnia that has emerged from the Dayton Peace Agreement, the executive powers exercised by various international organisations, in particular the Office of the High Representative (OHR), but also EUFOR and NATO, in Bosnia, and the time and resources devoted to discussing and addressing Bosnian matters by the wider international community. Given Bosnia's complexity, the legacy of the 1992–5 war and the many principles and interests involved in reconstructing any state after war, the international factor will remain critical to the country's evolution.

In theory, Bosnia's ethno-national composition presents one of the more stable frameworks for co-existence and effective democracy in a multi-ethnic state. It is certainly possible to devise power-sharing models based on guaranteed group representation that could both encourage inter-ethnic consensus and reward moderation, thereby making the state durable. In practice, however, this has not been the case.

The timing of Bosnia's move from totalitarian to democratic forms of government could hardly have been worse. In the months leading to multi-party elections after nearly half a century of communist rule, as well as in their aftermath, events elsewhere in the Yugoslav Federation, in Croatia, Serbia and Slovenia in particular, had a momentum of their own and effectively shaped the future for Bosnia and its citizens. Once war had engulfed Bosnia, ethnic-cleansing campaigns killed or driven vast numbers of its citizens from their homes, and the international community recognised the former Yugoslav republic as an independent country, there could be no going back. By the time the fighting was brought to a halt at the end of 1995, the Bosnian Question was far more complex than it had been in 1991. The already multifaceted issue of how to reconcile the interests of Bosniaks, Croats and Serbs was exacerbated by the legacy of armed conflict. The new country and the international community also had to address the consequences of nearly four years of war, of ethnic cleansing and of genocide. Moreover, the peace agreement instituted internal territorial divisions, cumbersome decision-making structures and mechanisms for power-sharing that might have been necessary to end the war but complicated the prospects for effective government.

Given the length of the Bosnian War, the extent of its consequences and the differing, even diametrically opposed interpretations of its causes, almost every aspect of the country's reconstruction has been controversial. All reforms, privatisations and agreements with other states or groups of states are seemingly hostage to the wider question of what kind of country Bosnia should be. As a result, the first question most politicians ask when confronted with change is how it might impact the position and outlook for his or her community. Even in areas where there appears to be consensus, such as the necessity of building a closer and deeper relationship with the European Union, ethno-national considerations crowd out all others, making genuine progress almost impossible.

The impasse caused by this zero-sum politics contributed to the international community taking decision-making away from domestic institutions. Moreover, it makes it extremely difficult for the international community to step back from the intrusive role it has played without the entire post-war structure disintegrating. While almost all actors, domestic and international, agree that the way forward lies in integration with the European Union, this can only be achieved if Bosnia's institutions become genuinely self-sustaining. And this requires finding a better framework to reconcile the interests of Bosniaks, Croats and Serbs, within both Bosnia and the wider region.

Ethno-national identities and rivalries

Anyone who has spent any length of time in Bosnia rapidly realises that most Bosnians have multiple identities: that someone can feel and profess to be Bosniak, Bosnian and European at the same time. The issue of identity—what makes us what we are—is complex. In Bosnia, three distinct ethno-national identities evolved in parallel following the Ottoman conquest in the fifteenth century and the introduction of structures that institutionalised religious divisions. Moreover, these identities remained fundamental to most of the population up to the 1992–5 war and have subsequently been reinforced by that war and the climate of ethno-nationally charged politics in the years since the end of armed hostilities.

Before the Ottoman conquest,[2] Bosnia had both Catholic and Orthodox populations, as well as followers of a schismatic Bosnian church. Today's Bosniaks, Croats and Serbs are not, however, necessarily the direct descendants of these peoples. Bosnia's population was fluid over many centuries, changing according to the shifting fortunes of the Habsburg Monarchy and the Ottoman Empire in war. Settlers, usually Orthodox but also Catholic and Muslim, were often brought in from elsewhere in the Ottoman Empire to repopulate frontier regions. Muslims fleeing European territories that had been lost to the Habsburgs sometimes settled in Bosnia and Catholics and Orthodox migrated the other way. In the nineteenth and twentieth centuries, Orthodox also migrated to Serbia and Muslims to other Ottoman lands, including Turkey.

Under Ottoman rule, Muslims were governed according to Islamic law. Non-Muslims—Jews as well as Catholics and Orthodox—lived within semi-autonomous communities, or millets, in which they were partly governed by their spiritual leaders and, in return for tribute, were able to practise their own religion with limited restrictions. People were in effect defined by their faith, with the result that, over the centuries, religion and ethno-national identity became inextricably linked. Since the Orthodox community came under the authority of the Serbian patriarch of Peć in Kosovo, the Serbian Orthodox Church was able to nurture a Serb national consciousness among the Orthodox community in Bosnia as well as in Serbia. The Franciscans were spiritual leaders as well as temporal governors of Bosnia's Catholics. Moreover, each community was homogenised by this system of rule, irrespective of where its members originally came from.

Many Slavs in Bosnia converted to Islam under Ottoman rule with the result that Bosnia had a Muslim majority by the early seventeenth century and became self-governing in borders that are almost identical to those of today. Reasons for this large-scale conversion are varied, but one motivating factor would certainly have been the opportunity to enjoy the economic and political benefits of belonging to the Ottoman Empire's dominant religion. Conversions also took place

18

between other faiths at times, especially between Catholics and Orthodox in an attempt to escape persecution.

Under the Ottoman Empire, therefore, Muslims were privileged while Catholics and Orthodox had an inferior status. Catholics in particular had a hard time during the early centuries of Ottoman rule since the primary Ottoman enemy, the Habsburg Monarchy, was also Catholic and they therefore represented a potential fifth column. Indeed, large numbers of Catholics left Bosnia in the 1690s in the wake of Ottoman regrouping, following earlier Habsburg military successes.

Although the Ottoman Empire initially sought to build up the Orthodox community as an ally against the Habsburgs, the emergence of Serbia as an independent entity in the nineteenth century came to present the most immediate threat to Ottoman authority in Bosnia. By the mid-nineteenth century, Serbs, most of them peasants working for Muslim landowners in a feudal-style relationship, comprised a similar proportion of the total population to Muslims but were increasingly alienated from and resentful of the Ottoman administration.

The majority of Croats and Muslims were also peasants working the land and conditions for all three communities were similar. There was, however, minimal interaction among them. Croats lived in Croat villages, Muslims in Muslim villages and Serbs in Serb villages. In the countryside, the communities kept to themselves and, despite speaking the same language, lived parallel lives. This was not the case in the cities. There, all three communities as well as Jews intermingled, though Muslims were the most numerous and each community lived in its own quarter.

The end of Ottoman rule in Bosnia in 1878 was triggered by Serb uprisings, and Russian intervention against and victory over the Ottoman Empire in support of Bulgarian independence. This led initially to the Treaty of San Stefano between Russia and the Ottoman Empire and later to the Congress of Berlin, involving all of Europe's great powers. Under the Treaty of San Stefano, Bosnia was to be self-governing with a parliament whose deputies were to be 20 per cent Croat, 40 per cent Muslim and 40 per cent Serb, reflecting roughly the proportions of each community in the overall population. Following the Congress of Berlin, Bosnia was to be administered by Austria-Hungary. It was *de facto* a Habsburg land, but *de jure* remained part of the Ottoman Empire until its annexation in 1908 by Austria-Hungary.[3]

Habsburg rule marked the end of Muslim dominance in Bosnia. It also introduced a degree of modernisation, including railway construction and the foundation of many newspapers, as well as some urbanisation and industrialisation. Advances in communication technology opened up greater opportunities for contact among Bosnia's communities, but Habsburg attempts to inculcate a Bosnian regional identity, by, for example, promoting a 'Bosnian' language and dissolving confessional schools, failed. In the case of newspapers, most catered exclusively to one or other of Bosnia's communities.

According to the first Habsburg census in 1879, Serbs had become the most numerous community in Bosnia, comprising nearly 43 per cent of the population. This followed an exodus of Muslims, who still comprised close to 39 per cent. Croats made up just over 18 per cent. The religious divisions institutionalised under Ottoman rule in millets evolved into ethno-nationally based political parties in line with the rest of Austria-Hungary in the years running up to the First World War, with Muslims founding the Muslim National Organisation (Muslimanska narodna organizacija, or MNO), Serbs the Serb National Organisation (Srpska narodna organizacija, or SNO) and Croats the Croat National Union (Hrvatska narodna zajednica, or HNZ). Each community also had its own cultural society—the Muslim Gajret, the Serb Prosvjeta and the Croat Napredak.

The Habsburgs initially brought in civil servants from elsewhere in Austria-Hungary to administer Bosnia, rather than recruit locally. Bosnia's administration changed overnight from being essentially Muslim to Christian, comprising primarily Catholics, but also some Orthodox, including Croats and Serbs from elsewhere in Austria-Hungary, though not Bosnian Croats or Bosnian Serbs. Over the years of Habsburg rule, the proportion of foreign-born civil servants declined to around 60 per cent on the eve of the First World War. By this time, Croats, though numerically still the least numerous of Bosnia's communities, were best represented in the administration, followed by Serbs, with Muslims the most under-represented.

Although Habsburg rule was not the preferred system of government for Bosnia's Muslim elite, who had lost many of their privileges, the Habsburgs were prepared to leave them in control of the land they owned in return for their loyalty. By neglecting agrarian reform until the eve of the First World War, however, the Habsburgs failed to address the greatest grievance of the Serb peasantry, who effectively remained serfs until Austria-Hungary's demise and resentful of the Muslim landowning class.

Austria-Hungary's annexation of Bosnia in 1908 was spurred by the Young Turk Revolution in the Ottoman Empire of the same year. The Young Turk Revolution restored the Ottoman constitution and led to similar constitutional demands within Bosnia, which was still formally part of the Ottoman Empire. In response, the Habsburg emperor granted Bosnia a constitution in 1910, though it was drawn up without the participation of the two largest political parties, the Muslim National Organisation and the Serb National Organisation. The 1910 constitution gave Bosnia a parliament in which seats were distributed among the religious communities in proportion to their share of the overall population. Of seventy-two elected seats, thirty-one were designated for Orthodox, twenty-four for Muslims, sixteen for Catholics and one for the Jewish community.[4] In addition, twenty non-elected seats were allocated to notables of all four confessions from the fields of religion, law and commerce. In this way, representation amounted to a compromise between equality among the religious communities and residual Muslim social dominance.

The Bosnian parliament functioned briefly before the outbreak of the First World War and its actions were characterised by demands for greater power and autonomy on the one hand and ethno-national bickering on the other. Whereas Muslim and Serb elites had tended to work together under Habsburg rule in the hope of obtaining greater autonomy within an Ottoman structure, this co-operation came to an end after Austria-Hungary's annexation of Bosnia. Instead, Croat and Muslim elites began to co-operate, as both had a vested interest in the best possible arrangement within a Habsburg structure. Serbs, by contrast, were increasingly attracted by the possibility of union with Serbia, whose full independence had been recognised in 1878 at the Congress of Berlin and whose borders had expanded greatly after the Balkan Wars of 1912 and 1913 to incorporate Kosovo, parts of Sandžak and much of Macedonia. Although the proverbial shot that triggered the First World War was fired by a Serb, Gavrilo Princip, in Sarajevo, Bosnia's Croats, Muslims and Serbs had minimal influence over the fighting that followed, which pitted them as part of Austria-Hungary against Serbia. To an extent, Franz Ferdinand, the heir to the Habsburg throne, was tempting fate when he decided to visit Sarajevo on St Vitus Day, 28 June 1914. The date was emotionally charged as it was the anniversary of the 1389 Battle of Kosovo, the event that heralded the end of the medieval Serbian Empire, and any visit on that day could be interpreted by Serb nationalists as provocative.

In the aftermath of Franz Ferdinand's assassination, anti-Serb sentiment ran high throughout Austria-Hungary and boiled over into regime-sponsored, anti-Serb pogroms both in Bosnia and in Croatia. Most Serb cultural organisations were closed and some Serb civilians were deported from strategically sensitive areas and interned. Despite this, the Bosnian Serb elite took pains to demonstrate loyalty to the Habsburgs and supported the war effort. Indeed, many Serbs served in the Habsburg armies until the disintegration of Austria-Hungary in the autumn of 1918. Following Austria-Hungary's rapid demise, the Bosnian political elite took Bosnia into the Kingdom of Serbs, Croats and Slovenes, which was formed via union with Serbia of most of the Habsburg lands that had a South Slav majority. In this way, the Bosnian Question became an integral part of the wider Yugoslav Question of how to balance the interests of the many peoples now living together in the new state.

In theory, the Yugoslav state provided the best possible framework for co-existence for all three of Bosnia's communities as both Croats and Serbs were united with their ethno-national kin and Muslims continued to live together.[5] In practice, however, the absence of a foreign overlord proved a mixed blessing. The new

22

state was not a union of equals, but a Serb-dominated affair. The first provisional cabinet, comprising thirteen Serbs, four Croats, two Slovenes and one Muslim, presided over the administrative extension of Serbia across the whole of the country during its twenty-one-month existence until the final post-war territorial settlement was agreed in Paris and elections were held. In Bosnia, the purge of the administration was almost as comprehensive as it had been in 1878, only this time the civil servants brought in were Serbs from Serbia.

Bosnia's Muslims were now vulnerable and almost invisible in the administration. In the anarchy that reigned following the collapse of Habsburg authority, some Serb peasants turned on landowners in a rampage that degenerated into violence against the Muslim population and resulted in some 2,000 deaths.[6] Serfdom was formally abolished in February 1919 and land ownership transferred to the former serfs with minimal compensation for the former landlords. Although Croat and Muslim peasants were also beneficiaries, agrarian reform represented a significant transfer of economic power from Muslims to Serbs.

In response to the pressure they were under, Bosnia's Muslims rallied behind the Jugoslovenska muslimanska organizacija (Yugoslav Muslim Organisation, or JMO) and its leader Mehmed Spaho. The JMO used its electoral weight to protect Muslim interests, supporting the Serbian political parties' centralist vision of the Kingdom of Serbs, Croats and Slovenes in return for whatever concessions it could obtain. To this end, it backed the 1921 constitution in return for a guarantee that Bosnia would be administered within its historic borders. The need for JMO support also helped moderate some of the agrarian reforms—to the disappointment of Serb peasants. As a result, Bosnian Serb political support was split between the Serbian political parties and Bosnian Serb parties representing the interests of farmers. Bosnian Croat political support shifted to the Hrvatska seljačka stranka (Croatian Peasant Party, or HSS), which already dominated Croatian politics.

Politics in the Kingdom of Serbs, Croats and Slovenes divided along ethno-national lines, paralysed the work of government and sometimes turned violent, especially in Bosnia where paramilitary groups linked to political parties physically attacked and occasionally murdered rivals. Indeed, this violence spilled into the Belgrade parliament in June 1928 when a Montenegrin deputy shot and killed five deputies of the HSS, including its leader, Stjepan Radić. The ensuing chaos persuaded King Alexander to establish a royal dictatorship in January 1929 and to rename the country Yugoslavia (land of South Slavs).

King Alexander divided Yugoslavia into administrative units or *banovinas* that bore minimal resemblance to historic or ethnonational entities. In this way, the territory of Bosnia was divided among four *banovinas* that extended into neighbouring Croatia, Montenegro and Serbia. Elected officials at a local level were dismissed and replaced with appointees. A new constitution was imposed in 1931 that was designed to avoid conflict among ethnonational parties and ensure that real power remained with the monarch. Bosnia's Muslims found themselves divided among four *banovinas*, two with a Serb majority and two with a Croat majority. They were also often squeezed out of local administration. In response, the JMO began to advocate federalism on the basis of historical units, among them Bosnia.

King Alexander was assassinated in Marseille in 1934 by a Bulgarian working for the Ustašas, a Croat revolutionary organisation created five years earlier that operated out of Benito Mussolini's Italy. In the wake of his death, King Alexander's cousin, Paul, became Prince Regent and maintained the dictatorship, while modifying approaches to the national question. A new ruling party, the Jugoslovenska radikalna zajednica (Yugoslav Radical Union, or JRZ), was formed based on a coalition of the most powerful Serbian party, the JMO and the most powerful Slovene party, but excluding Croat political representatives. This provided the JMO with almost five years of unprecedented influence on the territory of Bosnia, to the dismay of Bosnia's Croats and Serbs. This came to an end when the JRZ lost the December 1938 elections.

Having failed to build stability via a coalition of Serbs, Muslims and Slovenes, Prince Paul sought accommodation with the Croats. This manifested itself in the Cvetković-Maček Agreement or *Sporazum* of August 1939, which created an autonomous Croat *banovina* within the Yugoslav state. The settlement was negotiated and agreed by Prime Minister Dragiša Cvetković and HSS leader Vladko Maček behind the backs of Serb and Slovene parties as well as the JMO. Moreover, it effectively divided Bosnia into Croat and Serb territories. Of a population of 4.4 million in the Croat *banovina*, 866,000 were Serbs and 164,000 were Muslims. The creation of a Croat *banovina* was supposed to be followed by the creation of Slovene and Serb *banovinas*. However, the *Sporazum* itself was never properly implemented and the Slovene and Serb *banovinas* were never created because of the onset of the Second World War.

Brotherhood and unity

The Second World War had a greater impact on Bosnia, scene of the most savage and prolonged fighting, than any other part of Yugoslavia. It was also in Bosnia that Tito's communist partisans emerged as the most capable indigenous fighting force, sufficiently strong to establish their authority throughout the territory that had made up Royal Yugoslavia and to annex some adjacent Slav-populated territory from Italy after the defeat of Nazi Germany. Had there been no war, the communists would not have been in a position to come to power. Had there been no communists, it would have been extremely difficult to rebuild the country that disintegrated in 1941 because of the scale of the killing.

That Bosnia should become the killing field it did was not pre-ordained. Rather it was a consequence of the regime imposed on it by Adolf Hitler. Yugoslavia had not been on Hitler's agenda and few preparations for the country's occupation had been made in advance of the invasion. Hitler intervened in Greece following a bungled invasion of that country by Mussolini's Italy and negotiated an agreement with Prince Paul by which Germany would be able to use Yugoslav territory to transport supplies and equipment to Greece, but not military personnel. Hitler decided to invade Yugoslavia at the eleventh hour after junior officers in the Yugoslav Air Force, objecting to the transit agreement, staged a coup d'état.

Following Yugoslavia's rapid collapse, Hitler hived off whatever territory he could to neighbouring countries with territorial claims against it.[7] The problematic regions that could not be hived off—inner Serbia, a truncated Croatia, a piece of Vojvodina and Bosnia—remained. Here Hitler looked for quisling leaders. In Serbia, he found General Milan Nedić, a senior officer in the Yugoslav Army and member of the pre-war elite, who was convinced that Germany had already won the war. In Croatia, however, Hitler's task was more difficult, since the vast majority of Croats backed Maček who refused to co-operate, in part because he believed that Germany was going to lose the war. In the absence of an alternative, Hitler handed power to the Ustašas, the terrorist group led by Ante Pavelić responsible for the assassination of King Alexander.

There was no precedent for the Ustašas. When they came to power Maček broadcast a statement advising Croats to obey the new authorities, before withdrawing from political life and retiring to his home village. Maček could not anticipate what the Ustašas were about to do. Serbs living in the Nezavisna država Hrvatska (Independent State of Croatia, or NDH) would almost certainly have endured Ustaša rule had they been given the opportunity. Indeed, even when the Ustašas began wiping out Serb villages, some survivors went to Zagreb to alert the authorities to what was taking place, convinced that the government could not be involved. But the government was involved. Moreover, it was pursuing a policy of genocide, brazenly setting out to kill a third of the Serb population, expel a third and convert the remaining third to Catholicism.

The Ustašas were terrorists who would never have been able to form a government under normal circumstances but were handed absolute power over lands in which Croats formed only a little more than half the population. The NDH included all of what would become Bosnia after the Second World War, as well as Syrmia, part of which would be in Vojvodina and part in Serbia, as well as a corner of what would be Slovenia. But the NDH did not include much of what would become the Republic of Croatia, since Istria and much of Dalmatia were under Italian rule and Međimurje and Baranja were under Hungarian rule. In this way, the NDH included about 750,000 Muslims and 1.9 million Serbs.

When they assumed power, the Ustašas lacked popular support, since even according to their own estimates they only had some

40,000 followers. Independence helped raise the Ustašas' standing among Croats. However, by initiating a needless conflict with the Serb population, they spawned rebellion among Serbs, reprisals against Croats and an environment of savagery in which ultimately all communities committed atrocities. This multi-sided conflict was exactly what the Germans would have preferred to avoid since it made the entire region unstable, but it was also the consequence of giving absolute power to a terrorist group. Indeed, so appalling was Ustaša rule that the Ustašas also alienated substantial parts of the Croat population and could not trust the regular Croatian Army unless accompanied by Ustaša units. Even mild expression of opposition was punished by internment in a concentration camp.

The unprovoked and premeditated slaughter carried out in the name of Croatia by the Ustašas in the summer of 1941 has understandably left a scar on Serb consciousness that remains to the present day. It also set in motion a cycle of massacres that continued throughout the Second World War and would probably have shattered prospects for the reformation of a Yugoslav state had it not been for the presence and ideology of the communists. Tito's partisans presented a non-nationalist alternative to the narrowly sectarian outlook of other belligerents. It was an alternative that did not exist in the 1990s.

Since Serbs fleeing Ustaša atrocities provided a reservoir of recruits for the communists, the partisan rank and file was initially disproportionately Serb. Its leadership, by contrast, was always multi-ethnic and included many professional revolutionaries like Tito, himself half-Slovene and half-Croat. Moreover, it was by appealing to all Yugoslavia's peoples, in the spirit of 'brotherhood and unity', that the partisans were able to build the popular constituency so critical to waging a guerrilla campaign. As the war dragged on, the composition of the partisans in Bosnia changed as Croats and Muslims swelled their ranks.

On 25 and 26 November 1943, Bosnia's communist-dominated Country Anti-Fascist Council for the People's Liberation of Bosnia (ZAVNO BiH),[8] in which Serbs formed a majority, gathered for the first time in the Central Bosnian town of Mrkonjić Grad and passed a resolution proclaiming Bosnia to be 'neither Serb nor

Croat nor Muslim but Serb and Croat and Muslim'. Three days later, on 29 November 1943, the Anti-Fascist Council for the National Liberation of Yugoslavia (AVNOJ)[9] held its second convention in Jajce, also in Central Bosnia, to set the foundation for what was to become the Socialist Federal Republic of Yugoslavia, built on a 'democratic, federative principle as a state community of equal nations' with Bosnia one of six republics.

As long as the partisans were comparatively weak, they were prepared to accept former foes into their ranks. As the tide turned, however, they began to focus on consolidating their hold on power, imposing a Marxist-Leninist blueprint on society and eliminating all opposition. Indeed, the war in Yugoslavia continued for a full week after the end of hostilities on other European fronts as anti-communists of all ethno-national origins attempted to fight their way out of the country, determined to surrender to British or US forces rather than fall into Tito's hands. Those who failed to make it to Austria or Italy, as well as many who made it but were handed back by the British Army, were often summarily executed.

The official number of war dead, which was supposed to exclude those fighting for the Axis Powers, was 1.7 million. This figure was a rough calculation arrived at immediately after the war for reparations and propaganda purposes. Tito aimed both to maximise war compensation from Germany and to demonstrate to the world that the heroism and suffering of Yugoslavs during the Second World War surpassed that of all other peoples save only the Soviets and perhaps the Poles. However, in nationalist circles on all sides, operating on the principle 'the more the better', estimates of the dead extended even higher.

Academic studies indicate that the number of war dead is, mercifully, well below the official figure. During the 1980s, independent research into the question by two men, Bogoljub Kočović, an émigré Serb, and Vladimir Žerjavić, a Croat, produced very similar results.[10] Both investigations were based not on body counts or survivors' recollections but on computer analysis of census returns and demographic indices. According to Kočović, whose figures are marginally higher than those of Žerjavić, a total of about 1,014,000, or 6.4 per cent of Yugoslavia's 1941 population, died during or in the immediate aftermath of the Second World War on all sides. In absolute terms, Serbs (487,000), Croats (207,000), Muslims (88,000), Jews (60,000) and Montenegrins (50,000) were the biggest losers, while in relative terms Jews (77.9 per cent), Roma (31.4 per cent), Montenegrins (10.4 per cent), Serbs (6.9 per cent) and Muslims (6.7 per cent) lost the largest part of their respective communities. When Kočović's figures are further broken down by republic, the highest percentage losses were recorded in Bosnia (11.8 per cent), Montenegro (10.2 per cent) and Croatia (7.3 per cent).

Among Serbs, the vast majority of casualties were from the NDH, where one in six perished. According to Kočović's estimates, 125,000–17.4 per cent of the pre-war Serb population–died in Croatia and another 209,000–16.9 per cent of the pre-war population–died in Bosnia. While shocking, these figures do not necessarily reflect the horror of the war from the perspective of those on the receiving end of the Ustašas' brutality. A high proportion of victims were killed between June and August 1941, when they were not even aware of any conflict. The violence then continued at concentration camps. At Jasenovac, the most notorious camp, extermination was not a regulated process along Nazi lines. Instead, inmates were generally killed by beating, stabbing or starvation. The manner of death was brutal, though the number of victims was less than propagandists claim, or most people believe. According to Žerjavić's calculations, about 85,000 people in total lost their lives at Jasenovac.[11]

An open discussion of the Second World War in its immediate aftermath might have put relations among Croats, Muslims and Serbs in Bosnia on a more secure footing. At the very least, a better understanding of the conflict should have dispelled many of the myths that are still widely believed today. But the ideological beliefs of the victorious communists ruled out such a discussion. The end of capitalism was supposed to herald the end of national oppression. All anti-communists were labelled collaborators, irrespective of their allegiance or whether they had fought at all. The Second World War was interpreted as an epic anti-fascist struggle and proletarian revolution, but not a civil war. This simplistic version of the events of 1941–5 became the official communist history of the war. However, an alternative history was passed on by word of mouth to succeeding generations, ensuring that open wounds continued to fester.

The country's first communist constitution of 1946 was modelled on that of the Soviet Union drawn up by Josef Stalin. The division into federal units[12] was not meant to divide the country but to create as equitable a balance as possible among Yugoslavia's peoples and to prevent conflict over disputed territories. Inter-republican borders could only be altered after negotiations among the republics themselves with the agreement of all sides. In addition, each republic had the right to secession and self-determination, although clearly these rights were never meant to be exercised.[13] The communist revolution was supposed to be the culmination of a historical process and there was certainly no provision for a possible break-up of Yugoslavia. The country's peoples had exercised their right to self-determination 'once and for all' during the national liberation struggle, when they chose to live together in a multi-national federation.

In reality, although not mentioned anywhere in the constitution, all power lay with the Communist Party, just as in the Soviet Union. The division into federal units that was to become so objectionable to Serb nationalists in the 1980s was relatively uncontroversial in the 1940s. This was in part because Serbs dominated the Communist Party apparatus in Bosnia and elsewhere as a result of their numerical preponderance among the partisans. This remained the case for the first two decades after the Second World War. More-over, during these years, regions that were home to partisans enjoyed the state's largesse, benefitting from investment in heavy industry; regions that were not, did not. In this way, Western Herzegovina, the Ustaša homeland, was singled out for special treatment, with a particularly harsh police regime, minimal state investment and the changing of place names.

Yugoslav communism was hostile to all the parochial nationalisms of the peoples of Yugoslavia,[14] attempting instead to cultivate a multinational and thoroughly Yugoslav patriotism emanating from the wartime struggle for national liberation. This narrative was supposedly part of a wider, ongoing revolution aspiring to universal, socialist goals that could only be achieved through the unity of all working people. National equality was fundamental and extended as far as participation in the national liberation struggle. According to the official interpretation of the Second World War, all Yugoslavia's peoples had contributed equally to the defeat of fascism. While, strictly speaking, this may not have been the case, it was an attempt to wipe the ethno-national slate clean and allow all peoples to join the new state free from any historical mortgage.

The Communist Party, or League of Communists, as it was renamed after the break with the Soviet Union, was a club that anyone could join. In this way, its ethno-national composition changed over the years to reflect more closely the ethno-national composition of Bosnia itself, so that by 1984 its membership was 42.1 per cent Serb, 34.6 per cent Muslim and 11 per cent Croat.[15] At the same time, Bosnia's ethno-national composition was also changing, with the proportion of Muslims rising and those of both Serbs and Croats declining.

The proportion of Serbs declined in the first instance because of greater wartime losses. In the immediate aftermath of the Second World War, large numbers of Serbs also moved from Bosnia to the Banat region in Vojvodina to settle land where ethnic Germans had lived until 1945 when they fled with the retreating German Army. Subsequently, Croats and Serbs moving to urban centres often migrated to Croatia and Serbia. Croats, in particular, also emigrated in search of a better life outside Yugoslavia. Muslims, by contrast, tended to remain in Bosnia where their numbers were swelled both by immigration of Muslims from Sandžak and, above all, a higher birth rate. By the 1971 census, Muslims formed the largest community, comprising 39.6 per cent of the population; Serbs made up 37.2 per cent; and Croats made up 20.6 per cent.

The official status of Muslims was also changing. In the 1948 census, they had the option of declaring themselves Croat-Muslims, Serb-Muslims or ethno-nationally undeclared Muslims. In 1961, the category of 'Muslims in the ethnic sense' was introduced. In 1963, the preamble to the Bosnian constitution listed Croats, Muslims and Serbs as constituent peoples. And in 1971, the status of Muslims was officially elevated to that of one of Yugoslavia's constituent nations on a par with those peoples with a home republic: Croats, Macedonians, Montenegrins, Serbs and Slovenes.

Yugoslavia was changing rapidly and Bosnia was changing with it. Both Croats and Muslims rose within the League of Communists of Bosnia and were also able to build careers at the federal level.[16] In addition, as a result of Yugoslavia's prominent position in the Non-Aligned Movement, Muslims were considered an asset in the country's diplomatic service and often sent to serve in Muslim countries, where companies from Bosnia also competed for contracts for large construction projects.

Urbanisation was slowly transforming Bosnia. New housing estates were increasingly ethno-nationally mixed, intermarriage especially among Croats and Serbs was on the rise and a generation was growing up as aware of its urban roots as its ethno-national affiliation. Sarajevo was host to the 1984 Winter Olympics, the films of Sarajevo director Emir Kusturica were among the most acclaimed of the 1980s in Europe and Sarajevo bands Bijelo dugme, Plavi orkestar and Zabranjeno pušenje, Sarajevo singer Zdravko Čolić and Brčko singer Lepa Brena were Yugoslavia's most popular performers. For just over two decades before the disintegration of the communist Yugoslav state, all three of Bosnia's peoples had more or less equal status, arguably for the first and only time in Bosnia's history.

3

DISINTEGRATION

'The first democratic elections in the history of the republic produced
a deeply divided political system. As the republic became politically
polarised from within, the external environment became chaotic.'

Steven L. Burg and Paul S. Shoup[1]

End of communism

The stability that both Bosnia and the rest of Yugoslavia enjoyed
under Tito was built on shifting sands. Despite the esteem in which
Tito was held at home and abroad, the state he created outlived
him by less than a third of the time that he had ruled it. Although
Tito's Yugoslavia had evolved a long way since the 1948 split
with Stalin and the rest of the communist world, it remained
fundamentally a *nomenklatura* society[2] with an extensive security
apparatus and powerful mechanisms for social and economic
control. The Achilles' heel was the economy, and economic collapse
preceded political disintegration and war.[3]

Despite the rhetoric of socialist workers' self-management,
Yugoslavia's economy suffered from the same ailments as Europe's
other communist countries. However, because of its unique
geopolitical position between East and West, Yugoslavia could draw
on lines of credit that were not open to other communist countries.

Instead of reforming, Tito preferred to maintain tight political control over the economy and to borrow. In the wake of hikes in oil prices starting in 1973, Yugoslavia's balance of trade deteriorated and its foreign debt rocketed from under $3.5 billion in 1973 to more than $20.5 billion in 1981.[4]

The crunch came around the time of Tito's death, when the loans dried up and Yugoslavia had to begin repaying its debt. This coincided with recession in Western Europe, stemming from the second oil shock of 1979, while the debt burden was aggravated by high interest rates and an exceptionally strong dollar. Living standards began to slide and inflation took off. Between 1982 and 1989, the standard of living fell nearly 40 per cent and in December 1989 inflation peaked at more than 2,000 per cent. The nail in the coffin of communist credibility came two years earlier when Agrokomerc, a Bosnian food-processing company, disintegrated. It had been the twenty-ninth largest company in Yugoslavia and had survived bankruptcy for years through a series of political loans. When it went under, it had almost $900 million of unpaid promissory notes in a scandal implicating the Central Committee of Bosnia's League of Communists and especially the businessman-politician Fikret Abdić. The Agrokomerc debacle was arguably the extent of Bosnia's contribution to Yugoslavia's demise. Though Bosnia's citizens were to bear the brunt of the fall-out from the country's break-up, the key decisions leading to it were being taken elsewhere, especially in Belgrade and Ljubljana, where very different visions for the country's future were being articulated.

The end of capitalism had not heralded the end of national oppression, as the communists once believed. The communists therefore developed mechanisms to balance the competing interests of Yugoslavia's many peoples. To this end, they promulgated four constitutions that reflected the country's transition from a centralist state on the Stalinist model to a federation of eight units—six republics and two autonomous provinces—with many trappings of a confederation.

The solution to the national question was supposed to be scientific. The country's peoples were split into nations and national minorities. The nations corresponded to those peoples with a home republic—Croats, Macedonians, Montenegrins, Serbs and Slovenes—and, from 1971, Muslims. Meanwhile, all other peoples living in Yugoslavia were classified as national minorities. Albanians, for example, were considered a national minority, even though there were more of them in Yugoslavia by the 1980s than Macedonians, Montenegrins or Slovenes. Each constitution listed the nations and national minorities living there and officially both nations and national minorities had the same rights and duties. In this way, everyone was formally classified according to his or her ethno-national identity and it was in theory possible to ensure equitable representation for each community.

The 1974 Constitution, Yugoslavia's sixth and last, was the longest constitution ever written, with 405 clauses. It described an intricate series of checks and balances designed to prevent any individual acquiring as much power as Tito himself had held and to prevent any peoples from dominating the country. All Yugoslavia's republics were sovereign. Foreign affairs, defence and essential economic matters remained the prerogative of the federal centre, but still required consensus among the federal units. Otherwise, the republics and provinces were able to pursue their own policies. The unifying elements that tied the country together were Tito himself, the armed forces, which Tito had created and still dominated, and the League of Communists of Yugoslavia, which Tito had purged two years earlier. Although this constitution was ostensibly designed to cater for life after Tito's death, in reality it made Tito even more indispensable to Yugoslavia than he had been to date.

Federal institutions, from the presidency and National Bank to cultural and sporting bodies, contained representatives from each federal unit. Offices were rotational so that every republic and autonomous province had equal access to positions of power. While the system was designed to be manifestly fair, it exacerbated the post-Tito malaise. Federal presidents and office-holders were aware of the failings of the Titoist system, but had neither the time nor the authority to improve it. At the same time, republican leaders were wary of moves to increase the authority of the federal centre at their expense and used their representatives in the federal institutions to maintain the status quo.

As Yugoslavia's economy crumbled, the country's communist authorities were unable to respond and could only justify their monopoly on power by reference to their revolution some forty years earlier. They were locked in a time warp, trapped by their ideology and increasingly powerless to influence their own destiny. It was a recipe for disaster.

The Titoist settlement was eventually challenged and overturned by Slobodan Milošević, the president of Serbia's League of Communists. Milošević used his position at the centre of the Party apparatus, responsible for patronage and appointments, to purge it and revive its fortunes by injecting it with nationalism. He then set about using the Party structure to recentralise the Yugoslav state. While the Serb nationalist programme was not originally Milošević's,[5] he took control of the narrative via mass rallies and tight media control at a time of declining living standards and diminished expectations. It was an extremely dangerous ideology for a multi-ethnic state in which Serbs had the manpower to destabilise the country, but not to dominate it.

According to the 1981 census, carried out a year after Tito's death, Serbs made up about 36 per cent of Yugoslavia's population. Of these, close to 2 million lived outside the Republic of Serbia while another 1.3 million lived in Serbia's autonomous provinces, Vojvodina and Kosovo, in addition to the 4.9 million Serbs of inner Serbia. Given the choice, most Serbs would probably have preferred to live within a centralised state, just as most non-Serbs would have opted for a federation or confederation.

Having consolidated power in Serbia, Milošević turned his attention to Vojvodina and Montenegro. Following an intense media offensive and mass demonstrations, unpopular authorities were ousted in October 1988 and January 1989 respectively and the state apparatus was purged in the same fashion as in Serbia. Then, in March 1989, Kosovo's constitution was forcibly changed, a state of emergency was declared, and twenty-eight demonstrators died in violent clashes. In the same month, Serbia's constitution was also changed to incorporate Kosovo and Vojvodina and introduce a new interpretation of sovereignty. Whereas hitherto, each Yugoslav republic had been sovereign and republican leaders had represented all people living in their territory, Milošević claimed the right to represent all Serbs throughout Yugoslavia. Since large Serb communities lived in six of Yugoslavia's eight federal units, this direct appeal was an extremely powerful weapon that Milošević used to undermine republican authority in Bosnia and Croatia.

During Milošević's assault on Tito's Yugoslavia, the federal authorities and other republics did little to stop him, opting for the path of least resistance because of their own lack of a popular mandate. Indeed, their acquiescence had been necessary for the imposition of a state of emergency and constitutional changes in Kosovo. Croatia's leadership had effectively been silent since Tito had purged nationalists in the early 1970s. Bosnia's communists were discredited following the Agrokomerc scandal. And Macedonia's leadership sympathised with Belgrade over Kosovo as a result of strained relations between ethnic Macedonians and Albanians in that republic as well. Eventually, Slovenia's communist leadership decided to break ranks and stand up to Milošević. This was largely a result of the pressure it was under within Slovenia from an increasingly confident opposition movement that was pushing for an end to single-party rule.

Developments in Slovenia were broadly in line with the rest of Eastern Europe, where the fall of the Berlin Wall on 9 November 1989 had spelled the end of one-party rule. The republic's communist leadership decided that it could not stem the tide of democracy and opted for a multi-party system. However, any attempt at introducing multi-party democracy in Slovenia would be scuppered if Milošević succeeded in recentralising Yugoslavia. As a result, the Slovene leadership began to espouse a confederal arrangement in which each republic could choose its own form of government. According to this vision, republics would be able to choose to remain communist or to evolve into multi-party democracies.

Milošević called an extraordinary fourteenth Congress of the League of Communists of Yugoslavia in January 1990. This event was billed as the clash of concepts for Yugoslavia's future. In the event, however, the Slovene delegates were shouted down and unable to present their proposals. They had, in any case, already committed themselves to multi-party elections in April. As it became clear there would be no discussion, they walked out. In the absence of the Slovene delegation, Milošević attempted to resume the Congress, but when the Croatian delegation walked out as well, the Bosnian and Macedonian communists were no longer prepared to continue and the meeting was suspended. In the short term, the tide of democracy that had just swept Eastern Europe would thwart any further attempts by Milošević to recentralise Yugoslavia via the League of Communists. But in the longer term, it was actually Yugoslavia's undoing.

Until this time, Yugoslavia had occupied a position of geopolitical significance between East and West, which Yugoslav politicians had relied upon as insurance against economic and political disaster. They had calculated correctly that the West would not stand by and watch Yugoslavia founder. But Yugoslavia's status changed when the Soviet Union chose not to intervene to restore communist rule in Eastern Europe. In the absence of the Soviet bogey, Yugoslavia lost its geostrategic importance and Yugoslavs could no longer rely on Western support to bail them out. Meanwhile, the focus of Western attention and financial aid switched to the emerging democracies that had just thrown off the Soviet yoke.

Democratic dawn

For almost forty-five years, communism had been the glue holding Yugoslav society together. In its absence, Yugoslavia remained intact, though the country Tito had built was no more. In a climate of goodwill it would likely have been possible to erect a third Yugoslavia out of the ruins of the Titoist state. In effect, the demise of communism had merely reopened the 1920s debate as to the best form of government for a common state. While the experience of the interwar period did not bode well for the prospects of a third Yugoslav incarnation, the country had come a long way. Having learned about each others' cultures and traditions in school for the previous forty-five years, Yugoslavs had grown more aware of the ethno-national complexity of their country and should have been more tolerant of one another. The number of people who chose to declare themselves 'Yugoslav', either out of conviction or because they were the progeny of mixed marriages, rather than Serb, Croat or another Yugoslav nationality, rose with each census and appeared to augur well.[6] At the same time, the logic that had made Yugoslavism so powerful a political philosophy during the nineteenth and twentieth centuries was as compelling as ever. The country was still a mosaic of nationalities whose destinies could not be separated. A single Yugoslav state enabled the vast majority of South Slavs to live within the same country and ensured that rival claims to ethno-nationally mixed territories would not spill over into conflict.

The first non-communist group to emerge was the Udruženje za jugoslovensku demokratsku inicijativu (Association for a Yugoslav Democratic Initiative, or UJDI). Founded in March 1989 by the Croat intellectual Branko Horvat, UJDI included many of the most impressive thinkers in every republic and sought to address the many issues that Yugoslav society was facing. In an effort to stave off the ethno-nationalisation of politics, UJDI came up with a form of democracy tailored to Yugoslavia's needs. Under UJDI's proposal, the country's future parliamentary system would be restricted to two parties, one communist and the other non-communist, but neither constituted along ethno-national lines.

Also in March 1989, Ante Marković, who was to be Yugoslavia's last prime minister, came into office at the head of a government of technocrats determined to address Yugoslavia's economic ills. Marković reasoned that since the political crisis was rooted in the economic downturn of the 1980s, the solution, too, would be found in the economy. Despite a trade war between Slovenia and Serbia, the Marković reforms, which included a wage freeze and price liberalisation, generated impressive results, slashing inflation from more than 2,000 per cent at the end of 1989 to below 10 per cent in just two months and doubling the country's foreign currency reserves.

Marković aimed to capitalise on his economic successes by founding his own non-communist political party, with which he hoped to contest as yet unscheduled federal elections. He reasoned that if he could organise nationwide elections he might be able to give the federal government a democratic mandate and legitimacy, which the republics, all still governed by communists, lacked. For the initiative to have any chance of succeeding, Marković needed to hold federal elections before any of the republics went to the polls. But since Slovenia's communists had already committed themselves to multi-party elections in April 1990, he needed to persuade them to delay their poll, which he was unable to do.

As far as Slovenia's communists were concerned, any move aimed at increasing the authority of Yugoslavia's federal centre was a potential threat, and they were not prepared to commit Slovenia's future to the outcome of elections that had not yet been organised and might evolve into another vehicle for Serb nationalism. The atmosphere of fear that Milošević had created through mass rallies, hysterical media reporting and police rule in Kosovo had set their course. By holding multi-party elections at a republican as opposed to a federal level, Slovenia's communists were setting a precedent whose consequences would be felt elsewhere.

Since Slovenia's population was predominantly Slovene, the choice of electoral system was not controversial. Political representation was, nevertheless, built in for Hungarian and Italian minorities via designated seats to ensure them a voice in parliament, though not for Yugoslav citizens who had moved to Slovenia from elsewhere.[7] In the parliamentary election, which took place before Marković was able to form a party, a coalition of six opposition parties defeated the reformed communists, though in the presidential election the reformed communist candidate hung onto power.

In Croatia, where elections took place two weeks after Slovenia, the choice of electoral system was extremely important, given that a quarter of the population was not Croat, that nearly 12 per cent was Serb and that Serb political representation had been a prominent feature of the communist system in that republic.[8] In retrospect, the majoritarian, first-past-the-post system was not best suited to the republic. It was, however, deliberately chosen by the communists, now calling themselves the Party of Democratic Change (Stranka demokratskih promjena, or SDP), in the mistaken belief that it would work to their advantage. Although the former communists polled well, the system worked against them. An ethno-national party, the Hrvatska demokratska zajednica (Croat Democratic Union, or HDZ), led by Franjo Tuđman, a Titoist general turned nationalist dissident, won an absolute majority of parliamentary seats on a minority poll.[9]

Whether or not a more appropriate electoral system would have made any difference to the evolution of Yugoslavia's disintegration is debatable.[10] What is clear is that the advent of democracy transformed the relationship between Croats and Serbs in Croatia. Whereas the communist system had bent over backwards to make Serbs feel secure in Croatia, political power had now been transferred to a political party that represented exclusively Croat interests. Moreover, it had won its votes by promising to stand up to Serb nationalism and would rapidly change the republic's constitution to downgrade the status of Croatia's Serbs from that of a 'nation' to that of a 'national minority'. The issue of Serb rights in Croatia was real,[11] even if Belgrade's actions only aggravated the situation.[12]

The Croatian poll set the scene for Bosnia's elections that took place in November and December 1990 and the party system that subsequently became entrenched. A month before the Croatian poll, the Bosnian parliament, aware of the potential dangers of ethno-national politics, adopted an Election Law that banned political organisation on the basis of ethno-national identity. The key provision was, however, declared unconstitutional by the Constitutional Court and removed from the legislation under which the elections were eventually conducted.[13] As a result, the parties that registered were overwhelmingly ethno-national, the three most successful of which were to be the Stranka demokratske akcije (Party of Democratic Action, or SDA), the Srpska demokratska stranka (Serb Democratic Party, or SDS) and the HDZ.

Since the SDA was registered in March 1990 before the provision banning ethno-national parties was struck down, the party's name did not carry an ethno-national prefix. It was, however, clearly a Muslim party. The SDA was headed by Alija Izetbegović, a man who had been imprisoned by the communists in the 1940s and 1980s and had authored a 1970 *Islamic Declaration*, which extolled the virtues of an Islamic state. The SDS was formally founded in Bosnia in July 1990 and led by Radovan Karadžić. It bore the same name as the Serb ethno-national party that had already contested the Croatian election because that party's leader, Jovan Rašković, had contacted Karadžić, his professional colleague, to encourage him to create it. Both men were psychiatrists. The HDZ was created in August 1990 as a branch of the ruling party in Croatia. The three ethno-national parties campaigned together against the Savez komunista-Socijalistička demokratska partija (League of Communists-Social Democratic Party, or SK-SDP) and Marković's newly formed Savez reformskih snaga Jugoslavije (League of Reform Forces of Yugoslavia, or SRSJ).

In November and December 1990, several elections took place in Bosnia—to the 130-member Chamber of Citizens, the 110-member Chamber of Municipalities, the seven-member presidency and the municipal assemblies—each with a different electoral system. Deputies to the Chamber of Citizens were elected in seven large, multi-member districts in which seats were distributed proportionally on the basis of the total number of valid votes cast. Deputies to the Chamber of Municipalities were elected on a majoritarian basis in each municipality, with a second round of voting if necessary. The ethno-national composition of the Bosnian parliament resulting from these elections had to be within a 15 per cent deviation of the ethno-national composition of the population as recorded in the 1991 census. At the presidential level, each voter was able to cast seven votes to elect two Croats, two Muslims, two Serbs and one Other to the presidency. The candidates who were elected were those in each group who obtained the most votes. At the municipal level, seats were awarded on a proportional basis.

Commentators at the time described the November and December 1990 polls as more of a census than a contested election.[14] More than 80 per cent of voters opted for the three main ethno-national parties in what were well-organised, free and fair elections despite a high proportion—more than 20 per cent—of invalid ballots. Moreover, the electoral system helped these three parties to an even greater share of seats at all but the municipal level.

Bosnians were not voting for the wholesale destruction of their home republic. Rather, they were seeking security at a time when the demise of communism and the emergence of Serb and Croat nationalism made ethno-national security an issue. Fear was one of the most important motivating factors, since anyone not voting for his or her own ethno-national representatives would effectively be increasing the ethno-national representation of the other communities. In this way, the vote of the smallest community, the Croats, was most homogenised behind the HDZ, that of the Serbs somewhat less homogenised behind the SDS and that of the largest community, the Muslims, most fractured, though still largely homogeneous.

Given Bosnia's ethno-national composition, a mixed government working together would have been in the interests of the vast majority of the population. Moreover, having joined forces to defeat the former communists, the three ethno-national parties agreed to form a governing coalition together. But apart from agreeing to purge the former communist administration, replacing cadres loyal to the Titoist system with their own apparatchiks, most of whom were former communists, the three ruling ethno-national parties could find no common ground.

Key offices were divided among the ruling parties. Alija Izetbegović became president;[15] Jure Pelivan of the HDZ prime minister; and Momčilo Krajišnik of the SDS speaker of the parliament. Beyond this division of spoils, however, the coalition partners found it virtually impossible to co-operate. As a result, Bosnia's democratic institutions failed to function. In municipalities where one ethno-national party held a majority of seats, it formed its own ethno-nationally pure government. In municipalities where no ethno-national party had an absolute majority, their representatives proved incapable of working together. The exception was Tuzla, where non-nationalists had won the municipal election and formed a multi-ethnic administration that continued to function to some extent even after war had broken out.

Under communism, Croats, Muslims and Serbs had been guaranteed proportional representation in all socio-political bodies, but mechanisms to protect vital national interests—such as the need for super-majorities as opposed to simple majorities to pass certain legislation—did not exist. In anticipation of controversy, a series of constitutional amendments was passed in July 1990. This included the formation of a Council for Questions of the Establishment of Equality of the Nations and Nationalities of Bosnia to review any act of the National Assembly should twenty or more deputies consider it to undermine ethno-national equality. However, this body did not become operational. A Constitutional Commission was, nevertheless, formed at the beginning of 1991 to determine how decisions should be taken on constitutional issues, whether by consensus or by majority vote. Here, however, agreement could not be reached on the nature of the Bosnian state, whether it was a republic of citizens or of nations, or even on how power could be exercised by the various tiers of government.

The advent of multi-party democracy left Bosnia both polarised and paralysed. The interests of the republic's communities could not be reconciled or protected within the existing institutions. The result was that politics rapidly degenerated into a zero-sum equation, in which issues were viewed strictly in terms of winners and losers and efforts to develop compromise solutions were interpreted as a sign of weakness. At the same time, each ethno-national ruling party was developing its own parallel power structures, re-creating the *nomenklatura* system along ethno-national lines. In October 1990, even before the elections had taken place, the SDS had formed a Serb National Council to serve as an alternative decision-making authority. Meanwhile, the broader Yugoslav political environment continued to deteriorate.

Descent into war

Discussions on the Yugoslav state failed to generate any results in the course of 1990. This was in large part because Serbia felt it had no need to make concessions. Milošević was dictating the course of events, controlling four out of the eight positions in the federal presidency, including the post of president, during the critical year between 15 May 1990 and 15 May 1991. He was also able to use and abuse the Serb communities outside Serbia, in whose name he claimed to speak, secure in the knowledge that he alone could back up positions by force.

As communism was defeated in multi-party elections in Slovenia, Croatia and then Bosnia, the Jugoslovenska narodna armija (Yugoslav National Army, or JNA), which was constitutionally committed to preserving the 'gains of the revolution' and to a unitary state, disarmed the territorial defence forces of each republic in turn.[16] The JNA then formed a Serbian alliance by default, since only Milošević appeared committed to both communism and a unitary state. Indeed, in the run-up to the December 1990 election in Serbia, which Milošević could not avoid, hard-line communists, including Milošević's wife Mira Marković and senior JNA officers, created a new Communist Party, the Savez komunista-Pokret za Jugoslaviju (League of Communists-Movement for Yugoslavia, or SKPJ), and endorsed Milošević's newly renamed Socijalistička partija Srbije (Socialist Party of Serbia, or SPS) as the party to vote for.

Milošević's SPS retained power in a contest in which the main opposition, Vuk Drašković's Srpski pokret obnove (Serb Renewal Movement, or SPO), appeared, if anything, even more nationalistic. Milošević succeeded where other former communist leaders failed by maintaining tight control of the media, using a first-past-the-post electoral system (requiring only a relative majority of votes for an absolute majority of seats), and by a healthy electoral bribe, in the form of hefty wage and pension increases, on the eve of the elections.[17] Although the vote was not overtly rigged, the opposition alleged fraud and organised street protests against the biased reporting of state television. These culminated in a Belgrade rally attended by more than 150,000 people on 9 March 1991 that degenerated into street fighting, required the deployment of the JNA to restore order, and cost the lives of one protester and one policeman.

The events of 9 March 1991 were significant on many levels. Firstly, they revealed how determined Milošević was to hang on to power. Secondly, they led to renewed attempts by Milošević to generate crises elsewhere in the Yugoslav Federation, especially in Croatia, to divert attention from the situation within Serbia. And thirdly, they confirmed to Slovene minds the need to extricate Slovenia as quickly as possible from the quagmire into which the rest of Yugoslavia was heading.

On the same day that Milošević's SPS won Serbia's elections, 23 December 1990, Slovenes went to the polls in an independence referendum.[18] Three days later the Slovene parliament declared its intent to secede from Yugoslavia in six months, if there were no progress towards a negotiated settlement of the country's future. The JNA's 1989 intervention in Kosovo and the ongoing suppression of the province's Albanian majority had a huge impact on Slovene attitudes to the rest of the Yugoslav Federation, stoking fears of a similar scenario within Slovenia itself. Moreover, events in Croatia, where a Serb revolt had begun in the aftermath of the April and May 1990 elections, appeared to be heading in a similar direction.

The advent of multi-party democracy and the possibility of the fragmentation of Yugoslavia opened up questions about how to regulate relations among communities and develop appropriate mechanisms for autonomy and cultural rights that needed to be addressed. However, the way Milošević set about resolving these questions on behalf of the Serb communities of Croatia and Bosnia could only exacerbate the situation, alienating the country's other peoples and working against the longer-term interests of the very people he claimed to represent.

Having faced hostility in the Croatian parliament in Zagreb, SDS MPs in Croatia formed a separate Union of Communes of Lika and Northern Dalmatia, with its own assembly, the Serb National Council, in Knin. This body's first move was to proclaim the sovereignty and independence of the Serb nation. It then severed relations with Zagreb and announced a Serb referendum on autonomy to be held over a two-week period in August and September 1990. Croatian government attempts to intervene and halt the referendum were blocked by the JNA.

The majority of Croatia's Serbs—especially the urban population—had largely ignored Milošević's propaganda offensive, which started in the 1980s and included ceremonies commemorating Serb dead at sites of Ustaša atrocities during the Second World War. They also voted for the reformed communists in the 1990 election. Most were acutely aware of their vulnerability should conflict break out with the Croat majority and would have preferred not to have to choose camps. However, they had little choice as hostilities escalated. The Serb revolt was at first confined to shooting at trains and harassing foreign tourists in the region around Knin, which became known as Krajina (border region).[19] But each month it intensified, non-Serbs moved out, shooting incidents became more frequent, and bombs began going off elsewhere in Croatia. By autumn 1990,[20] Croatia was locked in a spiral of violence that was pushing the republic steadily towards bloodshed.

As the security situation in Croatia deteriorated, Milošević tried repeatedly, together with Borisav Jović, the federal president and head of the country's armed forces, to impose a state of emergency on the country. Following the 9 March 1991 demonstrations in Belgrade, Jović called a meeting of the federal presidency that was also attended by military leaders. Representatives of the four federal units controlled by Milošević voted for imposition of a state of emergency, but required one more vote to put it into effect. They anticipated that the vote would come from the Bosnian member of the presidency, Bogić Bogićević, who was a Serb. However, despite being put under intense pressure, Bogičević remained steadfast and blocked the imposition.

On 15 March, in the wake of failure to impose a state of emergency, Jović resigned together with the representatives of Montenegro and Vojvodina claiming that the balance of power within the presidency was leading to the break-up of the country. Jović returned to the presidency six days later without any explanation. The same night, Milošević went on Belgrade television to state that Serbia would no longer obey the federal presidency and was mobilising police reservists to avert rebellion in Kosovo and Sandžak. He also urged Serbs to unite behind him to defend themselves. The next day, the Serb National Council in Knin proclaimed the secession of Krajina from Croatia and Serbia's prime minister informed the Serbian parliament that Bosnian and Croatian forces were preparing an offensive against Serb-populated towns.

As important as what was actually happening in Yugoslavia during 1990 and the first half of 1991 were public perceptions. This did not depend on real events but on the atmosphere created by political rhetoric and rival media, since a climate for war existed months and possibly years before anyone was killed. The first showdown took place on 2 March 1991 in Pakrac, a Serb-majority town in Western Slavonia, where armed Croats and Serbs faced each other with the JNA in the wings. It was the culmination of several weeks' struggle over control of the police station and, though shots were fired, the day passed without casualties. Despite this, Serbian media reported that some forty Serbs had been killed. This deliberate misinformation was presumably designed to generate a pretext for intervention, but failed because local Serbs were fearful of the consequences and exercised restraint.

In Pakrac, the Serb and Croat militias were mainly made up of people from the town itself. Many had lived their entire lives there and knew their adversaries personally. A sense of community persisted and neither side could demonise the other sufficiently for fighting to break out. Indeed, had territorial disputes been left to the locals, they could have been worked out since all sides had too much to lose in the event of war. But outsiders, who did not have the same sense of community or of the potential losses involved, including Serb paramilitary forces loyal to warlord-politicians Željko Ražnjatović-Arkan and Vojislav Šešelj, increasingly dictated the pace of events.

In the next showdown, on 31 March 1991, a Croatian policeman and a Serb rebel died as the Krajina militia clashed with Croatian police over control of Plitvice National Park. After a day's fighting, the Croatian police had captured twenty-nine Serb fighters. That night, the federal presidency met in emergency session and, at Jović's insistence, ordered the JNA to take control of the situation to prevent further bloodshed. It was the beginning of a pattern, which was to last until the autumn, when the JNA gave up all pretence of neutrality.

Three days before the Plitvice clashes, Yugoslavia's six republican presidents began a series of weekly summits aimed at resolving the crisis. Though Bosnia and Macedonia were eager to agree anything that might hold Yugoslavia together,[21] the gulf between the Serbian position and that of Slovenia and Croatia could not be bridged. Meanwhile, the pattern of Serb provocation and Croat reprisal acquired a self-perpetuating momentum in Croatia. On 2 May, twelve Croatian policemen were killed in Borovo Selo, a Serb village just outside Vukovar in Eastern Slavonia, and several of their bodies were mutilated by paramilitary forces loyal to Šešelj in the first atrocity to be committed in the conflict. That night, after another emergency session of the presidency, JNA units were again deployed to separate warring factions. The next day, Tuđman went on television to announce that war had begun.

The Borovo Selo massacre was the last occasion when Jović could use his position as president to direct federal policy. His mandate ran out on 15 May 1991 when he was due to hand over to Croatia's representative on the presidency, Stjepan Mesić. The handover should have been a formality as every year on 15 May a new president was appointed and the office went to each federal unit on a rotational basis. However, though it was Croatia's turn to head the presidency, the Serbian bloc rejected Mesić's appointment. The presidency was divided, Mesić was not elected and the institution that served as Yugoslavia's head of state and commander-in-chief of the armed forces was left in limbo.

The toxic combination of escalating violence in Croatia and political deadlock added to the resolve of Slovenia's leaders to distance themselves from the rest of the country and spurred their preparations for independence. Fearful of the prospect of being left behind, Croatia's leaders decided to follow Slovenia and, in a hastily arranged referendum on 19 May, the vast majority of Croatia's population voted for independence.[22] Since the Serbs of Krajina had organised their own plebiscite two months earlier, in which they voted unanimously to remain part of Yugoslavia, Tuđman was aware that an independence declaration appeared to play into Milošević's hands. However, he viewed it as the least of many evils, deciding that the risk of remaining part of a rump state without Slovenia was greater than that of declaring independence. The date set for the formal declaration was 29 June 1991, three days after Slovenia's proposed date, to give Tuđman time to see how Serbia and the JNA reacted to it, and, in the intervening month, Croatia joined Slovenia in intensive lobbying of international opinion.

Hitherto, the international community had played no direct role in the Yugoslav drama and had no intention of becoming involved. While the major powers were aware that the country was disintegrating, they could see no easy solutions and felt no obligation to try and resolve the internal problems of another country. Yugoslavia had lost its strategic importance as a buffer state between

East and West, and diplomats lost patience with the country's seemingly irrational obsessions and intractable problems. Eastern Europe's emerging democracies became the focus of diplomatic activity and foreign investment in the region, while events in the Middle East, Iraq's invasion of Kuwait and the Gulf War, eclipsed all others.

Nevertheless, international opinion mattered greatly. Yugoslavs looked abroad, and especially to the European Community, for help in the transition from communism. One of the European Community's preconditions for assistance was that Yugoslavia stay together. The European Community was loath to see Yugoslavia fragment into mini-states for two reasons: divorce was likely to be messy, and it could become an unwanted precedent for the Soviet Union, which at the time also appeared to be on the verge of disintegration. Although the European Community expected a resolution of Yugoslavia's internal conflict without recourse to violence, its insistence on the status quo inadvertently contributed to the deadlock in the country's constitutional talks. By insisting on a single entity, the European Community appeared to be backing Serbia and the JNA, giving Milošević little reason to compromise.

While Slovenia and Croatia sought to internationalise Yugoslavia's internal conflict to improve their position in relation to Serbia, the meagre international engagement only undermined their position. Rather than urging moderation on Serbia and the JNA, diplomatic efforts focussed on pressuring Slovenia and Croatia into abandoning their independence declarations. Though well-intentioned, such moves bolstered the resolve of the Yugoslav military and risked legitimising their use of force. Indeed, it may have been the eleventh-hour intervention by US Secretary of State James Baker, designed to head off Slovenia and Croatia's independence declarations, which pushed Yugoslavia over the edge into war.

Five days before Slovenia was due to declare independence, Baker, who was on an official visit to Albania, made an unscheduled stop-over in Belgrade to make the US position on Yugoslav matters clear. During his one-day visit he met with Yugoslavia's republican leaders and military chiefs and declared that the United States would not recognise Slovenia or Croatia 'under any circumstances'.

DISINTEGRATION

The message the various Yugoslav leaders perceived from Baker, whether or not this was his intention, was that the United States was prepared to accept military action to hold Yugoslavia together.

Despite Baker's warning, the leaders of Slovenia and Croatia pressed ahead with independence declarations. Indeed, as they got wind of JNA plans, both republics brought the date forward to 25 June. Just over a day later, in the early hours of 27 June, the JNA dispatched tanks to secure Slovenia's border crossings and Ljubljana Airport. It was the beginning of the Wars of Yugoslav Dissolution, an armed conflict that would suck in the entire country over the next decade, with the most serious consequences in Bosnia, the most ethno-nationally mixed republic. Two days after war broke out, the international community became formally involved as the *troika* of foreign ministers co-ordinating the European Community's foreign policy arrived, hoping to help mediate a solution.[23]

4

WAR AND PEACE

'The Yugoslav War of Dissolution was about statehood, sovereignty, self-determination and, effectively, the meaning of "nation", as well as the identity and future of particular nations.'

James Gow[1]

Self-determination, legitimacy and hostilities

The war in Slovenia lasted ten days,[2] ending with the Brioni Accord of 7 July 1991 under which the JNA halted all actions on Slovene territory and Slovenia and Croatia froze their independence declarations for three months. This moratorium was designed to buy the time to give Yugoslavia's leaders a second chance to resolve their differences with the assistance of the European Community (EC). To this end, the European Community established a Peace Conference on Yugoslavia in The Hague on 7 September under the chairmanship of Lord Peter Carrington, the former British foreign minister and NATO secretary general.

EC efforts to contribute to a peaceful solution are often ridiculed by reference to the unfortunate comment of Jacques Poos, the Luxembourg foreign minister and leader of the original EC *troika*, that the hour of Europe had dawned.[3] However, the EC Peace Conference was, in theory, exactly what Yugoslavia needed, since it aimed to consider the country as a whole and to develop a coordinated approach to the region's conflicts, rather than dealing with flashpoints such as Slovenia in isolation. All Yugoslav peoples, including the Albanians of Kosovo and the Hungarians of Vojvodina, were able to make their own representations, and the condition of Bosnia and Macedonia was from the outset supposed to be as much part of the agenda as the more pressing crises in Slovenia and Croatia.

Although the European Community wanted the Yugoslavs to reach a solution among themselves without recourse to violence, such a prospect was by this stage extremely unlikely. Another round of inter-republican meetings across the summer, brokered by Macedonia's representative on the federal presidency, Vasil Tupurkovski, failed to make progress against a backdrop of ever-escalating violence in Croatia. Even at the height of the war in Slovenia, the conflict in Croatia had been more intense and the fighting heavier, though, at Milošević's insistence, the Brioni resolutions were restricted to Slovenia. As a result, EC observers were only able to monitor the ceasefire in Slovenia and had no mandate to extend their operations into Croatia.

Although hostilities began in Slovenia, the future of that republic was hardly contested since Serbia had no territorial pretensions against it.[4] Indeed, Slovene President Milan Kučan had discussed the prospect of a peaceful divorce in bilateral talks with Milošević at the beginning of the year. In declaring independence, the Slovene leadership had not been severing all ties with the rest of the country but setting in motion a process of what it called 'dissociation' under which it had already prepared plans for a restructuring of the JNA and the apportioning of Yugoslavia's debt, among other issues that needed resolution. This process was accelerated when the JNA decided on 18 July 1991 to withdraw unilaterally, completing the task by 25 October 1991, one week over the three-month deadline it had set for itself. The ease with which Slovenia disentangled itself from the Yugoslav Federation was to prove deceptively reassuring.

The complexity and urgency of the Yugoslav crisis were almost certainly more than the European Community was equipped to deal with at the time. The EC Peace Conference on Yugoslavia was operating in areas in which the European Community had no prior experience and no diplomatic machinery to deploy. Yet the European Community had to decide who the legitimate interlocutors were, to be a credible mediator and, ultimately, to adjudicate on the competing claims of Yugoslavia's republics and peoples. To provide the EC Peace Conference with legal advice, a five-member Arbitration Commission was created on 27 August 1991. Headed by Robert Badinter, president of France's Constitutional Court, and including his peers from Belgium, Germany, Italy and Spain, the Commission would issue a series of opinions between then and the middle of 1993 to assist the European Community in its decision-making.

The Badinter Commission's opinions remain controversial in the former Yugoslavia to this day. One reason is that they sought to address the issues at the heart of the conflict. Views as to how and why war broke out essentially boil down to competing interpretations of the right to self-determination. Critical to this debate are competing definitions of 'nation'—whether all people living within the territorial boundaries of a given political community or all members of a particular ethno-national group. Leaders of each community had a different view as to where sovereignty lay—whether in a geographic entity or in the ethno-national group—and how self-determination should be implemented. This reflected the geographic distribution—whether concentrated in certain republics or spread out across much of the country—and status—whether a nation or a national minority—of the community they represented.

The Serb position on these matters was clear. Sovereignty lay in the ethno-national group. If other nations sought self-determination and wished to secede from the common Yugoslav state, they were entitled to do so. However, they would not be able to take territory with them on which Serbs lived, irrespective of internal, administrative borders. In the event that nations, nevertheless, sought to secede and take territory with them on which Serbs lived, Serbs, too, had the right to self-determination and would seek to remain part of Yugoslavia. If Croats in Croatia or Croats and Muslims in Bosnia had the right to secede from Yugoslavia, by the same logic Serbs had the right to secede from Croatia and Bosnia and to remain part of Yugoslavia. It was and remains a powerful argument, albeit one that was ultimately rejected by the Badinter Commission, in legal opinions that paved the way for the international recognition of Yugoslavia's constituent republics as independent states.

The Badinter Commission's opinions have helped fuel conspiracy theories about international plots to destroy Yugoslavia.[5] This is ironic, since, despite poor omens for Yugoslavia for several years,[6] the international community did its best to ignore the country's plight right up until June 1991 in the hope that somehow Yugoslavs would resolve their differences and the problem would go away. This policy of neglect was facilitated by Iraq's invasion of Kuwait in August 1990 and the subsequent Gulf War, which eclipsed all other conflicts for the best part of a year. What international involvement there was in Yugoslavia was aimed at holding the country together.

US Secretary of State James Baker's eleventh-hour intervention was part of a flurry of diplomatic activity on the eve of the independence declarations. A day before Baker's visit to Belgrade, the Conference on Security and Co-operation in Europe (CSCE) reiterated support for Yugoslavia's continued territorial integrity and on 23 June EC foreign ministers agreed unanimously not to recognise the independence of Slovenia and Croatia if they seceded unilaterally from Yugoslavia. Earlier, at the end of May, an EC delegation to Belgrade, headed by Commission President Jacques Delors, promised Marković generous financial aid if the country remained together, though by this stage Marković had minimal influence over the course of events. The EC Peace Conference on Yugoslavia was also seeking to broker an arrangement by which the country would remain together so that it would not be necessary to make rulings on what were mutually exclusive positions.

The EC Peace Conference on Yugoslavia presented a document entitled *Arrangements for a General Settlement* to the concerned parties on 18 October 1991 seeking to reconcile their positions with principles of human rights and the peaceful settlement of disputes as enshrined in international treaties and CSCE and UN resolutions. Under these proposals, Yugoslavia's successor states would form a loose confederation consisting of the former republics within their existing boundaries, but under obligation to protect human rights, including the collective rights of minorities.[7] They would also be offered a 'European perspective': the prospect of a closer relationship with the European Community, with recognition tied to compliance with European political norms. Although the document contained much of what Slovenia and Croatia had been proposing before the beginning of hostilities, it was drafted in such a way that republican borders could be redrawn on the basis of peaceful negotiation and that a federal Yugoslavia could be formed among those republics wishing it, in an attempt to persuade Serbia to sign on. It also deliberately avoided any reference to the situation in Kosovo. Despite this, Serbia rejected the proposal on 5 November 1991,[8] arguing that it presupposed the disappearance of Yugoslavia as an independent state, effectively turning Serbs outside Serbia into minorities.

Meanwhile, armed Serbs were in a position to forge mini-states in both Croatia and Bosnia. Despite Lord Carrington's diplomatic efforts, the contours of succession were being decided by force on the ground. Moreover, in the absence of coercive powers, the EC Peace Conference on Yugoslavia was little more than a bystander to these events. At this point, the European Community did briefly consider dispatching a military force to Croatia. The Dutch presidency proposed deployment of an 'interposition force' and France an intervention force to impose a ceasefire. But these proposals were ruled out by the United Kingdom at a meeting of EC foreign ministers in Brussels on 19 September and with them any military involvement. In practice, therefore, EC mediators were not in a position to address the Yugoslav crisis on its merits, but found themselves dealing exclusively with the belligerents in the increasingly forlorn hope of persuading them to observe a ceasefire. Having threatened to impose sanctions on any party that did not accept the outline peace agreement, the European Community suspended trade and aid agreements with Yugoslavia on 8 November and then restored those benefits to the 'co-operative republics' on 2 December, that is to all but Serbia and Montenegro.

The actions of all sides were depressingly predictable, reflecting the military hardware, resources and manpower of each. Initial Serb victories in both Croatia and Bosnia were down to an imbalance in firepower that became a near-permanent feature of the conflict after the UN Security Council imposed an arms embargo on the whole of Yugoslavia on 25 September 1991. In the long run, however, the situation in terms of resources and manpower favoured Croats in Croatia and Muslims in Bosnia, especially as sanctions began to take their toll on the economy of Serbia and Montenegro.

Krajina Serbs were well-armed because they had been supplied with weapons by Serbia during 1990 and 1991.[9] They were therefore able to extend the territory under their control, especially during the summer of 1991 when Croatian government forces lacked similar firepower. These were, however, illusory victories, since Croatian government resources were incomparably greater than anything available to the Krajina Serbs who were dependent on the support of Serbia and the JNA. Moreover, they served, above all, to shatter relations between Croats and Serbs, the majority of whom lived outside Krajina.

Given Croatia's initial military weakness and the threat this posed to his own position, Tuđman was eager to negotiate with Milošević. Indeed, hoping to take advantage of Milošević's weakened position after the 9 March riots, Tuđman sought a meeting with him to discuss possible solutions. While the precise contents of the 25 March meeting between the two men at Tito's former hunting lodge in Karađordevo in Vojvodina have never been published, it is clear that Tuđman proposed the division of Bosnia as a way of avoiding conflict between Croats and Serbs. At the time, Tuđman's ideal solution was the 1939 *Sporazum*, or Cvetković-Maček Agreement, which established a Croat *banovina* incorporating most of Yugoslavia's Croats, though he was aware that his negotiating position was weak because of the military imbalance. Indeed, it appears that Tuđman was even willing to offer parts of Croatia, including regions where Croats formed a majority, such as Vukovar, in exchange for a peaceful settlement. Though this proposition was largely at the expense of Bosnia's Muslim community, it seemed to Tuđman to be both logical and preferable to war.

The fact that Tuđman and Milošević could brazenly discuss the partition of Bosnia was a reflection of the situation on the ground a year before the formal outbreak of hostilities. Since the ethno-national parties that had won the election were unable to work together, the state had ceased to function. The centralised administrative structure bequeathed by the communists did not correspond to the new ethno-national realities. It was therefore bypassed as each ethno-national ruling party built its own alternative structures. Serb autonomous authorities became the effective government across much of the republic. Croat administrative bodies took charge in Western Herzegovina and some other Croat enclaves. Moreover, the centralised tax system disintegrated as revenues were effectively appropriated by ethno-national administrations at the local level, leaving the central government increasingly short of resources. Although Izetbegović formally represented Bosnia at meetings of republican presidents, his government in Sarajevo had little influence over much of the republic.

The Serb cause, which was strong in both moral and legal terms if taken at face value, was undermined, above all, by the way in which it was prosecuted. While propagandists made all sorts of claims about what was happening during the war in Croatia, an impartial record of events was compiled in real time by the EC Monitoring Mission. At the beginning of September, Milošević had been persuaded to extend its mandate to Croatia and the observers produced a confidential report on the war, which was leaked to the media by diplomatic sources sympathetic to Croatia. The report accused the JNA and Serb irregulars of a systematic campaign of terror, killing, looting and ethnic cleansing across Croatia and pointed out that, whereas the Croatian authorities had allowed the observers to carry out their investigations freely in Croat-held territory, the JNA and Serb irregulars had barred access to many areas. It concluded that, though Croats had also committed atrocities, the overwhelming majority had been committed by Serbs against Croats.

This was the highly charged atmosphere in which the Badinter Commission began issuing opinions. The first, issued on 29 November 1991, determined that the Socialist Federal Republic of Yugoslavia was 'in the process of dissolution'.[10] The second, issued on 11 January 1992, determined that the 'Serb population in Bosnia and Croatia is entitled to all the rights concerned to minorities and ethnic groups... and that the republics must afford the members of those minorities and ethnic groups all the human rights and fundamental freedoms recognised in international law.'[11] And in the third opinion, also issued on 11 January 1992, it determined that 'the boundaries between Croatia and Serbia, between Bosnia and Serbia, and possibly other adjacent independent states may not be altered except by agreement freely arrived at... Except where otherwise agreed, the boundaries become frontiers protected by international law.'[12] This was justified on the basis of *uti possidetis*, the international legal principle meaning 'as you possess' in Latin that had been used to set borders of newly independent states following decolonisation. These opinions provided the legal underpinning to the European Community's policy of recognition. In effect, republics had the right to self-determination, but not nations or national minorities.

Recognition and recrimination

The Badinter Commission was acutely aware that the opinions it presented would also be applicable to and set precedents for the Soviet Union, which was also in the process of dissolution. It was therefore attempting to devise universal solutions that would help foster maximum stability through commitment to human rights and minimal redrawing of borders. It was also seeking to provide coherence for the European Community, whose own members had been divided as to the best course of action.

As fighting escalated in Croatia, a rift emerged between countries such as Germany, which believed the way to end the war was to confront Serbia and punish it by recognising Croatia, and the United Kingdom, which preferred to avoid taking sides and was unwilling to extend recognition to any state that did not control its own territory. Increasing evidence of Serb atrocities and the failure of the EC Peace Conference brought most EC countries over to the German position. After a nine-hour meeting on 16 and 17 December 1991, EC foreign ministers agreed to recognise on 15 January 1992 any Yugoslav republic seeking recognition that also fulfilled the human rights standards set out in the EC's *Arrangements for a General Settlement*.[13] The Badinter Commission would advise on each application.

In addition to Slovenia and Croatia, both Bosnia and Macedonia applied to the Badinter Commission, as did the unofficial Albanian government of Kosovo. In the case of Slovenia and Croatia, recognition was little more than a formality and the Badinter Commission duly recommended that both republics be recognised, though Zagreb was asked to improve its minorities legislation. The Commission also recommended that Macedonia be granted recognition, but ignored the Albanian application since Kosovo was not a republic. Bosnia was deemed more complex and the Commission decided that evidence of the state of public opinion should be gathered, 'possibly by means of a referendum', before it could consider the matter further. Meanwhile, another conference was set up within the EC Peace Conference on Yugoslavia specifically to mediate a way forward among increasingly hostile rival ethno-national elites in Bosnia, again under the chairmanship of Lord Carrington.

The decision to recognise Slovenia and Croatia generated widespread criticism at the time and is blamed in some quarters for the carnage that followed. Indeed, both Lord Carrington and Cyrus Vance, his UN counterpart who had been appointed special envoy in early October, opposed recognition of Slovenia and Croatia in January 1992, and Izetbegović also requested it be withheld for fear of the impact on Bosnia. However, the only comprehensive, academic study of this issue, by Richard Caplan, deems recognition policy to have had minimal impact, arguing that 'the forces of violence in the region were to a large degree operating independently of the factor of recognition.'[14] Indeed, given what was happening on the ground, any attempt to blame recognition policy for triggering war in Bosnia is, at best, simplistic. By contrast, as Caplan points out, recognition opened up opportunities for more effective international action, and it was the 'failure to seize those opportunities, rather than the strategic effects of recognition, that best explains the tragic events that ensued'.[15]

As much as Yugoslavia desperately needed an overall settlement, the EC Peace Conference was not remotely close to reaching one. Moreover, by working towards so broad an agreement it risked prolonging the Croatian War almost indefinitely since resolution would be hostage to even more intractable issues such as that of Kosovo and the status of its Albanian population. Although the plight of Serbs outside Serbia was the focus of discussions on minority rights at the EC Peace Conference, the conditions in which Croats, Hungarians and other minorities in Vojvodina, Muslims in Serbia's Sandžak or Albanians in Kosovo lived were incomparably worse. Croatian government representatives were always happy to offer identical rights to Serbs within Croatia as those enjoyed by non-Serbs in Serbia.

The key factor that ensured that the seventeenth internationally brokered ceasefire of the Croatian War held, thereby bringing the fighting to a halt in January 1992, was neither the prospect of international recognition nor the skill of mediators, but the situation on the ground. By the time Vukovar, scene of the heaviest fighting, fell on 18 November, the military equation was very different to that in the summer when large-scale hostilities erupted. Although the balance of firepower was still weighted against the Croatian government, the tide of battle was turning. Indeed, it had begun to turn at the beginning of that month when Croatian government forces went on the offensive for the first time, recapturing a swathe of territory in Western Slavonia. The formation of a Croatian Army and the performance of the JNA were critical to the turn-about in military fortunes. The Croatian Army, whose core were JNA-trained officers, benefitted from rising morale and had acquired sufficient weaponry to be able to hold their own. The JNA, by contrast, had haemorrhaged non-Serb soldiers, was suffering desertions among Serbs, and was struggling to call up reservists in Serbia and Montenegro, where mobilisation orders were often ignored.

Even though Serbs had formed the majority of the population in Western Slavonia, the JNA retreated in the wake of the Croatian Army's offensive and local Serbs chose to flee rather than face reprisals. These now displaced Serbs were then moved to Eastern Slavonia, adjacent to Serbia, where the Croat and Hungarian populations, which had formed the majority, had already been expelled. The result was more compact Serb-held territories, corresponding to about 22 per cent of Croatia, that could best be held by a truce that froze the front lines. To this end, Milošević called on the United Nations—not the European Community—to prepare a treaty.

The agreement ending the Croatian War was duly put together by Vance and signed in Sarajevo on 2 January 1992. It envisaged deployment of 14,000 peacekeepers and the demilitarisation of contested regions. Serb forces were expected to give up captured territory where Serbs did not live, and the peacekeepers would, in time, enable all people to return to their homes. The Sarajevo Accord was not a definitive solution because it left the final status of Serb enclaves vague, enabling Zagreb to understand that they remained within Croatia and Belgrade to believe that they would be independent and self-governing. It suited both Zagreb and Belgrade, but not the leaders of the self-proclaimed Republika Srpska Krajina (Republic of Serb Krajina, or RSK). They feared reintegration into Croatia on any terms and had already declared independence on 19 December. Moreover, their subsequent failure to comply with the agreement and rejection of all other proposals would help ensure that it would amount to no more than a protracted ceasefire.

Although the headquarters of the UN Protection Force (UNPROFOR) was scheduled to be in Sarajevo, the situation in Bosnia was arguably already more precarious. Indeed, the JNA and Serb irregulars had used Bosnian territory to launch attacks against Croatia during the Croatian War; Croats and Serbs from Bosnia had been fighting against each other in Croatia; and increasing armed incidents in Bosnia risked spiralling out of control. Already in early October 1991 the predominantly Croat village of Ravno in Eastern Herzegovina had been attacked and severely damaged by the JNA and Serb irregulars who went on to attack Dubrovnik. A month later, several hundred Muslims fled the town of Šipovo in Central Bosnia after a Muslim was killed by Serb police. Meanwhile, the JNA moved arms and munitions from Slovenia and Croatia to Bosnia and placed heavy weapons in strategic locations throughout the republic.

The situation was so grave that on 12 November 1991 Izetbegović appealed to the United Nations for the immediate deployment of UN peacekeepers to prevent impending violence. This and other similar appeals in the following weeks and months, including private pleading from Lord Carrington and other mediators, fell on deaf ears at the United Nations and in capitals with the capabilities to make a difference. Meanwhile, Bosnia continued to fracture along ethno-national lines. Six Serb Autonomous Regions were created between September and November, a Bosnian Serb Assembly was formed in October, and an exclusively Serb referendum was held in the Autonomous Regions, backing the formation of a Republic of the Serb People of Bosnia that would remain joined to Serbia and Montenegro.[16] The Republic was formally proclaimed on 9 January 1992.

Karadžić was not putting forward proposals for discussion, but presenting facts on the ground, secure in the knowledge that he had the backing of the JNA and Serb irregulars, whose behaviour was increasingly provocative. To be sure, each ethno-national elite was positioning itself as best it could. Izetbegović himself was happy to use the preponderance of SDA and HDZ deputies in the Bosnian parliament to push significant measures through that were opposed by the SDS and of dubious legality, including a memorandum on Bosnian sovereignty on 15 October 1991 that led to a walkout of SDS deputies.[17] The Croat Community of Herzeg-Bosnia was formed in Western Herzegovina on 18 November 1991 as a separate Croat governing structure in Bosnia.

The positions of the three ethno-national parties were evident in the discussions over the memorandum on Bosnian sovereignty. The SDA was sympathetic to Slovene-Croatian advocacy of a confederal arrangement for Yugoslavia and did not wish Bosnia to remain in a Serb-dominated rump state. HDZ positions were more complex and reflected the attitudes both of Croats living in areas where they formed a minority among Muslims and Serbs and of Croats living in areas where they formed a majority. The party took its lead from Zagreb and supported the concept of a sovereign Bosnia, rather than remaining within a Serb-dominated Yugoslavia, but also claimed the right to self-determination for Croats. The SDS wanted Bosnia to remain within Yugoslavia and together with Serbia, insisting on self-determination for Serbs in any other eventuality. These were mutually exclusive positions and the memorandum was passed by 142 votes out of 240 in the absence of the SDS deputies, even though they had wished to put the matter to the Council for Questions of the Establishment of Equality of the Nations and Nationalities of Bosnia (which had been announced but not created). In effect, Serb deputies had been outvoted on a matter of vital national interest in a manner that was at odds with the constitution. As a result, the SDS leadership decided that Serb representatives would not participate in the work of republican governmental bodies until that decision was annulled.

The decision was not, however, annulled and served as a precedent for the vote to organise a referendum on independence. The decision to hold a referendum was again taken in the absence of the Serb deputies. It was taken at 4.30am on 25 January—one-and-a-half hours after Momčilo Krajišnik, the SDS speaker of the parliament, had adjourned the session—by a unanimous vote of the 130 deputies still present. Although the Badinter Commission had sought evidence of public attitudes to independence and suggested that a referendum might provide a way to assess this, the kind of referendum that was being organised would not. The independence referendum took place in the absence of any vision of the kind of state Bosnia would be, how it would be structured and what sort of relationship it would have with the rest of what had been Yugoslavia. No details had been agreed and Bosnia's existing structure was already disintegrating.

In the event, the referendum took place on 29 February and 1 March 1992 with EC financial support despite SDS objections and a Serb boycott. The result was 99.7 per cent support for independence on a turnout of 64.4 per cent, roughly the proportion of Croats and Muslims in the population. Before the results came through, a Serb was shot dead on his way to a wedding in Sarajevo and within the hour masked Serb gunmen had erected barricades around the city in a co-ordinated move. A dozen people died that day as Karadžić presented six demands, including the formation of ethno-national police forces and media. Although the way in which Karadžić and the SDS made their point was brutal, the point itself was valid. How was it possible to vote on independence when the organisation of the state itself had not been determined?

Amid escalating violence, especially in Eastern Bosnia, Lord Carrington worked together with the Portuguese diplomat José

Cutileiro, now that Portugal had assumed the presidency of the European Community, to find a structure for Bosnia that would be acceptable to all. In the absence of any mechanism to prevent the use of force, the options amounted to little more than determining the minimal SDS positions and seeking to persuade the SDA-dominated Bosnian government and HDZ to agree to them. The proposed solution was 'cantonisation', that is the division of Bosnia into 'three constituent units, based on national principles and taking into account economic, geographic and other criteria'.

Under what became known as the Cutileiro Plan, Bosnia was to have a parliament with two chambers, one elected directly and the other formed by an equal number of representatives from each community. Central government would have responsibility for defence and foreign policy, economic and financial policy, basic utilities and infrastructure, but each community would be able to veto in the parliament anything it judged to be against its interests. The 'constituent units' would be responsible for all other matters, so long as their actions did not impinge upon the independence and territorial integrity of Bosnia. The arrangement would be overseen by a Constitutional Court, which would include international judges to act as non-partisan arbiters in disputes.

The problem with the Cutileiro Plan, which was agreed in principle on 18 March 1992, was how to divide Bosnia into three 'constituent units'. Of Bosnia's municipalities, thirty-seven had an absolute Muslim majority, thirty-two an absolute Serb majority and thirteen an absolute Croat majority. A further fifteen municipalities had a simple Muslim majority, five a simple Serb majority and thirteen a simple Croat majority. With the exception of Croat-populated Western Herzegovina, an absolute majority rarely accounted for more than 70 per cent of the population, and as often as not adjacent municipalities had majorities of one of the republic's other peoples. Dividing Bosnia into ethno-national territories would inevitably be messy and require massive population transfers. The agreement was first rejected by the HDZ as it became clear that close to two thirds of Croats would be living in Muslim or Serb constituent units. And then it was rejected by the Bosnian government. This was in part because of the implications for Bosnia of the territorial carve-up, and in part because of expectations that the European Community and the United States would, in any case, recognise Bosnia's independence and then, presumably, support the newly independent state.

The European Community and the United States did, indeed, recognise Bosnia on 6 and 7 April 1992, but only after hostilities had already broken out and without providing the assistance that might have helped the new state to survive. On 1 April, paramilitaries loyal to Željko Ražnjatović-Arkan entered Bijeljina, a town in North Eastern Bosnia adjacent to Serbia, ostensibly to prevent a massacre of Serbs but actually murdering several dozen Muslims. Four days later, armed Serbs fired indiscriminately from the top of the Holiday Inn Hotel in Sarajevo at anti-war demonstrators who had gathered to profess their commitment to a multi-ethnic Bosnia, killing two of them. That evening Serb heavy artillery began its bombardment of Sarajevo. From the European Community's perspective, recognition held out the possibility of a quick-fix solution and had, therefore, been worth trying. But when the policy failed to halt the fighting, the fact that Bosnia had officially become a fully-fledged member of the international community did not mean that any state was going to come to the aid of the government or even that the arms embargo would be lifted.

Recriminations over diplomatic failure in Bosnia are essentially redundant, since persuasion alone could not have prevented the conflict escalating into another war. The only strategy that might have averted bloodshed, namely timely military intervention, had been ruled out during the war in Croatia. In theory, had Bosnia been recognised together with Slovenia and Croatia on 15 January 1992, a peacekeeping force could have been deployed in a preventive capacity. But since no country was prepared to send its own troops to neutralise the military imbalance, diplomats could only observe how the imminent catastrophe, which all Yugoslavia experts had been predicting, unfolded.

Peace-brokering amid ethnic cleansing

The hostilities that erupted at the beginning of April were in many ways a rerun of the Croatian War. The tactics were identical to those deployed in and around Dubrovnik and Vukovar, though the scale was larger because the numbers involved were greater. The initial *blitzkrieg* campaign was, above all, about expelling non-Serbs to create ethno-nationally 'pure' Serb territory, hence international adoption of the term *etničko čišćenje* or ethnic cleansing to describe what was taking place. As in Croatia, it was launched by paramilitaries, including some of the same individuals, willing to commit atrocities in a deliberate attempt to shatter relations between communities. The more barbaric the killing, the greater the incentive for non-Serbs to flee. Indeed, both the nature of the killing and the logic behind it were reminiscent of the summer of 1941, when the Ustašas descended on defenceless Serb villages. The difference was that this time Serbs were the perpetrators of the atrocities, and Croats and especially Muslims were the victims. Moreover, in contrast to the Second World War, there was no non-nationalist, multi-ethnic military option, akin to the partisans, available to Bosnians.

The fighting would create the ethno-national territories that 'cantonisation' had implied, but that had not hitherto existed. It was by definition a life-or-death struggle both for the individuals whose lives were on the line and their wider communities. Many factors influenced the decision to launch the ethnic-cleansing campaign. These included personal ambition and greed, since the masterminds also benefitted in terms of status in the new ethno-nationally pure society that was being created and of wealth, having appropriated the possessions of the expelled populations. Fear and hatred were also factors in the wake of many years of propaganda. However, it was, above all, the imbalance in firepower between Serbs and non-Serbs that made it possible for Serb leaders to calculate that it would be possible to succeed with such a campaign, much as in Croatia, presenting both Bosnia's other communities and the international community with a *fait accompli*. Any delay in launching the campaign would turn the odds against them, since it was increasingly clear that the Croat and Muslim leaderships had very different visions for Bosnia and that they too were preparing for war.

The work of many organisations, including in particular the International Criminal Tribunal for the former Yugoslavia (ICTY), the International Commission on Missing Persons (ICMP) and

Sarajevo's Research and Documentation Centre (RDC), has helped provide an accurate record of the events and casualties of the Bosnian War. Evidence and data collected generally substantiate the apocalyptic impressions presented at the time by Western media covering the war, including the existence of a network of concentration camps, widespread rape and the systematic eradication of non-Serb culture in areas where the non-Serb population had been expelled.[18] Moreover, the extent of Serbia's involvement in Bosnia, both before and after the formal withdrawal of the JNA on 19 May 1992, made it possible for the Bosnian government in 1993 to bring a charge of genocide against Serbia in the International Court of Justice in The Hague. That said, the number of people killed in the war is considerably lower than the figure of 250,000 that was presented by the Bosnian government and largely accepted at the time. Extrapolating from *The Bosnian Book of the Dead*, a comprehensive study of war victims compiled by the RDC, the total figure would likely be somewhere between 100,000 and 110,000.

The Bosnian Book of the Dead, which was published in a semi-final format in 2007, is a body count of individuals whose deaths were a direct result of the war. The preliminary total of 97,207 represented a minimum figure. Since this figure is broken down in terms of time and place of death as well as the ethno-national identity, gender, age and status (civilian or military) of victims, it also sheds much light on the nature of the Bosnian War. The greatest number of deaths came in the first few months of hostilities in 1992 in Eastern Bosnia (Podrinje), around Prijedor in North Western Bosnia and in Sarajevo, as well as in Srebrenica in July 1995. Among civilian deaths, 33,070 (83.33 per cent) were Muslim, 4,075 Serb, 2,163 Croat and 376 Others. 51.6 per cent of Muslim dead were civilians, as opposed to 27.8 per cent of Croat dead and 16.4 per cent of Serb dead. Interestingly, 436 Croats, 381 Serbs and sixty-nine Others died in the ranks of the Bosnian Army, close to 3 per cent of the total; 487 Muslims, seventy-three Serbs and seventeen Others, 10 per cent of the total, died as soldiers in the Hrvatsko vijeće obrane (Croat Defence Council, or HVO); and 272 non-Serbs, just over 1 per cent of the total, died in the ranks of the JNA or the Vojska Republike Srpske (Army of Republika Srpska, or VRS).

Despite the imbalance in firepower and the pre-emptive nature of the initial ethnic-cleansing campaign, there were too few Serbs to make a success of the enterprise. The Serb offensive succeeded in establishing Serb control over about 70 per cent of Bosnia's territory. However, it came unstuck in the cities, where the proportion of Muslims was greater and, especially in Sarajevo, where many Serbs chose to stay put and resist the Serb forces claiming to fight on their behalf. Although the arms embargo against Yugoslavia helped reinforce the imbalance in firepower, the provision of humanitarian aid helped keep non-Serbs both alive and in Bosnia. The urban population was also swelled by an influx of displaced persons from the countryside. As it became clear to Serb forces that they would not be able to capture urban centres without incurring massive casualties, they chose to surround enclaves. The result was a series of sieges, most notably that of Sarajevo where the daily carnage was broadcast instantaneously around the world. Though lacking weapons, the Bosnian government was not short of manpower or commitment and in time this enabled it to build the strength to strike back.

Though Croats and Muslims were ostensibly on the same side in the early months of hostilities, the conflict, if not the fighting, was three-sided from the beginning. The initial alliance was one of convenience and self-preservation. Indeed, even at the height of the initial Serb offensive, Croat and Serb leaders, Mate Boban and Karadžić, met up to discuss tactics, including on 6 May 1992 at Graz Airport in Austria. Croats and Muslims formed separate fighting formations, the HVO and the Bosnian Army, and had different outlooks on the nature of the Bosnian state. Both communities had voted for independence in the referendum because neither wished to remain part of a Serb-dominated Yugoslavia. But whereas the Muslim leadership remained wedded to the concept of a centralised Bosnia, a position the Bosnian government continued to present in the peace negotiations, the Croat leadership's vision for Bosnia was closer to that articulated by their Serb counterparts.[19]

Media reporting and especially television images clearly had an impact on international policy-making, though no-one was prepared to intervene on behalf of one side, as the Bosnian government hoped. The UN Security Council imposed economic sanctions against Serbia and Montenegro and, by extension, the Bosnian Serbs, on 30 May 1992—three days after the broadcast of television images of the Sarajevo bread queue massacre in which twenty-two people died. On 6 June 1992, UN Secretary-General Boutros Boutros-Ghali recommended the extension of UNPROFOR into Bosnia to support the delivery of humanitarian aid via Sarajevo Airport. That was eventually made possible following the visit of French President François Mitterrand to Sarajevo on 28 June. And the mandate and size of the UN force were steadily increased, often in the wake of media revelations, to help contain the conflict and ensure delivery of humanitarian supplies.

Television images of cadaverous prisoners cowering in terror broadcast by Britain's Independent Television News on 6 August 1992 and subsequently throughout the world generated public outrage on an unprecedented level and persuaded Britain's prime minister, John Major, who had recently taken the chair of the European Community, to organise an international conference on Bosnia in conjunction with the United Nations. The resulting London Conference on 26 and 27 August marked the end of the EC Peace Conference on Yugoslavia and the beginning of a new International Conference on the Former Yugoslavia (ICFY). This was created in permanent session in Geneva to resolve all issues relating to Yugoslavia's dissolution under the permanent co-chairmanship of the presidency of the European Community (soon to become the European Union) and the secretary-general of the United Nations, represented respectively by Lord David Owen, another former British foreign minister, and Vance. The London Conference also drew up, among other documents, a 'Statement of Principles' including non-recognition of advantages gained by force as well as respect for the independence, sovereignty and integrity of Bosnia's borders. In the wake of the London Conference, the UN Security Council established a Commission of Experts to gather evidence of war crimes perpetrated in the former Yugoslavia.[20]

Despite talk of military intervention and war-crimes trials, the momentum generated by the London Conference rapidly dissipated in the absence of muscular follow-through to match the rhetoric. Moreover, the ICFY rapidly had to shelve attempts to deal with all issues emanating out of Yugoslavia's dissolution in favour of a policy focussed on Bosnia. Nevertheless, the document that eventually emerged as the Vance-Owen Plan[21] was impressive in as much as it sought to balance the interests of Croats, Muslims and Serbs via a complex constitutional plan designed by the Finnish diplomat Martti Ahtisaari. Although it, too, envisaged a territorial division, the division was not into ethno-nationally pure provinces. Moreover, provinces that were predominantly populated by one ethno-national group were not contiguous, denying the Bosnian Serbs the key gains of ethnic cleansing. To be sure, predominantly Serb regions in the west of Bosnia were to be connected by internationally secured highways to predominantly Serb regions in the east.

The Vance-Owen Plan envisaged a weak central government responsible for foreign affairs, international commerce and citizenship, and taxation for these purposes with economic and other functions usually within the remit of central government assigned to independent authorities, comprising representatives of the provinces. In total, there were to be ten, largely autonomous provinces, each with its own police force. Sarajevo was to have a special status as the capital and each community would have equal representation in political structures. In the remaining nine provinces, offices would be divided among communities according to the results of the 1991 census. There were also provisions for the separation of forces, for control and monitoring of heavy weapons by UNPROFOR and the demilitarisation of Sarajevo, even the eventual, progressive demilitarisation of the entire country, as well as for the return of displaced persons and protection of minority rights. Implementation would have required an international military force of between 50,000 and 70,000 soldiers, for which NATO and the United Nations were already preparing.

Critics of the Vance-Owen Plan were quick to describe it as rewarding ethnic cleansing. It was, nevertheless, a step away from the ethno-national segregation envisaged in cantonisation and arguably as good a blueprint for a peace process as possible after a year of fighting, in the absence of any international appetite for coercive intervention. Indeed, leaders on all sides—including Karadžić—were persuaded to sign onto it and the Plan was supported in both Zagreb and Belgrade. It was, however, rejected by the Republika Srpska National Assembly, which had hastily organised a referendum among Bosnian Serbs to back its stance, because the Plan envisaged giving up Serb-held territory. While the Republika Srpska National Assembly's rejection might have been circumvented via proposals for progressive implementation and Serbian pressure on the Bosnian Serbs, the greatest obstacle to its success was Washington. The Vance-Owen Plan ultimately failed because it was not supported by the United States, whose participation in the implementation force would have been vital, and which viewed it as a betrayal of the Bosnian Muslims.

In the wake of the collapse of the Vance-Owen Plan, Thorvald Stoltenberg replaced Vance as the UN Secretary-General's special envoy at the ICFY and diplomatic efforts to end the fighting resumed. However, given the mediators' lack of leverage and the logic of the conflict, proposals became increasingly divorced from the London Principles and prospects of a breakthrough ever more remote. Although the Vance-Owen Plan had apparently not been sufficiently favourable to the Bosnian Muslims for Washington to commit, subsequent plans—the Owen-Stoltenberg[22] and Contact Group Plans[23]—were considerably less favourable. The lesson that all sides took from the failure of the Vance-Owen Plan was that each could only rely on itself. This contributed to the breakdown of the Croat-Muslim alliance, three-way fighting and increasing radicalisation, ethno-national homogeneity and reprisals on all sides. It had become a war of attrition for ethno-national survival, whose logical conclusion involved the defeat and therefore disappearance of one or more communities. Meanwhile, the United Nations found itself caught in the middle, deploying 36,000 peacekeepers, attempting to alleviate suffering and committed to protecting six 'safe areas'[24] it was not configured to defend. As international acrimony increased, countries with peacekeepers deployed on the ground even threatened to withdraw their contingents.

Getting to Dayton

The possibility of a complete withdrawal of UN forces was real in the spring and summer of 1995 after more than three years of war, repeated humiliations, in particular at the hands of the Bosnian Serbs, and no end to hostilities in sight. It did not come to this, as a result of changes in the balance of forces on the ground, limited international military intervention against the Bosnian Serbs and single-minded US diplomacy to broker a peace agreement backed up by the genuine threat of force.

US policy-making, whether under President George H.W. Bush or President Bill Clinton, had always had the potential to make a difference, but was circumscribed by fears about being drawn into a quagmire.[25] The risks of engagement in what Clinton's secretary of State Warren Christopher described as a 'problem from hell' appeared excessive as long as the conflict could be contained so that it did not spread beyond Bosnia and did not spill over into other areas of policy-making.

Having avoided engagement to the greatest extent possible during both the Croatian War and the formative months of the Bosnian War, the outgoing Bush administration changed tack at the end of 1992 and named Radovan Karadžić, Slobodan Milošević, Ratko Mladić, Željko Ražnjatović-Arkan and Vojislav Šešelj, among others, as war criminals. The incoming Clinton administration promised a more hands-on approach but was unwilling to risk deploying US ground troops. In this way, as discussed above, it fatally undermined the prospects of the Vance-Owen Plan. Instead, it proposed an end to the arms embargo that penalised the Bosnian Muslims in particular—'levelling the killing field' in the words of British Foreign Minister Douglas Hurd—and air strikes against Bosnian Serb positions—a policy that UNPROFOR troop-contributing countries could not countenance since it would have exposed their forces to unacceptable levels of risk and jeopardised the humanitarian effort. Indeed, it was only when UNPROFOR appeared on the verge of disintegration, and acrimony over diplomatic failure in Bosnia was beginning to affect relations among NATO allies, that the United States focussed its resources and efforts to end the war.

As in Croatia in 1991, a change in the military situation on the ground, which had been largely static since the beginning of 1994, paved the way for a peace agreement. Power had shifted away from Serbia and Montenegro, both subject to economic sanctions, towards Croatia, which, despite the arms embargo, had spent the intervening years building its military capabilities with tacit support from the United States in anticipation of the day when it would be in a position to recapture Serb-held territory. Zagreb was helped, above all, by the intransigence and obstructionism of the authorities of the Republika Srpska Krajina (Republic of Serb Krajina, or RSK). By refusing to implement key elements of the Sarajevo Accord, the agreement ending the Croatian War, blocking the return of displaced Croats and rejecting any form of integration, the leadership was making itself vulnerable to Croatian government offensives. These came in January 1993,[26] May 1995[27] and in particular August 1995, when the Croatian Army defeated and eradicated the RSK in four days as UN forces stepped aside.

The flight of between 150,000 and 200,000 Serbs[28] was the tragic end to a zero-sum conflict fought to create and preserve ethno-nationally pure territory. In the absence of Belgrade's support, the RSK leadership knew that it could not hold out against the Croatian Army and chose to organise an exodus of the Serb population rather than allowing them to remain and face reprisals.[29] By rejecting compromise,[30] most recently the so-called 'Z4 Plan' that would have entitled Krajina Serbs to autonomy and the moral high ground, the RSK leadership had effectively condemned the people it claimed to represent to exile. Zagreb was able to present its offensive as a move to save the beleaguered Bihać enclave, a UN safe area surrounded and under attack from both Croatian Serb and Bosnian Serb forces, from a similar fate to Srebrenica. That UN safe area had been overrun in July by the VRS and much of the male population summarily executed in the single worst atrocity of the Wars of Yugoslav Dissolution.

Croatia was able to intervene legitimately in Bosnia because Sarajevo had formally asked Zagreb to come to the rescue of the Bihać enclave at a meeting between Presidents Tuđman and Izetbegović in Split on 22 July 1995. The collaboration was made possible by the resurrection of the Croat-Muslim alliance, which itself was the result of concerted US diplomacy. The Washington Agreement that ended the Croat-Muslim War in Bosnia was formally signed on 18 March 1994, creating the Federation of Bosnia on Croat and Muslim-held territory as a first step towards a general settlement, as well as a confederation between Croatia and the newly created Federation. Although much of the detail, such as the nature of the confederation, was still to be worked out, the agreement was underwritten by the promise of financial assistance for post-war reconstruction and held sufficiently well to free up assets for the fight against the Bosnian Serbs.

In the wake of repeated humiliations at the hands of the Bosnian Serbs, including some 370 UN peacekeepers being held hostage in May 1995,[31] UNPROFOR was reinforced by the deployment of an Anglo-Dutch-French Rapid Reaction Force (RRF). The arrival of a combat-capable force in June 1995 was in effect a last roll of the dice for the UN mission. It was ready either to provide additional coercive options on the ground or to assist in the withdrawal of UN forces in case the US 'lift-and-strike' policy was put into action. In the event, the RRF took on a coercive role in support of concerted NATO air strikes that started on 30 August, two days after the second Sarajevo marketplace massacre in which forty-three people were killed and seventy-five were wounded, as soon as all UN troops had left Bosnian Serb-controlled territory. The air campaign, Operation Deliberate Force, lasted until 14 September with a short pause after the initial wave of attacks. During that time, it alleviated the three-and-a-half-year siege of Sarajevo and shattered VRS communications without a single NATO casualty, opening up greater opportunities for the advancing Croatian Army, HVO and Bosnian Army to exploit.

The offensive that began on 4 August 1995 around Bihać continued throughout that month and the next. In this way, the Bosnian Serbs were driven back until the territorial division approximated to the 51:49 split that had been on the table in the most recent peace plan, the Contact Group Plan, in which the Federation was slightly larger. Moreover, following the fall of the UN safe havens of Srebrenica and Žepa to the VRS in July, the division of territory appeared neater than it had been at the time of earlier proposals. While the Bosnian government was eager to maintain its offensive to capture as much Serb-held territory as possible, US diplomatic pressure forced it to call a halt amid concerns about the reliability of the Croatian alliance. At the time, the Croatian Army was bearing down on Banja Luka, the largest Serb-held town in Bosnia, and in a position to capture it, a move that would almost certainly have created several hundred thousand refugees and possibly forced Serbia to become engaged militarily.

In the absence of Zagreb's support, the Bosnian government reluctantly agreed a ceasefire—the thirty-fifth of the war—that went into effect on 10 October 1995, after one last push to capture additional territory. Many of the territorial issues that had sunk earlier peace plans had been resolved on the battlefield. That said, the most sensitive issues—the status of Sarajevo, divided between Serb-held and government-held territory; Federation access to Goražde, the one remaining UN safe haven in Eastern Bosnia; and the fate of the Posavina or Brčko corridor, the link between eastern and western portions of Serb-held territory—remained and would dominate the so-called proximity talks at the Wright-Patterson Air Force Base in Dayton, Ohio, that got underway on 1 November.

The Dayton talks and Accord were very much a US project, overseen and guided by Assistant Secretary of State for Europe Richard Holbrooke. The single-mindedness with which Holbrooke and the team he built around him drove the process was in sharp contrast to the more detached approach that had hitherto characterised US diplomacy towards the Bosnian War. This change was the result of many factors, including the prospect of a UN withdrawal; the impact of the Bosnian War on NATO, discussed above; a congressional resolution passed in July 1995 unilaterally to lift the arms embargo against the Bosnian Muslims; the Srebrenica massacre of July; the deaths of three senior US diplomats on the ground in Bosnia in August; and the personality of Holbrooke himself. Despite this change in approach, however, Washington remained cautious about placing US forces in harm's way and reluctant to enter into a long-term engagement, factors that would help undermine the early years of the peace process.

In driving forward the diplomatic process, Holbrooke engaged in tireless shuttle diplomacy, involving in particular Zagreb and Belgrade, and sidelined the ICFY, now chaired by Stoltenberg and Carl Bildt, a former Swedish prime minister who had succeeded Lord Owen as the EU representative in June. In the three months running up to the Dayton talks, Holbrooke obtained agreement on the 51:49 territorial division and a series of basic constitutional principles relating to issues such as power-sharing, elections, human rights and special parallel relations with neighbours that State Department lawyers then worked into a comprehensive draft accord. It was a draft that would also have to be agreed by the international institutions and countries that would have to become involved to oversee implementation.

The negotiating dynamic at Dayton differed from that at the ICFY in Geneva in that the Bosnian Serbs were represented by Milošević and the Bosnian Croats by Tuđman. This was especially significant on the Serb side, since Milošević was determined to bring the Bosnian War to an end to ensure that economic sanctions, by now biting, would be lifted against Serbia and Montenegro. As soon as agreement could be reached, sanctions would be suspended. Milošević was therefore willing to make compromises that the Bosnian Serb political and military leaders, Karadžić and Mladić, both of whom had been indicted for genocide in July by the International Criminal Tribunal for the former Yugoslavia (ICTY) and were therefore unable to attend the talks, were not. Indeed, he had already cut off much support to the Bosnian Serbs in the wake of their refusal to agree to earlier peace plans. Milošević was authorised to negotiate on their behalf as a result of an agreement brokered by the head of the Serbian Orthodox Church, Patriarch Pavle, at the end of August, the so-called 'patriarch paper'.

While Milošević's overriding aim at the Dayton negotiations was to end the sanctions, Tuđman's preoccupation was the fate of Eastern Slavonia, the remaining Serb-held territory in Croatia. Unlike Milošević and Izetbegović, Tuđman did not remain in Dayton, but came and went during the three-week negotiations, having obtained more or less what he wanted in Eastern Slavonia. Under the terms of what became known as the Erdut Agreement, after the place where it was signed on 12 November 1995, a transitional administration was established in Eastern Slavonia (UNTAES) to oversee the region's reintegration into Croatia. UNTAES would have a one-year mandate that could be extended for another year if requested by either party to the agreement.

In addition to the Erdut Agreement and the Dayton Peace Agreement itself, one other agreement was negotiated in Dayton, namely the Dayton Agreement on Implementing the Federation of Bosnia. This agreement, which was signed on 10 November 1995, enumerated measures for integrating the Federation economically, politically and socially; set out the separation of powers between the Federation and Bosnia's future central government; and provided an interim governing statute for the city of Mostar. As such, it provided some much-needed substance to the Federation and was a critical step towards the final peace accord.

Whereas Milošević and Tuđman were both eager to strike a deal to end the war, the Bosnian government, and Izetbegović in particular, was less committed and needed to be pressured into accepting the eventual agreement. It considered itself the injured party and felt the course of the war had only just changed in its favour. The Bosnian government, therefore, presented maximalist demands in the talks which, in line with the war that had been fought, were focussed on the territorial division of the country and military arrangements to the virtual exclusion of other issues that would be critical to the peace process.

The Bosnian government's hardline position paid dividends on all the most sensitive issues. This was a result of Milošević's willingness to make concessions that the Bosnian Serb delegates in Dayton, Nikola Koljević and Momčilo Krajišnik, would never have accepted, without even consulting them. In this way, he agreed to the extension of Federation territory into Eastern Bosnia via the construction of a dual-carriageway linking Goražde to other Federation territory, the transfer of the Serb-held suburbs of Sarajevo to the Federation[32] and, critically, at the very end of the talks, to deferring a final decision on the status of Brčko, the municipality linking the eastern and western parts of Republika Srpska, placing the issue in the hands of binding arbitration. To maintain the agreed 51:49 territorial division, the Federation agreed to hand back sparsely populated territory in Central Bosnia that had been captured in the last weeks of fighting. At the eleventh hour and under extreme pressure, Izetbegović caved in and agreed to what he described as an 'unjust peace'.

5

ELECTIONS AT ANY PRICE

'Dayton itself was as "maximalist" an agreement as possible; it aimed to create an ambitious blueprint for a new state. Yet many areas of Dayton's implementation have suffered from "minimalism", whether because of the limits placed on the instruments the agreement created for implementation, or because those responsible for implementation have interpreted their roles, responsibilities and powers narrowly. This tension between Dayton's ends and means created what some have described as an "enforcement gap" that slowed implementation immediately after the peace agreement and still plagues Bosnia to this day.'

Derek Chollet[1]

Peace or just a ceasefire?

Izetbegović's 'unjust peace' was initialled in Dayton on 21 November 1995 and signed on 14 December 1995 in Paris, bringing to an end more than three-and-a-half years of war. The General Framework Agreement for Peace, as it was formally called, was unjust from Izetbegović's perspective because it recognised the existence of Republika Srpska, thereby acquiescing in what had been obtained by ethnic cleansing and rewarding aggression. It is a view that remains prevalent among Bosniaks and their political leaders, as well as among many analysts of Bosnian affairs. Indeed, Holbrooke subsequently went on record to say that he regretted not making a stronger effort to remove the name Republika Srpska from the accord.[2] However, the settlement was a reflection of reality on the ground, as well as the level of risk that the international community was prepared to take on in relation to Bosnia at the time.

The war had not run its course when it came to an end. In the absence of intervention, it would have continued until either a territorial stalemate had been reached or until one or even two peoples had been definitively 'cleansed', as had been the case in Croatia. Some analysts believe that such outcomes make for more stable settlements, since multi-ethnicity need not enter the equation. Indeed, Croatia has generally been stable since the eradication of the Repulika Srpska Krajina (Serb Republic of Krajina, or RSK) and the reintegration of Eastern Slavonia. However, that stability came at the expense of the Serb population. Moreover, it would probably have taken some time to reach a similar stage in Bosnia, with the risk of contagion elsewhere in the region and other unforeseen consequences. It would also have created greater misery in terms of casualties and refugees and exacerbated already strained relations in the wider international community.

The Dayton settlement that Carl Bildt, the first high representative in Bosnia, described as 'part negotiated, part imposed' had much to commend it. It brought the war to an end; no people had been defeated; and the accord itself was sufficiently flexibly drafted to set in motion a process that held out the prospect of a better future for all Bosnians, without specifying the kind of country Bosnia would ultimately become. For this reason, there was great optimism as well as relief as the guns fell silent. The settlement was, nevertheless, predicated on a balance of terror, and littered with unrealistic deadlines aimed at providing an exit strategy for the international military presence. This meant that it risked amounting to a long ceasefire rather than a lasting peace, particularly as the Croat and Serb leaderships did not wish to be part of a common state.[3] And a key sweetener to Izetbegović to persuade him to sign onto the accord was the US-sponsored Train and Equip programme designed to build up Federation armed forces so as to end the imbalance in arms among the parties in Bosnia.

Though critical to securing Izetbegović's signature, Train and Equip was not part of the peace accord. Rather, it was a separate arrangement involving the United States, Germany and several Islamic countries allied to the United States, to boost the Federation's military capacities.[4] Its eventual impact was reflected in Annex 1B of the Dayton Peace Agreement ('Agreement on Regional Stabilization'), which created a comprehensive balance of forces among the Federal Republic of Yugoslavia, Croatia and Bosnia in ratios of 5:2:2. In this way, the Federal Republic of Yugoslavia would have two-and-a-half times more military hardware than Croatia; Croatia and Bosnia would have the same amount; and within Bosnia, the Federation would have two thirds and Republika Srpska one third of that entitlement. Although there were to be no arms imports for 180 days after the Dayton Peace Agreement came into force, the Federation would be entitled to build up its military capacity to those levels. Hence the justification for Train and Equip, which its US sponsors viewed as a way to supervise the Federation's arming, to develop professional armed forces and to help knit together the Bosnian Army and the Hrvatsko vijeće obrane (Croat Defence Council, or HVO).

Under Annex 1A of the Dayton Peace Agreement, a 60,000-strong, NATO-led Implementation Force, or IFOR, deployed in Bosnia with a one-year mandate. IFOR, one third of whose troops came from the United States, had what amounted to unlimited authority in theatre, which it used to oversee military implementation of the accord: the cessation of hostilities; the transfer of territory between the entities; the creation of a zone of separation; and the cantonment of heavy weapons. It was also able to take on additional tasks to create the conditions in which other actors could work on civilian implementation of the accord. However, it chose to interpret its mandate in limited terms.

Setting a one-year deadline on IFOR's presence and limiting its mandate appeared to have been politically necessary to secure its deployment. In practice, however, the obsession with avoiding casualties that characterised the initial troop deployment served only to preserve the wartime mindset among all parties in Bosnia, and undermine the prospect of civilian implementation of the Dayton Peace Agreement.

In the expectation that IFOR's deployment would be limited, all sides used the breathing space to prepare for an eventual resumption of hostilities. The Bosnian government, in particular, had taken note of the way in which Zagreb had captured Serb-held territory in Croatia and believed that it would be able to achieve similar victories in Bosnia as soon as it acquired the additional weaponry it was entitled to under the terms of the peace accord. On all sides, minefields were not cleared but 'harvested' so that the terrain remained treacherous, because some mines were left behind and those that were taken up could be laid elsewhere. A scorched-earth policy was pursued in all territory to be transferred from one entity to the other, removing or destroying anything of value and evacuating the population. Surplus weapons and munitions were hidden from IFOR in Republika Srpska. And the Bosnian government directed displaced Bosniaks to return to strategic areas in Republika Srpska.

In the event of a resumption of fighting, the Bosnian government would have been in a stronger position. The inter-entity boundary line would have been the new front line, and this, following the transfer of the Serb-held Sarajevo suburbs to the Federation, would have provided the Bosnian government with generally defensible positions. Meanwhile, Republika Srpska's geography made it extremely vulnerable, especially around Brčko, to a lightning offensive like those that had sealed the fate of the RSK in Croatia, given the Federation's superiority in manpower.

The Bosnian government had claimed to stand for a multi-ethnic vision of Bosnia during the war and there had certainly been Croats and Serbs in the wartime presidency and other prominent positions. By the end of the war, however, nobody in a genuine position of power represented multi-ethnicity. The positions that mattered were not in the formal institutions but in the ruling political parties, the Hrvatska demokratska zajednica (Croat Democratic Union, or HDZ), Stranka demokratske akcije (Party of Democratic Action, or SDA) and Srpska demokratska stranka (Serb Democratic Party, or SDS), each of which represented a mono-ethnic copy of the League of Communists.

Just as Serb leaders liked to present themselves as defenders of Yugoslavia, so Muslim leaders saw themselves as champions of Bosnia. Moreover, to emphasise the link between Muslims and Bosnia, they reintroduced the historic ethno-national name 'Bosniak' in place of 'Muslim' at the Second Bosniak Congress in September 1993. With Bosniaks driven out of their homes and killed simply for being Muslim and the survival of an entire people at stake, attitudes inevitably hardened. Believing that they had done everything the international community had asked of them and that they were therefore entitled to support, Izetbegović and his inner circle felt bitter and betrayed, fearing for the very existence of Bosniaks in Bosnia. As a result, they focussed efforts on salvaging what they could for their own community out of the country's ruins. Indeed, Izetbegović became so desperate that, in discussions over the Owen-Stoltenberg Plan, he even agreed to an eventual referendum in Serb-apportioned territory to determine its future status.[5]

Every problematic element of the peace process was on display in the transfer of the Serb-held Sarajevo suburbs to the Federation. Although the Dayton Peace Agreement held out the promise of return to all people who had been forced out of their homes in the course of the war, the number of displaced jumped by more than 60,000 within the first three months of it coming into force.[6] This was the result of a foreseeable and avoidable Serb exodus from the five suburbs that Milošević had traded for peace against the wishes of the Bosnian Serb leadership.[7]

The issue was security. Serbs might have been willing to stay had they felt that they would be secure under Federation authority. However, no one made any effort to reassure them that they would be safe. Instead, the Serb authorities did everything to force Serbs out, literally burning the homes of those reluctant to leave. Meanwhile, IFOR troops stood by watching, unable to intervene because of the limited interpretation of their mandate. When arsonists were arrested, for example, they were handed over to the Serb police who, as the instigators of the fires, promptly released them. The Bosnian government allowed rowdy mobs to enter suburbs as soon as they were handed over, making clear to any remaining Serbs that they were not welcome.[8] Departing Serbs generally sought to take all possessions with them and some even organised the exhumation of dead relatives and their reburial in Serb-held territory. In the wake of the Serb exodus, prospects for reconstructing the diversity Sarajevo had once been celebrated for were severely damaged.

ELECTIONS AT ANY PRICE

Contours of the settlement

Although the focus of the Dayton talks had been on the territorial division and the military aspects of implementing the settlement, the bulk of the peace accord covered civilian issues. Indeed, military matters only featured in the first ('Annex 1A: Agreement on Military Aspects of the Peace Settlement' and 'Annex 1B: Regional Stabilization') and second ('Annex 2: Agreement on Inter-Entity Boundary Line and Related Issues') of eleven annexes. The remaining nine addressed civilian implementation, providing a blueprint for post-war reconstruction as well as for the state of Bosnia, including, in Annex 4, its constitution. Given how little time was devoted to drafting civilian aspects of the accord and how irreconcilable the differences, the final text was a remarkable document. In addition to an end to hostilities, it appeared to hold out the promise of return for people who had been expelled from their homes, of political regeneration and justice in terms of elections and war-crimes trials, and international assistance to get the country back on its feet. As such, it provided a starting point for a process that in theory had the potential to lead to a functional and self-sustaining state.

The drafters of the Dayton Peace Agreement were, nevertheless, under no illusions about the settlement. It was a means to end a war, not the basis of a permanent solution to the Bosnian Question. After all, the accord, which included the constitution, was prepared, agreed and officially published in English and not in any of the languages of the country;[9] the status of Brčko remained open; and the governing structures bequeathed to Bosnia, in addition to being extremely complex, were so expensive to maintain that servicing the settlement alone risked undermining the country's longer-term prospects. Bosnia's ability to move on would, however, depend on how the peace accord was implemented.

Under the Dayton constitution, Bosnia inherited the political independence, territorial integrity and sovereignty of what had hitherto been called the Republic of Bosnia and was defined as a single state divided into two entities—the Federation of Bosnia, and Republika Srpska—with three constituent peoples, Bosniaks, Croats and Serbs, as well as Others. The country's central institutions were so weak in relation to those of the entities that entity structures were arguably more important to the prospects for long-term peace. Bosnia's central institutions were exclusively responsible for the following areas: foreign policy; foreign trade policy; customs policy (setting import tariffs though not gathering the revenue); monetary policy through the Central Bank; finances of Bosnia's state institutions and the country's international obligations; immigration, refugee and asylum policy and regulation; international and inter-entity law enforcement, including relations with Interpol; establishment and operation of common and international communications facilities; regulation of inter-entity transportation; and air traffic control. In addition, however, Bosnia could take on other responsibilities under certain circumstances and specifically 'shall assume responsibility for such other matters as are agreed by the Entities, are provided for in Annexes 5 through 8 to the General Framework Agreement; or are necessary to preserve the sovereignty, territorial integrity, political independence and international personality of Bosnia. Additional institutions may be established as necessary to carry out such responsibilities.' In effect, therefore, Bosnia's central institutions had the potential to become considerably more significant. Indeed, within six months of the constitution coming into force, the entities were supposed to 'begin negotiations with a view to including in the responsibilities of the institutions of Bosnia other matters, including utilization of energy resources and co-operative economic projects'. Other matters, including tax collection, were left for the entities.

The entity constitutions and government structures were the product of their respective creations. Republika Srpska's constitution was drafted in February 1992 and promulgated on 27 March of that year—before the beginning of the war—with a host of amendments enacted six months later, including adoption of the name 'Republika Srpska'. It set out details of a centralised 'state of the Serb people and all its citizens' without any mention of Bosniaks and Croats. The Federation's constitution was drawn up in 1994 following the end of the Bosniak-Croat War. It sought to balance the interests of Bosniaks and Croats—both described as constituent peoples—but not Serbs, who did not feature.[10]

ELECTIONS AT ANY PRICE

The Republika Srpska constitution was drafted for what its architects intended to be an independent, sovereign and, above all, Serb state. Although specific references to independence and sovereignty were eventually removed after the Dayton Peace Agreement came into force, the constitution nevertheless sought to convey the impression that Republika Srpska was a state in its own right. It possessed all the attributes of a state—armed forces, national bank, constitutional court, supreme court, parliament, government and president—and its territory was 'unique, indivisible and unalienable'. Power was concentrated in the government that was headed by a prime minister, who was appointed by a directly elected president, and answerable to an eighty-three-member National Assembly. The offices of president and vice president, elected together on a single ticket, were largely symbolic—though, in addition to appointing the prime minister, the president appointed a fifty-five-member Senate, which had an advisory role. The only other tier of government was at municipal level. Here officials were directly elected but responsibilities were restricted to implementation and administration of policies determined by the National Assembly. The constitution also guaranteed 'human freedoms and rights in accordance with international standards', 'assurance of national equality' and 'protection of the rights of... minorities', as well as a raft of social rights, such as the right to health care and employment. Moreover, there was no possibility of extradition, providing a safe haven for those wanted by the International Criminal Tribunal for the former Yugoslavia (ICTY).

The Federation constitution had much in common with the state constitution. This was in part because it, too, had been drafted by US State Department lawyers; in part because it had originally been intended as a blueprint for a country-wide settlement; and in part because it sought to balance the interests of peoples who had been at war with each other and whose leaderships remained reluctant to co-operate. In addition to Bosniaks and Croats, the constituent peoples, the category of 'Others' featured as a specific category as well as 'citizens of Bosnia', implying some kind of special representation for non-Bosniaks and non-Croats, though not specifically for Serbs.

In contrast to Republika Srpska, the Federation was designed to be about as decentralised as possible. There were three tiers of government—federal, cantonal and municipal—as well as special regimes in certain cantons and in the cities of Mostar and Sarajevo. The federal tier had minimal authority and was responsible for defence; making economic policy at the federal level; regulating finances and fiscal policy at the federal level; combating terrorism; inter-cantonal crimes; drug trafficking and other forms of organised crime; making energy policy; allocating frequencies for radio and television broadcasters; and financing these activities. In addition, the federal tier shared responsibility with the cantons for human rights; public health; environmental policy; communications and transport infrastructure; tourism; and social welfare policy.

The Federation parliament consisted of two chambers, a directly elected House of Representatives with 140 members and a House of Peoples made up of the same number of Bosniak and Croat delegates, thirty each, elected from among members of cantonal assemblies, together with some twenty Others. Key offices, such as president and vice president of the Federation, parliamentary speaker and deputy speaker were to be divided up evenly between Bosniaks and Croats. Equal ethno-national representation was also a feature of the judicial system, with the same number of Bosniak and Croat judges in all courts—constitutional, supreme and human rights—as well as an appropriate number of Others. Legislation affecting the 'vital interests' of either constituent people required a majority of both Bosniak and Croat delegates in the House of Peoples, as well as a majority of all delegates, to be passed. In the event that the invocation of 'vital interest' by a majority of either the Bosniak or the Croat delegates was opposed by a majority of the remaining delegates, the disputed legislation would be referred to a joint commission of Bosniak and Croat delegates. If that failed to find a solution after a week, the matter would be referred to the Federation Constitutional Court.

Of the three tiers of government, the middle, cantonal level was the most significant and each of the ten cantons—five predominantly Bosniak, three predominantly Croat and two 'mixed'—had its own government responsible for policing; education; public housing; culture; information and broadcasting; land use; business regulation; energy resources; social welfare; health; tourism; and financing these activities.[11] In practice, areas of shared responsibility with the federal tier were assumed by the cantons. Each canton had its own constitution, a directly elected assembly, a governor elected by members of the assembly and a government headed by a prime minister.

The two 'mixed' cantons, Central Bosnia and Neretva,[12] had special regimes in which responsibility for education, culture, radio and television, local business and tourism was devolved to the municipal level. Moreover, as in the Federation parliament, 'vital national interest' could be invoked by a majority of either Bosniak or Croat delegates, in which case a majority of both Bosniak and Croat delegates was required for legislation to pass. If invocation of 'vital national interest' was opposed by a majority of the remaining delegates, the matter would be referred to a joint commission of Bosniak and Croat delegates, then to the highest cantonal court and finally to the Federation Constitutional Court. In addition, offices such as those of governor, deputy governor and ministerial posts were carefully divided between Bosniaks and Croats.

The municipal tier of government had a relatively limited role with two exceptions. The first was where a number of municipalities made up a city administration, as in Mostar and Sarajevo. The second was where the ethno-national composition of a municipality was different to that of the canton it was in. In the first instance, the city had its own statute, council and mayor operating in parallel to the cantonal and municipal authorities. In the second instance, education, culture, tourism, local business and charitable activities were devolved to the municipal level.

The ethno-national composition of the police had to reflect the ethno-national composition of both the canton and the municipality. The right of refugees and displaced to return to their homes was guaranteed in the constitution. A human rights court was created and three ombudsmen, one Bosniak, one Croat and one Other, appointed to help address human rights issues. Every conceivable international human rights convention and agreement was incorporated into the Federation constitution, as, indeed, it was in the Dayton constitution.

Under the Dayton constitution, which could only be amended by 'a decision of the Parliamentary Assembly, including a two-thirds majority of those present and voting in the House of Representatives', the entities were able to establish 'special parallel relationships with neighbouring states'. However, these had to be 'consistent with the sovereignty and territorial integrity of Bosnia'. With the consent of the Parliamentary Assembly, the entities could enter into specific agreements with states or international bodies. The Federation might, therefore, form special links with Croatia, and Republika Srpska with Serbia.

The Parliamentary Assembly of Bosnia had two chambers, the House of Peoples and the House of Representatives. The former had fifteen members, five from each constituent people—ten (five Bosniaks and five Croats) from the Federation and five (Serbs) from Republika Srpska. The Bosniak and Croat members were appointed from the House of Peoples of the Federation and the Serbs were nominated from the Republika Srpska National Assembly. A minimum of nine delegates, three from each community, had to be present for a quorum. The House of Representatives has forty-two members, twenty-eight of whom are elected from the Federation and fourteen from Republika Srpska. A majority of those present in both chambers was the basic requirement for taking decisions in the Parliamentary Assembly. However, each constituent people had the right to declare any prospective decision 'destructive of a vital interest', in which case the proposal required 'a majority of the Bosniak, of the Croat and of the Serb Delegates present and voting'. In such a way, decisions were to be made by broad consensus and not against the declared vital interest of any community.

The 'vital-interest' mechanism was also a feature of the three-person presidency that was made up of one Bosniak and one Croat, both directly elected from the Federation, and one Serb, directly elected from Republika Srpska. Although the presidency was expected to reach decisions by consensus, a majority decision was in theory possible. In the event of a two-to-one decision, any presidency member could, in the following three days, declare a decision to be 'destructive of a vital interest', in which case the decision would be referred to either the Republika Srpska National Assembly, or either the Bosniak or the Croat members of the House of Peoples in the Federation. A vote of two thirds of the relevant group within ten days rendered the decision null and void. The presidency appointed the chair of the Council of Ministers, in effect the government, of which no more than two thirds of ministers could come from the Federation and deputy ministers were not to be of the same constituent people as the minister.

Taken together, all these mechanisms meant that the system required broad agreement and consensus to function. However, given the animosity and absence of trust after three-and-a-half years of war, and the fact that both Croat and Serb political leaders continued to aspire to union with Croatia and Serbia respectively, such consensus did not exist. The peace accord therefore built in provision for international involvement in all aspects of the peace process, with its overall co-ordination entrusted to a high representative, an ad hoc position specifically created to oversee civilian implementation ('Annex 10: Agreement on Civilian Implementation of the Peace Settlement.').

The Organization for Security and Co-operation in Europe (OSCE) had a three-pronged mandate. It was to monitor the human rights situation ('Annex 6: Agreement on Human Rights'), to oversee arms reduction ('Annex 1B: Agreement on Regional Stabilization'); and supervise elections ('Annex 3: Agreement on Elections'). The Office of the UN High Commissioner for Refugees (UNHCR) was to prepare a repatriation plan to enable refugees and displaced persons to return to their homes ('Annex 7: Agreement on Refugees and Displaced Persons'). And a UN International Police Task Force (IPTF), initially made up of 1,500 unarmed foreign police officers, was to 'assist, advise, monitor and observe the work of local police' ('Annex 11: Agreement on International Police Task Force').

International influence was equally crucial in a host of ostensibly domestic institutions. An international human rights ombudsman was appointed by the chairman-in-office of the OSCE for the first five years of peace implementation ('Annex 6: Agreement on Human Rights'); eight of fourteen members of a Human Rights Chamber were internationals appointed by the Committee of Ministers of the Council of Europe (also Annex 6); three out of nine commissioners on what became the Commission on Real Property Claims of Displaced Persons and Refugees were internationals appointed by the president of the European Court of Human Rights ('Annex 7: Agreement on Refugees and Displaced Persons'); three of the nine judges on the Constitutional Court were internationals appointed by the president of the European Court of Human Rights ('Annex 4: Constitution'); and the governor of the Central Bank was an international appointed by the International Monetary Fund for the first six years (also Annex 4); two out of five members of a Commission to Preserve National Monuments were internationals appointed by the director-general of the United Nations Educational, Scientific and Cultural Organisation for five years ('Annex 8: Agreement on the Commission to Preserve National Monuments'); two of five members of a Commission on Public Corporations were internationals appointed by the president of the European Bank for Reconstruction and Development ('Annex 9: Agreement on Establishment of Bosnia Public Corporations').

Civilian mobilisation

The many countries and organisations with a stake in the peace process came together as the Peace Implementation Council (PIC)[13] at a conference in London on 8 and 9 December 1995. This was an ad hoc grouping to succeed the ICFY and manage the peace process, setting direction and mobilising resources. It was not answerable to the United Nations but invited the UN Security Council to endorse its decisions. The United Nations was largely bypassed because it was perceived to have failed during the war. Indeed, it was barely mentioned in the Dayton Peace Agreement and might have been written out entirely if any other organisation had been prepared to take responsibility for policing. At the London meeting, Bildt was formally appointed high representative and an agenda was set aiming to create a climate of stability and security; to establish new political and constitutional arrangements in a framework of democracy and the rule of law; to protect and promote human rights and the early return of refugees and displaced persons; to establish an open, free-market economy; to kick-start economic reconstruction; and to create 'a direct and dynamic contractual relationship between Bosnia and the European

Union within the framework of a regional approach'. On 20 and 21 December, the European Commission and World Bank hosted a donors' meeting in Brussels to begin putting in place what became in March 1996 a $5.1 billion, five-year reconstruction programme.

The PIC had an especially important role to play because international commitment to Bosnia's reconstruction had to be on an almost unprecedented scale to begin to address the consequences of three-and-a-half years of war and the legacy of forty-five years of communism. Moreover, budgetary resources for peace implementation had not been identified during the Dayton negotiations, nor had the various tasks of the many international agencies involved on the ground been properly divided up. And despite the extraordinary role he had played in getting the settlement agreed, as well as the relationships he had with the key players, Holbrooke left government service in February 1996 to work in the private sector.

When the Dayton Peace Agreement came into force, more than half the pre-war population of 4.3 million were either internally displaced within Bosnia (1.1 million) or living as refugees abroad (1.2 million), in addition to the 100,000 or so who had been killed. Of some 3 million people remaining in Bosnia, some 2.4 million or 80 per cent were dependent on international humanitarian aid. Physical destruction marked the entire country, with religious buildings particularly hard hit,[14] infrastructure shattered[15] and just under a third of the housing stock damaged or destroyed. Moreover, more than half a million mines remained in the ground. Meanwhile, GDP per capita had slumped to less than $500 or about 20 per cent of the pre-war level as production collapsed. The heavy industry that had formed the backbone of Bosnia's pre-war economy was, in any case, dated and much of it redundant. Moreover, communist structures needed an overhaul in line with the rest of Eastern Europe to enable the country to move from a socialist to a capitalist economy.

The physical challenge of reconstruction was great but surmountable given the level of international aid. The transition from a socialist to a capitalist economy was more complex, but again it could be achieved with a combination of aid, training and expertise. By contrast, the political challenge involved in piecing Bosnia back together, if only in the form envisaged under the Dayton Peace

Agreement, was of another order of magnitude. Implementation of the accord and in particular Annex 7 ('Agreement on Refugees and Displaced Persons') effectively entailed reversing the results of ethnic cleansing, which had been the primary war aim of some of the belligerents.

Although the parties to the peace accord were also expected to implement it, the chances of them doing so voluntarily were minimal. Power was concentrated in the hands of individuals who had a vested interest in maintaining the ethno-national divisions that had become institutionalised in the war, since they had created them themselves and were the principal beneficiaries. Some had already been indicted by the International Criminal Tribunal for the former Yugoslavia (ICTY). Others must have suspected that they, too, would be indicted. In the case of Republika Srpska leaders, the peace accord had been negotiated and agreed despite them. Moreover, if the accord were implemented to the letter, if refugees and the displaced were able to return to their homes, if war-crimes suspects were brought to trial, and if Bosnia were to become a functioning democracy governed by the rule of law, their power bases would be no more. Indeed, many would probably find themselves serving lengthy terms in international prisons.

The likely consequences of attempting reconstruction without reforming the wartime power structures were apparent in Mostar even before the Dayton Peace Agreement brought the war in Bosnia to an end. The Herzegovinian city had been home to the country's most famous landmark, the Old Bridge or *Stari most*, which had been one of five bridges spanning the Neretva River in Mostar before its destruction in November 1993. Mostar had also been the scene of the heaviest and most prolonged fighting between Bosniaks and Croats, with a front line that ran through the city centre. In the wake of the Bosniak-Croat War, the European Union put together an ambitious programme to rebuild and reunite the city. An EU Administration of Mostar (EUAM), headed by Hans Koschnick, a former mayor of Bremen in Germany, arrived in Mostar in July 1994 and remained until January 1997, together with a contingent of international police under the auspices of the Western European Union. In the course of its two-and-a-half years' existence, the

ELECTIONS AT ANY PRICE

EUAM spent some 300 million German marks (€150 million), or about 5,000 German marks per inhabitant. This was international aid on an unprecedented scale, for which the EUAM could show a series of new constructions, including two bridges over the Neretva, but little progress on political reunification or reconciliation. As commentators remarked at the time, the EUAM was able to build physical bridges, but not to join two halves of a divided city.

The EUAM's failure to bridge the political divide was not for want of trying or lack of courage. Rather, it reflected the extent of the vested interests that needed to be overcome to reunify the city. Koschnick himself was fortunate to survive physically unscathed after two attempts on his life. The first was in September 1994, soon after he arrived, when his apartment in the EUAM's headquarters, Hotel Ero, was rocketed in the early hours of the morning. The second was in February 1996 when a mob surrounded and attacked him in his car. The second incident came soon after Koschnick unveiled plans to create a large central zone that he hoped would be a step towards reuniting the city and rebuilding its multi-ethnic character. Koschnick resigned a month later after an emergency meeting of EU foreign ministers decided to make concessions to the Croat leadership, who had instigated the attack, rather than support his position.

As high representative, Bildt would face the same systematic obstructionism at the state level that Koschnick had had to deal with in Mostar. In addition, he had to build a new international organisation in extremely difficult conditions; to co-ordinate the work of the other international organisations, most of which were also being set up from scratch; and to present a case for appropriate resources and interpretation of mandates in key capitals.

At the end of hostilities, the ruling ethno-national political parties controlled almost all aspects of society and were easily able to manipulate a destitute population. They had inherited the mechanisms of social control—the *nomenklatura* system—from the former communist regime. However, whereas the communists had become increasingly reluctant to use the coercive means at their disposal, their ethno-national successors had no such qualms. Indeed, many of the individuals who dominated the ethno-national

95

parties, and especially the SDS, had risen to positions of authority because of the ruthlessness with which they had waged the war, and were determined to manipulate the party apparatus to retain their privileges and status. Media were slavishly obedient to political authority and continued to stoke the flames of ethno-national hatred; the economy was in the hands of individuals linked to the ruling ethno-national parties; housing and other benefits were allocated by local authorities who used this power to enforce strict loyalty; and there was no transparency in decision-making.

Reality in Bosnia at the end of the war was three ethno-national mini-states, each with its own armed forces, police, media, administration, official documentation and vehicle licence plates. Separate currencies circulated in each ethno-national mini-state, the Serbian dinar in Republika Srpska, the Croatian kuna in Croat-held Federation territory, the Bosnian mark in government-controlled Federation territory, with the German mark accepted everywhere. There were no telephone lines between the entities, let alone bus routes, postal services or other means of communication.

In terms of the wider region, both Croatia and the Federal Republic of Yugoslavia retained a large capacity to influence events in Bosnia and undermine the state. Although both Milošević and Tuđman had played important, even constructive roles in the Dayton negotiations and were signatories to the peace accord, they also had their own agendas in Bosnia. Both Belgrade and Zagreb benefitted from an end to hostilities, yet neither was committed to the terms of the peace accord and both continued to finance critical elements of their respective communities' power structures, including, in particular, security forces. Meanwhile, although the ICFY was wound up, the regional approach leading to a 'direct and dynamic contractual relationship between Bosnia and the European Union' envisaged at the PIC's London meeting failed to materialise.[16]

On the ground in Bosnia, by contrast, Bildt managed to put together a functioning office in a remarkably short period of time given the conditions. To ensure a high calibre of staff, he personally oversaw much early recruitment. He also insisted on the use of the latest information technology, including email at a time when it was still uncommon. By getting the Office of the High Representative

(OHR) off the ground so rapidly, through his stature as a former prime minister of Sweden and the enormous energy he brought to the post, Bildt became the focal point of the international civilian effort. However, his mandate was weak.[17] It was about monitoring, co-ordinating and facilitating, with specifically no authority over IFOR. Unless IFOR was willing to play a more interventionist role, the international presence risked achieving little in the face of near total obstructionism.

Given the reluctance of the local authorities to comply with civilian aspects of the peace accord, some form of political revitalisation was clearly necessary before implementation could begin in earnest. Moreover, the Dayton Peace Agreement stipulated the holding of elections six to nine months after it came into force, which, in theory, could have served as an agent of change. After all, competitive elections are critical to democratic processes and in most countries provide a means to change the faces of those in power. In the event, however, the elections that took place as scheduled on 14 September 1996, nine months to the day after the Dayton Peace Agreement was signed, failed to achieve any political rejuvenation. Worse still, the manner in which they were held and the abuses that were tolerated helped entrench an insidious political system, undermining prospects for multi-ethnicity, reconciliation and a self-sustaining peace process.

Elections, pseudo-democracy and institutional paralysis

The debate over whether elections should take place in the timeframe specified in the Dayton Peace Agreement, which dominated the early months of the peace process, was part of the wider debate over the ultimate goal of peace implementation. Should the international community be seeking to rebuild multi-ethnicity in Bosnia, and if so in what way? Or would the settlement be more durable if, in practice, it cemented ethno-national partition? The peace accord was ambiguous and could be read either way, though 'multi-ethnicity' did not explicitly feature.

While the peace accord appeared to hold out the promise of return to refugees and displaced persons, it actually presented two solutions: return or compensation for lost property. While the peace accord appeared to be seeking to rebuild multi-ethnic political institutions based on the country's pre-war demography, in that people were expected to vote in their pre-war municipalities, it also offered the possibility of voting elsewhere. Moreover, there were no provisions for how multi-ethnicity was supposed to work below the state level. How, for example, should the Republika Srpska National Assembly make decisions in matters relating to the interests of Croats and Bosniaks, or the Federation parliament with Serbs? And how should municipal councils and governments take the views of all communities into consideration, and not just the views of the majority?

A compelling case could be made for proceeding with elections as envisaged in the Dayton Peace Agreement. The polls—for the House of Representatives of Bosnia, for the presidency of Bosnia, for the House of Representatives of the Federation, for the National Assembly of Republika Srpska, for the presidency of Republika Srpska and, if feasible, for cantonal assemblies and municipal governing authorities—were necessary to put in place the political institutions set out in the peace accord. Moreover, the key annex ('Annex 3: Agreement on Elections') contained a series of safe-guards ostensibly designed to prevent the process from being abused, including conditions for free and fair elections such as a politically neutral environment, freedom of expression and of the press, freedom of association and freedom of movement. In addition, the process was to be supervised, not simply overseen, by the OSCE, which also had to certify whether elections could be 'effective under current social conditions in both entities' in advance of the polls and, via a Provisional Election Commission (PEC), would draw up electoral rules and regulations.

The issue was one of standards. The international community, in the form of the OSCE, had the authority to delay elections and to insist that these standards be met. It was also in a position to craft an electoral system that might contribute to inter-ethnic accommodation by, for example, building in mechanisms to provide ethno-national security or encourage voters to cross the ethno-national divide, as in functioning multi-ethnic democracies. But standards and appropriate systems depended on the level of risk and engagement that the international community was prepared to take on, as well as on a political calculation of what the local 'market' was willing to bear. In the absence of the political will to take on local power structures, the local 'market' was not going to make any effort to meet even minimal standards. In the event, the line of least resistance was adopted, standards were ignored and a flawed poll was rammed through.

Advocates of multi-ethnicity as the best long-term solution for Bosnia were most opposed to the holding of precipitate elections, which they considered likely to cement the results of ethnic cleansing. But those advocates were not represented in any of the three ruling mono-ethnic political parties, the only local parties represented in the PEC with a voice in designing the system, whose overriding concern was to secure and maintain ethno-national homogenisation.

The electoral timeframe may or may not have been necessary to ensure that the US public perceived Washington's engagement as a success. Since Bob Dole, the Republican nominee for president, supported greater and concerted US engagement in the former Yugoslavia to help resolve the many outstanding issues, there was actually bipartisan support for the US troop deployment. Nevertheless, the perception in Bosnia was that the Clinton administration had decided that in the run-up to a US presidential election it would not take any unnecessary chances and that therefore elections would take place in Bosnia, irrespective of the consequences.[18] Moreover, the OSCE's decision was effectively pre-empted by a series of statements from the US State Department, the Contact Group and even the Italian presidency of the European Union to the effect that elections would take place according to the Dayton schedule.

On 25 June 1996, the OSCE Chairman-in-Office Flavio Cotti certified that elections should proceed taking into consideration the 'global context', giving the green light to a 14 September poll. He also pointed out that the preconditions set out in the Dayton Peace Agreement had not been met and that if they were not met in the intervening period, the elections ought not to take place, as they would lead to further tensions and 'pseudo-democratic legitimisation of extreme nationalist power structures'. He stressed the need to eliminate 'every single possibility of direct or indirect exertion of influence by indicted war criminals', urging both the parties to the accord and the international community to redouble efforts to meet minimum conditions.

Cotti's warning was prophetic, as the already unsatisfactory conditions deteriorated between certification and the day of the vote. The precedent was again Mostar, where a municipal election had taken place on 30 June 1996. Although the poll itself passed without incident, it did not contribute to the creation of meaningful and functioning political institutions that might help reunite the city. Instead, in the absence of preconditions for a free and fair poll, it served to cement the ethno-national divide and entrench wartime leaders in power, formally instituting political deadlock.

The Mostar poll was, nevertheless, different to what was about to happen on 14 September in several key respects. The EUAM had already been in place for close to two years and was a well-resourced mission. It was therefore on top of voter registration and alert to potential abuses of the poll. Indeed, it devised an innovative electoral system specifically to avoid fraud and help reconstruct multi-ethnicity in the city. The ethno-national results of the election were set in advance in such a way that sixteen Bosniaks, sixteen Croats and five Others would be elected to the city-wide council,[19] irrespective of how many voters actually cast ballots for the various ethno-national political parties.

As a newcomer to the international scene, the OSCE did not have the institutional ability to hire staff or borrow money for operations and was dependent on personnel and money offered by member states.[20] This left the Bosnian mission understaffed and underfunded during its early months and, even when the full contingent had supposedly arrived, short of experts in elections, human rights and, most critically, information technology. The OSCE would have struggled to organise elections in the prescribed timeframe even in a favourable climate. In the pressure-cooker environment of post-war Bosnia, it was obliged to pander to the ruling ethno-national parties to ensure that the poll would take place.[21] As a result, it proved largely powerless to prevent massive and flagrant abuses, whose impact would be more far-reaching than any other aspect of the peace process.

The most glaring abuses took place in voter registration. Had a similar system been in place to that used in Mostar, including predetermined ethno-national results, there would have been no electoral advantage in manipulating voter registration, and the elections might even have contributed to reversing the effects of ethnic cleansing. Predetermining the ethno-national results of an election is not uncommon in functioning multi-ethnic states. Indeed, certain ethno-national results were already set in the Dayton constitution, such as for the presidency and the House of Peoples, as described above. However, since the ethno-national results of the elections were left open and there were no 'vital interest' mechanisms at municipal level (or indeed at the level of Republika Srpska or even for Serbs in the Federation), the key electoral challenge for the ethno-national parties was to create ethno-national majorities by 'packing' strategic municipalities.

In 1991, the territory that became Republika Srpska had a population that was 28.77 per cent Bosniak, 9.99 per cent Croat, 54.3 per cent Serb and 7.53 per cent Other. The territory of what became the Federation had a population that was 52.09 per cent Bosniak, 22.13 per cent Croat, 17.62 per cent Serb and 8.16 per cent Other. By the end of the war, the figures were 2.19 per cent Bosniak, 1.02 per cent Croat and 96.79 per cent Serb in Republika Srpska and 72.61 per cent Bosniak, 22.27 per cent Croat, 2.32 per cent Serb and 2.38 per cent Other in the Federation.[22] If, therefore, people were to vote in their pre-war municipality, some councils would be elected with majorities representing the communities that had been expelled.

Under the Dayton Peace Agreement, most displaced Bosnians were expected to vote in the municipalities in which they had been living in 1991 to start the process of reintegration. Voting elsewhere was to be the exception.[23] Under the PEC's electoral rules and regulations, displaced persons wishing to vote somewhere other than where they had been living in 1991—either in the municipality in which they were currently living or in a different municipality in which they intended to live—had to fill out a so-called P-2 form, apply to the PEC and then vote in person on the day. Whereas displaced Bosniaks and Croats generally registered to vote by absentee ballot in the municipalities in which they had been living in 1991, almost all displaced Serbs registered to vote in their current place of residence. Had these displaced Serbs chosen to switch their vote themselves, this might have been acceptable. However, the Bosnian Serb authorities systematically pressured them into registering to vote in Republika Srpska and not where they had been living in 1991 by withholding housing, humanitarian aid and other benefits until they produced a P-2 form. In this way, the exception became the rule. Manipulation of voter registration among refugees in the Federal Republic of Yugoslavia went still further, so much so that the OSCE was eventually obliged to postpone municipal elections. In total, 123,007 Bosnian Serb refugees registered in the Federal Republic of Yugoslavia via the P-2 form to vote in person on the day of the election in municipalities in Republika Srpska in which they supposedly intended to live. All were registering in municipalities where Bosniaks and Croats had formed the majority of the population before the war, in a co-ordinated campaign to ensure Serb majorities on the municipal councils.[24]

The manipulation of voter registration reflected prevailing attitudes to democratic government as well as the critical importance of the electoral system in shaping political behaviour. The ethno-national parties had a very clear understanding of what winning more than 50 per cent of votes meant, namely ethno-national rule by the community with the majority at the expense of the other communities. While elections are a key feature of democracy, an inappropriate electoral system in a multi-ethnic state can prove extremely destabilising. Certain features of Bosnia's post-war electoral system—such as separate polls in the two entities for the joint institutions as well as the explicit stipulation that voters would only be able to vote for one member of the presidency—were a manifestation of the Dayton settlement. But most were left for the PEC to determine. However, given the timeframe it was working to, minimal thought was given to system design. As a result, parliaments were elected by party-list proportional representation because this was the only system that could be put in place in the limited time available.[25]

The electoral campaign was extremely nationalistic. Moreover, it effectively involved three separate contests, one in Bosniak-controlled territory, another in Croat-controlled territory, and another in Serb-controlled territory in which the level of debate and number of competing views reflected the relative size of each community. Of the three contests, the one in Bosniak-controlled territory was most open, with a genuine division between the ruling SDA and two alternatives: the Stranka za Bosnu i Hercegovinu (Party for Bosnia, or SBiH), which had just been founded by Haris Silajdžić, a former SDA leader who had served as foreign minister for most of the war and was prime minister during the Dayton negotiations; and the Združena lista (Joint List, or ZL), a coalition of parties that had evolved out of the League of Communists, that is the Socijaldemokratska partija (Social Democratic Party, or SDP) and the Unija Bosansko-Hercegovačkih socijaldemokrata (Union of Bosnian and Herzegovinian Social Democrats, or UBSD), the successor of Ante Marković's Savez reformskih snaga Jugoslavije (League of Reform Forces of Yugoslavia, or SRSJ). The SBiH appeared to represent a country-wide outlook in contrast to the sectarian approach of the SDA, and therefore sought to appeal to non-Bosniaks who believed in a Bosnian state, in addition to Bosniaks. The ZL attempted to represent a genuinely multi-ethnic outlook as befitted the inheritors of the communist tradition, even though the vast majority of its supporters were Bosniaks.

In Croat-controlled areas, the HDZ tolerated almost no dissent and ignored rules and regulations concerning the conduct of the polls, much as in the earlier Mostar vote. Although the degree of repression was probably not necessary in the absence of any alternative, it ensured ethno-national loyalty among Croats.

In Republika Srpska, voters had different parties or coalitions to choose among, though almost all appeared to share the same programme, with the only issue being how best to preserve and strengthen Republika Srpska. One minor but serious party in a coalition of parties that had evolved out of the League of Communists did, nevertheless, appear to be different, namely the Stranka nezavisnih socijaldemokrata (Party of Independent Social Democrats, or SNSD) of Milorad Dodik. While Dodik did not overtly advocate a multi-ethnic Bosnia, his party did not carry an ethno-national prefix and he and eleven associates had formed the opposition to the SDS in the Republika Srpska National Assembly during the war. Moreover, Dodik had constructive relations with various politicians in the Federation, which he maintained even during the war.[26] He appeared committed to a peace process, unlike the ruling SDS, which had refused international assistance and portrayed the poll as a referendum on independence, and whose leader, Radovan Karadžić, had been indicted for war crimes.

The one situation that might have held up the elections was the continued presence of Karadžić on the political scene. Although unable to stand as a candidate because of his indictment (unless he surrendered to the ICTY), Karadžić remained president of both Republika Srpska and the SDS and his ongoing influence and liberty were extremely embarrassing for international officials involved in the peace process. Karadžić stepped down and agreed not to appear in public or in broadcast media on 19 July 1996—eight weeks before the elections—after talks with Holbrooke, who had returned to the Balkans at the request of the Clinton administration.[27] Karadžić was succeeded by Biljana Plavšić, who was viewed at the time as the most uncompromising of the SDS leaders. Despite formally withdrawing from public life, Karadžić's image was everywhere.

Given the vice-like grip of the ruling ethno-national parties, the election results were never in doubt. International agencies attempted to level the playing field with a series of initiatives, such as the launch of internationally funded media, including a television station on the eve of the vote, and by distributing up to 375,000 German marks to each political party to enable them all to finance a campaign. But the reality was systematic intimidation in the run-up and widespread fraud on the day.

The ruling ethno-national parties did not need to stuff ballot boxes to win the elections, but did so anyway. The scale of the fraud only emerged when the votes were counted and the overall total—2,486,050 in the election for the House of Representatives of Bosnia—was greater than 100 per cent of the electorate physically able to vote either by postal ballot or in person. The Election Appeals Sub-Commission, a juridical body set up by the PEC to ensure compliance with election rules and regulations and to adjudicate in the event of complaints, decided that the turnout was 'so high that it raises a significant possibility of double voting, other forms of fraud, or counting irregularities' and recommended a complete recount of all votes cast and other measures to investigate the matter. However, the PEC chose to ignore the recommendation, certified the election results and hastily destroyed all ballots, making independent investigation impossible.[28]

Certification had several immediate consequences. Firstly, it lifted the already suspended sanctions against the Federal Republic of Yugoslavia and Republika Srpska. Secondly, as a result of the abuse of voter registration, it helped cement the ethno-national division created by the war. Thirdly, it entrenched the ruling ethno-national parties in power with a democratic mandate and renewed legitimacy. And fourthly, it set in place an invidious political system that would help fuel conflict rather than mitigate it. Moreover, the 'Dayton' institutions that were supposed to come together in the wake of the elections failed to materialise in a meaningful form.

Almost exactly a year later, on 13 and 14 September 1997, the postponed municipal elections took place. The conditions had hardly improved in the intervening period, though a rift had opened up among the leadership in Republika Srpska between pragmatists prepared to work with the international community led by Plavšić, on the one hand, and Karadžić loyalists, on the other. The opportunity for ballot fraud had been greatly reduced as a result of a comprehensive voter registration carried out over nearly two months both in Bosnia and in the many countries where refugees were living. In total, 2,520,217 voters registered, of whom 2,174,765 cast ballots over an orderly two-day period, confirming the scale of the fraud a year earlier.

The opportunity for voter-registration fraud had been somewhat reduced, but could not be eliminated because local authorities were again issuing falsified documents to 'pack' strategic municipalities (especially Brčko) with voters from the desired community. Indeed, the scale of the fraud was so great that voter registration had to be halted after four weeks for additional staff training. The PEC gave each of the ruling parties a CD-ROM of the complete list of voters and the municipalities in which they had registered three weeks before the vote. After this, the parties combed through the names of people registered in strategic municipalities, counting the numbers of Bosniaks, Croats and Serbs, easily identifiable from their names, to determine the likely results.[29] Once again the elections made a mockery of democracy and served, above all, to reinforce the ethno-national divide.[30] In the wake of a second flawed poll, therefore, the task of piecing Bosnia back together and creating a self-sustaining settlement was even greater than it had been at the beginning of the peace process. Moreover, it required a major shift in international strategy towards Bosnia, one that was already coming together.

6

OVERRIDING 'DEMOCRACY' TO IMPLEMENT DAYTON

'The international community, and specifically the United States, is in the odd position of pretending to build democracy while vigorously ignoring the consent of the governed, at least as manifested by the victors in elections that the international community has mandated and supervised.'

Robert M. Hayden[1]

Changing course

Had the NATO-led peacekeeping force withdrawn from Bosnia one year after its deployment as scheduled, there would likely have been a rapid resumption of armed hostilities. Although the military annexes of the Dayton Peace Agreement had been implemented more or less as planned, their implementation alone was not sufficient to prevent a return to war. In the absence of a long-term military commitment, there was no prospect of a durable settlement. This reality was reluctantly recognised by decision-makers who in November 1996 agreed to extend the military presence for an additional eighteen months, and eventually—after two years of the peace process—for as long as required.

Prolonging the international military presence and removing artificial deadlines for its withdrawal was an important first step towards bringing peace to Bosnia. However, the extension of the NATO-led force's mandate by itself would have achieved little more than turn the inter-entity boundary line into a border. In order to see other elements of the Dayton Peace Agreement implemented, and especially provisions relating to refugee returns, a new interpretation of the mandate was required. The focus of the mission had to shift from preventing a resumption of hostilities and force protection to creating the conditions in Bosnia for civilian implementation of the peace accord. This is precisely what happened in the course of 1997 and 1998.

The change in interpretation of the military mandate reflected a wider shift in international strategy towards the peace process. This shift was the result of various factors, including a realistic assessment of where Bosnia was headed after the first year of peace implementation and changes in outlook in key capitals.

Although the Dayton Peace Agreement had been ambiguous about Bosnia's final status, events during the first year of its implementation pointed increasingly towards some form of ethnonational partition. Refugees were returning home, but almost exclusively to areas where they belonged to the community whose forces controlled the territory. Meanwhile, expulsions of remaining minority populations continued; violence against minority returnees was widespread; and even the shells of homes of displaced persons and refugees were being dynamited to ensure they could not be rebuilt and returned to. At the same time, there was minimal communication across the former front lines; the Dayton institutions that were eventually formed in the wake of massive international cajoling were deadlocked; and war-crimes suspects were able to go about their lives with impunity, confident that as long as they laid low for the duration of the international military presence they would escape trial.

Given the state of the peace process, it was hardly surprising that local leaders continued to contemplate war. This was especially the case on the Bosniak side. Indeed, in April 1997, maps appeared in the Sarajevo press of an alternative territorial division being discussed by the SDA leadership by which the eastern half of Republika Srpska would join rump Yugoslavia, predominantly

Croat parts of the Federation would join Croatia, and Bosnia would become what remained, that is predominantly Bosniak parts of the Federation and the western half of Republika Srpska. Such a division presumed the fall of the western half of Republika Srpska in a lightning strike much like Operations Flash and Storm in Croatia in May and August 1995, and would presumably have required Croatian support.

The Clinton administration had always been divided between a faction that believed in limiting involvement to provide space for local politicians to find their own solutions, and another that believed in a more proactive and longer-term approach to peace-building.[2] Elections had failed to put Bosnia on the road to a self-sustaining peace, but had opened up the possibility of another war in the wake of the withdrawal of the international military presence. The faction arguing for the interventionist approach—personified by new Secretary of State Madeleine Albright—began to get the upper hand in the months following Clinton's re-election in November 1996.

The shift in approach manifested itself spectacularly on 10 July 1997 in two snatch operations. British special forces arrested one war-crimes suspect, Milan Kovačević, and killed another, Simo Drljača, as he resisted arrest, in and around Prijedor, a town in the west of Republika Srpska. The impact of these snatch operations should not be under-estimated, for they brought an end to the cycle of impunity that had characterised the Wars of Yugoslav Dissolution and illustrated the new-found resolve of the international community. Moreover, there was minimal backlash against the international community beyond heightened rhetoric in SDS-controlled media. Fears of the potential consequences of such actions had clearly been exaggerated. The fact that the soldiers who carried out the snatch operations were British reflected a new commitment to the peace process and a willingness to take on risk in Britain. Tony Blair's Labour Party had come into government less than two months earlier with a large majority, promising an 'ethical' foreign policy. Indeed, Britain seized the moment to illustrate the point by funding construction of an additional trial chamber at the International Criminal Tribunal for the former Yugoslavia (ICTY) in The Hague.

A more pro-active approach had already been in place for several months. A decision had been taken to increase the size of the

BOSNIA'S PARALYSED PEACE

International Police Task Force from 1,500 to 2,500 at the London meeting of the Peace Implementation Council in December 1996, to begin to address the 'enforcement gap' created by the military's reluctance to take on policing tasks.[3] The Brčko Arbitral Tribunal[4] had made an interim ruling in February 1997 placing an international supervisor in Brčko to oversee Dayton implementation and not awarding the territory to either entity. Huge international pressure on local leaders had on 20 June 1997 helped persuade the newly formed Bosnian parliament to adopt a so-called 'quick-start' package of legislation drawn up by the OHR agreeing in principle to create a Central Bank, common currency, customs union and common external tariffs and, thereby, to begin knitting the country back together. And at the May 1997 meeting of the Peace Implementation Council in Sintra, Portugal, the first deadlines had been set for implementation of specific tasks, such as telephone connections between the entities. The implication was that if the local authorities failed to complete the tasks on schedule, IFOR's 32,000-strong successor, the Stabilisation Force (SFOR), would do it for them. The OHR was also empowered at Sintra to take measures against media that posed a threat to the peace agreement.[5] A new high representative, senior Spanish diplomat and former foreign minister, Carlos Westendorp, was appointed soon after.

The snatch operations helped to change the dynamics of the peace process, with the result that opportunities began opening up for the international civilian agencies. In addition, the international community was able to exploit a rift that emerged in the SDS between pragmatists led by Plavšić, who were willing to co-operate with the international community, and hardliners loyal to Karadžić, who were not. Each had a differing vision of what was best for both Republika Srpska and Serbs in general. The Karadžić faction, which was based in the Bosnian Serb wartime capital of Pale, just outside Sarajevo, and headed by Momčilo Krajišnik, the Serb member of the Bosnian presidency, had called the shots for the first year and a half of the peace process and, in addition to obstructing implementation of the peace accord, had refused international reconstruction assistance. The first $1.7 billion, which was pledged in 1996, had gone almost entirely to the Federation, since no representative of Republika Srpska had even attended the donors' conference.

The pragmatists, who were largely based in Banja Luka, feared for the future of Republika Srpska, or at least the western half of the entity, if its leadership continued to obstruct implementation of the Dayton Peace Agreement in the same manner as the Republika Srpska Krajina (Republic of Serb Krajina, or RSK) leadership in Croatia had blocked implementation of the Sarajevo Accord. The western half of Republika Srpska was extremely vulnerable to the kind of lightning strike that had eliminated the RSK and Bosniak leaders were known to be contemplating such an operation. Moreover, the many Serbs fleeing Operations Flash and Storm who had taken refuge in Banja Luka and surrounding areas were living testimony to the folly of the kind of obstructionism that the Karadžić faction was pursuing. The pragmatists were also concerned over corruption, as Karadžić and his closest associates lined their pockets via illegal sales of alcohol, coffee, fuel and tobacco at the expense of the entity coffers.

The death of Drljača in the 10 July 1997 snatch operation proved fortuitous for Plavšić, as he had been almost as powerful in the west of Republika Srpska as Karadžić in the east. At the end of June, Plavšić sacked the entity's interior minister and dissolved Republika Srpska's National Assembly. She was also planning to launch a new political party, the Srpski narodni savez (Serb National League, or SNS), to challenge the SDS, to the anger of her erstwhile colleagues in Pale who were looking for ways to oust her. Attempts to crush her revolt were thwarted by SFOR, which took over Banja Luka, expelled the secret police from its headquarters and stationed a liaison officer in Banski dvor (Plavšić's presidential palace). Moreover, as SFOR made it clear it would provide protection for Plavšić supporters, police stations throughout the west of Republika Srpska switched their allegiance to her over the summer.

Attempts to help Plavšić extend the territory under her control came unstuck at the end of the summer in Brčko and Bijeljina in the face of mob violence. In the ensuing confusion, US troops in SFOR found themselves holding a key television transmitter at Udrigovo near Bijeljina, but surrounded by civilians loyal to

Karadžić. After a five-day standoff, SFOR agreed to hand the transmitter back on condition that Srpska Radio-Televizija (Srpska Radio-Television, or SRT) refrain from incitements against SFOR and the international community[6] and that it open up the airwaves to alternative points of view. At the time, SRT was closely controlled by Krajišnik, who was chair of its governing board in addition to being the Serb member of the presidency. Moreover, its output was so obnoxious that the previous high representative, Carl Bildt, had described it as 'media that even Stalin would be ashamed of'. On 1 October 1997, as soon as SRT flouted the terms of the agreement by which it got the Udrigovo transmitter back, SFOR troops intervened at the request of the high representative to seize four transmission towers.

The seizure of SRT's transmission towers was another watershed in the peace process. By intervening in this way, the international community made clear that it would in future act to halt incitement of hatred and partisan interference in public broadcasting. The intervention, which was followed by the appointment of an interim international administrator at SRT, also ended the hardliners' monopoly over television in Republika Srpska, thereby helping create a more level playing field in the run-up to Republika Srpska's extraordinary elections in November.[7] And it heralded the beginning of comprehensive media restructuring throughout the country, not just in Republika Srpska.

November's extraordinary elections effectively ratified the new territorial division in Republika Srpska. Plavšić's new party and other alternatives to the SDS, including Dodik's SNSD, which together formed the *Sloga* (brotherhood) coalition, picked up votes in the west of Republika Srpska where they now controlled the levers of power, and the SDS remained dominant in the east where it retained its control over society. As a result of absentee ballots cast by Bosniaks and Croats, no party formed a majority. This made it difficult to form a government until the OHR, working closely with the US Embassy, acted to put together a coalition around Dodik, Plavšić's choice for prime minister, on the basis of Bosniak and Croat support.[8] Indeed, so involved was the OHR that it directed much of the critical session of the Republika Srpska

National Assembly on 18 January 1998, and even organised the return of a Croat deputy, who had already set off for Zagreb, for the key vote.

The OHR's role in helping Dodik form a non-SDS government reflected a new willingness to intervene. This was in large part the result of a robust reinterpretation of the authority of the high representative at the Peace Implementation Conference in Bonn, Germany, a month earlier. That reinterpretation was based on Article V of Annex 10 ('Agreement on Civilian Implementation of the Peace Settlement'), namely that 'The High Representative is the final authority in theatre regarding implementation of this Agreement on the civilian implementation of the peace settlement.' The executive authority that it conferred on the high representative, including the ability to impose legislation provisionally and to dismiss office-holders, became known as the 'Bonn Powers'.[9]

Introduction of the Bonn Powers was a response to more than a year of political deadlock in the wake of the September 1996 elections during which the country's elected representatives had failed even to agree a location for the joint institutions, let alone anything substantial. During this period, it became abundantly clear that the ethno-national parties were locked into a zero-sum mindset and would not implement what they had ostensibly agreed in the peace accord. As a result, the conclusions of the Conference contained sharp language criticising the ethno-national parties and lamenting the 'lack of strong multi-ethnic parties and a structured civil society'.

The conclusions of the Bonn Peace Implementation Conference also referred in the second paragraph to 'two multi-ethnic entities'.[10] This was the first such reference in any official document, including the Dayton Peace Agreement itself, relating to the peace process, and heralded an extremely significant shift in international strategy. In effect, the international community had decided after two years of systematic obstructionism that it would not be possible to build a self-sustaining peace in collaboration with the ethno-national parties. Rather, it would be necessary to take them on, dismantle their power structures and seek to build self-sustaining solutions in multi-ethnicity. This meant overruling or bypassing the democratic institutions whose creation had been the reason for the 1996 elections.

The problems inherent in such a strategy were immediately evident. How could the high representative and other international civil servants make decisions on matters of importance to Bosnians when they were not answerable to them and would not have to live with the consequences? How would decisions be implemented in the absence of local buy-in? How far could this process go without embedding a culture of dependency? Most importantly, was it possible to build democracy by undemocratic means?

In the months following the Bonn Peace Implementation Conference, the high representative began cautiously to impose decisions. Most of the early decisions were measures to promote Bosnian statehood, including a Law on Citizenship, a passport,[11] a flag, a currency,[12] a national anthem[13] and a coat of arms, none of which could be agreed by the country's elected representatives. One measure in particular—the introduction of a common vehicle licence plate—had an immediate impact on the dynamics of life in Bosnia. As soon as the ethno-national licence plates that had been introduced in the war were replaced with neutral plates, drivers were no longer immediately identifiable and began to venture outside territory controlled by the armed forces and police of their own community. Indeed, almost overnight, it became possible for Bosnians to travel throughout Bosnia, to visit areas they had not dared to go to for more than half a decade and to meet up with long-lost friends and former neighbours. Taken together, the new media environment, the introduction of a common vehicle licence plate and the reconnection of telephone lines between the entities greatly reduced tensions, which in turn paved the way for the beginning of a return process.

Promoting 'moderates'

In addition to helping install Dodik in office as prime minister of Republika Srpska, the international community propped up his government with the kind of financial assistance that the Federation had already been enjoying since the end of the war. Moreover, the

114

aid that began arriving was unconditional. Since international officials did not wish to risk undermining Dodik's popularity among Serbs, there was, for example, no obligation to welcome back displaced Bosniaks and Croats. Although Dodik had promised that 1998 would be the year in which 80,000 Bosniaks and Croats returned to Republika Srpska, the returns failed to materialise.

Plavšić initially, and then Dodik, were beneficiaries of a policy of favouritism simply because they represented an alternative to the SDS. Indeed, without international support—including bail-outs of Republika Srpska in 1998[14] and 1999 to ensure that the government, now firmly located in the new administrative centre of Banja Luka, could continue paying public-sector salaries—it is unlikely that they would have survived, let alone been able successfully to challenge SDS rule. They and their supporters were courageous at the time and international support for them also served international interests, as it helped to open up Republika Srpska for peace implementation to begin in earnest.

The policy of promoting non-nationalist favourites was not limited to Republika Srpska. More or less overt support to any alternative to the three principal ethno-national parties—the HDZ, SDA and SDS—as well as the SDS' even more extreme ally, the Srpska radikalna stranka (Serb Radical Party, or SRS),[15] became a *leitmotif* of international policy from this point until the 2002 elections. Although the OSCE had only been mandated to supervise the first post-war elections under the Dayton Peace Agreement, it retained its supervisory role until the adoption of a permanent Election Law in 2001 and even then retained some powers of oversight. In the 2002 poll, the ethno-national parties reasserted themselves at the ballot box in such a way that the international community was obliged to work with them. Moreover, the 2002 elections, the fourth post-war poll at the state level, conferred four-year mandates for the first time.

The ethno-national parties in the Federation had actually benefitted greatly from large-scale physical reconstruction and humanitarian aid in the early years of the peace process. This was because the international agencies involved in reconstruction operated much as they would have in the aftermath of a natural disaster, working in partnership with the local authorities to disburse funds as quickly as possible, thereby enabling the local authorities to direct much of the assistance. While this approach more or less succeeded in addressing the humanitarian needs of the population and improving material conditions, it also helped reinforce and legitimise the existing power structures. These same structures, which would now become the focus of international reform efforts, were also systematically blocking other aspects of peace implementation.

Not all international assistance served to reinforce the existing power structures. Support to independent media, civil-society groups and political parties (other than the HDZ, SDA and SDS) was designed to foster pluralism in the interest of building an environment in which democracy could begin to take root. That said, the impact of such support was modest in the early years of the peace process. This was in part the result of a lack of expertise among individuals and institutions making the grants; in part it was because the sums of money involved were too small to have much impact; and, above all, it was because existing power structures, whether inherited from the communist system or improvised during the war, were too repressive to countenance alternative power centres. Major reform was required in almost every domain just to begin to create the preconditions in which the peace accord might be implemented.

The international civilian agencies and the OHR in particular were in a position to take on the ethno-national parties, begin reforming Bosnian society and oversee implementation of the peace accord, as a result of SFOR's increasingly muscular posture. SFOR began systematically removing illegal checkpoints (in collaboration with the IPTF); arresting war-crimes suspects on a regular basis (though not Karadžić or Mladić); and, following deployment in August of a so-called Multinational Special Unit consisting of military police, intervening wherever necessary to maintain order and where possible to protect vulnerable communities. Although only just over half the size of its predecessor, SFOR was able to take on all these tasks without suffering a single fatality.

The OHR started operating on an ever-wider range of fronts to drive forward peace implementation. In the process, the organisation grew exponentially, jumping from fewer than 200 employees under Bildt to more than 700 by the time Austrian diplomat Wolfgang Petritsch became the third high representative in July 1999. To make progress, the OHR had to improvise and innovate. On the one hand, it sought to take advantage of political opportunities, like the power struggle in Republika Srpska, to push the peace process forward. On the other, it sought to address specific obstacles to peace implementation, establishing where problems lay and developing mechanisms to deal with them. In this way, the mission became a well-intentioned effort to do what was best for Bosnia, its peoples and in particular those individuals, such as the refugees and the displaced, who were the greatest victims of the war, in spite of the domestic authorities.

The policy of promoting 'moderate' favourites, like Plavšić and Dodik, to undermine the established ethno-national parties consumed a great deal of international time and effort, though ultimately the results were minimal. This policy involved systematic attempts to influence the outcome of state and entity elections in 1998, 2000 and 2002 and municipal elections in 2000 and 2004. Support included providing assistance to specific 'moderate' parties; public endorsements of certain candidates and parties by international dignitaries as well as threats and penalties, including removals, against others; post-electoral intervention to build 'moderate' coalitions, as after the extraordinary 1997 Republika Srpska National Assembly elections; and attempts to tinker with the electoral system to build incentives promoting moderation into the permanent Election Law.

At the 1998 elections, the policy of promoting international favourites came unstuck when Plavšić was defeated in the poll for Republika Srpska president by Nikola Poplašen, the SRS leader on a joint SDS-SRS ticket despite (or perhaps because of) her public endorsement by US Secretary of State Albright. In the wake of his victory, Poplašen refused to re-appoint Dodik prime minister, though the coalition Dodik headed had most support in the Republika Srpska National Assembly. Poplašen paid for his obduracy by being removed by the high representative in March 1999. Dodik therefore remained prime minister in what was effectively a caretaker capacity until the 2000 elections, even after his coalition fell apart and Republika Srpska remained without a president. Having failed to accept back expelled Bosniaks and Croats, to improve the entity's finances or to raise living standards, Dodik was defeated in the 2000 elections in which support for the SDS rebounded.[16] After the poll, a coalition government excluding the SDS—at the OHR's insistence—but reliant on SDS support was put together under Mladen Ivanić, leader of the comparatively minor Partija demokratskog progresa (Party of Democratic Progress or PDP), since Ivanić was deemed acceptable by the international community.

In the wake of the 2000 poll, it was, nevertheless, possible to put together 'moderate' coalitions at both federal and state levels, after three months of internationally brokered discussions. One reason for this was the electoral success of the SDP (a united party formed out of the ZL coalition that had contested the 1996 elections), whose share of the vote in the Federation rose above even that of the SDA. Together with the SBiH and eight smaller parties, it was therefore able to put together a wafer-thin governing coalition in the Federation called the Demokratska alijansa za promjene (Democratic Alliance for Change, or DAP) in which neither the HDZ nor the SDA participated. At the state level, the same parties, together with the SNSD and the PDP, were able to put together a coalition in which none of the three previously dominant ethno-national parties were represented.

The 2000 elections were contested under modified electoral rules and regulations developed largely by the OSCE. The modifications were generally modest attempts, discussed at length with all political parties though not agreed by them, to encourage accountability and build in incentives for moderation. In addition, one far-reaching change to the way in which delegates to the Federation's House of Peoples were chosen was imposed without discussion, a controversial move that contributed to a revolt against the international community by the HDZ leadership.

In the 2000 elections, open lists and multi-member constituencies were introduced at both state and entity level. In this way, electors were able to choose among candidates on party lists, thereby reducing somewhat the control of the parties over the voting process. At the same time, delegates were to represent specific regions, thereby creating a direct link between them and their constituents. To ensure that the overall results nevertheless approximated to the proportion of the vote obtained by each party, a complex system of compensatory mandates was also introduced. All these measures were then incorporated into the permanent Election Law that was eventually adopted in urgent procedure (that is, with limited discussion) in August 2001.

In the election for president (and vice president) of Republika Srpska, preferential voting was introduced in the hope that non-Serb voters would use their second choice votes to support moderate Serb candidates (Dodik himself in 2000) and swing the poll in their favour. Under this system, voters are able to rank candidates and, if no candidate obtains more than 50 per cent of the vote, the candidate with the fewest votes is eliminated and his or her ballots redistributed among the other candidates according to voters' second choices. The process is then repeated until a candidate obtains more than 50 per cent. In the event, preferential voting did not have the desired effect, in part because there were too few non-Serbs to have an impact, in part because non-Serbs were reluctant to vote for any Serb candidate. This reform was dropped after the 2000 election and not incorporated into the permanent Electoral Law, although it was introduced and retained in the 2004 mayoral elections.

The key change in the electoral rules that triggered conflict between the HDZ and the international community concerned the way in which Croat deputies to the Federation's House of Peoples were chosen. Hitherto, Croat members of the cantonal assemblies and Croat members alone had selected the thirty Croat members of the Federation's House of Peoples, just as Bosniaks had selected the thirty Bosniak members and non-Croats and non-Bosniaks had selected the twenty Other members. Under the amendment, all members of the cantonal assemblies were able to select all eighty members of the House of Peoples. While the same number of Bosniaks, Croats and Others would still be elected, the preponderance of Bosniaks in the cantonal assemblies would give Bosniaks a disproportionate say in selecting the Croats (and Others) and enable them to choose individuals whom the HDZ described as 'loyal Croats', thereby marginalising HDZ representatives. This was a fundamental change to the political system, introduced three weeks before the vote without prior discussion. In response, the HDZ organised its own referendum on the same day as the election, 11 November 2000, asking Croat voters if they approved of greater autonomy for Croat parts of the Federation. In the wake of this referendum, in which—according to the HDZ—70 per cent of voters opted for greater autonomy, the OSCE punished the HDZ by cutting ten HDZ mandates in cantonal assemblies. In February 2001, the HDZ asked the Constitutional Court to rule on the changes to the way in which delegates to the Federation's House of Peoples were elected. After the Constitutional Court decided that the matter was not in its competency and the HDZ was excluded from the Federation government, despite having received the votes of the vast majority of Croats, the HDZ created the Hrvatski narodni sabor (Croat People's Assembly, or HNS) in March. This was intended to be a governing body that would operate on an interim basis until the creation of a third Croat entity. In response, Petritsch removed Ante Jelavić, the HDZ leader and Croat member of the presidency,[17] and three other senior HDZ officials for violating the peace accord.

The drive for Croat self-rule following the 2000 elections was arguably the most serious challenge to the Dayton settlement since the end of the war. The power struggle with the international community was, however, one that the HDZ could not win, as a result of wider regional changes of immediate significance to Bosnia. The death of Tuđman in Croatia in December 1999 and the overthrow of Milošević in the Federal Republic of Yugoslavia in October 2000 had undercut hardline Croats and Serbs in Bosnia by curtailing the financial flows necessary to maintain para-states. After a change of government in Zagreb in January 2000 following the electoral defeat of the Croatian HDZ, the HDZ in Bosnia found itself increasingly isolated and short of money. The HDZ's financial difficulties were compounded in April 2001 following two SFOR raids on Hercegovačka banka, the primary conduit for HDZ financing, and the appointment of an international administrator to the bank, who froze all accounts and launched an audit of the bank's operations.[18] In the wake of this action, the promoters of Croat self-rule were no longer in a position to finance parallel structures. Although about half of Croat soldiers—some 7,500 men—had been lured to leave the Federation armed forces by the promise of a monthly salary of 750 Bosnian marks, they returned to barracks and swore allegiance to the Federation government after a two-month stand-off that ended on 15 June 2001. A legacy of mistrust was, nevertheless, created by an imposed reform that did not make its way into the permanent Election Law and was eventually withdrawn following more wide-reaching reforms emanating out of a landmark Constitutional Court ruling.

Attempts to undermine the ethno-national parties continued up to the October 2002 elections and beyond, though to a lesser extent. In the run-up to the 2002 polls, new High Representative Lord Paddy Ashdown, who had succeeded Petritsch in May, campaigned as if he were a candidate himself. He also wrote to every household in the country urging electors to 'vote for reform'—to no avail. Despite international support, the DAP had failed to impress the electorate in just over a year and a half in government at both federal and state levels. Its support fell back and it could not form a government, irrespective of international manoeuvring.

Building multi-ethnicity

Although attempts to promote moderation and multi-ethnic accommodation through the ballot box failed, the international community had other opportunities to build multi-ethnicity. This included, in particular, driving through the return of refugees and displaced persons; setting up a multi-ethnic administration in Brčko under international supervision; and following up an especially significant decision of the Constitutional Court on the constituency of peoples.

The return of displaced persons and refugees to areas where they did not belong to the dominant community was central to the peace process and a focus of OHR and international activity in general. Had all displaced and refugees returned to their homes, the ethno-national partition created by the war would have been overturned and, with it, the power structures that had created the divisions in the first place. But as long as those power structures remained intact, so-called 'minority returns' were extremely difficult to achieve. In the first two years of the peace process, there were fewer than 50,000 in total—44,398 to or within the Federation and only 1,125 to Republika Srpska. Numbers, nevertheless, picked up in 1998 and 1999, with more than 40,000 returning in both years—32,605 to or within the Federation and 8,586 to Republika Srpska in 1998, and 27,987 to or within the Federation and 13,020 to Republika Srpska in 1999—in spite of the impact of the Kosovo campaign, during which international agencies removed most staff from Republika Srpska. And numbers rose sharply between 2000 and 2003—during which time more than 300,000 returned home, including more than 130,000 to Republika Srpska—before falling back in 2004 to just under 15,000, since when it has been a trickle. In total, therefore, some 450,000 people officially returned to territory from which they had been expelled, and where they did not belong, or no longer belonged, to the dominant people, including more than 150,000 to Republika Srpska.[19]

These breakthroughs were achieved within the framework of the Return and Reconstruction Task Force (RRTF), an OHR-chaired inter-agency group founded in January 1997 that had a field presence and included all organisations involved in the returns process. The RRTF operated until 2003 and proved sufficiently flexible to mobilise international resources to support returnees and exert political pressure on local authorities where necessary.[20] The first removals of officials by the high representative, for example, involved individuals obstructing returns at the municipal level.[21] By addressing some of the overt discrimination returnees faced and by reversing discriminatory legislation relating to housing, returns became possible. New property laws were adopted under massive OHR pressure in April 1998 in the Federation and in December 1998 in Republika Srpska, which the OHR amended repeatedly to close loopholes, thereby enabling returnees to reclaim their former properties.[22]

Returnees who reclaimed their homes still faced systematic, institutionalised discrimination in other areas. Though property legislation had been altered, the judicial system remained antagonistic; police forces were mono-ethnic and hostile; social benefits were difficult to claim; the education system was discriminatory; the media ignored their plight; and they were unlikely to find employment in an environment where the ethno-national authorities could not provide sufficient jobs for members of the majority community. Reform was required in every area to make returns genuinely sustainable and to give returnees the real option of a future in their pre-war homes.

In Brčko, minority returns were more successful than anywhere else. The breakthroughs only came after the Brčko Arbitral Tribunal ruled in March 1999 that the entire pre-war municipality of Brčko should become a district under international administration.[23] This followed two interim rulings in February 1997 and March 1998 that had left the status open but placed an international supervisor,[24] who was also a deputy high representative, in the municipality to oversee Dayton implementation. Before the Arbitral Award, the returns record in Brčko was poor. Indeed, the failure of the Republika Srpska authorities, who controlled the town though only one third of the municipality, to accept back displaced Bosniaks and Croats or to create a multi-ethnic administration, paved the way for the Arbitral Award and the imposition of what amounted to an international protectorate.[25]

Brčko's ethno-national composition had changed significantly during the war. Of just over 87,000 pre-war inhabitants—44 per cent of whom were Bosniaks, 25.4 per cent Croats, 20.8 per cent Serbs and 9.8 per cent Others—two thirds had been displaced in the course of hostilities. At the time of the Arbitral Award in 1999, the OHR estimated the population to be about 35 per cent Bosniak, 15 per cent Croat and 49 per cent Serb as a result of the arrival of some 28,000 Serbs from elsewhere in Bosnia and Croatia, who were occupying the homes of displaced Bosniaks and Croats.

Under the terms of the Arbitral Award, the pre-war municipality was to be held in condominium by both entities simultaneously; that is, it would be part of both Republika Srpska and the Federation, and Brčko residents would be citizens of one or other entity as well as of the state. In this way, they were able to vote in entity and state elections and therefore have a voice in entity and state institutions, even though neither entity would be able to exercise any authority within the District. In effect, Brčko District became a third administrative unit in Bosnia, since only district and state law applied.

Brčko District was constituted with a twenty-nine-member District Assembly and was formally governed by a mayor. In reality, however, authority lay with the supervisor, whose powers were increased to make the office akin to that of an administrator. Indeed, until elections took place in October 2004, the supervisor appointed all members of the District Assembly. Moreover, the supervisor retained executive authority, including the power to dismiss officials and impose legislation, even after elections had taken place and an elected District Assembly formed. In this way, the supervisor was able to oversee large-scale minority returns—more than 21,000 in the five years leading to the October 2004 elections—and put in place a multi-ethnic administration, police force and education system.

The turn-around in Brčko was achieved by decree, not by negotiation with the existing power structures, and implementation was facilitated by generous financial support. Reforms, such as that of the police, began before the Arbitral Award, but the additional powers awarded to the supervisor enabled him to push through the kind of fundamental and comprehensive restructuring that had not been possible elsewhere in Bosnia. Indeed, Brčko's multi-ethnic police force, established in January 2000, was created from scratch. The supervisor appointed a police chief and two deputies, and all officers were recruited under IPTF supervision and paid about twice as much as they might have earned elsewhere in Bosnia.

In the field of education, the supervisor imposed laws ending segregated schooling and separate curriculums in 2001. The laws had earlier been rejected by the District Assembly on account of the opposition of Serb delegates. In this way, eight ethno-nationally segregated schools (three Bosniak, one Croat and four Serb) were consolidated into four integrated schools in which teachers earned better salaries than their peers elsewhere in Bosnia. While existing class years remained segregated, new classes were mixed from the beginning of the 2001 academic year. However, even in mixed classes, pupils were split up for sensitive subjects such as language and history.

Given the extent of the supervisor's authority, the system of government envisaged in the Brčko Statute was essentially academic until the supervisory regime came to an end. It was, however, designed to be ethno-nationally blind. There are no formal power-sharing arrangements, quotas or 'vital-interest' mechanisms, and minimal reference to ethno-national identity, in contrast to the system elsewhere in the country. The only exception is that three seats are reserved for each of the three constituent peoples on the District Assembly, a measure that was conceded reluctantly by the supervisor though in practice it changed nothing. Otherwise, the District Assembly is elected according to the same system as in all other municipalities in Bosnia, namely by proportional representation. Civil servants are appointed on the basis of 'professional merit', though the public administration and key positions 'shall reflect the composition' of the District's population. In practice, this has meant that great effort has been made to apportion posts in line with Brčko District's ethno-national structure.

A series of measures relating to decision-making and in particular the need for supermajorities for key decisions and appointments nevertheless help ensure that no community is in a position to dominate the others. The election of the mayor, for example, requires a three-fifths majority among delegates to the District Assembly.[26]

A three-fifths majority is also required in other areas. This includes the passing of legislation; the District budget; changes to the rules of procedure, election and dismissal of all persons elected by the District Assembly, including its president; and appointment and removal of officials where the District Assembly's consent is required, such as the police chief. Decisions concerning adoption and amendment of the Statute itself require a three-quarters majority of the total number of deputies.

These measures effectively ensure that Bosniaks and Serbs cannot be outvoted, given the size of both communities, though Croats can. However, the need for 60 per cent support for all laws has in practice made legislating extremely difficult. As a result, the supervisor has had to impose much key legislation in a similar fashion to the high representative elsewhere in Bosnia. And even though the Statute is ethno-nationally blind, the party system is not. The same ethno-national parties operate in Brčko as elsewhere in Bosnia and the electorate divides along the same ethno-national lines, creating the same problems in the District Assembly as in the state parliament and the Mostar city council, the only other assemblies without built-in ethno-national majorities.

The issue of ethno-national representation in the various entity institutions and assemblies came to the fore in the wake of a landmark ruling by the Constitutional Court, the so-called decision on the constituency of peoples. The decision (composed of four partial decisions published between January and August 2000) emerged out of a case put to the Court in February 1998 by the chair of the presidency, Alija Izetbegović, following lobbying by a group representing Serbs who had remained in government-controlled territory during the war, the Srpsko građansko vijeće (Serb Civic Council, or SGV). Izetbegović asked the Court to evaluate the consistency of the entity constitutions with the state constitution and, in a supplemental request the next month, specified those provisions of the entities' constitutions that he viewed as unconstitutional. In effect, the case put the discriminatory elements of the entity constitutions in the dock. In its ruling, the Constitutional Court agreed with Izetbegović that several articles—twelve provisions of Republika Srpska's constitution as well as the preamble and four articles of the Federation's constitution—were unconstitutional, thereby opening up questions of ethno-national rights, representation and decision-making mechanisms.

The decision was controversial in that it was supported by the three international judges and two Bosniak judges on the Court, but opposed by the two Croat judges and the two Serb judges, who published dissenting opinions. The key issue was whether Bosniaks, Croats and Serbs were 'constituent peoples' throughout the country or whether Bosniaks and Croats were 'constituent peoples' in the Federation and Serbs the 'constituent people' in Republika Srpska. The dissenting judges argued that since Bosniaks, Croats and Serbs were only listed as constituent peoples in the preamble to the state constitution, rather than the body, that this was not legally binding and not in conflict with the entity constitutions. The decision stood, since there is no ethno-national veto in the Constitutional Court and a simple majority of judges is all that is required.

The Constitutional Court decision on the constituency of peoples is a thoughtful analysis of the inconsistencies and short-comings of the Dayton settlement in terms of the institutional discrimination experienced by members of non-dominant groups.[27] The ruling went beyond the narrow issue put to it to discuss the principles of the structure of multi-ethnic states, and systems for balancing interests of different peoples on the basis of international instruments for protecting human and minority rights, which form an integral part of the state constitution. It not only examined the texts of the state and entity constitutions, but also considered the actual situation on the ground in both entities, highlighting the experiences of non-dominant groups and contrasting reality with the letter of the law, thereby exposing the hypocrisy of the counter-arguments. This included, for example, the presentation of data concerning the proportion of members of non-dominant groups in institutions such as the judiciary and police force, and the actual experience of returnees.

The decision was critical of the constitutions and, by extension, structures of both the Federation and Republika Srpska, arguing that the concept of ethno-national segregation as enshrined in the entities failed to meet democratic principles, effectively calling the division into question. Moreover, it concluded in Article 60 that 'the constitutional principle of collective equality of constituent peoples following from the designation of Bosniaks, Croats and Serbs as constituent peoples prohibits any special privilege for one or two of these peoples, any domination in governmental structures or any ethnic homogenization through segregation based on territorial separation.'[28] The Court had problems both with the absence of group-specific rights in the constitution of Republika Srpska and with the extent of the group-specific rights granted to Bosniaks and Croats, though not to Serbs, in the constitution of the Federation, because of discrimination against both Serbs and citizens who were not Bosniaks, Croats or Serbs. Thus there were also implications for the state institutions.

The Constitutional Court did not propose a solution for those sections of the entity constitutions that were incompatible with the state constitution; it simply declared them invalid. Since domestic institutions failed to take any steps to amend the constitutions, the high representative appointed in January 2001 two sixteen-person commissions, one in each entity, to make recommendations on implementing the Court's decision.[29] After the commissions had drawn up proposed constitutional amendments, leaders of the largest political parties met in Mrakovica, Prijedor municipality, in January 2002 and Sarajevo in February, to negotiate a mutually acceptable compromise without international supervision. Given the importance of these amendments to Bosnia's future, High Representative Petritsch wished to see agreement among Bosnians and avoid imposing a solution. However, the changes had to be in place by 19 April 2002 when the October elections were to be called, since the new structures envisaged in the amendments had to be reflected in the electoral system.

The compromise package was signed by most party leaders on 27 March 2002, although not by the HDZ and SDA. Although political leaders from the Federation had initially sought symmetry in the negotiations, that is, more or less identical mechanisms to protect the rights of Bosniaks and Croats in Republika Srpska as for Serbs in the Federation, they settled for less in the interest of finding a compromise. Despite this, the Republika Srpska National Assembly introduced a number of changes into the package before adopting it. As a result of the changes, some of which were at odds with the earlier agreement and the Constitutional Court ruling,[30] the House of Peoples in the Federation was not willing to adopt the amendments as earlier agreed. As a result, the high representative imposed the amendments to the Federation's constitution, corrections to the Republika Srpska constitution and amendments to the Election Law to bring it into line with the respective constitutions.

The imposed solution established ethno-national power-sharing arrangements in both entities, including fixed ethno-national representation and office-distribution arrangements in key institutions; it defined the areas where vital national interests applied and procedures to protect them; and it introduced proportional representation in all public authorities. In addition, it established full language equality among the three nations and altered the discriminatory self-definition of the entities, removing special references to Bosniaks and Croats in the Federation constitution and the many references to the Serb nation in the Republika Srpska constitution.

According to the revised governmental structures that began to be put in place following the October 2002 elections, the governments of both entities became multi-ethnic for the first time. In Republika Srpska, the government was composed of a prime minister and sixteen ministers (eight Serbs, five Bosniaks and three Croats). The prime minister had two deputies, each from a different constituent people selected from among the ministers. In the Federation, the government was composed of a prime minister and sixteen ministers (eight Bosniaks, five Croats and three Serbs). Again the prime minister had two deputies from different constituent peoples selected from among the ministers.[31] These arrangements were to remain in place until Annex 7 ('Agreement on Refugees and Displaced Persons') of the Dayton Peace Agreement was fully implemented, at which point a minimum of 15 per cent of government members must come from one constituent people, a minimum of 35 per cent from two constituent peoples, and one government member from the group of Others. Each entity would in future have a president and two vice presidents, each from a different constituent people. In addition, the posts of prime minister, speaker of the Federation House of Representatives/Republika Srpska National Assembly, speaker of the Federation House of Peoples/Republika Srpska Council of Peoples, president of the Supreme Court, president of the Constitutional Court and prosecutors were divided up so that no more than two posts in each entity could be filled by representatives of any one constituent people or of the group of Others.

Henceforward, the House of Peoples in the Federation contained as many Serbs as Bosniaks and Croats, with additional representation for Others. In addition, a Council of Peoples was created in Republika Srpska in which again all constituent peoples were represented equally, with additional representation for Others. All legislation in the Federation had to be passed by both Houses. Any legislation involving vital national interests had to be passed by both the

Republika Srpska National Assembly and the Council of Peoples. Moreover, vital national interests of constituent peoples were defined for the first time.[32] Any matter in which vital national interest was invoked needed to be resolved by consensus. In cases where this was not possible, the matter would be put to a Vital National Interest Panel of the entity's Constitutional Court, whose membership consisted of seven judges, two from each constituent people and one Other.

In public institutions—defined as ministries of the Federation government, of the Republika Srpska government and of cantonal governments, municipal governments, cantonal courts in the Federation and district courts in Republika Srpska, and municipal courts in the Federation and Republika Srpska—constituent peoples and Others were to be proportionally represented. Moreover, proportional representation would be based on the 1991 census, until Annex 7 had been fully implemented. There was no indication of when or how this process would be considered complete.

These changes constituted a significant restructuring of the system of government set out in the Dayton Peace Agreement, addressing, in part, the institutional discrimination contained within it. In theory at least, they helped put Serbs on a level footing with Bosniaks and Croats in the Federation and establish a greater degree of inclusion for Bosniaks and Croats in Republika Srpska, thereby making the overall settlement appear fairer.[33]

Justice

Irrespective of the fairness of the settlement, the issue of justice risked undermining it unless and until it was addressed. Although this question is often viewed in terms of the work of the International Criminal Tribunal for the former Yugoslavia (ICTY), it has always been multifaceted. As such, it goes beyond punishing individuals responsible for committing crimes to include matters such as establishing a record of events; finding graves; identifying remains and burying them properly; recognising the loss of surviving family members, as well as broader war-related losses, and providing compensation; and vetting the administration to prevent compromised individuals from holding public office.

The campaign of atrocities in the spring and summer of 1992 that brought the term 'ethnic cleansing' into the international political lexicon also spawned two legal responses, one from the international community, the other from the Bosnian government. In October 1992, in the wake of the London Conference, the UN Security Council established a Commission of Experts to gather evidence of rapes, tortures and murders perpetrated in the former Yugoslavia. This led in May 1993 to the creation of the ICTY, an ad hoc tribunal based in The Hague and mandated to prosecute and try persons responsible for serious violations of international humanitarian law—grave breaches of the 1949 Geneva Conventions on violations of the laws or customs of war, genocide and crimes against humanity—committed in the former Yugoslavia since 1991.[34] Two months earlier, in March 1993, Bosnia had filed a case at the International Court of Justice (ICJ),[35] also in The Hague, against what was by then a rump Federal Republic of Yugoslavia, arguing that the latter 'planned, prepared, conspired, promoted, encouraged, aided and abetted and committed' genocide against Bosnia's population. It was eventually heard in 2006, thirteen years later, and ruled upon in February 2007.

These two parallel processes, both unprecedented, were connected yet distinct. Whereas the ICTY sought, initially at least, to hold individuals accountable for their actions and thereby to individualise guilt, the ICJ proceedings involved putting a country on trial for the actions of its leaders and was therefore very much about collective guilt. To be sure, at the time it was initiated, the ICJ case was, above all, an attempt to draw international attention to what was taking place in Bosnia, to generate pressure for intervention to bring the war to an end. Moreover, by developing a doctrine of 'joint criminal enterprise'[36] to prosecute the Serbian leadership, a doctrine that was subsequently extended to the Croatian leadership, the ICTY effectively came to make a case for collective responsibility of political and military elites.

International backing for the ICTY was slow to materialise. The Commission of Experts initially struggled to persuade the United Nations and its leading members of its merits. The special rapporteur appointed to the Commission, Cherif Bassiouni, was starved of conventional funding but managed to begin compiling a war-crimes database thanks to donations from the Soros Foundation, the charity set up by international financier and philanthropist George Soros. Talk of war-crimes trials during hostilities appeared to some diplomats and mediators to undermine the prospects of reaching a settlement, though it was only after Karadžić and Mladić had been indicted for genocide that a peace accord was actually agreed. Similar fears contributed to IFOR's reluctance to arrest war-crimes suspects. Indeed, ICTY representatives were not invited to the December 1996 London Peace Implementation Conference, the official review of the first year of the peace process, although Richard Goldstone, the original prosecutor, chose, nevertheless, to show up.

Despite facing repeated funding crises, hostility from local authorities, lukewarm international support and a dearth of suspects in custody in its early years, the ICTY evolved into a major, albeit controversial, actor, both in Bosnia and the wider region. The ICTY's fortunes changed in the wake of the 10 July 1997 snatch operations as, belatedly, it found itself in a position to begin putting some of the individuals it had indicted on trial. Its staff grew to more than 1,200. Its budget jumped from $276,000 in 1993 to $95 million in 1999 and $272 million in 2004–5, the last year it issued indictments, with additional, external funding for exhumations and an outreach programme to explain the ICTY's work in the region. Moreover, in spite of its slow start and the fact that its most notorious indictees, Karadžić and Mladić, remained at liberty until July 2008 and May 2011 respectively,[37] the ICTY was able to hold certain individuals to account for their actions, to give victims the opportunity to face their persecutors in court and, via a series of landmark rulings, to establish a legal record of what had taken place.

Various trials were of special significance. The first was that of Duško Tadić, a Bosnian Serb indictee who was arrested in February 1994 in Germany and put on trial in May 1996. He was convicted in May 1997 of thirteen counts of crimes against humanity and war crimes and subsequently sentenced to twenty years in prison. A rape charge against him was dropped. In February 2001, three Bosnian Serbs—Dragoljub Kunarac, Radomir Kovač and Zoran Vuković—

were convicted of crimes against humanity—torture, slavery, outrages upon human dignity and the mass rape of Bosniak women in Foča in 1992.[38] It was the first time that an international tribunal had brought charges exclusively for crimes of sexual violence against women. And in August 2001, General Radislav Krstić, commander of the Drina Corps of the VRS, became the first person to be convicted of genocide, later reduced on appeal to aiding and abetting genocide, for his role in the Srebrenica massacre of July 1995.[39] In this way, the ICTY had also ruled that legally the massacre constituted genocide, the deliberate and systematic destruction of an ethnic, racial, religious or national group.[40]

In addition to these landmark rulings, the leaderships of Serbia, the Bosnian Serbs, the Bosnian Croats and the Croatian Serbs were among the ICTY's 161 indictees,[41] as were key individuals in the Croatian military establishment and several Bosnian government military leaders. ICTY investigations of Izetbegović and Tuđman were halted after their deaths.

Milošević was indicted by the ICTY in May 1999 during the Kosovo War while president of Yugoslavia, initially for war crimes committed in Kosovo. He was overthrown in October 2000 in the wake of election rigging, and arrested by the new authorities in March 2001. He was extradited to the ICTY to stand trial on 28 June 2001, St Vitus Day,[42] and eventually charged with crimes against humanity, violating the laws or customs of war, grave breaches of the Geneva Conventions and genocide for his role during the wars in Bosnia, Croatia and Kosovo, as part of a joint criminal enterprise.[43] The trial started in February 2002 and ended prematurely with his death in March 2006. Others allegedly involved in the same joint criminal enterprise included Vojislav Šešelj, the SRS leader. He travelled to the ICTY voluntarily in February 2003 and was put on trial in November 2007 on charges of war crimes and crimes against humanity, boasting that he alone had advocated a Greater Serbia.[44]

Croatian Serb leader Milan Babić testified to the extent of Milošević's involvement in the Croatian War early in the Milošević trial as part of a plea-bargain. He also pleaded guilty to one crime against humanity and expressed 'shame and remorse' before being sentenced in June 2004 to thirteen years in prison. He subsequently committed suicide in the ICTY detention unit in The Hague, having returned there to testify in the trial of fellow Croatian Serb leader Milan Martić. Martić himself was sentenced in June 2007 to thirty-five years in prison for, among other things, having been part of a joint criminal enterprise and helping organise an ethnic-cleansing campaign of Croats and non-Serbs in Krajina.[45]

In Bosnia, the Serb wartime leadership was also found to have been part of the same joint criminal enterprise, specifically seeking to 'ethnically recompose the territories targeted by the Bosnian Serb leadership by drastically reducing the proportion of Bosnian Muslims and Bosnian Croats through expulsion'. On learning of her indictment, Biljana Plavšić surrendered voluntarily to the ICTY in January 2001. Though charged with genocide among other crimes, she plea-bargained, pleaded guilty to one crime against humanity and expressed remorse. In this way, she was eventually sentenced to eleven years in prison.[46] Her former colleague and rival, Momčilo Krajišnik, was arrested by NATO forces in April 2000. The highest-ranking official to have been tried to the end, he was convicted in September 2006 of extermination, murder, persecution, deportation and forced transfer of non-Serbs, but acquitted of murder as a war crime, genocide and complicity in genocide, and sentenced to twenty-seven years in prison. On appeal, the charges of murder and extermination were dropped and the sentence was reduced to twenty years.[47]

Senior Bosnian Croats who were indicted and surrendered voluntarily to the ICTY in the 1990s, including Tihomir Blaškić, Mario Čerkez and Dario Kordić, were tried, convicted and sentenced before the doctrine of joint criminal enterprise had been developed. Three Croatian officers behind Operation Storm—Ivan Čermak, Ante Gotovina and Mladen Markač—and the Bosnian Croat wartime political and military leadership were, by contrast, tried on charges relating to their participation in a joint criminal enterprise.

Generals Čermak, Gotovina and Markač went on trial in March 2008 for their roles in a joint criminal enterprise together with Tuđman, former Croatian Defence Minister Gojko Šušak, former Croatian Chiefs of the General Staff Janko Bobetko and Zvonimir

Červenko, all of whom had died in the intervening period. The enterprise was aimed at the 'permanent removal of the Serb population from the Krajina region by force, fear or threat of force, persecution, forced displacement, transfer and deportation, appropriation and destruction of property and other means'. Whereas Čermak and Markač surrendered voluntarily on learning of their indictments, Gotovina spent four years on the run before being arrested on the Spanish island of Tenerife in December 2005. The Croatian government participated in the defence to challenge the doctrine of joint criminal enterprise in Operation Storm. Čermak was acquitted at the original trial in April 2011, while Gotovina was sentenced to twenty-four years in prison and Markač to eighteen years. In November 2012, however, the ICTY's Appeals Court overturned these verdicts and Gotovina and Markač were released.

Six leading Bosnian Croats including Jadranko Prlić, former prime minister of the Croat Republic of Herzeg-Bosnia,[48] all of whom surrendered voluntarily to the ICTY, went on trial together in April 2006 charged with grave breaches of the Geneva Conventions, violations of the laws or customs of war and crimes against humanity. These resulted from their participation in a joint criminal enterprise to 'politically and militarily subjugate, permanently remove and ethnically cleanse Bosnian Muslims and other non-Croats who lived in areas on the territory of the Republic of Bosnia which were claimed to be part of the "Croatian Community (and later Republic) of Herzeg-Bosnia" and to join these areas as part of a "Greater Croatia".' (Others allegedly involved in the joint criminal enterprise included Tuđman, Šušak, Bobetko and Mate Boban, the Bosnian Croat wartime leader, who could not be tried as they had already died.) In May 2013, all six were convicted and sentenced to prison terms of between sixteen and twenty-five years with Prlić receiving the longest sentence. These six have appealed and the matter of a joint criminal enterprise will be re-examined. Moreover, the prospect of the verdict being overturned on appeal is real, given that judges at the original trial were themselves divided on the issue, with the lead judge issuing a dissenting opinion.

In addition to overturning the first-instance verdict against Gotovina and Markač, the ICTY Appeals Court overturned the first-instance verdict against Momčilo Perišić, former chief of the general staff of the Yugoslav Army. Perišić was initially convicted of crimes against humanity and violations of the laws or customs of war in September 2011 and sentenced to twenty-seven years in prison. However, the judges at the original trial were divided, with the lead judge issuing a dissenting opinion. On appeal, Perišić was acquitted, with the Appeals Court judges concluding that the military help that the Yugoslav Army had provided to Bosnian and Croatian Serbs aimed to support their general war efforts and not war crimes.

The ICTY's success in processing the 161 suspects it indicted is in part the result of arrests carried out by SFOR in Bosnia, in part the result of international pressure on local authorities, and in part because ten died before they could be brought to justice. SFOR arrested twenty-eight war-crimes suspects between 1997 and 2003 and killed two who were resisting arrest.[49] Pressure on Belgrade, Zagreb and especially the Bosnian Serb leadership has, at times, been intense. Indeed, High Representative Lord Ashdown deliberately used his executive powers to ratchet up pressure on the Bosnian Serb authorities and undermine indictees' support networks, freezing the bank accounts of both the SDS and specific individuals linked to the support networks, and dismissing Bosnian Serb officials, including fifty-nine in a single day on 30 June 2004.[50]

In 2002, the ICTY unveiled a completion strategy that foresaw the end of its work and therefore its closure by the end of 2010, pre-supposing detention of the most important indictees, with the last indictments to be issued at the end of 2004.[51] This did not mean that everyone who had committed crimes during the Wars of Yugoslav Dissolution would have been brought to justice, but that the useful role of the ICTY would be over. In future, war-crimes trials would continue to take place, but primarily in Bosnia, Croatia and Serbia. Indeed, several indictees in custody at the ICTY were repatriated to face trial in the countries in which their alleged crimes had been committed. The scale of the task in Bosnia, where estimates of the number of potential suspects extend as high as 16,000,[52] was, however, enormous. As part of the judicial reform process, therefore, additional capacity has had to be built in the court system and a strategy for dealing with these cases developed.[53]

Domestic war-crimes trials had already taken place in Bosnia with the ICTY's blessing.[54] Under the so-called 'Rules of the Road' procedure, agreed in February 1996, an arrest warrant for a war-crimes suspect in Bosnia could only be issued after the case file had been reviewed and approved by the ICTY prosecution. This was to prevent local authorities detaining individuals without credible evidence. The ICTY prosecution reviewed 1,419 cases against 4,985 individuals and gave approval for 848 individuals to be arrested on war-crimes charges. The review process was transferred to Bosnia's State Prosecutor's Office in October 2004.

The most eagerly awaited verdict in the region was not from the ICTY, but from the ICJ: the Bosnia versus Serbia and Montenegro genocide case, which was delivered on 26 February 2007. It was the first case in which one country accused another of genocide, dating back almost fourteen years to the first year of the war. The ICJ had responded to Bosnia's initial filing by issuing an interim judgement ordering the Federal Republic of Yugoslavia to do everything in its power to prevent genocide from being committed in Bosnia. The case had subsequently become extremely controversial since the post-war Bosnian Serb leadership, which had not been involved in initiating the case, exerted maximum pressure to have it withdrawn.

In its ruling, the ICJ's fifteen-member panel of judges decided that what had occurred throughout Bosnia did not constitute genocide, though widespread and systematic atrocities had undoubtedly taken place. It, nevertheless, found that the July 1995 Srebrenica massacre was an act of genocide in line with the earlier ICTY verdict in the Krstić trial. However, it ruled that this was the work of the Vojska Republike Srpske (Army of Republika Srpska, or VRS) and various paramilitary units, rather than Serbia, the legal successor of the Federal Republic of Yugoslavia. The ICJ recognised that Serbia gave substantial military and financial support to the VRS and that this had likely been used to commit genocide. However, since it could not be proved that Serbia was aware that its assistance would be used in this way, Serbia was found not to have committed, taken part in or abetted the genocide. The ICJ, nevertheless, ruled that Serbia had failed both to prevent the genocide and to punish those responsible for it, violating the Convention on Genocide Prevention and Punishment. It also decided that Serbia should immediately comply with the Convention, transfer individuals accused of genocide to the ICTY and otherwise co-operate with the ICTY.[55] The ICJ's ruling disappointed some legal scholars, since it appeared to have set an extremely high burden of proof and to have been made without access to key evidence. The ICJ had failed to obtain sensitive sections of the records of Serbia's Supreme Defence Council, the key decision-making body in matters relating to the Bosnian War. These documents had been made available to the ICTY for the Milošević trial and had been used by prosecutors to link Milošević with specific events in Bosnia. However, they had been made available on condition that they would remain under seal at the ICTY to protect Serbian national security. This meant they did not form part of the evidence that the ICJ could consider.[56] Moreover, ICJ Vice President Awn Shawkat al-Khasawneh issued a dissenting opinion.

In Republika Srpska, an official Srebrenica Commission was formed in October 2003 in the wake of a ruling by Bosnia's Human Rights Chamber and, critically, a decision issued by High Representative Lord Ashdown. The Chamber had ruled in March 2003 that the human rights of forty-nine relatives of Bosniaks who had 'disappeared' in and around Srebrenica in July 1995 had been violated by the refusal of the Republika Srpska authorities to assist their search, accusing the authorities of 'indifference to the suffering of the Bosniak community'. It ordered the Republika Srpska authorities to disclose all information relevant to establishing the fate and whereabouts of the missing, including the location of mass graves containing the bodies of Srebrenica victims, to conduct an investigation into the events at Srebrenica and to publish its findings by the beginning of September 2003. In addition, Republika Srpska was ordered to pay immediate compensation of 2 million Bosnian marks (€1 million) to the Srebrenica-Potočari Memorial Foundation and Cemetery for the collective benefit of the families of all Srebrenica victims, as well as to make annual payments of 500,000 Bosnian marks for the next four years. The Srebrenica-Potočari Memorial Foundation and Cemetery had been created by decision of the high representative in May 2001. The land had also been procured by decision of the high representative in October 2000. The first remains of victims were due to be buried in the Cemetery in March 2003.

The report that the Srebrenica Commission eventually released in October 2004 was about as different as it could be to the Republika Srpska government inquiry of two years earlier. The 2002 report had concluded that the Srebrenica massacre had never taken place and that although some 2,000 Bosniaks had died, they had all been soldiers in the Bosnian Army. The 2004 report, prepared under intense international pressure, listed 8,731 missing and dead by name, as well as the locations of thirty-two mass graves, twenty-eight of which were secondary; that is, containing bodies that had been removed from other sites, eleven of which had not been disclosed before. In the wake of the report's publication, Republika Srpska President Dragan Čavić made a televised address acknowledging that Bosnian Serb forces had killed several thousand civilians in violation of international law, and the Republika Srpska government issued an official apology. A year later, a government working group reported that more than 25,000 people had been involved in the massacre, including some 20,000 members of various armed formations, 892 of whom continued to hold positions in the administration.

Whether or not the apology was genuine is moot. As Bosniaks started burying the Srebrenica dead at the Srebrenica-Potočari Memorial Foundation and Cemetery in annual ceremonies on 11 July, the anniversary of the fall of Srebrenica and the beginning of the massacres, Republika Srpska established a 12 July commemoration of Serb dead in neighbouring Bratunac, 10km to the north. The Srebrenica-Potočari Memorial Foundation and Cemetery did, nevertheless, receive its start-up funding from Republika Srpska as ordered by the Human Rights Chamber in its March 2003 ruling. Together with other donations, including $1 million from the United States, this was sufficient to establish and maintain the Memorial Cemetery, but not to ensure its future. As a result, High Representative Christian Schwarz-Schilling, who had succeeded Lord Ashdown in February 2006, issued a decision to bring it under the authority and financing of Bosnia's joint institutions in June 2007.

In spite of the ICTY and ICJ verdicts in relation to Srebrenica, as well as the 2004 Srebrenica Commission report, genocide deniers have continued to question the official version of events in Srebrenica in July 1995. Attempts to conceal the extent and nature of the killings have certainly made the tasks of uncovering graves, exhuming bodies and identifying victims extremely difficult. However, techniques involving matching DNA extracted from victims' bones with DNA samples taken from the blood of surviving relatives, which have been pioneered in Bosnia since 2001 by the International Commission of Missing Persons (ICMP),[57] have made it possible to determine with some certainty the number of dead, as well as the elaborate measures that were taken to conceal the truth.[58] Moreover, identification and burial of remains have helped bring some form of closure for relatives.[59]

Another organisation that has contributed to providing an accurate record of atrocities committed during the Bosnian War, including in particular the number of war dead, is Sarajevo's Research and Documentation Centre (RDC). Founded in April 2004, it built on the work of the more partisan War Crimes Commission that had been created by the Bosnian presidency at the beginning of the Bosnian War. It has systematically collected and catalogued witness statements and other data, including video and photographic evidence, and compiled a comprehensive list of war dead in *The Bosnian Book of the Dead*.[60] Though the RDC is not a Truth and Reconciliation Commission, the documentary material it has collected would be important to such an institution if it were ever established.

Attempts to get a truth and reconciliation or recognition process off the ground have floundered. The earliest initiative, sponsored in 1998 by the US Institute of Peace, was scuppered at the first hurdle by ICTY opposition. Further attempts in 2001 and 2006 also failed, although a draft law to establish a Truth and Reconciliation Commission was prepared by a working group of legislators in the state parliament in May 2006, but never put into parliamentary procedure. A subsequent attempt, sponsored by the UN Development Programme (UNDP), again failed to make any headway. A Truth and Reconciliation Commission was formally established in Serbia and Montenegro by presidential decree in March 2001, shortly after

Milošević's removal. However, it failed to achieve any results and was dissolved within two years.

More than a hundred civil-society groups from Bosnia, Croatia, Kosovo, Montenegro and Serbia joined forces in October 2008 to work for the creation of a regional commission (RECOM) to determine and disclose the facts about war crimes and other gross violations of human rights committed in the former Yugoslavia. This regional coalition gathered a petition of more than half a million signatures in support of the project in one month in 2011, which it presented to presidents of all the Yugoslav successor states or their representatives. All endorsed the project by appointing envoys to examine the legal basis for a commission, with the exception of the Serb member of the Bosnian presidency, Nebojša Radmanović, and Slovenia's president, Borut Pahor. In response to feedback from these envoys, the regional coalition amended its statute in November 2014 with a view to establishing a RECOM.[61]

The only official commission in Bosnia to examine the war, apart from the Srebrenica Commission, was a Sarajevo Commission. Originally proposed in 2004 by Serb political parties, commissioners were formally appointed in June 2006 after the same parties threatened to boycott the country's joint institutions. Serb deputies wanted the Commission to focus on the plight of Serbs in Sarajevo during the war, while Bosniak deputies had wished to extend the remit of the Commission across the entire country. In the event, a compromise was struck whereby the work of the Commission was restricted to Sarajevo, but it would investigate 'the suffering of Serbs, Croats, Bosniaks, Jews and Others'. Given its political nature, it is perhaps no surprise that the Sarajevo Commission failed to produce any results, only recriminations over the compensation of commissioners and likely costs.

One issue that many Bosnians wanted the Sarajevo Commission to address was a system of compensation for losses—both material and emotional—that people experienced during the war. Although the issue was not on the agenda, it generates strong emotions.

The Dayton-created Commission on Real Property Claims of Displaced Persons and Refugees had focussed its efforts on determining property ownership. It did not seek to compensate people, for example, for damage to their property. Rather, foreign donors stepped in in some instances to repair, part-repair or provide materials for repairing damaged housing, but clearly not all. Since no universal criteria were developed for disbursing this kind of reconstruction aid, some people effectively had their homes rebuilt for them, while others received no assistance. Many groups of victims believe that they should be entitled to special compensation, with each group bringing what pressure it can on authority to this end. These groups include veterans who were obliged to serve in the war and put their lives on the line; women who were raped, sometimes repeatedly for prolonged periods; pre-war foreign-currency account-holders whose savings disappeared; individuals who lost relatives, often but not necessarily soldiers; and individuals who were maimed in the war.

Victims also generally feel that the perpetrators of crimes should no longer be allowed to hold positions of authority. In an attempt to remove these individuals from public office, international organisations helped establish vetting procedures. The UN International Police Task Force (IPTF) eventually vetted police officers systematically throughout Bosnia;[62] SFOR vetted military appointments above the rank of brigadier; the OSCE established a system of wealth disclosure for candidates standing for election; and the OHR began vetting candidates for ministerial positions at state, entity and cantonal levels. Moreover, vetting became a key element of institution-building, and was therefore fundamental to both public administration and judicial reform, as well as the work of the Civil Service Agency and the High Judicial and Prosecutorial Council (HJPC), the agencies set up to oversee these reforms.

Institution-building

The international community arrived at a co-ordinated institution-building strategy five years into the peace process. This approach, which was formally set out in the declaration of the May 2000 Brussels PIC meeting,[63] emerged out of the experience of the early years of peace implementation and ad hoc reforms designed to address the many obstacles. Having begun by helping form the basic

OVERRIDING 'DEMOCRACY'

institutions envisaged in the Dayton Peace Agreement in the hope that implementation of the accord's key principles would follow, the international community became increasingly focussed on overcoming obstructionism and, with ever more frequent recourse to the Bonn Powers, forcing through implementation in spite of the domestic authorities. Institution-building appeared to provide justification for the need to override the will of the population as expressed by the results of elections. Bosnia's democracy was immature, it was argued, because the country's institutions were weak, with the result that the international community needed to nurture domestic institutions until they were sufficiently robust for peace to become self-sustaining, at which point it would be possible to hand 'ownership' of the process to them.

The institution-building task covered all spheres of life, not just the political, economic, judicial and administrative institutions specifically listed in the Dayton Peace Agreement. Great efforts were invested early in the peace process into, for example, forming integrated sports associations to establish country-wide competitive leagues, to provide Bosnian sportspeople with the opportunity to compete on an international stage and, in theory, to give all Bosnians a national team to root for.[64] Invariably, it was the international community that, within the parameters of the Dayton Peace Agreement, drew up options, drafted relevant legislation and oversaw implementation, including initial financing, where necessary. In the process, almost all international agencies became involved in task forces set up to address specific issues. Moreover, the Council of Europe took on an especially important advisory role, as its European Commission for Democracy through Law, more commonly known as the Venice Commission, provided legal opinions to help ensure that proposals conformed with the European Convention on Human Rights and other relevant European legislation that formed an integral part of Bosnia's constitution. And as Bosnia's Constitutional Court established itself, it too ruled on matters put to it on reform issues.

Since the Bonn Powers were initially only envisaged as a temporary, emergency measure to break political deadlock at the state level, the international community devoted substantial time and effort to developing the Council of Ministers as an effective government for the country. Even persuading leaders of all communities to sit around the same table was an achievement when the body was formed in 1997. In its initial configuration, the Council of Ministers had two co-chairs who rotated every eight months, one Bosniak and one Serb, as well as a Croat vice-chair, and just three ministries: Civil Affairs and Communications, Foreign Trade and Economic Relations, and Foreign Affairs. Ministries were divided up on the basis of ethno-national parity and ministers had two deputies, each from a different constituent people. Decision-making was by consensus and four (of six) members of the Council of Ministers, including at least one from every constituent people, had to be present.

Appointing co-chairs had been necessary to get the Council of Ministers off the ground, but was in conflict with the structure set out in the Dayton constitution and declared unconstitutional by the Constitutional Court in 1999. The configuration of the Council of Ministers was subsequently changed on two occasions. First, in 2000, three ministries were added. Then, in December 2002, the high representative abolished co-chairs and replaced them with a single chair with two vice-chairs, each from a different constituent people; the number of ministries was expanded to eight,[65] each headed by a minister and one deputy from a different constituent people; and at least one minister or the general secretary of the secretariat had to represent Others. Decision-making remained by consensus, with at least two representatives of each constituent people and half its membership present to hold a session. Gradually, the Council of Ministers that was formed after the 2002 election with Adnan Terzić as its chair began to resemble a government. At the end of 2003, a ninth ministry, Defence, was also added, as part of the defence reform.[66]

Arguably, the most successful Dayton institution has been the Central Bank. Headed by an IMF-appointed international for the first six years,[67] it succeeded in establishing a new currency, the Bosnian convertible mark (konvertibilna marka), pegged in value to the German mark, that proved sufficiently stable that it drove out the four currencies—the Bosnian dinar, the Croatian kuna, the German mark and the Yugoslav dinar—that had been in circulation at the end of the war. Success was not pre-ordained, given the vested interests of the former warring parties in monetary 'sovereignty' and a history of currency failure and hyperinflation in the region. Rather it was the result of a currency board, tight monetary policy and effective, co-ordinated action by the key international institutions (the IMF, the OHR and the World Bank in particular). The IMF drew up the relevant legislation, ensuring that the Central Bank would be funded through its own activities thereby avoiding dependency on the state budget, and provided initial reserves of 25 million German marks. It also made liquidation of the existing National Bank a condition of its May 1998 standby arrangement with Bosnia.[68] This was also a precondition for disbursement of funds from other donors, including loans from the World Bank. The OHR imposed a design for the currency; banknotes were printed abroad and issued in July 1998; and the Bosnian mark was adopted as the currency of choice for transactions by the international institutions. Within a year, the existing National Bank had been liquidated, the Bosnian mark had become the primary currency in circulation throughout the country, and Central Bank reserves had swelled to more than 300 million Bosnian marks.[69]

The blueprint for the Central Bank contained in the Dayton Peace Agreement, including the currency board, almost certainly made monetary reform easier to introduce and implement than reforms in other areas such as the media, policing and the judiciary. Nevertheless, useful lessons were learned about deploying external expertise and appointing internationals to ostensibly domestic bodies. The IMF-appointed governor clearly helped generate confidence in the Central Bank's operations, as did the presence of internationals in key positions in other Dayton institutions, such as the Constitutional Court and the Human Rights Chamber. These then served as a precedent for the recruitment of internationals to interim positions in new institutions.

A process of comprehensive media restructuring began in the wake of SFOR's seizure of SRT's transmission towers on 1 October 1997. It was conceived and overseen by the OHR. Eventually, this consisted of five elements: media training; supporting independent media; developing appropriate libel and information laws; developing a regulatory framework; and reforming the public broadcasting system (PBS).[70]

Long-term media training included the creation of journalism schools with international partners, including the BBC, as well as programmes offering advice on media technology and business planning. While nominally independent media benefitted from international subsidies and equipment donations,[71] the bulk of international investment went into large-scale projects to develop multi-ethnic broadcasters, in particular the Open Broadcast Network.[72] Though this station failed to have any impact in the run-up to the original 1996 elections, for which it was created, it did begin to counter-balance the fabrications and distortions of the stations controlled by ethno-national parties in the period before more substantial restructuring could be introduced.

To promote the legal protection of journalists, the high representative struck down a provision allowing prison sentences for libel in July 1999. In October 2000, the state parliament adopted a Freedom of Information Law based on Western European practice, obliging authorities to make information available. A Law on Protection against Defamation was then passed in 2002, designed to provide journalists with additional safeguards.

With EU and US funding, an Independent Media Commission (IMC) dominated by internationals was created in June 1998 by order of the high representative. Modelled on regulatory agencies in Western Europe and North America, it sought to allocate licences in a transparent and non-partisan manner, encouraging fair competition among broadcasters. By promulgating a broadcasting code of practice and withholding licences, the IMC helped deter inflammatory broadcasts. Like the Central Bank, the Communications Regulatory Agency (CRA), which succeeded the IMC in 2001, was self-financing, since it was able to generate revenue via licence fees payable by telecommunications operators and broadcasters. A voluntary, self-regulating Press Council was also established in 2000 to protect and maintain standards in the press and deal with complaints from members of the public; and a press code was agreed in 2006.

Building a public broadcasting service out of an ethno-nationally segregated system was the most difficult aspect of media restructuring. Vested political interests sought to retain control over the remnants of Sarajevo Radio-Television, Bosnia's pre-war public broadcaster, whose assets had been divided into Bosniak, Croat and Serb components much as Karadžić had proposed on the eve of war. After months of negotiations with the country's three-member presidency, Westendorp persuaded the Bosniak and Croat representatives—but not the Serb—to agree a memorandum of understanding on the future of broadcasting. This document called for a new public broadcasting service that would respect religious tolerance and editorial independence and operate in a financially transparent manner, as well as a new service for the Federation. It also required broadcasters from Serbia and Croatia to abide by Bosnia's laws and regulations.

In practice, Belgrade and Zagreb ignored the memorandum's provisions; the SDA obstructed implementation of the reforms, since they extended beyond Republika Srpska to include the SDA-dominated Radio-Televizija BiH (RTV BiH); and the HDZ rejected them after a change in the Croat member of the presidency. A new multi-ethnic board of governors as well as an international supervisor at RTV BiH, was, nevertheless, appointed in July 1998, though their work was made difficult by the SDA. After a year of obstructionism, Westendorp imposed a new public broadcasting system (PBS) in July 1999 on his last day in office.

The OHR found legal justification for the creation of a state broadcaster in Article III of the Bosnian constitution, which refers to the state setting up communication facilities.[73] The decision created a loose structure designed to ensure that Bosnia's statehood was respected, that the SDA-dominated broadcaster would be succeeded by a genuine multi-ethnic service, and that a financially realistic model would be pursued. It also established a Federation broadcaster. The PBS replaced RTV BiH as a member of the European Broadcasting Union and the entity broadcasters only had access to international programming through it. The OHR appointed multi-ethnic management boards for the entity broadcasters in both Republika Srpska and the Federation. An expert from the BBC was then appointed to draw up an effective management structure, a process that was completed in 2003—by which time successive high representatives had issued fourteen decisions on media restructuring.[74] The new structure has, however, failed to come together as planned.

Obstacles encountered in implementing refugee return and other aspects of the Dayton Peace Agreement, as well as the need to build transparency in policing and the judiciary, led eventually to ever more ambitious reform and restructuring processes, almost invariably pushed through with the Bonn Powers.

The ethno-nationally divided, militarised and politicised police forces that emerged out of the war presented one of the greatest barriers to refugee return, peace implementation and the reconstruction of multi-ethnicity. Republika Srpska police were, for example, behind the arson in early 1996 in the Sarajevo suburbs, which were being transferred to the Federation, to drive out the Serb population. And as soon as the suburbs were handed over, Bosnian government police allowed mobs of Bosniak youths to rampage through them, effectively to finish the job. Police blocked reintegration in any number of ways, and the UN IPTF, which was charged with assisting the local police, initially had minimal influence beyond 'monitoring', despite the presence of 1,500 officers. The IPTF's mandate was, however, reinforced a year into the peace process in December 1996 by UN Security Council Resolution 1088 to include the power to conduct independent investigations into abuses by local police, and the number of officers increased to more than 2,000.

Initially, the IPTF was obliged to concentrate its reform efforts in the Federation because the Republika Srpska authorities refused to co-operate. Indeed, as long as the SDS remained in power, the IPTF was unable even to enter into a meaningful dialogue with the Republika Srpska Interior Ministry. In the Federation, by contrast, the IPTF signed an agreement on police restructuring in April 1996. Under this so-called Petersberg Agreement, the Federation authorities agreed to the creation of a unified Federation police force and recognised the authority of the IPTF over policing matters, paving the way for reform. A similar agreement, the Republika Srpska Framework Agreement, was eventually signed with the Republika Srpska authorities in December 1998.

Police reform can be split into three distinct but overlapping phases. In the years immediately following the signing of the Dayton Peace Agreement, the IPTF worked primarily at the level of individual police officers, focussing on training and vetting. In the second phase, starting in 1999, efforts shifted to structural improvements, police organisation, introducing greater accountability and improving democratic control. And in the final years of the IPTF engagement, and subsequently within the framework of European integration, reform focussed on bringing policing throughout the country under a single, over-arching structure.[75]

The framework agreements covered, among other areas, certification of officers, downsizing and the reintroduction of multi-ethnicity. To vet police, the IPTF developed a large bureaucracy to gather and store data, including educational qualifications, wartime records and violations of human rights or property legislation, on individuals who wished to remain or become police officers. In total, 16,700 police had been vetted by the end of the IPTF's mandate on 31 December 2002, of whom 800 were decertified. The number of serving police was reduced to 19,500, of whom 11,500 worked in the Federation and 8,000 in Republika Srpska. This figure remained high in proportion to the total population when compared with other European countries, but was, nevertheless, considerably lower than the 45,000 at the end of hostilities, 70 per cent of whom had become police officers during the war. In terms of the ethno-national structure of the police, the 1991 census served as the benchmark for the Federation, whereas in Republika Srpska it was the voting lists of the 1997 municipal elections.[76] In practice, however, few so-called minority police were recruited, despite enormous effort on the IPTF's part. By 2005, only 9.9 per cent of police officers in the Federation were Serbs and only 6.5 per cent of police officers in Republika Srpska were Bosniaks, with another 0.9 per cent Croats.

The most significant change that the IPTF introduced was the office of police commissioner (Federation) and police director (Republika Srpska), namely a professional police chief with separate competences to the interior minister and an independent appointment procedure. This move, which limited the power of entity and cantonal interior ministers, was opposed by all political parties, and the legislation had to be imposed in both entities and every canton by the high representative, requiring some twenty separate decisions, including amendments, in the course of 2002.

Nevertheless, by the end of the year and the end of the IPTF mission, all police bodies were headed by a professional commissioner or director.

Although the state of Bosnia did not have explicit policing authority under the Dayton constitution, it was responsible for preserving its sovereignty and territorial integrity and able to establish institutions 'necessary to carry out such responsibilities'. It was also mandated to deal with immigration, refugee and asylum policy, as well as international and inter-entity crime, including relations with Interpol. In line with these constitutional provisions and in an effort to make the state functional, therefore, the international community— primarily the IPTF and the OHR—helped facilitate the creation of state police forces to protect the country's borders and, following judicial reforms, to support the work of the State Prosecutor's Office, the State Border Service (SBS)[77] and the State Information and Protection Agency (SIPA) respectively.

The SBS was inaugurated in June 2000 on the basis of a law imposed by High Representative Petritsch five months earlier. The law had to be imposed because of Serb opposition. Serb leaders subsequently put the matter to the Constitutional Court, where it was dismissed a year later. The new law-enforcement agency, which had exclusive authority over a 10km strip of land running up to and including Bosnia's 1,551km of borders, as well as its international airports, was heavily subsidised in its early years, with international donors covering about half the €26 million annual costs. Given the scale of this investment, the international community maintained a tight grip on the project, ensuring that the SBS had taken control of all border crossings by the end of 2002.

Before the SBS' creation, entity and cantonal police had controlled Bosnia's borders and the entities had claimed customs revenues collected there. The borders had been among the most porous in Europe, with the result that tax avoidance, in terms of unpaid duties on goods such as alcohol, coffee, fuel and tobacco, had been endemic;[78] smuggling of people, drugs and weapons was rife; and war-crimes suspects were able to cross at will. In the years immediately after the SBS' creation, customs' receipts jumped 20 per cent and anecdotal evidence suggested that the level of smuggling dropped by at least as great a proportion.

The SBS was in November 2002 formally brought under the state Security Ministry that had just been created by High Representative Ashdown's decision, together with a still embryonic SIPA. The Security Ministry was to co-ordinate the two police forces, develop strategies for combating organised crime and terrorism and be responsible for international co-operation and relations with Interpol. SIPA had been created in June 2002 by legislation adopted by the state parliament with a limited mandate, namely to provide security for state dignitaries, state institutions and diplomatic missions, and to gather information on criminal offences falling under state competencies. In the wake of judicial reforms, this mandate would grow, in particular to support the newly created State Prosecutor's Office.

In 2002, the OHR embarked upon an ambitious reform of Bosnia's judiciary and legal system. This followed disappointing results of earlier, less comprehensive approaches. Several years of court monitoring by the UN Mission in Bosnia had exposed many shortcomings, as well as the extent of political and ethno-national bias in the system. An Independent Judicial Commission had been created in 2000 along similar lines to the Independent Media Commission, and a review of judges, based on complaint and investigation, and large salary increases were imposed, without having much impact on the quality of judges or justice. The new reform process sought to rationalise the court system, reducing the number of courts and harmonising juridical procedure and legal codes in the two entities, as well as instituting a complete overhaul of the judiciary, since all judges and prosecutors were obliged to resign and seek reappointment.

To oversee the judicial reform process, High Representative Ashdown established three councils, one at the state level and two at the entity level—the High Judicial and Prosecutorial Councils (HJPC) of Bosnia; of the Federation; and of Republika Srpska. These became operational with mixed international and national membership in September 2002.[79] In the wake of an assessment of needs, more than 30 per cent of first-instance courts were closed and the number of judges reduced accordingly. In terms of appointments, some 2,000 candidates applied for 953 judicial and prosecutorial posts, with the HJPC selecting the most qualified for each post within an ethno-nationally defined framework. Roughly 30 per cent of incumbents who applied for their posts were not reappointed, while others chose not to seek new mandates.[80] Since the ethno-national composition of the country in the 1991 census was taken as the basis for appointments, multi-ethnicity was re-established in the judiciary throughout Bosnia by completion of the reappointment process in September 2004.[81]

In October 2002, the high representative established the Court of Bosnia, usually referred to as the State Court, to address crimes relating to the country's sovereignty and territorial integrity, including organised crime, terrorism and war crimes. He followed this in January 2003 by imposing the Criminal Code and the Criminal Procedure Code of Bosnia,[82] both of which had been drafted within the OHR, as well as legislation to create the State Prosecutor's Office, the body mandated to investigate and prosecute perpetrators of criminal offences within the jurisdiction of the State Court. The creation of the War Crimes Chamber in the State Court, which began work in March 2005, and the Special Department for War Crimes in the State Prosecutor's Office completed the reforms.

In common with other new institutions, the State Court[83] and State Prosecutor's Office comprised both internationals and nationals with most early costs met by the international community and a timeframe for the reduction of the international presence and transfer to domestic funding.[84] International judges and prosecutors were initially appointed by the high representative. In July 2006, the HJPC of Bosnia took over this function, in addition to appointing the national judges and prosecutors. International judges outnumbered their national counterparts—with two internationals and one national on each of the five trial panels and the appellate panel—until 2008. After that, national judges formed the majority and the proportion of the overall budget covered by Bosnia exceeded the international contribution.[85]

To give the State Prosecutor's Office the necessary police support, a package of four laws was drawn up by the OHR in autumn 2003 designed to transform SIPA into a genuine state police agency with investigative powers unrestricted by the inter-entity boundary line. This included a new Law on SIPA, now renamed the State Investigation and Protection Agency, and a Law on Police Officers, as well as legislation on witness protection and money laundering. The state parliament enacted the new package into law in June 2004. Enactment followed intensive lobbying by both the OHR and the European Commission and the explicit linking of the passing of specific legislation to the prospect of forging a closer relationship with the European Union. In November 2003, the European Commission had presented its Feasibility Study on Bosnia, listing conditions that the country would have to meet to sign a Stabilisation and Association Agreement with the European Union, thereby putting the country on the road to eventual EU membership. Among those conditions was 'further reform and enhanced state-level enforcement capacity' to fight crime, including 'quickly making SIPA fully operational'.

Euro-Atlantic integration

Before publication of the Feasibility Study and the explicit linking of reforms to Bosnia's European future, legislation aimed at bolstering state institutions had been systematically opposed by Serb political representatives and frequently challenged (though without success) at the Constitutional Court. As a result, successive high representatives had increasingly resorted to the Bonn Powers to push key state-building legislation through. All were aware of the shortcomings of such an approach. However, they justified their actions as necessary short-term steps towards creating the self-sustaining institutions to help ensure that peace would take root. In this way, they argued, the international community would in time be able to give up the intrusive role it had been playing and hand ownership of the process to Bosnians. Adoption of the package of laws enhancing state law-enforcement capabilities, as well as legislation concerning defence, education and tax administration in the first half of 2004, represented a breakthrough, since it appeared to illustrate the potential 'pull of Brussels'; that is, the transformational power of the incentive of EU membership, as opposed to the earlier 'push of Dayton'.

Petritsch was the first high representative to present his approach in terms of working towards local ownership, and to articulate an 'entry strategy' for Bosnia into the European Union, as opposed to an exit strategy from Bosnia for the international community. The mantra was embraced by his successor, Lord Ashdown, who, in addition to serving as high representative, was appointed EU special representative in Bosnia to promote the European Union's policies and interests. Moreover, Lord Ashdown succeeded in galvanising the international community around an aggressive strategy aimed at embedding peace and stability by positioning Bosnia firmly on the road to membership in the European Union and NATO.[86] At the same time, he oversaw the deployment of the EU Police Mission (EUPM) and EUFOR, to succeed the UN IPTF and the NATO-led SFOR on 1 January 2003 and 2 December 2004 respectively, deepening the EU commitment to and stake in Bosnia.

The appeal of the European Union—and more generally Euro-Atlantic integration—was clear, since it appeared to offer the prospect of prosperity, stability and long-term security. Moreover, the PIC had set the creation of 'a direct and dynamic contractual relationship between Bosnia and the European Union within the framework of a regional approach' as one of the aims of the peace process at its London Conference in December 1995. What had been missing in the first half-decade of the peace process was a mechanism for this aspiration to be realised, and benchmarks to measure progress. This shortcoming was put right by the creation of a Stabilisation and Association Process for all countries in the Western Balkans aspiring to EU membership, together with a tailored Road Map for Bosnia in 2000, published as an annex to the May 2000 Brussels PIC meeting. Stabilisation and Association Agreements between the European Union and individual countries in South Eastern Europe were the equivalent of the Europe Agreements that had helped prepare Central and Eastern European countries for membership.

Even before Bosnia had completed the Road Map to the European Commission's satisfaction, the country was accepted into the Council of Europe. Membership of Europe's oldest institution and leading inter-governmental human rights body in April 2002 came one month short of a decade after Bosnia had first applied for guest status. It was a reward for progress in the field of human rights, even though many of the specific accession requirements the Council of Europe had set had not been met.

Bosnia had acquired observer status in the Council of Europe in January 1994 and applied for membership in April 1995. Just over four years on, in May 1999, the Council of Europe had laid out thirteen requirements, further sub-divided into forty tasks, which Bosnia had to meet to be admitted, based on the proposal of then High Representative Westendorp. Most of these requirements were eventually met, as in the field of judicial reform, though largely by imposition, rather than the legislative process. Since only eighteen tasks had been fulfilled by the time Bosnia formally became a member, the Council of Europe prepared a post-accession programme that was then further extended to help Bosnia meet all requirements. Where these requirements had still not been met, they became part of the broader preconditions set out in the European Commission's Feasibility Study.

The European Union's Road Map set eighteen preconditions that Bosnia had to meet before work on a Feasibility Study for the opening of negotiations on a Stabilisation and Association Agreement could begin. These covered political, economic and democratic measures[87] and were to be fulfilled by the end of June 2001. Although the Demokratska alijansa za promjene (Democratic Alliance for Change, or DAP) was in power at this time, the deadlines were missed. Eventually, by September 2002, fifteen out of the eighteen steps had been completed,[88] though once again largely by imposition. This, nevertheless, paved the way for the Feasibility Study on further European integration, published in November 2003.

The Feasibility Study drew up sixteen priority reform areas in which Bosnia was expected to make significant progress before the country could begin negotiating a Stabilisation and Association Agreement (SAA).[89] In addition, the European Commission prepared a so-called European Partnership for Bosnia, identifying other areas of reform,[90] giving a checklist by which progress could be measured, and providing a framework for financial assistance to support reform processes. In February 2004, leading political parties signed a common platform supporting the reforms required for the SAA process and began passing the necessary legislation, including the Law on SIPA.

Initially, Lord Ashdown used the Bonn Powers far more than any other high representative, to push an ambitious reform agenda dubbed 'Justice and Jobs' despite recalcitrant domestic politicians. This incorporated the judicial reforms described above as well as a series of measures to combat corruption, including the establishment of a special anti-corruption unit within the OHR, and steps to remove obstacles to business, improving the prospects for economic growth. Lord Ashdown also drew up and published annually a clear work programme called the Mission Implementation Plan (MIP), which that the OHR oversaw. As tasks on that work programme were completed, the MIP was redrafted and the OHR scaled back its operations, effectively handing responsibility for an ever-wider range of issues to domestic institutions.

In areas relating to the SAA, Lord Ashdown decided that he could not impose legislation, since Bosnia would have to demonstrate a capacity for self-governance in order to become a credible EU aspirant. Likewise, he resisted the temptation to impose legislation in the field of defence reform relating to membership of NATO's Partnership for Peace programme. Nevertheless, he kept a tight grip on the reform process by forming commissions that brought together all relevant local and international actors to draw up reform programmes in priority areas and then by massaging legislation through the domestic institutions, preparing the laws and engaging in intensive lobbying. The pushing agenda pursued by the OHR, on the one hand, and the pulling agenda of the European Union and to a lesser extent NATO, on the other, were complementary and mutually reinforcing.

The push-pull approach that Lord Ashdown pursued generated notable results, especially in the fields of intelligence, tax collection and defence, fundamentally altering key elements of the Dayton Peace Agreement in favour of a more centralised and, above all, functional country. But the limits of this approach were exposed in the field of police reform.

According to Holbrooke, the most serious flaw in the Dayton Peace Agreement was the continued existence of two opposing armies.[91] The actual situation was even less stable. Although the

Bosnian Army and HVO were expected to merge into Federation armed forces, the planned union failed to materialise. The NATO-led peacekeeping force oversaw large-scale downsizing of all three militaries and was able to reduce tensions via confidence-building measures and even to introduce some transparency into defence planning and budgeting. Nevertheless, the country remained divided into three mutually hostile military camps, which clearly posed a threat to long-term peace and stability. Moreover, although the number of men in military formations had declined from an estimated 430,000 at the end of hostilities to just 34,000 professional soldiers in 2002, the economic burden of that number in a population of under 4 million was still crippling.

In May 2003 Lord Ashdown created a Defence Reform Commission, bringing together all relevant security actors to draft the legal and constitutional changes necessary to turn Bosnia into a credible candidate for NATO's Partnership for Peace programme. The timing was auspicious, in part because it followed two high-profile security-sector scandals in Republika Srpska. The Orao Aviation Institute in Bijeljina was found in October 2002 to be supplying Iraq with parts for Mig-21 aircraft together with a Yugoslav company, in violation of a UN arms embargo in the run-up to the 2003 US invasion.[92] Then, following a series of SFOR raids on VRS bases in March 2003, it became clear that Republika Srpska's military intelligence service was spying on international organisations, Federation officials and its own citizens on a massive scale.

NATO insisted on the introduction of a civilian-led command-and-control structure including a Defence Ministry at the state level; democratic parliamentary control and oversight over the armed forces; transparency in defence plans and budgets; development of a Bosnian security policy; and common doctrine, training and equipment standards. In September, the Defence Reform Commission reached unanimous agreement on a 293-page report setting out the way forward and including draft changes to entity constitutions, three entity-level laws and two state laws, as well as proposals for two new laws, including a state Defence Law.

Constitutional and other legal changes made the state of Bosnia supreme in defence, established civilian control over the military and created a new state Defence Ministry, Joint Staff and Operational Command. New laws set out the roles and functions of key officials, established operational and administrative chains of command, and created new procedures for planning and co-ordinating defence budgets. Entity armies were made part of a single military establishment—the Armed Forces of Bosnia—commanded by a single operational chain of command. The state parliament created a Joint Commission on Security and Defence to oversee these new state institutions, officials and procedures. Entity defence ministers retained responsibility for manning, training and equipping entity armies.

In addition to the legal changes, active forces were reduced to 12,000 personnel, reserves were shrunk by 75 per cent to 60,000, and both the annual intake of conscripts and the length of their service were cut. Taken together, these measures, which helped achieve a 55 per cent reduction in the defence budget, constituted the greatest change to the Dayton settlement, including a specific transfer of competency from entity to state level. The drafting and agreeing of the Defence Reform Commission's report and the adoption of relevant legislation were followed up in an equally intense fashion. The Defence Reform Commission remained in place, overseeing implementation of the agreed reforms. The initial report heralded the beginning of a wider reform process that led to the creation of a second Defence Reform Commission in 2005 and an even more ambitious restructuring of the defence establishment.

In addition to creating the original Defence Reform Commission, Lord Ashdown formed an Expert Commission on Intelligence Reform, consisting of six national intelligence officers and an international chair. A draft law produced by the Commission, which again involved an official transfer of competency from the entities to the state, was passed by the state parliament in March 2004, a parliamentary oversight committee was created in May, and on 1 June the Obavještajna i sigurnosna agencija/Obavještajna i bezbjednosna agencija (Intelligence-Security Agency, or OSA-OBA) came into being through the merger of the two official and, in practice, three existing, intelligence agencies. OSA-OBA's 700 personnel were selected from among the existing employees of the disbanded entity intelligence agencies through a seven-month screening process designed to determine their level of professionalism and willingness to work for a state agency. A director-general and deputy were appointed after an international vetting process. Four multi-ethnic regional centres were created, each of whose competencies crossed the inter-entity boundary line. The Commission's international chair was appointed supervisor for intelligence reform to monitor, advise and assist the local authorities in implementing the law, a process that continued for the next two years.

The Defence Reform Commission's second report was unanimously agreed in September 2005, with its recommendations becoming law on 1 January 2006 with a strict timetable to be overseen by NATO. In the new structure, the entity Defence Ministries and armies were dissolved and conscription abolished; the Bosnian Armed Forces were further reduced in number to between 9,000 and 10,000 professional soldiers with reserves of half that number; and a single chain of command, running from the presidency to the defence minister, to the chief of the Joint Staff, to the commander of the Operational Command and commander of Support Command, and through them to subordinates, was created with all three constituent peoples equally represented at every senior decision-making level. There would, in future, be one state defence budget.

The new Defence Law established three multi-ethnic brigades with headquarters in Banja Luka, Mostar and Tuzla, in addition to three infantry regiments, each representing the military heritage and identity of the units from which they were descended, that is the Bosnian Army, the HVO and the VRS. In this way, the Bosnian Armed Forces were joint, rather than united, like the state they served. Nevertheless, in the wake of the reforms, the Armed Forces had arguably become the most multi-ethnic institution in the country and their structure was no longer an impediment to membership of the Partnership for Peace, to which Bosnia was invited in November 2006 at NATO's Riga Summit. The NATO precondition that Bosnia had failed to meet was full co-operation with the ICTY.[93] However, the country benefitted from an easing of ICTY-related conditionality towards Belgrade at that time, in an attempt to influence the results of forthcoming elections in Serbia by rewarding the comparatively moderate parties in government. In this way, Bosnia, Montenegro and Serbia were invited to join the Partnership for Peace at the same time.

Tax reform had been an international priority ever since the extent of tax evasion became clear in the immediate post-war years. Moreover, efforts to build transparency and efficiency in tax collection went hand in hand with efforts to reform the border police. In 2001, the European Commission began to insist that Bosnia take steps to replace existing sales taxes with a value-added tax (VAT) in line with European norms. VAT differs from sales taxes in that all purchasers of goods and services pay it, not just final consumers. Producers and distributors are then refunded any difference between the VAT they pay on inputs and the VAT paid on what they sell on. Since the tax is paid in a chain, all producers and distributors must participate in the system if they want to get their refunds, radically reducing the scope for tax evasion.

The chain-like structure of VAT required the creation of a strong central administrator capable of collecting payments and calculating and processing refunds. This meant moving the collection of indirect taxes from the entity to the state level via a transfer of competency. With international assistance, particularly from the European Commission and the IMF, an Indirect Taxation Authority (ITA), initially headed by an international, was created to administer the VAT and put all indirect taxes—including customs and excises—into a so-called 'Single Account'. The Single Account would fund the state budget and cover Bosnia's debt obligations, after which revenues would be divided between the entities and Brčko District. The ITA took responsibility for all operations of the old customs authority, as well as domestic excises and sales taxes from the Brčko District, Federation and Republika Srpska tax administrations on 1 January 2005, leaving them responsible for direct taxes only. A state VAT levied at 17 per cent replaced entity sales taxes on 1 January 2006. Entity governments and Brčko District argued for the best part of two years over the division of receipts from the new tax until a formula based on final consumption was agreed. Meanwhile, tax receipts surged as businesses that had previously been operating in the grey economy began paying taxes.

The introduction of VAT was a far-reaching reform bringing Bosnia in line with European norms and representing a genuine step towards meeting the conditions for the signing of a Stabilisation and Association Agreement set out in the European Commission's Feasibility Study. There were, however, numerous other reform areas in which the European Commission also expected to see progress, including in particular reform of the police. It was, above all, the reality check provided by the failure of police reform that undermined the prospect of a smooth transition from the 'era of Dayton' to the 'era of Brussels' that Lord Ashdown had hoped would coincide with the tenth anniversary of the Dayton Peace Agreement.

Police reform did not need to become the obstacle that it did, nor the focus of so much time and effort. That it did was the consequence of a decision by Lord Ashdown to push a specific model of police restructuring. The Feasibility Study found Bosnia's system of law enforcement—fifteen police forces, operating at three levels of authority with minimal co-ordination—unfit to combat serious issues such as trafficking, organised crime and terrorism or to tackle corruption, and singled out the illogical structure as problematic, since it increased costs and hampered both co-ordination and effectiveness. And it concluded that Bosnia needed 'a structural police reform with a view to rationalising police service'. However, it did not present concrete proposals for institutional restructuring beyond the enhancement of law-enforcement agencies at the state level and better inter-agency co-ordination.

Following publication of the Feasibility Study, the European Commission tasked a team of consultants to assess the functionality of Bosnia's police as part of a wider analysis of priority reform areas. Their assessment, published in June 2004, was a technical review of the financial, organisational and administrative aspects of policing that compared the situation in Bosnia with that in EU member states. It found that the police were massively over-staffed and under-equipped, and managed according to an obsolete and illogical model in which there was no separation between political supervision and operational management. However, although it recommended the abolition of at least one layer of organisation, it did not present a specific proposal.

During the first half of 2004, the European Commission and the OHR campaigned for the adoption of six security-related laws, including the Law on SIPA. After all six had been passed, Lord Ashdown issued at the beginning of July a decision establishing a Police Reform Commission, tasked with preparing a proposal for the creation of 'a single structure of policing for Bosnia under the overall political oversight of a ministry or ministries in the Council of Ministers'. In effect, though it was not explicitly stated, Lord Ashdown expected the entities and cantons to give up their law-enforcement competencies and transfer them to a jointly managed state institution. This was the most ambitious reform initiated by the international community, going well beyond anything called for in the Feasibility Study and raising the bar on signing a Stabilisation and Association Agreement extremely–arguable unnecessary–high.

Lord Ashdown's immediate motivation for creating the Police Reform Commission was NATO's Istanbul Summit at the end of June 2004, at which Bosnia was not invited to join the Partnership for Peace because of its, or rather Republika Srpska's, failure to deliver a single indictee to the ICTY. The Summit communiqué anticipated 'systematic changes necessary to develop effective security and law-enforcement structures' and triggered a series of actions, including the removal of fifty-nine officials. Buoyed by the success of the Defence Reform Commission, Lord Ashdown pressed ahead, arguing that the greatest obstacle to Euro-Atlantic integration was Republika Srpska's failure to co-operate with the ICTY, that this failure reflected the continuation of wartime practices, and that only by strengthening state police structures would it be possible to bring war-crimes suspects to justice.

The Police Reform Commission consisted of twelve members: three internationals, including the chair, former Belgian Prime Minister Wilfred Martens, and his deputy; and nine representatives of domestic authorities, all politicians. Three months into its work in October 2004, European External Relations Commissioner Chris Patten wrote to the chair of the Council of Ministers and both entity governments setting out the European Union's expectations, namely legislative and budgetary competencies for police matters to be vested at the state level; functional local police areas to be determined by technical policing criteria; and no political interference in operational policing. These points evolved into what became the three EU principles for police reform. The principles were also to become controversial after Lord Ashdown revealed in his Bosnian memoir that he had at times asked Patten to weigh in to say that certain reforms were required if Bosnia wished to join Europe, and that Patten had obliged.[94]

The Police Reform Commission's report, which became known as the Martens proposal, suggested constitutional amendments to transfer policing from entity to state level and included two draft laws for adoption by the state parliament. The Security Ministry was to have political oversight over the police, which would be divided into three bodies: SIPA; the SBS; and the Local Police Bodies. As the Local Police Bodies, of which there were to be ten, crossed the inter-entity boundary line, the proposal was rejected by Republika Srpska representatives and no agreement could be reached. After Martens submitted his report to the high representative and the chair of the Council of Ministers, the OHR launched a media campaign promoting the benefits of police reform, maximised pressure on the Republika Srpska authorities (including further dismissals ostensibly as a result of non-co-operation with the ICTY) and facilitated a series of political negotiations. However, the breakthrough that Lord Ashdown wanted before the tenth anniversary of the Dayton Peace Agreement and the end of his mandate failed to materialise.

Although Lord Ashdown had presented rejection of police reform in the starkest of terms—'choosing Belarus over Brussels'—the impact of failure to sign up to the Martens proposal was no greater than earlier failures to meet conditions set out in the Road Map or even for Council of Europe membership. To keep the process alive, Republika Srpska President Čavić and opposition leader Dodik drafted a resolution on police restructuring proposing the establishment of a state Directorate to draw up an implementation plan in accordance with the European Union's principles and Bosnia's constitution. Although this resolution did not constitute any actual reform, the European Commission considered its adoption by the Republika Srpska National Assembly on 5 October 2005 sufficient to open negotiations on a Stabilisation and Association Agreement. These started on 21 November 2005, the tenth anniversary of the conclusion of peace negotiations in Dayton, after the state and Federation parliaments adopted the resolution.

Given the circumstances in which it was created, it was not surprising that the Directorate would have no more success in breaking the deadlock than the original Police Reform Commission. Indeed, although the Directorate was created on the basis of the resolution drawn up by Čavić and Dodik, Republika Srpska representatives effectively boycotted its deliberations. This was the result of disagreement over decision-making procedures. The Directorate had a Steering Board in which decisions were to be taken by consensus, but if this was not possible, then by majority vote. Dodik, who had become prime minister in February 2006 after the collapse of the SDS government, argued that these procedures enabled Bosniaks and Croats to outvote Serbs and wanted them changed. When his objections were ignored on the grounds that the Directorate was a professional and not a political body, Serb representatives remained in the Directorate but only as observers.

Despite the Serb boycott, the Directorate published a final report in December 2006 that paved the way for further fruitless talks, in which Republika Srpska representatives rejected any moves to downgrade the status and authority of the Republika Srpska police. Indeed, it was only when the EU principles for police reform were dropped that it was possible to move to the signing of the Stabilisation and Association Agreement, which duly took place on 16 June 2008, very nearly four years after the creation of the Police Reform Commission. While the signing of a Stabilisation and Association Agreement was hailed as a breakthrough, heralding a new era for Bosnia, the mutually exclusive positions and outlooks of Bosnia's rival ethno-national leaders that had been exposed in police-reform discussions told a very different story.

7

RHETORIC AND REALITY

'Bosnians do not take ownership of their country's future, not because the foreigners won't let them, but because they do not agree among themselves what that future should be like,'

Tihomir Loza[1]

Assessing the process

The most difficult decision confronting the Peace Implementation Council (PIC) was how and when to bring the Dayton process to an end. That decision required a comprehensive assessment both of how the peace accord had been implemented and of Bosnia's ability to move forward on its own. If Bosnia's elected leaders were not capable of governing the country without the massive international support mechanism that had surrounded it since the end of the war, failure would bring into question both the international strategy pursued during the peace process and the entire Dayton project.

As long as the Office of the High Representative (OHR) maintained a firm hand on the peace process and drove through reforms, irrespective of the positions of Bosnia's elected authorities, it was always possible to make it appear as if the country was making progress. Moreover, there were some genuine achievements and breakthroughs, such as defence reform. However, the scale of

165

international involvement and the pressure brought to bear on seemingly every matter were so enormous that they masked the true state of affairs. Since the international community's self-proclaimed and overriding aim had been to develop self-sustaining institutions capable of taking Bosnia from the 'era of Dayton' to the 'era of Brussels', the ultimate test of the peace process was the ability of those institutions to function without continuous international intervention. When they were put to the test in 2006, they were found so wanting that it was not possible to close the OHR as planned.

The test came soon after Lord Ashdown was succeeded at the end of January 2006 by Christian Schwarz-Schilling as the fifth high representative and second EU special representative. Schwarz-Shilling, a seventy-four-year-old former German post and telecommunications minister, had resigned in 1992 after more than a decade in office in protest against the feeble international response to ethnic cleansing in Bosnia. Moreover, he had devoted much of the intervening period to a variety of Bosnian causes. He came into office committed to overseeing a transfer to local ownership of the peace process, as advocated by his two immediate predecessors, but never put into practice. This was symbolically to be realised by closing the OHR and restructuring the international presence in Bosnia in favour of a reinforced EU mission headed by the EU special representative to support the country's further recovery and to help guide it towards membership in the European Union. To achieve this, Schwarz-Schilling was expected to oversee agreement on police restructuring as well as other preconditions for the signing of the Stabilisation and Association Agreement, including implementation of public broadcasting system (PBS) reform, further public administration reform and co-operation with the International Criminal Tribunal for the former Yugoslavia (ICTY), all of which were supposed to set Bosnia irrevocably on the road to Euro-Atlantic integration.

There was, however, no progress in any of these areas and Schwarz-Schilling became a scapegoat for the sharp deterioration in the political environment in Bosnia during his seventeen-month mandate. But while the contrast between Schwarz-Schilling's apparent passivity and Lord Ashdown's seemingly boundless energy could not have been greater, Schwarz-Schilling was reaping the cumulative consequences of the failures of the peace process and the shortcomings of the settlement. Schwarz-Schilling's approach reflected continuity in as much as Lord Ashdown had himself changed tack towards the end of his mandate in preparation for the transition to local ownership. Lord Ashdown had reduced OHR staff from around 700 to below 300 in two rounds of cuts on 31 December 2004 and 31 December 2005; he refrained from using the Bonn Powers; and he began addressing many of the outstanding issues emerging out of the use of those powers for the best part of a decade, including lifting bans on individuals he or his predecessors had dismissed.

While Schwarz-Schilling wished to see Bosnia integrated as rapidly as possible into the European Union, he was also sceptical about the wisdom of giving up the high representative's executive powers. Publicly, he made it clear that as high representative he would only use the Bonn Powers in two situations: in the event of a threat to peace and stability or in matters relating to the ICTY. Privately, however, he argued on the basis of his experience of post-war Germany that executive powers should be retained irrespective of whether they appeared to be needed, since once given up they could not be reinstated. He pointed out that the Allies had retained executive powers in Germany for many years without using them, as an insurance policy in case events took a turn for the worse. He drew up option papers for the transition explicitly retaining the Bonn Powers, if possible within the person of the EU special representative, but if this was not acceptable to the European Union, within a residual OHR. In the event, the PIC decided in June 2006 on Schwarz-Schilling's advice to prepare for closure of the OHR on 31 June 2007, but to review that decision in early 2007 in light of developments in Bosnia and the wider region.

On becoming high representative, Schwarz-Schilling announced that he would step back and leave political processes to the domestic authorities, stressing the importance of the October 2006 elections for electing leaders equipped to secure Bosnia's European future. In contrast to his predecessors, he resisted the temptation to intervene even as the climate appeared to be deteriorating. He did this because he wished to establish with certainty whether Bosnia was capable of moving forward under its own steam before closing the OHR and, if it became clear that the country was not, to put or keep in place mechanisms to address the deficiencies that had been revealed. The issue was the underlying state of Bosnia after a decade of international supervision.

Strictly speaking, the situation should have been clear, given the level of international monitoring. PIC members had gathered periodically to review the peace process ever since the original December 1995 meeting in London. These gatherings had taken place at foreign-ministerial level every six months in the early years of the peace process and later at the level of political directors or their nominees every three months, with declarations or communiqués issued after each high-level meeting. In addition, PIC Steering Board ambassadors in Sarajevo met every week. While PIC declarations and communiqués should have presented an accurate picture of the situation in Bosnia, they were curious documents serving multiple purposes. Generally drafted by the OHR, they were part 'state-of-the-nation' reports, part work plans for the international community, part lists of expectations for the Bosnian authorities and part appeals to a variety of actors setting out philosophical visions of Bosnia's future. There was a pronounced tendency to use excessively diplomatic language, to exaggerate the extent of progress, and to heap praise on domestic authorities while placing responsibility for failure on them, too. By becoming the driver of reforms, the international community became an actor rather than an observer, with the high representative the most important decision-maker in Bosnia yet democratically unaccountable. As a result, the OHR had a vested interest in presenting a picture of success both in Bosnia and abroad, irrespective of reality on the ground.

The OHR and successive high representatives did not seek to distort reality. Rather, they were obliged, on the one hand, to balance the competing concerns and outlooks of all PIC members while, on the other, to spearhead efforts to transform Bosnia from an ethno-nationally divided, dysfunctional and war-torn country into a genuine candidate for membership in the European Union and NATO. They were operating in uncharted territory, forced to be innovative within the structures imposed by the Dayton Peace Agreement. Given the scale and complexity of the reforms, they could not expect immediate results.

Although the Bonn Powers were originally envisaged to break procedural deadlocks and to deal with specific and concrete threats to peace implementation, they evolved into the primary tool for advancing reforms. In the process, their usage soared. Whereas the Bonn Powers were only used once in 1997 and twenty-nine times in 1998, they were used ninety times in 1999, eighty-six times in 2000, fifty-four times in 2001, 153 times in 2002,[2] ninety-six times in 2003, 166 times in 2004,[3] ninety-one times in 2005 and eleven times during the first month of 2006 while Lord Ashdown was still high representative.[4]

Raw figures for the use of the Bonn Powers are useful in terms of year-on-year comparisons, as well as for comparisons among high representatives. However, they do not present a complete picture of their use or significance. On the one hand, they tend to exaggerate the scale of international intervention, since the same laws and amendments often had to be imposed not just at the state level, but also in the entities, cantons, Brčko District and municipalities, inflating the number of 'decisions'. On the other, the threat of imposition by the high representative frequently helped persuade domestic authorities to pass legislation that they might not have been willing to adopt otherwise. The Bonn Powers were systematically used to exert pressure on domestic leaders and effectively became a parallel legislative process. Whether or not imposed legislation was ratified in standard parliamentary procedure, a necessary first step before amendments could be made, decisions by the high representative became law as soon as they were published on the OHR website.

The Bonn Powers were primarily used to impose legislation and amendments to laws. They were also used to sanction political parties, to place financial controls on supporters of war-crimes suspects, to remove or suspend individuals from office and later to lift bans against them. And they were used to establish or extend the mandates of various bodies, such as the many reform commissions, as well as to appoint individuals to posts, usually in the judiciary, and then to extend or terminate their mandates. Over the years, the emphasis of decisions by the high representative shifted from return-related matters to rule-of-law issues, state- and institution-building measures, and later to decisions seeking to promote European standards of accountability, professionalism and transparency. Moreover, they were increasingly 'soft' impositions— impositions on issues where the domestic authorities recognised the need for particular solutions, but preferred not to be seen to be taking the decisions themselves.[5]

Use of the Bonn Powers nevertheless generated resentment, especially in Republika Srpska, where officials believed they had borne the brunt of decisions by the high representative. Lord Ashdown was especially reviled as a result of the many removals he had instigated, as well as the centralising tendencies of the reforms that he had overseen. The intense pressure Lord Ashdown brought to bear succeeded in forcing the Republika Srpska authorities to co-operate with the ICTY and in making the Dayton settlement more functional. However, ill feeling built up over many years helped create a backlash against reform processes and the international community in general. This manifested itself most obviously in the policies and rhetoric of Milorad Dodik, who returned to government as prime minister of Republika Srpska at the end of February 2006, less than a month after Lord Ashdown left Bosnia.

Dodik came back into government in the wake of a crisis in the Srpska demokratska stranka (Serb Democratic Party, or SDS), brought on largely by the sustained pressure that the party had been under for many years from Lord Ashdown. Although Dodik had been the beneficiary of massive international and especially US support over the years—and although he required the support of non-Serb deputies to form a government—he charted a course for Republika Srpska that brought him into conflict with the Bosniak political establishment, the international community and the new high representative. In part, Dodik's new course was electioneering, as he sought to present himself as the Serb champion in the run-up to October elections. In part, he was reacting to the new climate that Schwarz-Schilling's arrival had created. And in part, he was carried along by developments elsewhere: the failure of a constitutional reform initiative in Bosnia in April; the separation of Montenegro and Serbia following an independence referendum in Montenegro in May; and the prospect of independence for Kosovo. Dodik could pursue an increasingly independent and aggressive policy because of the financial position that he inherited. VAT revenues began to arrive in the month he became prime minister, providing him with a greater and more consistent revenue stream than any previous leader had enjoyed.

At the same time as Dodik wrapped himself in the mantle of Serb nationalism, Haris Silajdžić re-emerged as a political force among Bosniaks, marshalling opposition to the constitutional reform initiative in preparation for a third and ultimately successful attempt to be elected Bosniak member of the presidency in the October elections. As rhetoric among both Bosniak and Serb leaders began heating up, the reform process ground to a halt. Schwarz-Schilling addressed the state parliament on 24 May 2006 urging legislators to rise to the ownership challenge and pass a series of laws relating to the European Partnership, after which Serb parliamentarians walked out. The parliamentary boycott was in response to disagreements over the composition and mandate of the Commission to investigate suffering in Sarajevo, rather than the message contained in Schwarz-Schilling's speech. However, it lasted more than three weeks, bringing the work of the joint institutions, which could not function in the absence of deputies from Republika Srpska, to a halt. And it illustrated both fundamental flaws in the settlement and the fragility of the peace at the very time when the international community was planning to scale down its presence.

Limits of liberal peace-building

The Serb boycott should have set alarm bells ringing. The ensuing institutional paralysis highlighted the importance of external executive powers for the functioning of the country. Structurally, it was all too easy to paralyse the state institutions and, without the OHR, there was no obvious mechanism for resolving such situations. While it might be argued that such mechanisms would only be developed (and domestic politicians would only begin to behave responsibly) once the international community had given up its executive powers, the degree of risk involved in giving up those powers was considerable. That the PIC decided, nevertheless, to proceed with preparations for OHR closure was indicative of the prevailing mindset in capitals at the time. Policy was being driven by fatigue with Bosnia and frustration at the time and resources spent on the country, particularly as growing commitments in other parts of the world, and especially in Afghanistan and Iraq, sapped international resolve and capacity to develop alternative approaches.

International strategy as set out in the many PIC documents corresponded to what political scientists call the 'liberal peace model'. The international community, in the form of the European Union, the IMF, NATO, the OSCE, the World Bank and the many national development agencies as well as the OHR, had effectively sought to reproduce the Western liberal democratic model in Bosnia via, on the one hand, democratisation, including elections, civilian control over the armed forces and institution-building, and, on the other, the construction of a market economy, including tax reform, measures to build transparency and privatisation.

With the obvious exception of police restructuring, the major internationally supervised, institution-building projects had largely run their course by 2006; the limits of what could be achieved by decree had essentially been reached; and the period during which use of executive powers could be justified as emergency measures had expired. Yet even after more than a decade of intervention and investment on an unprecedented scale, and despite the incentive of eventual integration into the European Union and NATO, the results were modest. Bosnia's reality did not correspond to the rhetoric of progress and Euro-Atlantic integration. The fundamental cleavages, fears and mindsets that had initially paralysed Bosnian society between the 1990 elections and the outbreak of war continued to plague political life. Moreover, these cleavages scuppered the only serious, albeit modest, attempt to move beyond the Dayton settlement, the so-called 'April Package' of constitutional amendments that narrowly failed to be passed by the necessary two-thirds majority of the House of Representatives on 26 April 2006.

RHETORIC AND REALITY

Although no one considered the Dayton settlement to be an optimal solution—and everyone was aware it made for a dysfunctional and costly political system—successive high representatives chose not to open it up for fear of the potential consequences. The April Package evolved out of a considered analysis of constitutional issues in Bosnia prepared by the Council of Europe's Venice Commission. This was followed by nine months of discreet discussions involving representatives of all major political parties, facilitated and moderated by a specially formed team of Americans working in the non-governmental sector; and, after that, three months of intensive, higher-profile negotiations chaired by the US Embassy in Bosnia.

The Venice Commission published its report, 'Opinion on the Constitutional Situation in Bosnia and Herzegovina and the Powers of the High Representative', in March 2005.[6] It did so on the basis of a Council of Europe Parliamentary Assembly Resolution asking it both to determine how far the OHR's use of executive powers complied with Council of Europe basic principles, and to assess the conformity of Bosnia's constitution with the European Convention for the Protection of Human Rights and Fundamental Freedoms and the European Charter of Local Self-Government, as well as more generally the efficiency and rationality of the country's constitutional and legal arrangements. The report highlighted many of the shortcomings of both the existing constitutional structures and the workings of the OHR.[7] It also drew specific attention to the weakness of the state government in comparison with the entities in terms of Bosnia's capacity for European integration, concluding that it was 'unthinkable that Bosnia can make real progress with the present constitutional arrangements'. And it drew a link between the gradual phasing out of the power of the high representative and a parallel process of constitutional reform to make the legislative process more efficient.

Although the recommendations of the Venice Commission report were only advisory, they set the scene for nine months of constitutional reform discussions involving the country's eight most important political parties. These discussions took place within the framework of a working group comprising representatives of each political party and a three-man secretariat headed by Don Hays, a recently retired US diplomat at the US Institute of Peace, who had served in Bosnia as principal deputy high representative between July 2001 and March 2005.[8] The secretariat spent one week each month in Sarajevo during the spring and summer of 2005, organising a two-day session with the entire working group, followed by consultations with individual political leaders and international officials. Discussions took place in confidence, far from the media spotlight, and, despite huge differences in outlook and objective, the atmosphere was constructive.[9]

While the working group was able to establish consensus on the need for and scope of reform, negotiations had to move to the level of party leaders to have any chance of achieving a genuine compromise. Party leaders met in November 2005 in Brussels and again in Washington and Sarajevo in December, without achieving any breakthrough. In Washington, leaders nevertheless committed themselves to conclude an agreement on these reforms and to put it to the state parliament by March 2006, in time for changes to be incorporated in advance of the general election, scheduled for October 2006. Because of this urgency, the US Embassy in Sarajevo took over the role of the secretariat.

The constructive atmosphere that had characterised the early discussions disappeared as a potential agreement began to emerge. Indeed, the SBiH, whose representative had chaired the working group's meetings, withdrew from the process to campaign against the agreement over the issue of 'entity voting'.[10] The issue also led to a split within the HDZ. Deputies opposed to the agreement left to form their own party, the HDZ 1990, with the rump party henceforward referred to by its full name, namely the HDZ BiH. The April Package, which the presidency put to the Bosnian parliament on 25 March, was considerably more modest than Hays and the original sponsors of constitutional reform had hoped. Nevertheless, it, began to address several of the issues raised by the Venice Commission report with four constitutional amendments covering the distribution of competencies, the state parliament, the presidency, and the Council of Ministers.

The number of state competencies was to be expanded to include areas in which transfers of competency had already taken place, such as defence, security, intelligence, the State Court, the State Prosecutor's Office, the High Judicial and Prosecutorial Council, and the Indirect Taxation Administration. In addition, a new category of shared competencies was to cover areas such as taxation, elections and justice. Procedures were also drawn up for future transfers of competency. And a clause granting the state the authority to pass all legislation required for European integration was designed to create an effective tool for assuming necessary competencies.

An increase in the number of parliamentarians was proposed for both Houses. The House of Representatives was to grow from forty-two to eighty-seven members, twenty-eight from each constituent people and three representatives of Others. The House of Peoples was to grow from fifteen to twenty-one delegates, seven from each constituent people instead of five, who would be elected by the House of Representatives, not by entity parliaments. Speakers and deputy speakers in both Houses would no longer rotate but have four-year mandates, providing greater continuity. The House of Representatives was to have sole responsibility for passing legislation, with the powers of the House of Peoples limited to application of the procedure for protecting vital national interest. Critically, however, 'entity voting' was to remain for the House of Representatives, conditioning approval of legislation on the participation of at least one third of parliamentarians from each entity.

The presidency was to be reconfigured and its responsibilities reduced, at the same time as those of the Council of Ministers and its chair were to be increased. The three-person structure was to be retained, but members of the presidency would in future be elected by the parliament rather than by citizens. Members of the presidency would rotate every sixteen months, instead of every six months, and only three sensitive areas, including defence, were to require consensus. In this way, the president would have been primarily responsible for matters of protocol. The Council of Ministers Chair would have had a stronger role in forming the government and guiding ministers, and two additional ministries, for agriculture and for technology and the environment, would have been created.

The failure of the April Package to be adopted, despite intense lobbying, had a significance that went beyond the comparatively modest changes contained within it. For it exposed the depth of feeling and the scale of the task involved in amending the Dayton Peace Agreement using the mechanisms for change contained within it. Though a significant majority of parliamentarians—twenty-six out of forty-two—supported the amendments, and the Package fell only two votes short of being adopted, prospects of obtaining a two-thirds majority on anything more substantial were minimal. Moreover, the failure of the April Package coloured the political atmosphere in the run-up to the October elections, when Bosnians would be choosing the leaders meant to take ownership of the peace process after the OHR's closure.

Silajdžić spearheaded the SBiH campaign against the April Package, arguing that legitimising entity voting would reinforce the division of the country and bring Bosnia's very existence into question. The only reform the SBiH was prepared to support was one that weakened the entities, a position that was anathema to all political parties in Republika Srpska. Defectors to the HDZ 1990, which was led by Božo Ljubić, also challenged entity voting, interpreting it as a provision that selectively discriminated against Croats. This was because the procedure could be used by Serbs from Republika Srpska and Bosniaks from the Federation to block legislation, but not by Croats, since Croats did not constitute a sufficiently large proportion of the population. Moreover, they believed that any reduction in the competencies of the House of Peoples would make it more difficult to invoke vital national interest, thereby further weakening the Croat position.

Having staked out their positions in the debate over constitutional amendments, Silajdžić and Ljubić sought to present themselves as the respective Bosniak and Croat champions in the run-up to elections. Meanwhile, Dodik determined both that he would use the levers of power that he now controlled to maximise his chances of securing re-election and that he would not risk being out bid in ethno-national terms by the SDS or any other party, as he had been in the 2002 elections. He carried out a purge of those positions that he as prime minister controlled, replacing SDS nominees with SNSD supporters.[11] And, uncharacteristically at the time, he adopted the most extreme campaign rhetoric of any politician, raising the prospect of an independence referendum in Republika Srpska in the wake of Montenegro's May independence referendum, which had led to Montenegro's formal split from Serbia.[12]

The electoral campaign effectively started with the debate over the constitutional amendments and lasted for six months. During this period, the rhetoric was continuously ratcheted up and no legislation was passed on issues relating to Bosnia's European Partnership. Moreover, those politicians who took the most extreme positions were rewarded on polling day, with one exception: Željko Komšić, the SDP candidate for Croat member of the presidency. As a result of a quirk in the electoral system, he was elected by ballots cast by Bosniak and, to a lesser extent, Serb voters.[13] Dodik's SNSD won a landslide among Serb voters in the Republika Srpska poll; the SBiH and the HDZ 1990 made gains at the expense of the SDA and the HDZ BiH; Silajdžić became Bosniak member of the presidency; and the SNSD's candidate, Nebojša Radmanović, became the Serb member of the presidency.

Dark side of democracy[14]

Elections were a fundamental element of the peace process, starting with the September 1996 ballot that was mandated in the Dayton Peace Agreement and had been the focus of international effort during the first year. Indeed, one of the justifications for recognising and certifying that ballot, despite irregularities, was that it was seen as a learning process, and a step towards democratic governance. The October 2006 polls were the fifth general elections to have been held in Bosnia since the Dayton Peace Agreement came into force.[15] Had international officials known in 1996 that, ten years on, the most powerful individuals in Bosnian politics would have been Dodik and Silajdžić, and that the HDZ would have splintered, they would probably have viewed this as evidence that democracy was taking root and as vindication of their approach. After all, Dodik had been the most outspoken critic of the SDS and Silajdžić had left the SDA to form what had been viewed at the time as a more moderate and ostensibly multi-ethnic alternative. Had they known that the presidency would consist of Silajdžić, Radmanović, and Komšić, they would no doubt have been even more pleased, since not one of the wartime dominant, ethno-national parties would have been represented in the country's highest institution.

The problem with the 'learning democracy' strategy was that while the faces of the politicians in power and the names of their parties might have changed, the attitudes and policies had not. In effect, 'moderates' had transformed themselves into 'extremists' by behaving according to the logic of the electoral and political system to get elected. The October 2006 polls were supposed to bring to power individuals who would take ownership of the peace process and work to secure Bosnia's Euro-Atlantic future. In the event, however, they succeeded only in demonstrating the need for continuing international oversight in Bosnia, as rival party leaders were unable to form effective, multi-ethnic governments.

In the wake of the elections, it was easy to put together a government in Republika Srpska, where Dodik's SNSD was only one seat short of an absolute majority in the National Assembly. Dodik was obliged to appoint to his cabinet five Bosniaks and three Croats as a result of the amendments imposed by Petritsch in 2002 in the wake of the Constitutional Court decision on the constituency of peoples.[16] However, this did not slow the process. Government formation was more complicated at levels without built-in ethno-national majorities or where multi-ethnicity had to be incorporated comprehensively, as in 'mixed' cantons, in the Federation and at the state level. Schwarz-Schilling chose not to intervene in this process, in contrast to his predecessors, wishing to see how or whether it would be possible for governments to be formed without international pressure. After two-and-a-half months of seemingly fruitless negotiations, however, US Ambassador Douglas L. McElhaney decided to become involved. Eventually, just over three months after polling day, a grand coalition, involving all major political parties except the SDS and the SDP, came together under Dodik's choice for Council of Ministers chair, Nikola Špirić, who adopted the European Partnership document as its platform. It was the only platform acceptable to all parties.

The only political party to put forward a 'Western-style' political manifesto and campaign on 'bread-and-butter' issues of concern to all voters, as opposed to the national question, was the SDP. But with the exception of the vote for the Croat member of the presidency, the SDP fared poorly in the October 2006 elections. One factor contributing to the SDP's poor result may have been internal strife, as the party struggled to operate in a cohesive manner. In addition, the timing was inauspicious, given Montenegro's recent secession from Serbia, the imminent prospect of a decision on the future of Kosovo and the impending final ruling in Bosnia's genocide case against Serbia and Montenegro. However, a proper explanation for the electoral failure of both the SDP and moderate, non-national options has to consider the relationship between political parties, ethno-national identity and democracy in Bosnia.

Although political rhetoric was inflammatory in 2006, it was hardly more so than it had been in previous elections. Moreover, the time taken to put a coalition government together at the state level in the wake of the 2006 ballot was similar to that after earlier elections. The problem, of course, was that the parties in the governing coalition, each of which appealed exclusively to the interests of one people, had very different visions for the future of Bosnia. Irrespective of the number of times voters were able to cast ballots in elections, this was not going to change, as long as they perceived a threat to their ethno-national identity.

Discussion of the complexity of democratic governance in divided societies is almost as old as liberal political thinking. Indeed, this issue featured prominently in the writing of John Stuart Mill in the nineteenth century, notably in his exchanges with Lord John Acton.[17] Mill was extremely pessimistic about the capacity of what he called 'pluralistic societies' for representative government, writing that 'free institutions are next to impossible in a country made up of different nationalities. Among a people without fellow-feeling, especially if they read and speak different languages, the united public opinion, necessary to the working of representative government, cannot exist.'[18] Moreover, Mill's pessimism has all too often been borne out in multi-ethnic countries adopting democratic structures, sometimes with tragic consequences.

The debate on the capacity of pluralistic societies for representative government has, nevertheless, evolved greatly since the nineteenth century. In the intervening period, political scientists have developed a series of models for democratic co-operation in divided societies, based on empirical evidence that was not available to Mill. Bosnia's system of power-sharing—grand coalitions involving representatives of all peoples, the need for consensus in decision-making and proportional representation—corresponds to so-called consociationalism, a model associated with the Dutch-American political scientist Arend Lijphart. This form of government has proved durable in multi-ethnic societies such as Belgium, the Netherlands and Switzerland, and is credited by some analysts for the successful transition in South Africa. However, the conditions that Lijphart identified for consociational government, such as over-arching loyalties to the state and a tradition of elite accommodation, did not exist in Bosnia.[19]

The party system that was put in place in Bosnia in 1990 and effectively inherited from Croatia remains more or less intact today, two-and-a-half decades later.[20] International efforts to influence Bosnian politics since the end of the war succeeded in loosening the vice-like grip on power of the three ethno-national parties that emerged victorious in the 1990 elections and led their respective communities into war. But they failed to introduce structural reforms into the party system systematically to promote multi-ethnicity and reward moderation, which would have given democratic institutions the ability to evolve and flourish in the longer term. Rather, the electoral system chosen in 1996, coupled with various strictures in the Dayton Peace Agreement, reinforced many of the shortcomings of the original system.

Although international officials have repeatedly congratulated Bosnian authorities for the staging of elections in the post-war period, Bosnia's best-organised, most free and most fair polls were those that took place in 1990.[21] The pre-war elections were not marred by the inflammatory rhetoric that has featured prominently in all post-war polls. And the ethno-national parties that came out on top in the elections were able rapidly to form a government without external assistance. They had, after all, been in coalition against the former communists during the election campaign.

Even ethno-national leaders who have subsequently been indicted, put on trial at the ICTY and, in some cases, convicted of war crimes did not appear extreme in 1990. Plavšić, for example, was a respected academic, as was Nikola Koljević, the second SDS candidate to stand for the presidency. Had Plavšić appeared to non-Serb voters to represent a threat, they would have been able to vote for an alternative Serb candidate, as all voters were entitled to cast seven ballots for the presidency's seven members.[22] Moreover, there was little even in Karadžić's background in 1990 to foreshadow the turn his life was about to take.[23] He appears to have been a popular, gregarious and entertaining individual with friends from all ethno-national backgrounds. And before founding the SDS, he appeared interested in setting up the Green Party. Nevertheless, within less than a year of the original elections, he was warning Bosnia's Bosniaks in parliament that they faced annihilation, as politics descended into zero-sum rhetoric.[24]

Fears of the ethno-nationalisation of society in the wake of multi-party elections had led the Yugoslav intellectual group Udruženje za jugoslovensku demokratsku inicijativu (Association for a Yugoslav Democratic Initiative, or UJDI) to develop alternative models for democracy in the Yugoslav context, and the communist authorities in Bosnia to ban ethno-national parties—to no avail.[25] And it was the transformation in mindsets and attitudes in the course of 1991 as a result of the ethno-nationalisation of society that prepared the ground for war, ethnic cleansing and, ultimately, genocide. What was most remarkable about these developments was not how evil the individuals involved appeared, but how normal and unexceptional they were.

The grand coalition of HDZ, SDA and SDS that governed Bosnia in the wake of the 1990 elections contained representatives of all three of the republic's constituent peoples, all of whom had a democratic mandate, in terms of having won sufficient votes to win office. Yet the fact that the parties and their leaders could claim democratic legitimacy did not help shore up the republic and encourage them to work together for the common good. Quite the opposite.

Bosnia's original electoral system was democratic in as much as electors were able to vote for different candidates. However, it was also fundamentally flawed because of the ethno-national composition of Bosnian society. This flaw was a manifestation of an ambiguity at the heart of democracy, or rule by the people, where the 'people' do not correspond to the *demos*, that is the citizenry, but to the *ethnos*, namely those sharing a distinct culture. Since politicians were elected exclusively by the votes of one of Bosnia's peoples, they considered themselves answerable to that people and no other. In this way, each ethno-national party pursued its own agenda working narrowly to promote the interests of its people, irrespective of the consequences for Bosnia's other communities.

The ethno-national democratisation manifested in the 1990 poll results created a 'tyranny of the majority' at the municipal level and conflict at the state level. Ethno-nationally 'pure' municipal governments were formed; non-dominant communities were purged from the municipal administration and public companies; and other trappings of the ethno-national state were introduced at the local level. This was the case wherever the ethno-national parties—HDZ, SDA and SDS—had won power, though not in Tuzla, where a coalition of former communists held on to power. Almost overnight, ethno-national democratisation had massively increased the stakes in politics. In the absence of mechanisms to address the dangers presented by majoritarian politics, elections came, above all, to be about ethno-national hegemony. In the wake of the 1990 election, members of non-dominant communities found themselves systematically and institutionally marginalised. Moreover, the toxic combination of ethno-national democratisation and the wider regional conflict generated a vicious cycle of fear, insecurity and loathing that domestic institutions and actors, increasingly serving as echo-chambers for those fears and hatreds, were incapable of managing.

The logic behind Bosnian democracy in 1990, when the political system was created, was conflict. And that logic remains unchanged today. Hence the absence of 'bread-and-butter' issues, as well as the extreme rhetoric that characterises every election. Hence also the failure of a non-nationalist alternative to emerge in Bosnian politics, despite the obvious failings of the ethno-national parties. The only attempt to address some of the shortcomings of the political system was the reform process set in train by the Constitutional Court decision on the constituency of peoples. The package of resulting changes imposed by Petritsch helped provide a formal ethno-national balance at the entity and cantonal levels, but not at the municipal level. At the time of imposition, the process was supposed to go further, including both the municipal level and public companies, via additional, appropriate legislation. But no such laws were forthcoming, in part because of the change of high representative. When Lord Ashdown succeeded Petritsch as high representative, he allowed this matter to be placed on the backburner in favour of his own programme of 'Justice and Jobs'. Moreover, the democratisation programmes developed by international organisations such as the OSCE and non-governmental organisations such as the National Democratic Institute have failed to address these structural issues. Rather, by working within existing mono-ethnic structures, many well-intentioned democratisation programmes have reinforced and compounded the problem.[26]

Dodik and Silajdžić emerged as the most powerful individuals in Bosnian politics after the 2006 elections because both promised to defend the interests of their respective peoples more aggressively than their rivals. Neither made any effort to canvass votes outside his ethno-national group. And each grew more popular within their own communities by feeding off the inflammatory rhetoric of the other. In effect, the political system rewarded both men for the extremist positions they adopted. Moreover, although the SNSD and SBiH both joined the governing coalition at the state level, the two parties represented mutually exclusive and diametrically opposed visions of Bosnia's future, yet both could claim legitimacy on the basis of democratic mandates.

8

WHITHER BOSNIA?

'We can't have a process where Balkan countries pretend to reform and we pretend to believe them.'

Chris Patten[1]

Diplomatic autopilot

The debate over international engagement in Bosnia has generally been presented in terms of the continued existence of the Office of the High Representative (OHR) and whether or not the Bonn Powers should be used. It is, however, more complex and must at the very least also encompass the international military dimension. For it is the peace-enforcement mandate under Chapter VII of the UN Charter, emanating from Annex 1 of the Dayton Peace Agreement, that enabled the OHR to take on the intrusive role in Bosnian society that it played for much of the first decade of the peace process. Moreover, it is the international military presence, albeit greatly reduced, that provides the ultimate safeguard against a resumption of hostilities. The key question was whether, as successive high representatives had hoped, the 'pull of Brussels' would be sufficiently strong to replace the 'push of Dayton' as both the driver of reform and the glue holding Bosnia together. Despite Brussels' success in bringing eight former communist Central and

WHITHER BOSNIA?

Eastern European countries into the European Union in 2004, the prospect of a Stabilisation and Association Process and the aspirations of the majority of Bosnia's citizens, this was asking a huge amount. Indeed, even had international strategy towards Bosnia succeeded in creating genuinely self-sustaining institutions, OHR closure would have been complex, given the scale of the organisation's involvement in Bosnian life over more than a decade.

Having decided to review the decision to close the OHR at the end of June 2007, the PIC concluded in February 2007 that the timing was wrong and that the OHR should remain in existence. The risk involved in closing the OHR was judged too great to proceed, though the goal remained transition to an office run by an EU special representative (EUSR). The policy about-turn followed a sustained campaign by Schwarz-Schilling to persuade decision-makers in PIC capitals to keep the OHR open and to retain executive powers in Bosnia as an insurance policy. He had failed to persuade Brussels to entrust the EU special representative with such authority in the event of the anticipated transition to an EUSR operation. Having been widely criticised for presiding over the deterioration in the political atmosphere, Schwarz-Schilling sweetened the pill of the volte-face by offering to make way for another high representative, an offer that was hastily accepted.

The OHR's stay of execution was also influenced by concerns about the potential impact of two other factors: the International Court of Justice (ICJ) ruling in the Bosnia versus Serbia and Montenegro genocide case, and the decision on the status of Kosovo. One day before the PIC's decision, the ICJ ruled that the July 1995 Srebrenica massacre was an act of genocide, but that what had occurred over the whole territory of Bosnia did not constitute genocide. Moreover, this act of genocide was committed by the Vojska Republike Srpske (Army of Republika Srpska, or VRS) and various paramilitary units, but not by Serbia.[2] Irrespective of the merits or wisdom of the long-awaited ICJ ruling, PIC decision-makers could not at that stage anticipate what impact it might have on stability in Bosnia or the wider region. At the same time, the imminent decision on Kosovo risked being even more destabilising. The Kosovo decision had been expected by the end of 2006 based

185

on a negotiation process chaired by UN Special Envoy and former Finnish President Martti Ahtisaari. However, it had been delayed, as it had proved impossible to bridge the gap between Serbian and Kosovo Albanian positions.

In these uncertain circumstances, the PIC's decision was hardly controversial, even though Russia opposed the policy reversal and believed that the OHR could and should have been closed at the end of June 2007.[3] The decision was, nevertheless, only to postpone OHR closure. The issue was one of the timing of the transition from an OHR armed with the Bonn Powers into an EUSR operation equipped with an advisory mandate, not of the transition policy itself.

Having initially been viewed as the personification of local ownership, Schwarz-Schilling used his last four months in office to try to reinvigorate the OHR and the Bonn Powers. He used the threat of imposition to encourage local politicians to pass legislation; he fined political parties in Herzegovina-Neretva Canton for failing to form a government more than six months after elections had taken place; and, in his last week, he imposed a law bringing the Srebrenica-Potočari Memorial Foundation and Cemetery under the authority and financing of the joint institutions.[4] At the same time, Schwarz-Schilling sought to set in motion a constitutional reform process. He did this because he hoped to establish a formal link between constitutional reform and the phasing out of the Bonn Powers, as proposed in the Venice Commission's March 2005 'Opinion on the Constitutional Situation in Bosnia and the Powers of the High Representative'. This was necessary, he believed, to ensure the success of the transition to an EUSR operation, whenever that might come. However, after a handful of exploratory meetings, Schwarz-Schilling left office and the process ended.

Schwarz-Schilling's successor, Miroslav Lajčák, was a Slovak diplomat more than thirty years his junior who had risen to international prominence as Javier Solana's special envoy in Montenegro during the May 2006 independence referendum. His task was to put the peace process back on an even keel and oversee key reforms, such as police restructuring, necessary for Bosnia to sign a Stabilisation and Association Agreement (SAA) with the European Union and begin the long-anticipated transition. In contrast to Schwarz-Schilling, Lajčák cut a forceful figure. He made clear that he would use the authority of his office, if and when necessary. And he immediately used the Bonn Powers to remove an obstructionist police chief in Republika Srpska and to impose legislation confiscating the travel documents of ninety-three war-crimes suspects, thirty-five of whom were serving police officers, setting in train a series of arrests relating to the Srebrenica massacre. However, Lajčák's early momentum dissipated rapidly as a result of continuing deadlock over police reform.

Lajčák attempted to broker agreement on police restructuring by presenting the matter as a purely technical exercise. In a protocol put to party leaders at the end of August, he retreated from the position of his predecessor, who had stuck doggedly to the three European principles, in an attempt to strike a deal and allow Bosnia to move on—to no avail. In frustration, Lajčák reverted to the 'push of Dayton', preparing a number of coercive measures aimed at 'establishing a functional Bosnia'. He hoped that by putting in place a more efficient administration he would encourage political leaders to focus on steps to enhance EU integration, which he believed was what the majority of the population wanted. However, the first and only decision he sought to impose, on 19 October 2007, failed to achieve its aims in the face of Dodik's opposition[5] and insufficient backing from Brussels.

The issue that Lajčák ostensibly decided to address was that of decision-making procedures in state institutions. In reality, however, Lajčák was attempting to reassert the OHR's influence in Bosnian life after more than two years in which the Bonn Powers had only rarely been used. In this way, Lajčák both imposed amendments to the Law on the Council of Ministers[6] and instructed the joint collegium of the state parliament to change its rules of procedure in the interest of streamlining decision-making by 1 December 2007 or this would also be imposed.[7]

In part because the amendments had a direct impact on Republika Srpska's influence in Bosnia and in part because he did not wish to see the high representative re-establish himself as the decisive force in Bosnian politics, Dodik chose to call Lajčák's bluff. The Republika Srpska National Assembly organised a series of emergency sessions; Serb non-governmental organisations took to the streets in protest; and officials of Dodik's SNSD announced their intention to withdraw from state institutions. Council of Ministers Chair Nikola Špirić resigned, explaining that: 'If the international community always supports the high representative and not the institutions of Bosnia, then it doesn't matter if I am the head of that government or it is Bart Simpson.' Even Serbian Prime Minister Vojislav Koštunica entered the fray arguing that: 'Lajčák's measures and the Ahtisaari Plan for Kosovo are aimed at annulling UN Security Council Resolution 1244 [the Resolution providing for Kosovo's interim status] and the Dayton Peace Agreement, so that the independence of Kosovo could be proclaimed and Republika Srpska abolished.'

Since this situation had been triggered by a decision relating to outvoting in institutions, it appeared reminiscent of the October 1991 crisis when Serb representatives had formed their own legislative body, the Assembly of the Serb People in Bosnia, and some ceased attending the Bosnian parliament.[8] In response, ordinary Bosnians began panic-buying flour and cooking oil. And the EUFOR Commander, German Rear Admiral Hans-Jochen Witthauer, felt obliged to reassure the population that EUFOR would be ready to react in the event of another armed conflict.

Lajčák found himself increasingly isolated and cornered. He could not back down without damaging the legitimacy of the Bonn Powers. Yet he did not have sufficient international support to push ahead because of wider concerns for regional stability in the run-up to a decision on Kosovo's final status.[9] The crisis remained on the boil for more than a month during which fruitless negotiations took place between OHR lawyers and the Republika Srpska authorities.

Ultimately, it was a breakthrough on police reform that brought all sides back from the brink. The six party leaders who formed the governing coalition met with the high representative in Mostar on 28 October 2007 and drafted a declaration on police reform, consisting of the basic elements to which they could all subscribe, paying lip service to the three European principles, and leaving controversial areas for future negotiations. In essence, they agreed to put off addressing the sensitive elements of police reform for a later date within the context of a constitutional reform process, the parameters and timing of which still had to be decided. The six party leaders met again on 22 November in Sarajevo to draft and agree an Action Plan for Implementing the Mostar Agreement. The Action Plan defined a list of six institutions that leaders agreed to establish within six months at the state level. Legislation creating these institutions subsequently became the condition for the signing of an SAA with the European Union.[10]

Also at the Sarajevo meeting, Dodik presented new amendments to the rules of procedure of the state parliament. Although Dodik's proposal differed from the high representative's instructions, it was still considered an improvement and, after a week of further negotiations, was adopted with only minor modifications in the parliament.[11] Two days later, Lajčák issued an 'authentic interpretation' of the imposed decision to amend the Law on the Council of Ministers.[12] Although the high representative did not need to revise the wording of his existing decisions, the effect had clearly been changed. The key to resolving the crisis was, nevertheless, the Mostar Agreement and Action Plan. On 4 December 2007, the day these documents were adopted by the Council of Ministers, European Enlargement Commissioner Olli Rehn arrived in Sarajevo to initial the SAA. As soon as Bosnia adopted laws establishing the six institutions envisaged in the Action Plan, it would be possible formally to sign the SAA. This would put Bosnia's relationship with the European Union on a contractual footing, create additional opportunities for the country and all its citizens and, it was hoped, open a new and constructive chapter in terms of further European integration.

Although the police reform negotiations were effectively over, the scars remained. The Council of Ministers drafted two laws to create the bodies envisaged in the Action Plan. These were presented to parliament in March 2008 and adopted on 16 April.[13] In this way, Bosnia was deemed qualified to sign an SAA with the European Union, which it did on 16 June 2008, almost exactly four years after Lord Ashdown had set the police reform process in motion. The end result, however, was very different from what Lord Ashdown had set out to achieve. Whether or not it had been a strategic mistake to make the signing of an SAA contingent on police restructuring on the basis of the three European principles, both the reform process and the way in which it was eventually resolved were problematic in terms of the transformative potential of the incentive of European integration.

Although the three European principles had been presented as non-negotiable for more than three years, they were abandoned. At the same time, the other preconditions for the signing of an SAA— full ICTY cooperation, PBS reform and public administration reform—were set aside. Moreover, the eventual solution for police reform was, in the opinion of most experts, a step backwards in terms of effective policing, since it created an unnecessary administrative layer, shifted resources away from active policing into administrative structures, and risked provoking turf wars among agencies.[14] Indeed, as soon as the Action Plan was endorsed by party leaders, the EU Police Mission advised the European Commission to develop the document into a more comprehensive agreement so as to avoid adding 'a useless superstructure to the existing police structures and, instead, to create a state structure able to influence the status quo and to move the police restructuring forward'.[15] This did not materialise. The short-term need to neutralise Bosnia in the run-up to the decision on Kosovo had taken precedence over longer-term considerations.

Given the importance of credibility to the prospects of international operations, this short-termism was unfortunate. While opinion polls indicate widespread support among Bosnians of all ethno-national origins for European integration, the European Union, nevertheless, lacks credibility. This is due to its record during the Wars of Yugoslav Dissolution; a perception of weakness as a result of its focus on 'soft' as opposed to 'hard' power; and its ongoing debate over internal reform to cope with its increasing size and how this impacts future enlargement policy.

Failure to halt the fighting during the wars in Croatia and Bosnia has left the European Union with a credibility problem that cannot be resolved by public-information campaigns alone. Moreover, that problem is compounded in Serb minds by the perceived impact of the Badinter Commission on Yugoslavia's disintegration.[16] Although the European Union has developed its security and defence policy (the EU Police Mission was deployed in January 2003 and remained until June 2012, and since December 2004 EUFOR has been responsible for maintaining a safe and secure environment), it has not had to demonstrate its ability to use force. As a result, its resolve remains untested.

A perceived preference for 'soft-power' solutions and Brussels' reluctance to entrust the EU special representative with executive powers make the prospect of progress highly dependent on Bosnian political consensus and the effective use of conditionality. In the wake of the debacle over police reform, however, it would be difficult to persuade Bosnians to take EU conditionality seriously. The lesson Bosnian political leaders took from this experience was that as long as they were sufficiently obstructionist, the European Union would drop its conditions. Even if the European Union were able to use conditionality effectively, the 'pull of Brussels' would ultimately depend on whether the prospect for membership was realistic. This in turn depends on the appetite of member states for further enlargement, which was clearly waning. An EU constitution designed to rationalise the European Union for a membership of twenty-five or more was rejected in referendums in two of the original six member states in 2005, and there were later difficulties in persuading member states to sign a streamlined and less ambitious Lisbon Treaty. This was compounded by disappointment with the performance of Bulgaria and Romania following their admission to the European Union at the beginning of 2007, and concerns over the impact of bringing in relatively poor countries at a time of global recession and rising unemployment.

Credibility was also an issue for the OHR. The use of the Bonn Powers had always required tacit approval by local political leaders. Decisions by the high representative had already been challenged in a variety of ways, especially in Republika Srpska, with a raft of issues referred to the Constitutional Court. While most of these were rejected, one was not.[17] In July 2006, the Constitutional Court ruled that the absence of a right of appeal for individuals dismissed by the high representative was a violation of the European Convention on

Human Rights. The OHR managed to sidestep the implications of this ruling with a legal sleight of hand. The high representative provided the Bosnian authorities, specifically the presidency, with a process by which they would be able to comply with the ruling while, at the same time, 'upholding Bosnia's international obligations under Dayton and the UN Charter'; that is, recognising the authority of the high representative.[18] Dodik's challenge to Lajčák was, however, of another magnitude with correspondingly greater long-term consequences.

Although the EUFOR commander went on record during the November 2007 crisis to say that EUFOR would respond in the event of armed conflict, the international military presence was no longer sufficiently large for the high representative to look to it to back up his policies. EUFOR had been the same size as SFOR, namely 7,000-strong, between December 2004 and February 2007. It was then officially reduced to some 2,500 troops, 1,500 of whom were based in EUFOR's Butmir headquarters just outside Sarajevo, with the remainder deployed throughout the country in so-called Liaison and Observation Teams. In practice, however, EUFOR had already hollowed out to a little over 2,000 troops as contributing states failed to provide full contingents.[19]

Having attempted to use the Bonn Powers to take the political initiative and failed, Lajčák decided he could not proceed with coercive measures in the absence of international backing. Although temperamentally willing to adopt a confrontational approach, he considered it pointless without the right tools. As a result, Lajčák focussed on measures to make the transition as smooth as possible: launching a country-wide public-information campaign to promote the European Union and the benefits of European integration; defining criteria that needed to be met before the OHR could be closed and transition could take place; and lobbying Brussels for a well-resourced EUSR operation with an appropriate mandate.

Irrespective of the shortcomings of EU policy, transition to an EUSR operation was the only game in town. This was policy-making by default. Nevertheless, a series of benchmarks for transition—five objectives that needed to be delivered and two conditions that had to be fulfilled—were established at the February 2008 PIC meeting that became known as the 'five-plus-two' agenda.[20] The objectives were: acceptable and sustainable resolution of the issue of apportionment of property between the state and other levels of government; acceptable and sustainable resolution of defence property; completion of the Brčko Final Award; fiscal sustainability (promoted through agreement on a permanent ITA co-efficient methodology and establishment of a National Fiscal Council); and entrenchment of the rule of law (demonstrated through adoption of a National War Crimes Strategy, passage of the Law on Aliens and Asylum, and adoption of a National Justice Sector Reform Strategy). The conditions were signing of the SAA and a positive assessment of the situation in Bosnia by the PIC Steering Board, based on full compliance with the Dayton Peace Agreement.

The key condition, of course, was the second. In order for transition to proceed, even after all objectives had been delivered and the SAA signed, all members of the PIC Steering Board had to give Bosnia a clean bill of health and agree that the Dayton Peace Agreement had been implemented. This meant that the decision was going to be political. Given enduring US interest in Bosnia, it would ultimately depend on how the country functioned politically and whether the mechanisms that the European Union was able to put in place to ensure an EUSR operation would be equipped to deal with Bosnia's myriad problems and complexity.

Zero-sum politics and ever-rising tension

The signing of an SAA failed to have the desired impact on Bosnia in terms of building political consensus within the country and focussing minds on European integration. Indeed, the political climate continued to deteriorate during the second half of 2008. In its annual progress report on Bosnia published in November, the European Commission recognised that: 'Lack of consensus on the main features of state-building, frequent challenges to the Dayton Peace Agreement, and inflammatory rhetoric have adversely affected the functioning of institutions and slowed down reform, in particular since the middle of this year.' To be sure, the signing of an SAA was incidental to this further worsening in the political environment. It was partly a consequence of municipal elections that were held in October. Above all, however, it was a manifestation of the zero-sum attitudes that characterised Bosnian politics and the mutually exclusive positions adopted by rival ethno-national leaders in the absence of firm international oversight.

The inflammatory rhetoric that had marred the 2006 elections did not cease on polling day. Nor did it cease after rival ethno-national leaders formed a coalition government in the wake of the poll. Rather, as the extent of the international community's reluctance to move against elected leaders became clear, speech and actions that would once have provoked swift and severe responses from the OHR went unsanctioned and became increasingly common. Moreover, in spite of the sustained international effort to restructure the media landscape, media remained ethno-nationally divided and helped exacerbate and magnify tensions through increasingly partisan reporting.[21]

Silajdžić was the most open about his intentions. Having been out of Bosnia in Turkey for nearly three years before returning to enter the fray over constitutional reform, he was returning to fight the injustices that he perceived both in the Dayton Peace Agreement and in the way that it had been implemented. Republika Srpska had been created by genocide, he argued, and Bosniaks (and Croats) had been unable to return because the same genocidal structures remained in place and had blocked proper implementation of the Dayton Peace Agreement. He used every possible opportunity and forum to make this case in the hope that the international community would change tack and work to dismantle Republika Srpska. For example, he lobbied the Council of Europe Parliamentary Assembly to take a stance against entity voting, and he used his position as chair of the presidency to address world leaders at the UN General Assembly to call for righting the wrongs of the past, to address the genocide that had taken place and the 'ethnic apartheid' created by the division into entities.

Silajdžić took a legalistic approach to revising the Dayton settlement, hoping, in particular, to use the ICJ ruling in the Bosnia versus Serbia and Montenegro case to argue for the abolition of Republika Srpska. Like most Bosniaks, he had expected the ICJ to find Belgrade guilty of genocide throughout Bosnia. Though disappointed by the actual verdict, he nevertheless seized on the judgement concerning genocide in Srebrenica to press his case for overturning the Dayton settlement with the international community. To this end, he supported and possibly inspired calls by the municipality's Bosniak returnees for Srebrenica to be removed from Republika Srpska's jurisdiction. To be sure, Silajdžić was not the only Bosniak leader to make this case. Both Sulejman Tihić of the SDA and Zlatko Lagumdžija of the SDP also made similar arguments. And a group of Srebrenica returnees moved temporarily to Sarajevo where they set up a tent settlement to maintain pressure on local and international authorities.

In the end, Silajdžić failed to turn the ICJ ruling into a tool for revising Dayton. Republika Srpska granted Srebrenica the status of special economic development zone and Schwarz-Schilling appointed his own envoy, Clifford G. Bond, a former US ambassador, to serve as a contact point, to encourage additional international aid and investment. Bond remained for a year, helped generate extra funding for projects in and around Srebrenica, and defused the immediate crisis. For all his rhetoric, Silajdžić's position was weak. Although he could present a cogent case for the injustice of Republika Srpska's creation and continued existence, his only real weapon as Bosniak member of the presidency was moral indignation. He expected the international community to address this issue. And if the international community was unwilling to do so, Silajdžić had no other recourse.

By contrast, Silajdžić's nemesis, Dodik, was in a powerful position to undermine both the Dayton settlement and Bosnia's prospects of EU integration as prime minister of Republika Srpska, and it was Dodik's challenge that the international community had to take more seriously. Despite his inflammatory rhetoric and vulgar language, Dodik too adopted a legalistic approach, arguing that he sought only to uphold the Dayton Peace Agreement, no more and no less. And it was only when Federation politicians, and in particular Silajdžić, challenged that settlement, and by extension the legitimacy of Republika Srpska, that he raised the possibility of an independence referendum.

Since the Dayton settlement had given Republika Srpska a high degree of autonomy, Dodik set out, above all, to reinforce that autonomy. He did this by pursuing policies to strengthen Republika Srpska's economy; by challenging all previous reforms that had reduced the degree of autonomy set out in the Dayton Peace Agreement; and by blocking any reform that appeared to limit Republika Srpska's room for manoeuvre. He also sought to forge the best possible relationship with Russia, viewing a resurgent Moscow as a potential ally. This was against the backdrop of wounded Serb pride in the wake of Montenegrin independence and discussions on Kosovo's final status that culminated in its conditional independence.

In the economic field, Dodik pursued what initially appeared to be business-friendly policies, much as recommended by the international financial institutions. This was in contrast to policies pursued in the Federation and contributed to narrowing the gap in living standards between the two entities that had existed since the end of the war.[22] In addition, he sought to bring in strategic partners via the privatisation of key industries. This included sales of 65 per cent of Telekom Srpske to the Serbian state-owned Telekom Srbija for €646 million[23] and a large stake in Republika Srpska's oil industry to the Russian state-owned Zarubezhneft.[24] In this way, Dodik appeared to be putting the Republika Srpska economy on a more secure footing. He also generated the revenue to give him the financial freedom to adopt an increasingly independent posture. And he gave both Serbia and Russia a vested interest in developments in Republika Srpska.

Soon after returning to power, Dodik and other SNSD representatives began repeatedly asserting that more than fifty competencies had been transferred from entity to state level during the peace process. The implication was that these alleged transfers of competency undermined the autonomy Republika Srpska enjoyed in the Dayton Peace Agreement and should therefore be returned. Eventually, on 14 May 2009, the Republika Srpska National Assembly passed a series of conclusions calling, among other things, for a reassessment of sixty-eight competencies allegedly transferred from entity to state level (as well as related decisions imposed by the high representative).[25]

In reality, however, the majority of these items referred either to competencies expressly listed in the Dayton constitution as belonging to the state[26] or responsibilities not explicitly listed in the constitution, but which had been assumed by the state of Bosnia to fulfil its constitutional obligations.[27] There were, nevertheless, a handful of areas where transfers of competency had taken place based on formal agreement between the entities and the state, usually, but not always, brokered by the OHR.

Formal transfers of competency had taken place during Lord Ashdown's tenure as high representative in the fields of defence; electricity transmission; intelligence; the Indirect Taxation Authority; the High Judicial and Prosecutorial Council; and the Missing Persons Institute.[28] The OHR played a key role in the first five of these areas, but was unaware that a transfer of competency had taken place in the sixth area before Republika Srpska representatives began alleging ethno-national bias in the Missing Persons Institute and demanding its return to the entity level. The Institute had been established by the entities themselves with the support of the International Commission on Missing Persons, the international agency that had done most work in this field. While the international community considered these transfers of competency key to making Bosnia a more functional state governed by the rule of law, Dodik systematically sought to undermine the new institutions in order to reverse the centralisation process.

Dodik's hostility to the reforms overseen by Lord Ashdown was in part a reaction to the duress under which he believed the Republika Srpska authorities had agreed to the transfers of competency. More fundamentally, however, it reflected his opposition to any measure limiting Republika Srpska's 'sovereignty', a stance that had clear ramifications for the prospects of creating a more functional Bosnia through the process of European integration.

EU accession requires aspiring members to have the capacity to comprehend and assimilate a huge number of laws and to participate in a complex supra-national bureaucratic structure. While centralisation is not a goal in and of itself, it had proved an effective way of ensuring that reforms were implemented in the case of the eight Central and Eastern European countries that joined in 2004.[29] In practice, therefore, the process had helped centralise power in the executive branch of government in every new member state. While this appealed to Bosniak political leaders, it was anathema to party leaders in Republika Srpska. Indeed, Dodik repeated regularly during the police-reform negotiations that if presented with a choice between the European Union and Republika Srpska police, he would choose the latter every time. While he did not have to make that choice over police reform, because the issue was postponed for future constitutional reform talks, he faced what he considered limitations to Republika Srpska's sovereignty on most matters relating to Bosnia's European Partnership. In addition, therefore, to seeking to roll back earlier reforms transferring competency from the entity to the state, Dodik also ensured that Republika Srpska representatives in the joint institutions systematically blocked most laws relating to the European Partnership.

The legislative record at the state level was poor by any standard in spite of numerous capacity-building assistance programmes, and, in the case of legislation related to Bosnia's European Partnership, intensive international lobbying. In the course of 2008, for example, only thirty-seven out of 134 laws in the parliament's work plan were passed. The legislative record was better at entity level. However, many adopted laws ran counter to what international officials considered the best long-term interests of the country. This was the case, for example, when the Federation brought in a new system of benefit payments to veterans in the run-up to the 2006 elections. International institutions, led by the IMF, warned that the scale of the transfers would eventually undermine the solvency of the Federation. As a result of greater than anticipated VAT revenues, it was, nevertheless, possible to maintain these payments for the first two years. But as soon as the economy began to slow in response to the global economic downturn, the impact was precisely as the IMF had predicted.

The setting of objectives and conditions for OHR closure nevertheless helped break the deadlock. To find solutions to meet the PIC's objectives for transition and address constitutional reforms aimed at making Bosnia more functional and better equipped for European integration, Dragan Čović of the HDZ BiH,

Dodik and Tihić began a series of meetings in November 2008 known as the Prud process after the name of the village in Odžak, Northern Bosnia, where the three men initially gathered. Though hailed as a breakthrough and certainly contributing to progress in meeting the objectives for OHR closure,[30] the Prud process raised as many issues as it resolved. Constitutional proposals were interpreted differently by each side;[31] all three opened themselves up to accusations of treachery from rival ethno-national leaders; and it was far from clear whether any of them, and Tihić in particular, could actually deliver on anything that they had agreed.

The incentive for Dodik to engage in the Prud process was clear, namely to have the OHR closed. Relations with the OHR and especially with Raffi Gregorian, the principal deputy high representative, hit rock bottom in December 2008 when the Republika Srpska government filed criminal charges against Gregorian, as well as several journalists, non-governmental organisations, international prosecutors, judges and police officials, for being part of a 'joint criminal enterprise' conspiring to damage the reputation of Republika Srpska. This followed repeated requests for the government to hand to SIPA documents relating to various infrastructure projects, including motorway construction and a €110 million government building in Banja Luka, as required by a State Court order on behalf of the State Prosecutor's Office. Eventually, copies of the documents were handed over and the lawsuit was dropped. However, Dodik registered his irritation by saying that he considered it unacceptable for Muslim judges to probe into Republika Srpska's affairs.

In February 2009, SIPA submitted to the State Prosecutor's Office a report into the alleged criminal activities of Dodik and ten other officials and businessmen in Republika Srpska. These activities had allegedly cost the budgets of Bosnia and Republika Srpska more than €70 million. Dodik responded by portraying the report as an attack on Republika Srpska and alleging that Serbs in SIPA were being bypassed. While there may have been procedural irregularities in the way that the report was forwarded to the State Prosecutor's Office, it was the second such report. The first had been filed a year earlier based in part on documents provided by Transparency International, the Berlin-based anti-corruption watchdog.

Dodik was not the first or only leading politician to face corruption charges. Čović had been sentenced in November 2006 to five years in prison for abuse of office.[32] Mladen Ivanić, the former prime minister of Republika Srpska and future Serb member of the presidency, was sentenced in June 2008 to one-and-a-half years in prison for his role in a corruption scandal involving a publicly owned timber company.[33] And Nedžad Branković, the Federation prime minister at the time, was facing criminal charges related to the purchase of a luxury flat.[34] However, Dodik was in a stronger position than his peers. He was also determined to contest the grounds on which he could be indicted and effectively to challenge the entire legal system.

In the wake of the SIPA report, the Republika Srpska government decided that the charges were an illegal act forming part of a conspiracy to abolish Republika Srpska and that it would assess future co-operation with SIPA and the State Prosecutor's Office on that basis. It also announced that it would be conducting an analysis of the work of Bosnia's joint institutions, presumably with a view to withdrawing Serb representatives. At the same time, the Republika Srpska authorities co-operated less and less with the OHR, refusing to share materials, such as draft laws; rejecting the validity of decisions by the high representative, including imposed amendments to the Criminal Procedure Code; and writing directly to the UN Security Council to protest against the actions of the OHR and to challenge the authority of the PIC.

While Dodik was contesting the authority of the high representative, there was no high representative in the country. Lajčák accepted the post of Slovakia's foreign minister at the end of January 2009 with immediate effect. From that time until a successor was appointed at the end of March he only visited Bosnia occasionally and Gregorian took over as acting high representative. Lajčák's successor, the seventh high representative, was an Austrian diplomat, Valentin Inzko, who had been his country's first ambassador to Bosnia at the beginning of the peace process. Given the suddenness of Lajčák's departure, Inzko was obliged to jump into a tense and deteriorating situation with no time to prepare.

WHITHER BOSNIA?

Transitioning

If ever an international official in Bosnia was handed a poisoned chalice, it was Inzko. He became high representative with incomparably fewer resources than any of his predecessors, took over an institution lacking credibility and morale, and inherited a failing transition policy that remained in place because of the absence of an alternative. He was also facing a political challenge from Dodik unlike anything previously faced by the international community; the global economic recession had reached Bosnia and was beginning to bite; and the PIC was more divided than ever. Russia was pressing for immediate OHR closure; most EU countries were resigned to transition for want of an alternative, with the European Commission, France, Germany and Italy determined to hasten that process, and the UK most sceptical about the wisdom of this approach; Canada and Japan were ambivalent about continuing to pick up the tab for peace-building more than thirteen years after the end of the war; Turkey was wary of any move to give up the Bonn Powers; and the United States was concerned by the gravity of the situation yet unable to provide fresh momentum.

As Lajčák departed, he vented his frustration in a series of candid interviews. In these, he described a zero-sum political environment in which rival ethno-national leaders were incapable of working together for the common good; compared the international community to a 'dead horse', hopelessly divided over its approach and role; and made clear that, given the option of becoming Slovakia's foreign minister, he could not stay on as high representative. Although he repeated that the breakup of Bosnia would be 'unacceptable and impossible', describing any unilateral attempt to divide the country as creating a 'new Abkhazia'—a small, impoverished, unrecognised territory whose inhabitants lacked valid travel documents—his tone was not reassuring. Four months earlier, at the end of September 2008, Lajčák had compared the mood in Bosnia to that in Czechoslovakia on the eve of that country's dissolution or in Serbia and Montenegro at the time of Montenegro's independence referendum.

While Lajčák's choice of parallels may not have been wise, they reflected the perceptions of most Bosnians. The situation he described was also in stark contrast to the prevailing view in Brussels. While policy-makers prepared to bring the Dayton process to an end, a fatalistic pessimism set in among Bosnians. This was registered in increasingly negative attitudes towards the future in opinion polls. Indeed, in a poll commissioned by the OHR to provide Inzko with a comprehensive snapshot of attitudes across Bosnia as he took office, the proportion of people saying that the country was heading in the wrong direction was close to 75 per cent.[35]

The first challenge to Inzko's authority came in the form of the conclusions,[36] discussed above, adopted by the Republika Srpska National Assembly on 14 May 2009, which Inzko decided he was obliged to annul after his request for them to be rescinded had been ignored. On 20 June, therefore, he travelled to Banja Luka to explain to Republika Srpska's leadership why he was taking this step. Never before had a high representative felt it necessary to justify his action in this way. Inzko did so because PIC support was ambivalent. Moreover, Dodik was aware of divisions in the PIC, as the substance of PIC discussions was being relayed to him by the Russian ambassador. In addition to Russia, whose ambassador publicly announced his opposition to the Bonn Powers, France, Germany and Italy were reluctant to support the high representative. And EU officials in Brussels also wished to hasten the demise of the OHR so as to proceed with the transition that had already been in the offing for three years.

Double-hatted as both high representative and EU special representative, Inzko was juggling two roles that were increasingly incompatible. As high representative, he was answerable to the PIC and mandated to oversee implementation of the Dayton Peace Agreement, serving as its guardian and final interpreter. As EU special representative, he was answerable to EU High Representative for the Common Foreign and Security Policy Javier Solana and expected to nurture reform processes to assist the country on the road to European integration. The potential contradiction in these roles had not been so evident when OHR interventions served to help Bosnia fulfil the preconditions for an SAA. But when reforms overseen by the OHR in the course of the peace process appeared to be under threat, Inzko faced a dilemma. Should he, as high representative, intervene to prevent the rollback of reforms? Or should he, as EU special representative, give space to domestic authorities, irrespective of the immediate consequences, in the hope that the contractual relationship with the European Union embodied in the SAA would help Bosnians overcome their differences and establish integrative processes to take the country forward?

Dodik's challenge went beyond rhetoric. In addition to single-minded pursuit of maximum autonomy for Republika Srpska, he aimed to undermine the high representative. He did so because the high representative's executive powers represented the primary constraint on his actions and stood behind the State Court, whose prosecutors were conducting the criminal investigation into his affairs. To neutralise this threat, therefore, as well as to improve Republika Srpska's image more generally, Dodik invested heavily in lobbying, employing legal and public relations consultants and opening a series of representative offices in key cities around the world, including, in February 2009, in Brussels.[37]

In 2009 alone, Republika Srpska paid more than $4.6 million to US legal and public relations consultants, making it the third highest spending foreign government on lobbying in the United States. It employed the law firm Picard Kentz & Rowe and the lobbying firm Quinn Gillespie & Associates. Picard Kentz & Rowe deployed one of its partners in Republika Srpska's government building in Banja Luka, and Quinn Gillespie & Associates put retired US Ambassador Ralph R. Johnson, who had served as principal deputy high representative between July 1999 and July 2001, on the account. Republika Srpska also retained the services of public relations company Hill & Knowlton in Brussels.[38] The Republika Srpska government began to use well-argued legal analyses prepared by international lawyers to make its case in international forums, including, for example, submitting reports to the UN Security Council at the same time as the high representative presented his biannual update on the situation in Bosnia. Moreover, the lobbyists systematically met with decision-makers on both sides of the Atlantic to argue, among other things, that the high representative had been acting illegally; that the OHR represented the main obstacle to both Republika Srpska's and Bosnia's development and

Euro-Atlantic future; that Principal Deputy High Representative Gregorian was waging a personal vendetta against Dodik; and that Republika Srpska was a dynamic, vibrant and progressive state-in-the-making held back by being shackled to the rest of the country.

In 2009, one issue dominated the agenda, namely the mandate of international judges and prosecutors at the State Court. In the legislation establishing the State Court, this mandate was set to expire on 31 December.[39] However, the high representative was able to extend it, if he were to use the Bonn Powers. Since Dodik was himself under investigation, he had a vested interest in this decision. Moreover, he repeatedly made clear through the media and in private conversations with international officials that he considered any extension of mandate to be grounds for a referendum.

The head of the State Court and the state prosecutor held a very different view. They argued that the presence of international judges and prosecutors remained critical, both to the functioning and prospects of their institutions and more generally to the rule of law in Bosnia. They therefore wanted the high representative to extend the mandates. The ideal solution, from the international perspective, would have been for the parliament to adopt the necessary legislation. However, the domestic authorities were reluctant to do this, especially in relation to judges and prosecutors working on serious crime, as the targets of many of their investigations were politicians. As the deadline approached and uncertainty grew, international judges and prosecutors began to vote with their feet, applying for and accepting positions elsewhere.

Inzko understood the importance of extending the mandates of the international judges and prosecutors. He also believed that the Bonn Powers were an essential tool that needed to be retained and used to prevent further deterioration. Indeed, he demonstrated his willingness to use the Bonn Powers early on by removing two police officials engaged in illegal activities, including the wiretapping of OHR officials, on 8 June 2009.[40] He also chose to annul the Republika Srpska National Assembly's 14 May conclusions despite PIC members' ambivalence. However, Inzko felt exposed and, like Lajčák before him, let down, as the very people he believed should have supported him unconditionally were both demanding he take action and distancing themselves from those actions.

Before annulling the Republika Srpska National Assembly's conclusions, Inzko had a heated discussion on the matter with Solana who, together with other decision-makers in Brussels, was opposed to the use of the Bonn Powers, irrespective of the significance of the Republika Srpska National Assembly's conclusions. This position reflected frustration at the absence of progress on transition. The European Union was developing its foreign and security policy tools; it had a track record of success in the countries of Central and Eastern Europe; and it could bring resources to reform processes that no other institution or country could. Meanwhile, the OHR-driven process had failed to achieve what its advocates had hoped; the OHR was no longer pursuing a forward-looking agenda, but preparing for closure; and the 'five-plus-two' agenda was stuck. A change of direction was required to reinvigorate the process, which transition could provide.

When Inzko next used the Bonn Powers in September, there was no buy-in from Brussels, even though his impositions were designed to hasten transition. The issue was Brčko and, in particular, the supply of power to the district. Completion of the Brčko Final Award was the third objective for OHR closure and Principal Deputy High Representative and Brčko Supervisor Gregorian sought to end supervision before the next meeting of PIC political directors in November. To this end, he had been systematically addressing outstanding matters to ensure that the District's institutions were 'functioning effectively and apparently permanently' in line with the Final Award. Moreover, he succeeded in cajoling the parliament into adopting a constitutional amendment on 26 March 2009 bringing Brčko under the jurisdiction and protection of the state Constitutional Court.[41] However, he was unable to persuade the parties to agree to amend legislation on citizenship, the framework for electricity supply or the distribution of Bosnia's succession assets. To stick to the planned closure timetable, therefore, Inzko imposed eight measures, followed a day later by an executive order by Gregorian in his capacity as Brčko supervisor.

Diverging attitudes to these impositions illustrate the difference between OHR and EU approaches, priorities and concerns. Inzko and Gregorian were seeking to head off threats to the Final Award from Republika Srpska, which had been undermining the operations of the state electricity transmission utility, Transco. They feared that Republika Srpska's leadership was aiming to break the company up and sought both to make Transco's dissolution more difficult and to prepare contingency plans in case it were to happen. To this end, Gregorian stipulated in his executive order that if any side tried to dissolve, liquidate or incapacitate Transco, the company's property in Brčko would be considered the property of Brčko District. EU officials, by contrast, believed that the Brčko Final Award could have been completed without making an issue of power supply and that, in any case, the most durable, long-term solution was to create a free market in energy within the framework of EU accession. In the event, these differences were academic, as Dodik rejected the impositions, announcing that they would not be published in Republika Srpska's Official Gazette and would not become law.

The scene was set for another confrontation, as there would be no end to supervision in Brčko until the substance of the impositions was resolved. The anticipated clash did not, however, materialise, thanks to an EU-US initiative aimed at taking forward transition. The European Union and the United States came together to try to secure a series of constitutional changes to improve Bosnia's functioning, as well as to find agreement on the 'five-plus-two' agenda to facilitate transition to an EUSR-led process and closure of the OHR.

The hastily organised initiative was originally planned to be limited to a single, open-ended session at the EUFOR/NATO Butmir military base adjacent to Sarajevo Airport, in the hope that an intensive burst of high-level diplomacy might break the deadlock. As it became clear in the preparatory meetings that prospects of a breakthrough were minimal, the initiative evolved into what became known as the Butmir process. This culminated in two sessions of intensive talks on 8 and 9 and on 21 and 22 October 2009 between the highest-level international negotiating team ever assembled in the former Yugoslavia,[42] as well as representatives of seven of the eight political parties which had been involved in the 2006 April Package.Despite the credentials of the international negotiators and promises of accelerated Euro-Atlantic integration, the talks failed to generate any momentum and served, above all, to expose the gulf in positions between the rival ethno-national elites.[43]

Although the international negotiators had tried to reproduce the dynamics of the Dayton negotiations by holding the talks at a military base, the sense of urgency was lacking. One reason for this was timing. Had the Butmir process been launched six months earlier and linked to financial incentives rather than the prospect of Euro-Atlantic integration, the Bosnians might have responded more positively. In 2009, the global economic recession began to take its toll and the Bosnian economy contracted for the first time since the war. The economic downturn helped focus minds and generate the necessary consensus to negotiate a €1.2 billion, three-year standby arrangement with the IMF in May.[44] By October, however, the Bosnian leaders were no longer under any financial pressure and were each determined to project a powerful and uncompromising image exactly a year before the 2010 elections.

Unfortunate timing and poor preparations contributed to the failure of the Butmir process, but the fundamental reason for the deadlock was that the Bosnian leaders had mutually incompatible visions of their country and no incentive to compromise. Dodik was eager to see OHR closure, but unwilling to make the kind of concessions that would have reassured Bosniak and Croat leaders that it was in their interest. Bosniak and Croat leaders were not prepared to countenance OHR closure without the sort of constitutional reform that Dodik had rejected and which, in any case, the international negotiators had not put on the table. There were no quick fixes.

Although the Butmir process did not formally change anything, its consequences were profound, particularly for the OHR, which had effectively been circumvented. Despite preparing background material for the talks and providing logistical support, the OHR was not invited and its representatives were not present at Butmir. Inzko attended as EU special representative, but even in that capacity found himself marginalised. Meanwhile, the deadline for extending the mandates of international judges and prosecutors at the State Court was rapidly approaching.

Before Butmir, there appeared to be consensus in the PIC for the high representative to extend the mandates in the event that the parliament failed to adopt the necessary legislation. After Butmir, this was no longer the case. Rather than recognise that the process had failed, officials maintained the pretence that a deal remained within reach up to and even beyond the PIC political directors' meeting on 18 and 19 November 2009. To this end, they took responsibility for drafting the PIC communiqué away from the OHR to ensure that the final document did not offend the Butmir participants, so as to keep the process alive.

Although Inzko wished to use the Bonn Powers to extend the mandates and was implored to do so by both Bosnian and international judges and prosecutors in the State Court, he was not willing to proceed without international backing. In the wake of consultations in Brussels and Berlin, Inzko presided over an extraordinary, four-hour Sunday discussion of PIC ambassadors on 13 December 2009, at which it was decided that he would extend mandates in the War Crimes Chamber for a further three years—given the importance of the State Court to the ICTY's completion strategy—but that he should not extend mandates in the Organised Crime, Economic Crime and Corruption Chamber.[45] A day later, Inzko made the relevant impositions, announcing them at a press conference flanked by PIC ambassadors.

Dodik responded publicly to Inzko's impositions with another angry outburst and repeated his threat to hold a referendum. In reality, however, this was his greatest triumph. The parliament had not adopted the necessary legislation because the representatives from Republika Srpska had blocked it. And the international community had chosen to back down in the face of Dodik's threats, rather than confront him. The international prosecutor leading the investigation into Dodik and other prominent officials in Republika Srpska left the country and the dossier was passed to a local prosecutor. The case was then transferred from the State Prosecutor's Office to the Republika Srpska Prosecutor's Office in June 2011 and dropped in December of that year for lack of evidence.

The failure of the Butmir process did not herald a reassessment of international strategy. In its conclusions of 9 December 2009, the Council of the European Union formally linked 'transition of the OHR to a reinforced EU presence' to an application for membership in the European Union.[46] While this condition was left out of subsequent EU documents, the OHR had been humiliated. A cartoon on the front cover of the Sarajevo weekly *Dani* the week of the high representative's capitulation illustrated this by portraying Inzko as an executioner wielding an axe, with the US ambassador holding Gregorian's head on the chopping block and Dodik and other Bosnian politicians looking on approvingly. Having been the focal point of the international community and driver of peace implementation for thirteen years, the OHR was now little more than an observer.

Reforms and responsibility

The OHR continued to exist because there was no agreement on how to bring the process it had overseen to a conclusion. While some PIC members—notably the European Commission, France, Germany, Italy and Russia—advocated closure, others—in particular Turkey, the United Kingdom and the United States—were wary of giving up executive powers. In the absence of consensus in the PIC, the OHR was paralysed by its own Steering Board and increasingly passive in the face of challenges to the Dayton settlement. Moreover, the European Commission pressured the OHR via its budget, of which it provided more than 50 per cent,[47] obliging the high representative to cut his staff to a level where he no longer had the resources to fulfil his mandate.

The primary brake on transition was the European Union's unreadiness to take charge. This was complicated by changes to EU structures brought in as a result of the Lisbon Treaty, which entered into force on 1 December 2009, reorganising the European Union to cater to the needs of an enlarged membership. These changes included merging the posts of High Representative for the Common Foreign and Security Policy and the European Commissioner for External Relations into the post of High Representative for Foreign Affairs and Security Policy, and creating a European External Action Service, which was established a year later in December 2010, under that person. The first High Representative for Foreign Affairs and Security Policy, Lady Catherine Ashton, had her work cut out building structures and appointing staff, including determining the nature of the EU presence in Bosnia and identifying a new EU special representative.

Transition planning consisted of a series of internal papers for a 'reinforced EUSR'. The discussion on the size, scope and mandate of the EU presence in Bosnia was similar to that among US policy-makers in the 1990s. The issue, once again, was the extent to which responsibility for Bosnia's evolution should be left to the country's own leaders. Just as many in the Clinton administration had argued that the United States should limit intervention to providing a breathing space for Bosnians to reconcile their differences, many in the European Union believed that the country would only progress when Bosnians took responsibility for their destiny. To this end, they drew up proposals to downgrade EUFOR into a capacity-building and training operation; they opposed any use of executive powers by the high representative, or a more robust mandate for the EU special representative; and they were ambivalent towards the reforms that the OHR had overseen, many of which had been imposed.

In the absence of a 'reinforced EUSR', Inzko limped on as the double-hatted high representative and EU special representative with the OHR focussed on trying to complete the 'five-plus-two' agenda.[48] In addition, Inzko continued to report on the situation in Bosnia both to the PIC Steering Board and, twice a year, to the UN Security Council. In this way, he catalogued the ongoing deterioration in the country, including threats to reforms, but only intervened when the PIC Steering Board agreed that there was no alternative.

By 2010, it was clear that many reforms had been undermined and some new institutions were effectively hollow. The Council of Peoples in Republika Srpska, for example, had been a central pillar of the ethno-national, power-sharing arrangement that emerged out of the 2000 Constitutional Court decision on the constituency of peoples.[49] It comprised representatives of all constituent peoples and Others and had been designed so that any constituent people could block legislation deemed to violate its vital national interest. Having been constituted in 2004, it operated as intended to the end of the term of the 2002–6 legislature. Acting together, the Bosniak and Croat caucuses of the Council of Peoples could and did return any legislation they considered objectionable to the Republika Srpska National Assembly, much to the chagrin of Serb political parties, which were unused to having to take the interests of Bosniaks and Croats into consideration. After the 2006 elections, however, the SNSD found a way to neutralise the Council of Peoples.

At the 2006 elections, the SNSD placed three Croats high on its electoral list to ensure that they were elected to the Republika Srpska National Assembly. This, in turn, enabled the SNSD to appoint three of the Council of Peoples' Croat caucus. Since six out of eight members of a caucus had to support invocation of vital national interest, the SNSD now effectively had a veto over the Croat caucus, which stopped working together with the Bosniak caucus and only invoked vital national interest on extremely rare occasions. While the Bosniak caucus could still invoke vital national interest, the mechanisms designed to address their concerns had been neutralised by procedural rules of the Vital National Interest Panel of the Republika Srpska Constitutional Court. Although four out of seven judges—two Bosniaks and two Croats—generally supported Bosniak caucus invocations of vital national interest, that was not enough. Support of five out of the seven judges was required for an invocation to be upheld. The three remaining judges—two Serbs and one Other—routinely dismissed the Bosniak caucus' concerns.[50]

In 2009 Bosniak caucus invocations of vital national interest were repeatedly rejected, despite being supported by a majority of judges. In protest, the Bosniak caucus boycotted the Council of Peoples and appealed in vain to the entity's Constitutional Court to amend its rulebook. The Bosniak caucus was able to slow the passage of legislation in Republika Srpska, but not to block it. In the meantime, legislation on a wide range of issues, including land reform, taxation, policing and local government, was being adopted that Bosniaks and Croats considered detrimental to the prospects of their peoples in Republika Srpska.

Serb influence in the Federation was little greater than that of Bosniaks and Croats in Republika Srpska. The Serb caucus of the Federation's House of Peoples, the institution tasked with protecting the vital national interest of constituent peoples, was in theory in a stronger position than the Bosniak and Croat caucuses in the

Republika Srpska Council of Peoples, as the Federation's House of Peoples had to adopt all legislation—not just issues of vital national interest—before it could become law. However, the House of Peoples was primarily comprised of Serbs from political parties headquartered in the Federation who toed their parties' line. Indeed, the preponderance of SDP members among the Serbs in the Federation's House of Peoples gave the SDP additional influence over the legislative process in the Federation. Moreover, the Vital National Interest Panel of the Federation Constitutional Court did not have a quorum for many years as a result of a standoff over appointments to the Federation Constitutional Court.[51]

The constitutional amendments that Petritsch had imposed in 2002 to implement the Constitutional Court decision on the constituency of peoples had failed to achieve what had been intended. While the institutions envisioned under the amendments formally existed, they were unable in practice to address the institutional discrimination they had been designed to remedy. The arrangement required executive intervention to function as intended. However, the OHR was no longer in a position to do this, despite the responsibility it had for the constitutional amendments and the executive powers it still theoretically possessed, and institutional discrimination went beyond the issues covered in the Constitutional Court ruling. Indeed, another legal ruling, this time from the European Court of Human Rights, was about to challenge other aspects of the Dayton settlement.

The European Convention on Human Rights (ECHR) and its protocols formed an integral part of Annex 6 of the Dayton Peace Agreement.[52] As such, citizens who believed that their rights had been violated under the ECHR were able to take their country to the European Court of Human Rights (ECtHR) once domestic mechanisms for redress had been exhausted. While no one used this right in the first decade of the peace process, two Bosnian citizens did so in 2006 and 2007—Dervo Sejdić, a Roma, in June 2006 and Jakob Finci, a Jew, in January 2007—after Protocol 12, strengthening the ECHR by guaranteeing the right to equal treatment without discrimination, had come into force in April 2005. They argued that the country's constitution and Election Law were discriminatory as they restricted membership of the presidency and state House of Peoples to constituent peoples and prevented them from running for or being elected to these bodies.[53] The ECtHR merged the two cases and ruled on 22 December 2009 in favour of the plaintiffs.[54]

The judgement came as no surprise. The issues that the Sejdić-Finci case highlighted were obvious shortcomings of the Dayton settlement. The Council of Europe had wanted Bosnia to address these shortcomings at the time of its admission in 2002 and they formed part of Bosnia's post-accession programme.[55] They had also been preconditions for the European Commission's Feasibility Study for the opening of negotiations on an SAA. Although there appeared to be a consensus on the need to address the issues, they had not been considered a priority and were allowed to languish. The ECtHR judgement changed that. The Sejdić-Finci ruling moved to the top of the political agenda, as the European Union decided that the SAA would not enter into force until it was implemented. At the time, this was a hypothetical obstacle. The SAA still had to be ratified by all EU member states, and relations between Bosnia and the European Union were governed by an Interim Agreement. Moreover, elections were scheduled to take place in October 2010, so Bosnia had time to implement the ruling, given its significance for the legitimacy of the country's democracy.

While the Sejdić-Finci ruling was to take on serious implications in subsequent years, it did not represent an existential challenge to the Dayton settlement. Since the amendments required to address the ruling only concerned citizens who were not Bosniaks, Croats or Serbs, implementation did not need to undermine the existing power-sharing arrangement, unlike the 2000 Constitutional Court decision on the constituency of peoples.[56] However, whereas the OHR had held the authority to oversee implementation in 2000, this was no longer the case in 2009. After nearly four years of deterioration in the political environment, the prospects of agreement on any substantial change were minimal. The domestic authorities failed to agree to changes before the 2010 elections; the ballot, nevertheless, took place; and there were no consequences for political parties of the failure to implement the Sejdić-Finci ruling.

The elections also failed to generate positive change, although they did alter the balance of power among political parties. Dodik was elected president of Republika Srpska and his party, the SNSD, was able to form a government with a comfortable majority, continuing its existing coalition with the Demokratski narodni savez (Democratic People's Alliance, or DNS) and the Socijalistička partija (Socialist Party, or SP), despite winning fewer seats in the Republika Srpska National Assembly. The economic downturn probably contributed to the decline in Dodik's support, but had been cushioned by privatisation receipts and, in particular, the IMF standby arrangement. Moreover, Dodik's rhetoric appealed to many Serb voters who believed that he had delivered on much of what he had promised in 2006. Silajdžić, by contrast, had failed to deliver and was defeated in the contest for Bosniak member of the presidency by Bakir Izetbegović, son of the late Alija.

Dodik had not delivered a referendum, but he had gone beyond the rhetoric of secession and taken concrete steps in this direction. In the run-up to Kosovo's independence declaration, the SNSD adopted a set of conclusions, one of which claimed the right to self-determination, including secession. After Kosovo declared independence on 17 February 2008, the Republika Srpska National Assembly proclaimed that it had 'the right to determine a position on its legal status through... a referendum'. In February 2009, Serb political parties and the Republika Srpska government adopted a constitutional platform envisaging Bosnia as a 'union of independent states' and alluding to the possibility of entities holding referendums on secession. And on 10 February 2010, ostensibly in response to Inzko's extension of the mandates of international judges and prosecutors working on war crimes, the Republika Srpska National Assembly adopted legislation enabling Republika Srpska to conduct a referendum.

Having consolidated his hold on power after the 2010 elections, Dodik was emboldened to call the international community's bluff again. To this end, he proposed a referendum on the State Court and the 'anti-constitutional laws and activities of the high representative in Bosnia' that the Republika Srpska National Assembly adopted on 13 April 2011, together with a series of conclusions similar to those annulled by the high representative nearly two years earlier. The question on the ballot, which was tentatively scheduled for

June, was: 'Do you support laws imposed by the high representative in Bosnia, in particular the laws on Bosnia's State Court and Prosecution?' It was not a referendum on secession, but it was a direct challenge to the high representative's authority and the Dayton settlement and, as such, galvanised the international community. With the exception of Russia, the PIC rallied around Inzko, who had made the case for a robust response in Brussels, in Washington and at the United Nations. He specifically sought the intervention of Lajčák, his predecessor, now managing director for Russia, Eastern Neighbourhood and the Western Balkans in the European External Action Service, to help find a solution.

Dodik may have been surprised by the extent of opposition to the referendum, given how little backing Inzko had received to date. It rapidly became clear, however, that the international community could not afford to allow the proposed referendum to proceed and would endorse the use of the Bonn Powers in the event that Dodik refused to back down. In addition, the Federation parliament took an uncompromising stance, adopting a declaration rejecting the right of Republika Srpska to hold a referendum on a state competency.[57] The stakes were rising and Dodik needed a face-saving way out.

Lajčák's solution was to bring forward discussions between Bosnia and the European Union on judicial reform, even before the SAA came into force, to improve the rule of law in preparation for EU membership. It was ingenious in that it did not involve conceding anything of substance and yet Dodik could present it as an improvement on the status quo. It also helped put European integration at the top of the political agenda. And it even held out the prospect of accelerating EU accession, as it involved opening up one the most challenging fields for reform at the very beginning of the process. To seal the agreement, Lajčák travelled with Lady Ashton to Banja Luka on 13 May 2011 to meet with Dodik, who agreed to drop the referendum 'for now'. On 1 June the Republika Srpska National Assembly cancelled its earlier decision to hold a referendum. And on 6 June 2011, European Enlargement Commissioner Štefan Füle launched the Structured Dialogue on Justice at a two-day inaugural meeting in Banja Luka.

The fact that the European Union's most senior diplomat had journeyed to Banja Luka to negotiate with Dodik appeared to confer a level of credibility on Republika Srpska's president that many believed was not merited. Lady Ashton's intervention had, nevertheless, helped avert an unprecedented crisis. It also heralded the ascendency of the European Union among international organisations in Bosnia. And the outcome was satisfactory for much of the diplomatic community, though not the OHR. While Dodik backed down on the referendum, he would not budge on the Republika Srpska National Assembly conclusions. Moreover, the OHR was not invited to participate in the Structured Dialogue and thereby further marginalised.

To take the EU agenda forward, Peter Sørensen, a dynamic Danish diplomat, was appointed head of the EU delegation[58] and EU special representative from 1 September 2011. Inzko relinquished his EU special representative hat and the Office of the EUSR was decoupled from the OHR. This change resolved the contradiction in the two mandates that Inzko had held. However, by dividing capabilities, it had the unintended consequence of undermining the unity of purpose in the international community. Moreover, there was not much reinforcement in the EU presence. Staffing of the Office of the EUSR was modest by comparison with that of the OHR, at around eighty. The EU Monitoring Mission had already been closed at the end of 2007. The EU Police Mission was to be shut down at the end of June 2012. And although plans to give up EUFOR's Chapter VII peace-enforcement mandate were not approved, EUFOR was reduced to 600 soldiers in September 2012.

Deadlock, decay and debt

Sørensen was expected to bring the SAA into force as soon as possible, as, by this stage, it had been ratified by all member states.[59] The SAA had not come into force automatically due to failure to implement the Sejdić-Finci ruling, as it was felt that the SAA would have to be immediately suspended until Bosnia had resolved the matter to the satisfaction of the ECtHR. Instead, the EU Council decided that the SAA could come into force after adoption of a State Aid Law, adoption of a Census Law and 'credible effort' had been made toward implementation of the Sejdić-Finci ruling.[60] These were modest demands by any standards. Yet just over three years later, when Sørensen left the country, the SAA had still not come into force. Bosnia's political landscape remained deadlocked throughout his mandate; the country became increasingly dependent on borrowing; and the fabric of Bosnian society appeared to be decaying.

The extent of the failure was not a reflection on Sørensen's diplomatic skills, but of Bosnia's zero-sum politics and the short-comings of his mandate. Despite discussion of an 'EU toolbox', the options at Sørensen's disposal were limited and essentially consisted of advising, assisting, facilitating, monitoring and co-ordinating.[61] At the time of Sørensen's appointment, there had, nevertheless, been great optimism about the prospects of the 'reinforced EU presence'. This was the result of a breakthrough in visa liberalisation, which made it incomparably easier for Bosnians to travel abroad and appeared to herald more enlightened decision-making among Bosnia's political elite and to illustrate the benefits of adhering to the EU reform agenda.

The European Commission prepared a 'visa road map' for Bosnia (and four other countries in the Western Balkans) in mid-2008 with forty-two benchmarks that needed to be implemented for citizens to qualify for visa-free travel to 'Schengen Area' countries.[62] These included the introduction of biometric passports, the strengthening of law-enforcement capabilities and the adoption and implementation of relevant legislation, as well as harmonising aspects of entity and Brčko District criminal codes with the state criminal code. The reforms were negotiated, agreed and implemented in the course of 2009 and 2010 so that the European Union was able to reward Bosnians for completing a series of reforms with visa-free travel from 15 December 2010.[63]

In spite of optimism at the time, visa liberalisation did not herald a new dawn. The incentives that had spurred action were specific to visa liberalisation and the electoral timetable. A large proportion of Bosnian citizens had a tangible interest in visa-free travel and, as the October 2010 elections loomed, the electorate could punish political parties obstructing the process at the ballot box. Even so, Bosnia was slower than most of its Western Balkan peers in meeting the benchmarks. Moreover, the compromises reached were generally designed to circumvent controversial issues and avoid upsetting existing internal balances. The struggle to form a state government in the wake of the elections represented a more realistic indicator of the prospects for Bosnia with the support of a 'reinforced EU presence'. When Sørensen arrived in Bosnia, nearly a year after the elections, it had not been possible to form a new state government and the largest Croat political parties did not consider the Federation government legitimate. Sørensen was, therefore, stepping into the greatest governmental crisis the country had faced in the post-war period. Paradoxically, most international officials saw the results of the 2010 elections as more encouraging than those of 2006. Silajdžić had ceased to be a political force and Dodik's influence was reduced, albeit only slightly. Media tycoon Fahrudin Radončić launched a political party, the Savez za bolju budućnost (Union for a Better Future, or SBB), which picked up support among dissatisfied Bosniaks and appeared to present a pragmatic alternative to the SDA. The HDZ BiH polled poorly for a second successive election, albeit better than in 2006, and smaller Croat political parties appeared to be emerging from its shadow. And the SDP, the primary beneficiary of international political party support programmes, achieved its best post-war election results, becoming the largest political party, with its candidate for the Croat member of the presidency, Željko Komšić, re-elected with more than twice as many votes as Izetbegović, the Bosniak member.

The political deadlock at the state level that followed the 2010 elections was, in part, a consequence of the international community's unilateral retreat from the Bosnian political scene; in part, a result of political miscalculations and rash tactics by the SDP; and, in part, a manifestation of the clash of irreconcilable political agendas. Even after a government was formally established—sixteen months after the ballot—the deadlock continued throughout the four-year mandate as coalition partners squabbled, alliances shifted and inflammatory rhetoric polluted the political atmosphere.

The international community's retreat from the Bosnian political scene represented a fundamental change to the way the peace agreement had been implemented since December 1997 and left a vacuum in which unfulfilled agendas returned to the forefront of

Bosnian politics. Whereas once the OHR had set the parameters of acceptable behaviour in public life with the threat of impositions or removals, it now only intervened on the extremely rare occasions that the PIC Steering Board agreed no other course of action was possible. This greatly reduced the prospect of anyone holding political office being sanctioned. And it enabled political parties to revert to type and to focus energies on dominating the public sector so as to foster, maintain and control networks of patronage at a time of declining resources.

Flushed with electoral success, SDP President Zlatko Lagumdžija boasted that the poll had been the 'largest victory of the left in Bosnia since 1945' and promised to use the SDP's mandate to 'change the paradigm' in Bosnian politics. To this end, he made clear that he expected to be appointed chair of the Council of Ministers and agreed a political platform with two smaller, predominantly Croat parties—Hrvatska stranka prava (Croat Party of Right, or HSP) and Narodna stranka Radom za boljitak (People's Party for Work and Betterment, or NSRzB)—and the SDA to form a government in the Federation. This brought him into direct conflict with the HDZ BiH and the HDZ 1990, both smarting from Komšić's re-election to the presidency. The HDZs[64] believed it was the turn of a Croat to chair the Council of Ministers, as the incumbent was a Serb and his predecessor had been a Bosniak, and that only those parties for whom a majority of Croats had voted could legitimately represent Croats in government. The HDZs' position and that of Lagumdžija were mutually incompatible, exposing fundamentally contradictory interpretations of the Bosnian constitutional system. As Lagumdžija bulldozed forward, excluding both HDZs from the Federation government, Croat frustration grew, with implications for implementation of the Sejdić-Finci ruling.

The international community had no intention of becoming involved in government formation, but found itself dragged in when the ramifications of the conflict between the parties gathered around the SDP's platform and the HDZs became clear. To forestall the prospect of an SDP-led government, the HDZs delayed appointing delegates to the Federation House of Peoples. This was in violation of the constitution, but there were also no constitutional remedies for such a situation and without a House of Peoples it would not be possible to adopt a budget. To ensure that vulnerable groups continued to receive benefits in the coldest months, therefore, Inzko intervened on 26 January 2011 to impose temporary financing for the first three months of the year. To help find a compromise between the SDP and the HDZs, the OHR launched a mediation process in which key PIC ambassadors also participated.

The stumbling block, which ultimately proved too difficult to overcome, was the issue of Croat representation. The HDZs argued that as they represented the parties for which the majority of Croats had voted, they were the legitimate representatives of Croats and should be entitled to all governmental posts earmarked for Croats. The OHR persuaded the SDP to accept a compromise whereby eleven out of these posts went to the HDZs and two to the SDP. However, the HDZs were not prepared to compromise and the talks ended on 15 March. They had overplayed their hand in the expectation that the international community would not countenance the formation of authorities without them. This miscalculation may have been influenced by months of speculation that Germany, the country they considered most sympathetic to their cause, was planning a diplomatic initiative (that never materialised) in Bosnia. In the end, it fell to the German ambassador to explain to the HDZs that the international community would not stand in the way of the SDP forming a government without them.

The SDP moved ahead as expected and formed a government on 17 March 2011 together with the HSP, NSRzB and SDA. Živko Budimir of the HSP was elected Federation president with only thirty-three out of fifty-eight delegates in the House of Peoples sworn in. Budimir's predecessor, Borjana Krišto of HDZ BiH, challenged the legality of Budimir's election both with the Central Election Commission (CEC) and the Federation Constitutional Court.[65] Although not competent to make such a ruling, the CEC deemed the election to have been illegal at an extraordinary session on 24 March with a decision that was scheduled to come into force before the Constitutional Court reached its verdict. In response, Inzko suspended the CEC's decision in anticipation of the Constitutional Court's verdict.[66] But before the Constitutional

Court could pass judgement, Krišto withdrew her appeal.[67] This left the Federation government in place on the basis of a high representative's decision and the HDZs bitter and frustrated. The HSP and NSRzB inherited control over appointments in the public sector, including in public companies, at the Federation level, and HDZ officials lost their positions. The HDZs decried this outcome, rejected the Federation government as illegitimate, and revived the Hrvatski narodni sabor (Croat People's Assembly, or HNS), a body that had originally been created in 2001 as an interim step to a third entity.[68] Moreover, there were knock-on effects for relations between the entities. The Republika Srpska government adopted a conclusion stating that it considered the Federation government to be illegitimate and would, therefore, no longer work with it.

Lagumdžija had set out to build coalition governments 'on programmes rather than arithmetic', but his tactics had undermined the prospects of government formation at the state level and alienated the majority of Croats, who had not voted for the SDP or its partners. By seeking to chair the Council of Ministers, Lagumdžija had overturned the convention of rotation of the head of government among constituent peoples. Only when he relented, enabling Vjekoslav Bevanda, a Croat, to succeed Nikola Špirić, was it possible to form a government. Lagumdžija's belated motivation to compromise was the need for another standby arrangement with the IMF. Interest was scheduled to become due on disbursements from the 2009 standby arrangement in September 2012, and although Bosnia had only drawn on about a third of the €1.2 billion that the IMF had made available, it was not in a position to begin repaying. A Council of Ministers was formed in February 2012 comprising the HDZs, the SDA, the SDP and both the SDS and the SNSD, which had joined forces at state level to defend the interests of Republika Srpska. The new ruling coalition did not, however, stay together long, disintegrating within three months, as relations between the SDA and SDP broke down. Lagumdžija decided to end the coalition with the SDA in May after its delegates voted against the budget, and to seek accommodation with the SBB at the state level, and to bring the HDZs into government at the Federation level.

Lagumdžija succeeded in ousting the SDA at the state level so that a new Council of Ministers in which the SBB replaced the SDA was formed in November. However, he was unable to form a new Federation government with the HDZs, as the HSP, NSRzB and SDA used every possible legal and procedural mechanism to remain in office. SDA deputies in the Federation House of Peoples invoked Bosniak vital national interest, secure in the knowledge that the case could not be heard because of the absence of a quorum on the Vital National Interest Panel of the Federation Constitutional Court. Meanwhile, Budimir refused to resign as Federation president despite spending thirty days in custody in April and May 2013 before being indicted for allegedly accepting bribes in return for granting amnesties. The result was a governmental crisis in the Federation that lasted until the 2014 elections.

Although the Council of Ministers formally existed, the parties in the governing coalition had very different agendas, representing the very different visions they had of Bosnia. Moreover, relations between them were extremely fragile. Indeed, the SDS and the SBB were forced out of the ruling coalition in October 2013 and April 2014 respectively. The coalition partners had, nevertheless, been able to agree a new €380 million, two-year standby arrangement with the IMF in September 2012. This was critical to keeping the country afloat financially and enabled it to begin repaying interest on money borrowed under the 2009 standby arrangement.

In the month that the Council of Ministers was formed, February 2012, both the State Aid Law and the Census Law were adopted. All that remained for the SAA to be enacted, therefore, was 'credible effort' toward implementation of the Sejdić-Finci ruling. By this stage, however, two parliamentary commissions created to find a solution, the first formed during the 2006–10 parliament, had recognised failure. In the absence of a domestic institutional process to address the issue, the European Union found itself obliged to step in, making this the focus of EU efforts in Bosnia and working together with the leaders of the country's most powerful political parties to try and break the deadlock. However, despite establishing a High Level Dialogue on the Accession Process in June 2012, a solution proved elusive.

Although a multitude of potential solutions to the Sejdić-Finci ruling exist, the issue became complicated by red lines drawn by various parties and, above all, by the fallout from Komšić's re-election to the presidency. Party leaders from Republika Srpska insisted on direct election of the member of the presidency from Republika Srpska and most party leaders in the Federation were not prepared to accept an asymmetrical solution. This, therefore, ruled out indirect election of presidency members. Meanwhile, the leaders of the HDZs viewed the exercise primarily in terms of revising the way in which the Croat member of the presidency was elected so that only a candidate elected on the basis of the majority of ballots cast by Croats, thereby genuinely representing Croat opinion, would be able to win office.

As the proportion of Croats in the population declined, the HDZs feared for the future of Croats in Bosnia and the prospect of their marginalisation in a country increasingly dominated by Bosniaks and Serbs. They considered Komšić's re-election as Croat member of the presidency illustrative of their inability to shape their own destiny.[69] It was unconstitutional, they argued, because the presidency was not intended for any Bosniak, Croat and Serb, but the key representatives of the country's three constituent peoples. The HDZs also resented the reforms imposed by Petritsch in 2002 in the wake of the Constitutional Court decision on the constituency of peoples, believing that they undermined the Croat position in Bosnia. Moreover, their exclusion from the Federation government since the 2010 elections reinforced their sense of alienation and their determination to use the leverage they had in relation to the Sejdić-Finci ruling to change the settlement to their own advantage.

After endless rounds of negotiations, deadlines and unfulfilled promises, the European Union was obliged to give up. The 2014 elections took place under rules that did not comply with the Sejdić-Finci ruling. Although both the Council of Europe and the European Union had warned that elections would not be considered legitimate in the event they were held under the same discriminatory framework, there were, once again, no consequences. The major loser of the elections was the SDP, whose proportion of the vote fell from nearly 18 per cent to below 7 per cent, as Bosniak voters deemed them responsible for the failure of the past four years and punished them accordingly. A new left-leaning party, the

Demokratska fronta (Democratic Front, or DF) founded by Komšić after parting company with Lagumdžija, emerged on the political scene at the expense of the SDP. Dodik was re-elected president of Republika Srpska with a reduced margin and the SNSD remained the largest political party in Republika Srpska, despite losing significant support, and, with its existing coalition partners, the DNS and SP, was able to form a government with a narrow majority. Otherwise, the elections also saw the resurgence of the original ethno-national champions, the HDZ BiH, the SDA and the SDS. Meanwhile, the situation facing the new authorities was substantially more challenging than it had been four years earlier.

The 2009 and 2012 IMF standby arrangements succeeded in heading off a severe economic downturn. After declining by 2.9 per cent in 2009, the economy returned to growth, albeit modestly, in 2010 and 2011, declined modestly in 2012, and grew again in 2013 and 2014. In January 2014, the IMF extended the September 2012 arrangement for an additional nine months to June 2015 and increased it to €530 million. The standby arrangements did not, however, achieve as much as the IMF wished. The Bosnian authorities balked at implementing the reforms expected of them—including measures to improve tax collection, reduce public spending and improve the business climate—with the result that the IMF repeatedly froze its lending.

The Bosnian authorities found the reforms demanded by the IMF, as well as other internationally driven reform processes, painful in large part because they challenged the patronage networks in place. Transfers in wealth via the benefit system were high by international standards, but based on right, not on need. Veterans and other politically connected groups were major beneficiaries, while less than a quarter of benefits went to the poorest 20 per cent of the population.[70] Moreover, veterans were an especially vociferous and aggressive group. When the Federation authorities had attempted to reduce veterans' benefits in April 2010, to comply with the terms of the 2009 IMF standby arrangement, the veterans organised protests that turned violent.

Despite opposition, the IMF was more successful than any other international organisation in persuading the Bosnian authorities to initiate reform processes. This reflected both the scale of the need for budget support and the IMF's willingness to halt disbursements when commitments were not met. Nevertheless, the economic outlook remained poor. Debt soared from 18.7 per cent of gross domestic product in 2007 to 44.6 per cent in 2012 (improving to 42.5 per cent in 2013); unemployment rose from 23.4 per cent in 2008 to 28 per cent in 2012 (improving to 27 per cent in 2013); and foreign investment declined from a peak of €1.3 billion in 2007 to €307 million in 2010 and just €214 million in 2013.

The IMF's application of conditionality contrasted with the approach of the European Union. A European Partnership document defining the terms of Bosnia's path towards European integration had been adopted in February 2008.[71] This document set out short-term and medium-term reform priorities, criteria and conditions, including specific legislation at the state level, the strengthening of state institutions and the creation of new ones, including a Supreme Court. In the face of political resistance, however, the document was shelved. Instead, the European Union began in practice to support whatever the country's elites agreed among themselves, seemingly regardless of the implications. This played into the hands of the most obdurate party with the result that EU financing, using the Instrument for Pre-Accession Assistance (IPA), was increasingly channelled into projects promoting entity development rather than state development. In summer 2011, for example, the Republika Srpska government objected to planned IPA-funded projects designed to empower state institutions and was prepared to see Bosnia forego €96 million of IPA projects, rather than allow them to proceed. In order to retain the money, the Federation government agreed to replace the state-level projects with ones at the entity level.[72]

The 2011 EC progress report mentioned for the first time the need for Bosnia to develop a co-ordination mechanism 'within the country's institutions at every level' to take its relationship with the European Union forward.[73] Hitherto, the Council of Ministers and its Directorate for European Integration had been responsible for this relationship but had been unable to deliver a country-wide position. A co-ordination mechanism would place the onus for developing common positions on the Bosnian authorities so as to avoid repeating the IPA funding crisis and ensure that the country communicated with one voice. It also constituted a large concession to the Republika Srpska leadership, which interpreted it as representing an alternative path to European integration, circumventing the need for reform of internal political structures and the prospect of centralisation.

The importance placed on implementation of the Sejdić-Finci ruling and the time spent on it did not preclude progress in other areas. Yet there was no progress. Annual EC progress reports, often referred to as 'no-progress reports' by EU officials themselves, catalogued the consequences of political deadlock. These amounted to stagnation at best, and decay at worst. In October 2012, the Zemaljski muzej (National Museum) closed its doors as a result of budget cuts and disagreement over the financing of national cultural institutions.[74] In September 2013, Bosniak returnees in two parts of Republika Srpska removed their children from school, demanding changes to the curriculum to accommodate their ethno-national identity. Even the Structured Dialogue was not immune. In December 2011, Republika Srpska adopted a Law on Courts that weakened the authority of the state-level High Judicial and Prosecutorial Council (HJPC), was at odds with state legislation and undermined the independence of the judiciary.

Despite deadlock in most areas, ethno-national political elites were able to find common ground on matters in which they had a vested interest. In July 2012, for example, the parliament amended a Law on Conflict of Interest that had been imposed by the high representative, watering down the definition of conflict of interest and sanctions. And in November, the SDP and SNSD reached agreement on an agenda to transfer powers from independent bodies like the HJPC, the Central Election Commission and the Civil Service Agencies, all established under international oversight, to politicians.

Although the substance of the SDP-SNSD Agreement was never realised, it contributed to a growing perception that political elites were out of touch, unaccountable and corrupt. While a large proportion of the population faced hardship, falling living standards and declining prospects, their leaders appeared focussed on feathering their nests, ensuring that they would face no repercussions and avoiding responsibility. As frustration grew, conditions were ripe for street protests. The first large-scale demonstrations, which were triggered by a dispute over identity numbers and documents, took place in front of the state parliament in Sarajevo in June 2013 and remained peaceful. The next large-scale demonstrations, in February 2014, which started as protests of employees of bankrupt public companies in Tuzla, spread across the country and erupted into violence in several cities in the Federation.

The June 2013 demonstrations were christened the *bebolucija*, or baby revolution, as they were motivated by concerns for newborns who were not being issued identity numbers as a result of failure to implement a Constitutional Court ruling. Protesters gathered in front of the parliament to pressure deputies into agreeing a compromise so that newborns would receive identity documents. The issue galvanised around the death of a baby girl, whose departure for urgent medical treatment abroad had been delayed because of the dispute. Deputies from Republika Srpska insisted on different identification numbers for Republika Srpska. Deputies from the Federation opposed this solution, since it went beyond the Constitutional Court's ruling.[75] A temporary solution was agreed to assuage the protesters and, six months later, the parliament adopted the legislation after Federation deputies caved in and accepted different identification numbers in the two entities.

Popular protests began in Tuzla on 4 February 2014 and turned violent a day later. More protesters gathered on 6 February in cities throughout the country in solidarity. On 7 February, Mostar, Sarajevo and Zenica experienced large-scale riots and the burning of landmark buildings, including the presidency in Sarajevo. In the wake of the riots, the governments of Sarajevo, Tuzla and Zenica-Doboj Cantons resigned and citizens spontaneously established plenums to try and channel the protesters' anger in a positive direction. The plenums drafted lists of demands and programmes and protestors continued to gather most days for several weeks, though the numbers dwindled over time.

One of the protesters' motivations was deep-seated frustration at poor governance. This was again in evidence in May when catastrophic flooding across much of the country killed twenty-five people, displaced another 40,000 and affected an estimated 1.5 million. Authorities at all levels failed to rise to the challenge, leaving stricken communities to fend for themselves. In an impressive demonstration of solidarity, ordinary people stepped in to help their less fortunate fellow citizens on both sides of the inter-entity boundary line, with plenums, non-governmental organisations and religious communities spontaneously organising relief efforts. The international community was also quick to respond. The IMF doubled to €191 million the money made available to Bosnia in June to ensure that the authorities had the means to react. The European Union, United Nations and World Bank oversaw a damage assessment exercise, which estimated the destruction to have been greater than €2 billion. A donors' conference was also organised in Brussels in July, generating pledges of €138 million in donations and €670 million in soft loans. However, in the ultimate indictment of post-war reconstruction, most donors insisted on implementing projects themselves rather than entrusting them to local authorities.

Prospects

As Bosnians went to the polls in October 2014, the sense of despair was palpable. According to the 'Global States of Mind 2014' study published that month by Gallup, Bosnia's government was the least popular in the world. It had an approval rating of just 8 per cent with 91 per cent of the population believing government corruption to be rampant. The country had regressed for more than eight years and had been deadlocked for the past four. Moreover, the authorities had been unable to provide a co-ordinated response to the flooding and were now squabbling over how to divide the aid that had been pledged. In the wake of February's unrest, street protests and plenums, many in the international community were hopeful that Bosnians would vote for change. They therefore financed another get-out-the-vote campaign. Inzko, much criticised for his inaction in the face of challenges to the Dayton settlement, urged Bosnians to use their own 'Bonn Powers' at the ballot box. However, the elections failed to set a new course for the country.

In spite of their pessimism about the future, most Bosnians opted to re-elect the same ethno-national parties that had presided over their country's decay. While most would have preferred to see change, few believed they had the luxury to vote for a non-nationalist alternative. This was, above all, because they expected voters from other communities to choose the most extreme option available to them and preferred not to risk undermining their own community's position in the face of that threat.[76] The logic was the same as it had been in every preceding election, serving to perpetuate the cycle of fear, insecurity and loathing the country had been stuck in since the 1990 elections and heralding further zero-sum politics.

Pessimism also reflected the discrepancy between the rhetoric of international policy-makers and Bosnia's reality. International officials urged, implored and occasionally pleaded with Bosnians to see reason, build consensus and focus on their country's European future—to no effect. Bosnia's trajectory since 2006 was a consequence of the fact that the Dayton process appeared to be coming to an end; decision-making was increasingly in the hands of domestic authorities and yet the fundamental issues that had led to war had not been resolved. In these circumstances, Bosnian political leaders behaved as if they were approaching the endgame, jockeying for position in advance of the day when the Dayton settlement had to be opened up.

Endgame or not, Bosnia's evolution would depend on a host of factors. These included developments within the country, in the wider region, and beyond the region in capitals where the mandates of the international community and the policies to be pursued were determined. The behaviour of domestic actors was depressingly predictable. However, the regional situation was incomparably better than at the end of the Bosnian War. The neighbouring states retained an influence, but generally had an interest in stability. Croatia joined NATO in April 2009 and the European Union in July 2013. Serbia started membership negotiations with the European Union in January 2014 and agreed an Individual Partnership Action Programme with NATO in January 2015. This turn-around was clearly positive, though not necessarily permanent.[77] The greatest variable was the international factor. The international community had invested greatly in the peace process and, at times, been engaged to such an extent that it had altered the country's trajectory. For the past decade, however, it has appeared stuck on autopilot and fixated on the process of European integration as the only possible strategy, irrespective of the results.

The OHR's long, drawn-out retreat from Bosnian political life accelerated with the arrival of the 'reinforced EUSR'. PIC ambassadors began meeting on alternative weeks, rather than every week. The PIC Steering Board began meeting twice a year at the level of political directors instead of three times. The OHR no longer prepared reports for these meetings, as they were timed to follow publication of the high representative's biannual UN Report, and even relinquished control over the communiqué-drafting process. In August 2014, the high representative lifted all remaining bans on individuals who had been removed by his predecessors, having already lifted fifty-eight bans in May 2011 in the wake of the arrest of Ratko Mladić. The OHR had also closed its office in Brčko on 31 August 2012, suspending though not formally ending the supervisory regime that had been in place since March 1999.[78]

The decision to retain the Brčko Arbitral Tribunal was the result of a compromise between the European Union, on the one hand, and Turkey, on the other. The European Union had been determined to end supervision for many years and the OHR had worked systematically to make that possible without undermining the achievements of the supervisory regime. This involved finding sustainable solutions for the issues, such as electricity supply, which Inzko had sought to impose in September 2009, as well as obtaining formal recognition of Brčko's status in Republika Srpska. While the Republika Srpska authorities never formally endorsed the Arbitral Award, the government did adopt a decision changing the entity's official map from one in which Brčko was presented as an integral part of Republika Srpska to one in which Brčko was marked as distinct.[79]

In spite of assurances on Brčko, Turkey remained sceptical about Republika Srpska's sincerity. Moreover, both Turkey and other PIC members had concerns about the wisdom of ending supervision, for fear that Brčko might become a magnet for organised crime.

Corruption was endemic, the economy was declining and the District was outside the jurisdiction of either entity. In effect, it was an independent municipality. With Croatia scheduled to become an EU member in July 2013, Brčko was divided from the European Union only by a river and was less than 20km from the Serbian border. To be sure, the supervisory regime had failed to resolve the issue of corruption and its retention would have made little difference to the District's economic prospects. The consequences if Brčko were to become a haven for organised crime would be primarily felt in the European Union, whose representatives appeared willing to take the risk.

By asserting itself in the PIC, Turkey succeeded in placating Federation opinion and retaining an insurance policy of sorts in the event of a challenge to Brčko's status. The Federation parliament had adopted a declaration on 'non-acceptance of termination of supervision for Brčko District' and senior figures were lobbying PIC members to that effect. The Arbitral Tribunal was, in any case, a strange institution by this stage, consisting solely of the Arbitrator, Roberts B. Owen, who was retired and in his eighties. Despite this, Owen, or whoever might replace him, retained the authority to change the Arbitral Award and to give the District to either entity.

Turkey's growing assertiveness reflected frustration at the course of the peace process, disappointment with the OHR's passivity and dismay at the seeming indifference of the European Union to the rollback of reforms. In pursuing diplomatic goals that diverged from the EU consensus, Turkey was following the example set by Russia in the PIC, albeit in a more constructive and less overtly partisan manner. As the high representative's authority declined, Russia tied its colours to Dodik's mast, presenting his positions to the rest of the PIC, arguing against any form of sanction and refusing to sign onto joint positions.[80] Turkey, by contrast, did not align itself with any individual politician, but sought more generally to voice the concerns of Bosniaks to the PIC.

Turkey wanted to maintain a robust OHR for two reasons: because OHR efforts to turn Bosnia into a functional country tallied with most Bosniaks' desire to preserve an integral Bosnia; and because the Dayton structure was so loose that Turkey feared Republika Srpska would attempt to secede in the event of OHR closure. Turkey wanted to see the OHR reinforced so that it could safeguard reforms and, in particular, deal with the many unresolved issues. Moreover, Turkey was particularly concerned by issues relating to the plight of the Bosniak community in Republika Srpska. These included measures to expropriate Bosniak-owned land by stealth;[81] voter registration, especially in relation to Srebrenica;[82] the construction of provocative churches and monuments;[83] failings of the legal system that allowed convicted war criminals to abscond;[84] and discrimination within the education, health and social systems.

While the plight of Bosniaks in Republika Srpska was without doubt grim, all minority communities faced similar pressures, whoever and wherever they were. Moreover, the magnitude of decay throughout the country was so great that an extremely large proportion of the population was socially excluded.[85] Bosnian society was in deep crisis, which manifested itself in rising divorce and falling marriage rates, declining fertility, increased consumption of antidepressants and rising emigration, with opinion polls consistently indicating that more than 70 per cent of the young intended to leave. Meanwhile, the country's institutions were deadlocked and issues were not being discussed, let alone addressed.

In common with Bosniak opinion, Turkey wished to see Inzko use his authority to unblock institutional deadlock as high representatives had done before 2006. Its diplomats argued that the OHR formed an integral part of the peace settlement and had a responsibility to prevent paralysis unless the Dayton Peace Agreement was reformed so that the system could no longer be blocked. Moreover, by not unblocking institutional deadlock, the OHR was helping Dodik to achieve his stated ambition of undermining Bosnia. The OHR now limited its activities to monitoring, occasional mediation and efforts to find solutions to the remaining objectives for OHR closure. The high representative had intervened in January 2011 to suspend legislation adopted in Republika Srpska in September 2010 on state property until the Constitutional Court could rule on its legality.[86] Beyond that, the OHR sought to avoid engagement, but could not prevent its Sarajevo headquarters becoming a focal point for protesters. These included the parents of Bosniak children from Konjević Polje in Republika Srpska, who spent four months sleeping in tents in front of the OHR between 9 October 2013 and 31 January 2014, demanding changes to their children's curriculum to cater for their heritage.[87]

The February riots were a rude wake-up call and exposed the extent of long-term international failure. In response, the European Union developed a six-point Compact for Growth and Jobs, shifting the focus of its efforts to economic and social reforms that it expected the new authorities to work on after the October 2014 elections.[88] In the wake of the vote, the British and German Foreign Ministers, Philip Hammond and Frank-Walter Steinmeier, drew up a joint initiative for Bosnia, which was endorsed as EU strategy in December 2014. Presented as a last chance, the strategy involved changing the sequencing of what was expected from Bosnia to take the process of European integration forward. The presidency and party leaders were expected to adopt a declaration on Bosnia's EU orientation and make a verbal commitment to reform, including eventually implementing the Sejdić-Finci ruling. In return, the European Union would put the SAA into force. Bosnia would be expected to start working on the reform agenda, and the European Council would invite Bosnia to apply for EU membership after the country had made unspecified progress. The European Commission would provide an opinion on the membership application on the basis of how reforms had been implemented, including the Sejdić-Finci ruling. In essence, the issue of constitutional change was shelved to improve prospects of progress in other areas.

The need for economic and social reform was overwhelming. In addition, successful reform processes would help improve the political climate and possibly pave the way for political reform at a later stage. However, given the vested interests in the existing system, it was far from clear that any progress could be made on economic and social issues without fundamental political reform. Moreover, the EU strategy immediately faced obstacles. Dodik rejected a draft declaration prepared by the presidency. And newly elected Croatian President Kolinda Grabar-Kitarović made clear that she was unimpressed with it, since it failed to address the problems faced by Bosnian Croats. A revised declaration, which Dodik considered acceptable, was subsequently adopted by the presidency on 29 January 2015, signed by leaders of all political parties represented in the Bosnian parliament on 12 February, and endorsed by the parliament on 23 February. The EU General Affairs Council announced on 21 April that the SAA would come into force on 1 June 2015.

The prospect of SAA activation may have helped spur the formation of governments at state and Federation levels, as both a Council of Ministers—comprising the DF, HDZ BiH, PDP, SDA and SDS, but not Dodik's SNSD—and a Federation government—comprising the DF, HDZ BiH and SDA—took office on 31 March. Beyond that, however, it failed to reverse Bosnia's trajectory. The failure of the Bosnian authorities to agree a justice reform strategy led the European Commission to cut funding for some 140 prosecutors and support staff investigating war crimes from the beginning of 2015. On 15 January 2015 SNSD deputies in the state House of Representatives began walking out of every session in protest against rejection of their proposal to discuss the removal of the House's Bosniak speaker on account of war-crimes allegations. The Republika Srpska National Assembly adopted a declaration on 17 April pre-empting a decision of the Constitutional Court in a case relating to the Republika Srpska Law on Holidays brought in 2013 by the Bosniak member of the presidency, Bakir Izetbegović, announcing that the National Assembly would not implement the ruling if it did not support the Republika Srpska position. Moreover, the declaration also challenged the presence of international judges in the Constitutional Court and the legitimacy of decisions in which they had been involved.[89] And on 25 April the SNSD passed a resolution at its annual congress to hold an independence referendum in 2018 unless Republika Srpska succeeded in strengthening its autonomy by the end of 2017.

Two days later, on 27 April, a twenty-four-year-old Bosniak entered a police station in Zvornik in eastern Republika Srpska, shot dead a police officer and wounded two others before being killed by police returning fire. This was one of the most serious acts of terrorism since the war and responses to it only exacerbated the situation. Media speculated, among other things, that the attack was belated vengeance against Republika Srpska by the radicalised, returnee son of a Bosniak executed by Serb forces in 1992. Dodik announced that Republika Srpska might withdraw from Bosnia's state security institutions. A week later, the Republika Srpska police raided sites throughout the entity and detained thirty allegedly radicalised Bosniaks in an operation that was not co-ordinated with other policing bodies. Bosniak politicians claimed they were targeting returnees. Dodik justified the action in terms of the defence of Republika Srpska and wrote to UN Secretary-General Ban Ki-moon telling him that Islamic terrorism was a major problem in Bosnia and that the country was the largest exporter of Islamic fighters in the region.

Assessing the threat of Islamic terrorism in Bosnia is difficult. Apart from the Zvornik attack, there had been two other major instances of Islamic terrorism since the end of the war, both in the Federation. The first was an attack on a police station in the Central Bosnian town of Bugojno in June 2010 in which one police officer was killed and six were wounded. The second was a shooting incident in November 2011 in front of the US Embassy in which one police officer and the gunman were wounded. Both incidents involved Bosniaks, one from Sandžak, who had converted to a Wahhabi ideology imported by foreign fighters during the Bosnian War.[90] Some 700 foreign fighters who served with the Bosnian Army are believed to have settled in Bosnia after the war, six of whom were surrendered to US intelligence officials in January 2002 and transported to Guantánamo Bay. Bosnian media report that some 200 Bosnian citizens have travelled to Iraq and Syria to join the Islamic State. Legislation criminalising both participation in and recruitment of Bosnian citizens for conflicts abroad was adopted in 2014 and Bosniaks have been put on trial for these offences. Moreover, the Islamic community has been careful to distance itself from any possible connection to terrorism.

SAA activation was no more successful in improving the political climate than the initial signing seven years earlier. In an unrelated development, the Federation government collapsed within days of the SAA entering force. A week later, Dodik rejected the European

Union's reform agenda, refusing to sign its action plan and obliging new European Enlargement Commissioner Johannes Hahn to cancel his planned visit to Bosnia. And on 15 July 2015 the Republika Srpska National Assembly voted to hold a referendum on the judicial system and the authority of the high representative. Voters in Republika Srpska were to be asked whether they supported the 'anti-constitutional and unauthorised laws imposed by the high representative of the international community, especially the laws imposed relating to the Court and the Prosecutor's Office of Bosnia and Herzegovina'. In a rerun of the 2011 referendum crisis, tensions began rising again.[91]

Even before the new EU strategy was formally adopted, the European Union faced another challenge in Bosnia whose ramifications may prove both significant and sinister. Russia abstained in the November 2014 annual vote in the UN Security Council on extending EUFOR's mandate. The official explanation for this position was that the text had been misused to push Bosnia towards the European Union and NATO. However, since it had never been a problem before, the abstention probably represented a deliberate attempt to undermine Western policy, in retaliation for sanctions against Russia over its actions in Ukraine. In effect, Moscow was making the point that, as a permanent member of the UN Security Council, it decided on EUFOR's future. And it was putting the European Union and the United States on notice that it might choose to bring the EUFOR mandate to an end.

As long as the international community retains a Chapter VII peace-enforcement mandate in Bosnia, it should be in a position to deal with any contingency that might arise. If the mandate were ended, however, the consequences would inevitably be destabilising.[92] Talk of a return to war had grown in direct proportion to the discrepancy between international policy and the gravity of the situation on the ground. Even though Bosnia has had a single army since the beginning of 2006, the country joined NATO's Partnership for Peace at the end of the same year, and little heavy weaponry remains, the possibility of a return to hostilities, albeit very different to the Bosnian War, cannot be ruled out.[93] Indeed, Bosniak and Serb leaders accuse each other of rearming surreptitiously via the proliferation of unregulated hunting clubs, veterans' associations and private security companies. Whether or not any rearmament has taken place—and both sides deny it has—discussions of how a new war might play out are increasingly common and reminiscent of the discussions that took place in 1997, when it appeared that SFOR would withdraw at a time when civilian implementation of the Dayton Peace Agreement had hardly begun.[94]

Issues that risk triggering new hostilities include premature conclusion of the Dayton process and the secession of Republika Srpska. Deciding when the Dayton Peace Agreement has been fully implemented is, of course, subjective. The SDA, still by far the largest and most influential Bosniak party, made a formal declaration on this matter in September 2008 in the run-up to municipal elections. In this document, the SDA presented its analysis of Dayton implementation and listed the areas it believed remained outstanding. It concluded that if the OHR were to close before everything had been implemented, the country would revert to the pre-war constitution of the Republic of Bosnia.[95] In other words, there would be no division into entities and Republika Srpska would cease to exist.

The thinly veiled threat was tantamount to a declaration of war in the event of the OHR's premature closure. Although there is little doubt that Bosniaks would feel under great pressure to return to war in the event of Republika Srpska's secession, it is less clear whether Dodik or any other Serb leader would be reckless enough to take such a step, regardless of the rhetoric. Bosniaks appear most prepared to return to war because they believe that they would be righting a historical wrong, and some feel confident that they would be able to make rapid gains at minimal cost. Many believe that the tide of battle had turned by November 1995 and they were winning the war when it was brought to an end. They have the edge in terms of manpower and view Republika Srpska as extremely vulnerable, especially around Brčko and Sarajevo, to the kind of lightning strike that overwhelmed the Republika Srpska Krajina (Serb Republic of Krajina, or RSK) in Croatia in 1995.[96]

Despite Dodik's rhetoric, it is not clear what he has to gain from secession. He has done well politically out of Bosnia as currently configured. He has been the country's most powerful politician and has effectively controlled state politics as a result of the SNSD's dominance among Serbs, political divisions in other communities and existing decision-making mechanisms. He has also presented himself as the defender of the settlement that ended the war. By contrast, if he were genuinely to attempt to lead Republika Srpska to secession, the consequences could be personally disastrous. He would lose the moral high ground and risk losing territory. At best, he would lead a truncated Republika Srpska into the Abkhazia-style situation Lajčák described. At worst, that truncated territory would be annexed by Serbia. Rationally considered, Dodik is best off continuing to behave much as he has in recent years.

The problem in such an event is the degree of consensus required for Bosnia's political system to function. The most likely eventuality is continuing institutional paralysis, ever-rising tensions and further crises. Under these circumstances, the most optimistic scenario for Bosnia is probably that of Mostar, the divided city that many observers view as a byword for ethno-national extremism and intolerance. Mostar remains effectively partitioned into a Bosniak east and a Croat west more than twenty years after the end of the war there, with minimal numbers of Serbs living on either side. Children attend segregated schools, even where they are educated under the same roof.[97] Mostarians tend to keep to their own side of the city. The partition is, nevertheless, soft. Mostarians cross from one side to the other and ethno-nationally related incidents are rare.

In January 2004, Lord Ashdown enacted a Mostar City Statute in the hope of unifying the city and making it more functional. The six separate municipalities were merged into one city council, with one mayor, budget and administration. However, the city remained mired in zero-sum politics. After the October 2008 elections, it took more than fourteen months and high representative intervention to appoint a mayor. Nor was it possible to organise an election in Mostar in 2012, at the same time as local elections in the rest of the country, as a result of failure to implement two rulings of the state Constitutional Court in relation to the electoral system.[98] Moreover, a subsequent OHR-led facilitation process failed to break the deadlock. The result is that Mostar is governed by a caretaker mayor, lacks a city council, and is increasingly paralysed—nearly four years after elections should have taken place.

As pessimistic as the Mostar scenario might appear for the whole of Bosnia, it might actually be overly optimistic in terms of the prospects for multi-ethnicity. With the exception of Brčko, where the international community effectively imposed multi-ethnicity throughout the municipality in the form of integrated education and quotas in all parts of the administration, Mostar is the only city where different communities live in such close proximity under the same administration and none is dominant.

The most damning element of the Mostar experience is that it indicates that time and money are not healers in the existing political framework. The peace process started earlier in Mostar than anywhere else in Bosnia; more money has been spent per capita than anywhere else apart from Brčko; and there have been more internationally sponsored reconciliation projects per capita than anywhere else.[99] Yet results have been meagre. Attitudes have become entrenched; there is minimal trust between communities; and the city appears to be almost permanently on the edge. The danger is that in the absence of a robust international security presence, incidents may boil over into violence with knock-on effects elsewhere in the country. While the level of tension in Mostar is greater than elsewhere in the country, the underlying political contradictions are much the same at the state level.

While the international community has been reluctant to open up the Dayton settlement for fear of the consequences, that day will eventually come. Ideally, it should come in the form of a well-prepared, inclusive and structured constitutional reform process. Alternatively, it might be forced upon the country in the wake of further ECtHR rulings.[100] Or it might emerge by default out of the complete breakdown of the existing system. However it comes, the relative merits of partition or reintegration will be up for discussion. Dodik, or whoever is in power in Republika Srpska, will seek the maximum degree of autonomy and, ideally, internationally sanctioned secession; the Bosniak leadership will aim for the greatest possible integration and, ideally, the abolition of entities; and the Croat leadership will seek the best formula for protecting the interests of the country's dwindling Croat population, including the creation of a third entity or even internationally sanctioned secession of predominantly Croat areas. It is a recipe for paralysis at best and renewed conflict at worst. As a result, the international community will have to remain engaged, to steer the process and, ultimately, to make difficult decisions about the structures that are most likely to provide long-term stability.

9

CHANGING THE LOGIC
OF BOSNIAN POLITICS

'Among the laws that rule human societies, there is one which seems to be more precise and clear than all others. If men are to remain civilized or to become so, the art of associating together must grow and improve in the same ratio in which the equality of conditions is increased.'

Alexis de Tocqueville

Recognising failure

It is almost impossible to be optimistic about Bosnia's future, if one takes the existing political framework as a given and assumes that international strategy will remain unchanged. Although Bosnian political leaders may, with the benefit of international micro-management, agree to declarations on their country's EU orientation or even satisfy the five objectives set for OHR closure, their outlook and aspirations are so fundamentally different that the country will remain mired in zero-sum politics. Unless this self-destructive calculus can be broken, the peace process will remain paralysed. And unless and until the international community is able to recognise the extent of the failure in Bosnia, it will not be possible to address the systemic nature of the country's malaise.

As things stand, international officials continue to repeat the mantra that there is no alternative to Bosnia's European path and urge the country's leaders to see reason, to temper their rhetoric and to carry out internationally approved reforms. At the same time, they are aware that Bosnia will not be able to make genuine progress unless the country develops a very different constitution and transforms its governing structures. Opinion polls indicate that the vast majority of Bosnians would welcome any initiative to confront the shortcomings of the constitutional structure, if this would allow them to live in a 'normal country'.[1] And yet no one has been prepared to take the lead in guiding such reforms. As a result, international officials find themselves reiterating, on the one hand, that the Dayton Peace Agreement must not be violated and, on the other, that if and when a new constitution is adopted, it must be agreed by local parties.

Despite the reluctance of international officials to re-enter constitutional discussions, the international community will have to take the lead in reforming Bosnia's political system to avert the drift back to conflict. The country's existing institutions are not equipped for the task, and the differences in outlook and aspiration among Bosnians are too great. Moreover, the longer this task is delayed, the more difficult it becomes. Violence remains a risk because of myriad unresolved issues, zero-sum politics and incompatible positions of rival ethno-national leaders. Republika Srpska may be recognised as an integral part of Bosnia in the Dayton settlement, but its continued existence in the absence of the wholesale refugee returns also anticipated in the peace accord leaves a sour taste in the mouths of non-Serbs. Few Bosniaks and Croats who used to live on the territory that is now Republika Srpska have returned and those who have ventured back to stay, as opposed to rebuilding properties to sell, are mostly old and often live in miserable conditions. Many have not returned because return was not a genuine option under the pre-vailing political system, notwithstanding massive international efforts. While the number of people who are still, two decades after the end of the war, interested in return is minimal, the failure of the returns process leaves open wounds.

Recognising the extent of failure in Bosnia is the starting point for developing a more effective strategy, because it is only by understanding that failure and with it the limits of liberal peace-building that it is possible to chart a different course. Unfortunately, the international community finds this difficult because it appears to reflect badly on its work to date. The irony is that it is possible for the performance of individuals and institutions to be good even when the results are meagre—simply because the overall strategy is wrong. The OHR, for example, became an efficient, effective and enterprising institution able to steer the peace process with comparatively modest resources in a remarkably short space of time. Its *raison d'être*, however, was overseeing implementation of a peace agreement that contained so many inconsistencies that it could not provide the basis for a functional state. Bosnia needed to move beyond the Dayton Peace Agreement as rapidly as possible, but international mandates were derived from that same document. As a result, efforts were focussed on specific tasks emanating from the peace accord, rather than on developing effective mechanisms for balancing the interests of Bosnia's communities to move away from zero-sum approaches and help make peace self-sustaining.

Recognising failure requires an audit of the peace process to understand the shortcomings of the OHR's use of the Bonn Powers, as well as a realistic analysis of the consequences of existing trends and policies. And it requires a willingness to remain engaged in the long-term with a very different strategy, rather than handing owner-ship of a dysfunctional and discredited political system to political elites who are the products and beneficiaries of that system.

Recognising failure also requires a fundamentally different approach to presenting and interpreting data—one that highlights where problems are rather than one that focuses on progress. Returns data, for example, are presented in terms of the number of people who have reclaimed their properties rather than the number who have chosen to stay in areas where they belong to a minority community. Yet in terms of rebuilding multi-ethnicity, which has rhetorically been an international aim since 1997 and could be key to longer-term stability, the latter is far more relevant. To be sure, it would be difficult to present returns data in such a way until the results of the October 2013 census have been collated. The ethno-national information has proved sensitive because of the implications for recognising or reifying the results of ethnic cleansing. Until data from the new census are published, the last Yugoslav census of 1991 remains the only benchmark for the division of posts according to ethno-national identity.

There is, nevertheless, a new ethno-national reality in Bosnia. Although homes and places of worship have been rebuilt throughout the country, multi-ethnicity has not been reconstructed. Bosnians have returned to areas where they belong to the ethno-national majority, but only rarely to areas where they would become part of a minority.[2] Instead, they have reclaimed property and sold it on, often to people in a similar situation from a different community, to buy something comparable in areas where they would belong to the majority. This process of ethno-national homogenisation, which assumed horrific proportions in the war, has continued in its aftermath even in areas, such as Sarajevo, where the vestiges of multi-ethnicity remained.[3] Few are prepared to endure the institutionalised discrimination of another community, which goes well beyond anthems, flags and coats of arms (all of which have been challenged in cases brought to the Constitutional Court).[4] Meanwhile, Bosnians of mixed ethno-national origins or in mixed marriages, often well-educated professionals, have emigrated in disproportionate numbers.

One key component of ethno-national rule is the education system. This helps form and reinforce identity and attitudes among the dominant ethno-national group and fails to cater to minority communities. The international community had no specific mandate to intervene in this field under the Dayton Peace Agreement, but the OSCE, under the remit of democratisation, took it upon itself in 2002 to monitor developments and to seek to create more progressive and inclusive approaches—to little effect.[5] With the exception of Brčko, where schools have been integrated since 2001 on the basis of a supervisory decree,[6] schooling remains largely segregated, which in terms of attitudes of the younger generations represents a virtual time bomb.[7]

Despite their publicly antagonistic rhetoric, Bosnia's current generation of political leaders tends to get on well on a personal level[8] in part because they shared a common Yugoslav upbringing and many attended the same schools and universities. Even if they did not attend the very same schools, they were educated in the same classrooms as the country's other communities according to the same, ethno-nationally neutral curriculum. They are therefore able to relate to each other as individuals. This is not the case for children and young adults who have attended school after 1992. Indeed, ten school years have already completed their entire schooling in segregated schools. The result is minimal contact with their peers from other communities and a marked tendency towards chauvinistic stereotyping.[9] Whether by design or simply as a by-product of segregation, the attitudes that have been inculcated in children for the best part of two decades will almost certainly make it more difficult for future generations to work together and to reach compromises.

Polls indicate more extreme attitudes among younger Bosnians who have not grown up and been educated together than among their older compatriots, and a desire to leave the country. The latter is, above all, a result of the lack of opportunities at home, where youth unemployment is close to 60 per cent. But it is also indicative of the failure of post-war reconstruction to create a sound basis for economic growth, in spite of an estimated €10 billion of international aid since the end of the war.[10] Four separate parliamentary commissions have been formed to investigate what happened to the donations Bosnia received in 1996, in 2003, in 2009 and again in 2010. The 2003 commission presented a preliminary report to the parliament in which it concluded that Bosnia received a total of €7.5 billion between 1996 and 2005, of which only €3.5 billion could be accounted for. It failed, however, to complete a final report, in part because of political pressures. Subsequent commissions have suffered a similar fate.

Irrespective of the mixed fate of international aid to Bosnia, the economic burden imposed upon the country by the Dayton structures was such that merely servicing the settlement has always risked bringing it down.[11] Internationally sponsored reforms, especially the introduction of value-added tax, have helped the various tiers of government generate more revenue via more efficient tax collection, and have reduced corruption by improving accounting and increasing

245

transparency. They have also succeeded in cutting defence spending. However, they have not reduced the cost of administration. Indeed, they have occasionally added to the burden by setting salaries for specific groups, such as judges, at levels that are considerably higher in relative terms than in other countries, and establishing additional co-ordination bodies and mechanisms to compensate for the dysfunctionality of the Dayton structures.

Despite the high cost of the administration and international efforts to help reform it, Bosnians are generally poorly served. This is, in part, a result of the country's internal divisions. It is, for example, easier for citizens of Republika Srpska to receive medical treatment in Serbia than in the Federation because medical insurance in one entity does not cover the cost of care in the other. Twenty years after the war, it remains bureaucratically difficult to claim pensions and other benefits when moving from one entity to the other, a situation that is far worse for people who do not belong to the dominant ethno-national group.

While many joint institutions exist, they tend to operate in a dysfunctional manner, despite international monitoring and the presence of embedded international advisors. Instead of working as cohesive units with single chains of command, most joint institutions effectively operate with three internal, ethno-national structures and hierarchies. The result is a massive loss of efficiency. The Foreign Affairs Ministry may be the most extreme case of this syndrome, with diplomats representing, above all, the ethno-national group or political party to which they belong, and the entity they come from, with the foreign minister frequently at odds with colleagues in the Council of Ministers. But the situation is little better in other ministries or state agencies.

One feature of several Dayton institutions, as well as of bodies created in the wake of internationally engineered reforms, has been a built-in international presence. This component of ostensibly domestic institutions has at times proved controversial. It is clear, for example, that the 2000 Constitutional Court decision on the constituency of peoples was the result of the presence of international judges on its bench.[12] The international presence in most bodies has, nevertheless, been designed to be of limited duration, as in the case of the State Court.

While the presence of international judges and prosecutors helped provide additional capacity in the State Court and reinforced its credibility during the early years, an analysis of the results is sobering. With the exception of the trial of Republika Srpska's wartime interior minister, Momčilo Mandić,[13] high-level corruption trials have failed to result in convictions, or, where they have, plaintiffs have managed to avoid imprisonment on appeal. The record is better in war-crimes trials, though still worse than had been hoped when the ICTY began referring cases to Bosnia. That said, political opposition, especially in Republika Srpska, to the continued presence of international judges and prosecutors, was probably indicative of the importance of their contribution to the State Court.

The prospective demise of the OHR brings into question all reforms the institution has overseen, not just those in the judicial field. This is because there are no mechanisms, in the absence of the Bonn Powers, to ensure entity co-operation either with the structures that have been created as a result of these reforms or even with the joint institutions created under the Dayton Peace Agreement. Co-operation depends, above all, on goodwill, of which there is little. Moreover, the very logic of electoral politics in Bosnia appears to be pulling in the opposite direction.

Without doubt, the most important area in which to recognise failure is that of democratisation. While elections take place at regular intervals with minimal fraud, the democratic process has failed to build stability or reconciliation within Bosnia. Rather, it has helped reinforce ethno-national divisions and reward extremist behaviour that undermines the prospects for multi-ethnicity. The results of democratisation must not be measured in terms of voting, but in terms of creating a functional political system in which politicians are accountable to the entire electorate, the provision of effective representation for Bosnians who do not belong to the ethno-national majority, and the establishment of conditions in which multi-ethnicity can not just survive, but thrive.

Salience of ethno-national security[14]

Despite international reluctance to recognise failure in Bosnia, the day will eventually dawn when it becomes impossible to ignore the gravity of the situation. When that day arrives, the international community will have to begin addressing the shortcomings of the peace process. This in turn—whether under the auspices of a high representative, an EU special representative or another mediator— will involve opening up the Dayton settlement. So why, despite the enormous outlay in terms of time, energy and resources, the failure? And how might that failure be belatedly addressed?

There are several explanations for failure, all of which are contributory factors. Building durable peace in the wake of ethno-national war is always a difficult undertaking. The facts that the war lasted for more than three-and-a-half years, that half of the population were driven from their homes and that genocide took place would have made reconciliation and reconstruction extremely challenging in any circumstances. The basic structures of the Dayton Peace Agreement itself, the division into entities, the decision-making processes and administrative burdens made Bosnia as dysfunctional as a country can be. During the first year of the peace process, the focus on holding elections and the refusal to address other issues, such as the liberty and ongoing influence of indicted war criminals, made an already challenging task yet more difficult. Instability in Kosovo and elsewhere in the region, as well as interventions from neighbouring countries, contributed to an environment of near-permanent tension. The use of the Bonn Powers beyond their originally modest conception helped to give the impression that progress was being made, when that progress was often illusory. The 'pull of Brussels' has not proved a sufficiently strong incentive to set in train self-sustaining reform processes to overcome zero-sum, ethno-national politics and to help turn Bosnia into a functional state. And, in recent years, the international community has failed to focus on Bosnia as a result of competing priorities elsewhere in the world.

There is, however, a more fundamental explanation for failure, namely that the liberal peace-building model, which has under-pinned international strategy towards Bosnia, is not sufficient to address the problems of a society emerging from ethno-national war. Indeed, it might even be argued, given the framework provided by the Dayton Peace Agreement, that this approach has exacerbated tensions among Bosnia's peoples, undermining the long-term prospects for peace. Policy-makers have focussed on 'what should be' in a Western liberal democracy, rather than 'what is' in a country where concerns about ethno-national security and survival are paramount. Moreover, they have not been sufficiently courageous or innovative even to attempt to reform the structures into which they have put so much effort, thereby largely neglecting the issue of ethno-national security that is at the heart of the Bosnian Question.

In the wake of ethno-national war, ethno-national identity, however it may have been created, takes on a salience that is far greater than it would have been under other circumstances. Moreover, it will remain the key mobilising factor as long as group members and elites continue to feel that their ethno-national identities are threatened.

In Bosnia, ethno-national security, or what political scientists call the 'societal security dilemma',[15] became an issue in 1990 as the country prepared for multi-party elections. This was in part a consequence of the electoral system, which paved the way for the ethno-nationalisation of politics. At the same time, an already tense situation was made worse by events elsewhere in the Yugoslav Federation and, in particular, violence between Croats and Serbs in Croatia, which spilled over into Bosnia. The electoral system put in place after the war under OSCE supervision, in conjunction with various restrictive provisions of the Dayton Peace Agreement, exacerbated the shortcomings of the original system, making ethno-national identity even more fundamental to politics.[16] And the ethno-national political representatives of each constituent people themselves constituted the threat to the ethno-national identities of the others, in what has become a vicious cycle of fear and loathing.

Well-intentioned state- and nation-building reforms led by the international community may also have had unintended consequences in terms of the societal security dilemma. While generally presented as benign, rational and indispensable, reforms have often been perceived as threatening by one or more community, since they appear to confer advantages on another ethno-national group. Given the centralising tendency of most internationally sponsored reform processes, they have generally appealed to Bosniaks and been opposed by Serbs, with Croats less categorical, but generally hostile. Hence the backlash against internationally sponsored reform processes in Republika Srpska as soon as the international community stopped routinely deploying the Bonn Powers, began downgrading its presence and relaxed its grip on Bosnian processes. Hence, also, opposition to reforms relating to Bosnia's European Partnership. While Schwarz-Schilling, Lajčák and Inzko have all received their share of criticism for appearing to lose control or failing to reassert authority over the peace process, they were, above all, reaping the consequences of the failure to address the societal security dilemma earlier in the peace process. This is best illustrated in terms of the attitudes of both the elites and the wider population in 2005 when Lord Ashdown was still high representative and the peace process was apparently progressing nicely. These attitudes were recorded in extensive opinion polling that formed part of the research for the doctoral thesis of Bosnian-Swedish academic, Roland Kostić.[17]

Had the peace process been on the right track in 2005, ten years after the end of the war, one might reasonably have expected perceptions of threat to Bosnia's ethno-national groups to have diminished. This, however, was not the case. Political leaders from all parties believed that the threat to their own community was great.[18] Moreover, ordinary Bosniaks, Croats and Serbs shared this perspective in as much as it related to their community as a whole throughout Bosnia, even if most indicated that they themselves felt secure and free to express their own culture, religion, language and national symbols in their local environment. In essence, Bosnians of all ethno-national origins felt secure where they belonged to the majority people. Given the extent of post-war ethno-national segregation in Bosnia, this was the case for most Bosnians in most of the country. However, they did not feel secure in areas where they did not belong to the majority and where they considered their people to be under threat.

Identity-related issues are complex and generally alien to the mostly Western officials who have helped guide the peace process. Indeed, the international community has a preference for individual as opposed to group rights, which, despite their prominence in the Dayton Peace Agreement, are often viewed as part of the problem, rather than the solution. The international community has sought to entrench legal safeguards in Bosnian law derived from international human rights legislation relating to minorities. It has also systematically intervened to limit overtly discriminatory practices, and taken measures to make certain aspects of the Dayton settlement more equitable in terms of ethno-national security, in the wake of the 2000 Constitutional Court decision on the constituency of peoples.[19] However, the legal human rights guarantees have failed to persuade many Bosnians that they can live in security under the ethno-national rule of another people. Discriminatory practices reappear as soon as the international community reduces pressure on domestic authorities. The Constitutional Court ruling led to changes at state and entity levels but not at municipal level or in public companies, where it should have had the most impact.

If the peace process is examined through the prism of ethno-national security, it is possible to see the rationality of political behaviour that has perplexed the international community; it is also possible to predict attitudes, likely reactions and trends. While international officials wish to see Bosnians of all ethno-national persuasions join with one another in a common European cause, Croats and Serbs are, above all, fearful of the prospect of domination by or assimilation among Bosniaks. In this context, it is easy to understand Croat leaders' insistence on separate languages and media and the devolution of authority to levels at which they form a majority. Hence also Croat moves towards self-rule in 2001 and enduring aspirations for a separate Croat entity. And hence, too, Serb insistence on the legitimacy and integrity of Republika Srpska, the pre-eminence of the entities over the state and the maintenance of maximum entity autonomy. In Bosnia's ethno-democracy, the ethno-national security of one people is achieved via the ethno-national rule of that people over specific territory at the expense of the others.

Bosnians and their political representatives were, nevertheless, reassured by the international military presence. The peacekeeping force, still some 7,000 troops in 2005, provided the ultimate guarantee that there would be no return to war. Moreover, external security guarantees were welcomed by the elites of all three communities.[20] This was in contrast to all other areas of peace-building. While the predominantly Bosniak political parties SDA and SBiH were positive about external intervention in general and the OHR in particular, as well as external support for nation-building, their Croat and Serb counterparts were universally negative (as was the predominantly Bosniak SDP). Moreover, these views reflected the attitudes of the wider Bosniak, Croat and Serb communities.

Attitudes to issues such as the nature of the Bosnian War and the work of the International Criminal Tribunal for the former Yugoslavia (ICTY) reflected the massive cleavages in Bosnian society, which have not narrowed in the course of the peace process. Predominantly Bosniak political parties and Bosniaks in general considered the Bosnian War to have been a war of aggression, some seeing it waged by both Serbia and Croatia, others holding Serbia alone culpable. Their Croat and Serb counterparts, by contrast, considered it to have been an internal conflict or civil war. Predominantly Bosniak political parties, and Bosniaks in general, considered the ICTY to have had a positive impact on reconciliation, whereas their Croat and Serb counterparts considered its impact to have been negative, viewing the institution as unjust and politically biased against them.[21]

Despite conflicting views of the recent past and the work of the ICTY, there was near consensus on the possibility for peaceful co-existence. All political parties except the Srpska radikalna stranka (Serb Radical Party, or SRS) believed that Bosnia's communities could live together. Most believed they could even live side by side, a position supported by the vast majority of the population of all communities. And the SDP and SNSD members believed in a more interactive co-existence.[22] There should, therefore, be a way of organising Bosnia that enables citizens of all ethno-national origins to live together. This, however, requires opening up the Bosnian Question, namely the issue of relations among Bosniaks, Croats and Serbs, and a degree of inventiveness and innovation that has hitherto been lacking.

The formula of one country, two entities and three constituent peoples was not a solution to the Bosnian Question. It was simply what could be agreed by Alija Izetbegović, Slobodan Milošević and

Franjo Tuđman and their negotiating teams in three weeks of talks after more than three-and-a-half years of fighting. In reforming the settlement, it will be necessary to change paradigm and to address, above all, the issue of ethno-national security. This requires moving beyond the consociational structures that have failed to function in the absence of the necessary consensus. And it means, in particular, addressing the consequences of the country's ethno-democracy, that is, the contradiction between the *demos* and the *ethnos* that generates ethno-national conflict, as well as developing a framework for co-existence, building in a process of reconciliation and thereby changing the logic of Bosnian politics. This task should have been carried out much earlier in the peace process when international resources were greater and attention keener, when the world economy was doing better and there were fewer competing priorities. But even now, it is possible to turn the country around and resurrect the peace process.

Revisiting the Bosnian Question

Revisiting the Bosnian Question involves re-opening all the points of contention that formed the backdrop to the war: statehood; self-determination; sovereignty; definitions of 'nation'; and the institutions of representative democracy. Given that every issue impacts every other, reluctance to open up the settlement has been understandable. The key issue, nevertheless, remains how best to organise relations among Bosniaks, Croats and Serbs in both Bosnia and the wider region to balance the legitimate interests of each community. What makes the process so complex today is the legacy of the past twenty-five years.

While every issue has to be on the table, the process should aspire to concrete goals. Above all, it should seek to create a settlement that is affordable and self-sustaining, in which the international community is not obliged to play an intrusive role. Ideally, it should also ensure that ethnic cleansing is not rewarded. This requires designing a system acceptable to all three communities that also provides ethno-national security and fosters political responsibility. Given the positions of today's ethno-national leaders, the task is akin to squaring a circle. Moreover, the failure of even modest constitutional reform proposals in 2006 would suggest that reform is not likely to be achieved by incremental change.

The point of departure remains the March 2005 Venice Commission's 'Opinion on the Constitutional Situation in Bosnia and Herzegovina and the Powers of the High Representative' that inspired the 2006 attempt at constitutional reform.[23] The enduring significance of this report is that it examined the shortcomings of the Dayton constitutional arrangement in its entirety, viewing the authority of the high representative as an integral part of the settlement. Though critical of the Bonn Powers 'when exercised without due process and the possibility of judicial control', it also recognised the achievements of the high representative, whom it credited with most of the progress that had been made in Bosnia. Moreover, it recommended that the Bonn Powers should be phased out, 'preferably in parallel with a constitutional reform' and that, in the meantime, an advisory panel of independent lawyers should be created to address high representative decisions directly affecting the rights of individuals.[24]

The sophistication of the arguments in the Venice Commission's report was in marked contrast to the subsequent debate over transition from an OHR armed with the Bonn Powers and supported by a military mission with a peace-enforcement mandate to a 'reinforced' EUSR with neither executive powers nor military clout. In the absence of constitutional reforms advocated by the Venice Commission, a shift of such magnitude constituted a radical change to the existing settlement and to the balance of power within the country. For this reason, Serb leaders have been very eager to see the back of the OHR while their Bosniak and Croat counterparts have generally opposed such a move. Although deployment of the Bonn Powers in the manner in which they were used before 2005 is not realistic, the degree of risk involved in giving up all executive mandates is so great as to necessitate some middle course.

The precedent for maintaining long-term executive mandates comes from Austria and Germany in the wake of the Second World War. In both countries, the Allies retained executive powers for decades, though they were not used. Indeed, it was only in March 1991, more than five months after German unification, that the Allies finally relinquished all executive powers.[25] The great difference between the situation in Austria and Germany after the Second World War and Bosnia today is that the Third Reich had not only been defeated but had surrendered unconditionally. The Allies were therefore able to build structures from scratch. In this way, they were able to focus on getting their political, economic and social systems right, to develop blueprints for functioning democracies and to make sure they worked before stepping back. And even then, given the horror of the conflict, executive powers were retained as long-term insurance policies against the possibility of any resurgence of extremist politics.

Although the scale of the Bosnian War is not comparable to that of the Second World War, the conflict was sufficiently traumatic to merit the long-term retention of safeguards against the possibility of further ethnic cleansing and genocide. Bosnia has failed to achieve the degree of responsible governance and stability that Austria and Germany had achieved long before the Allies gave up their executive powers. Bosnia is not a self-sustaining democracy, and the political system remains as insidious and virulent as it was before the outbreak of hostilities.

Brussels' reluctance to entrust the EU special representative with executive powers is understandable if executive powers are assumed to be synonymous with the Bonn Powers. If the role of the EU special representative is to help Bosnia prepare for EU membership, he cannot, at the same time, be overruling domestic political actors and removing individuals from public life. If, however, executive powers are considered a mechanism to head off developments that could lead to ethnic cleansing, only to be used in extreme circumstances, their retention should be acceptable. Moreover, there is an emerging norm in international law known as the 'Responsibility to Protect' (R2P) that would provide the justification for their possible use and help reassure Bosnians that the European Union would not allow a repetition of the events of the first half of the 1990s.

According to the principles of R2P, if a state is unwilling or unable to prevent genocide, war crimes, ethnic cleansing or crimes against humanity, the international community then has a responsibility to step in. Moreover, that responsibility is divided into three parts: the responsibility to prevent, to react, and to rebuild. The concept was developed in a report of the same name compiled in 2001 by the Canadian-funded International Commission on Intervention and State Sovereignty, which was set up originally to examine humanitarian intervention in the wake of NATO's 1999 Kosovo campaign.[26] It was endorsed by world leaders at the September 2005 World Summit, marking the sixtieth anniversary of the founding of the United Nations, in the outcome document.[27]

R2P is relevant in terms of rebuilding after ethnic cleansing and genocide and of preventing any repetition. Moreover, it remains relevant twenty years after the end of the war because of the country's ethno-democracy; because ethno-national political parties are incapable of taking into consideration the interests of other communities; and because the human rights provisions in the Dayton Peace Agreement, as well as the vital-national-interest mechanisms developed in the wake of the 2000 Constitutional Court decision on the constituency of peoples, risk being ignored or removed. Indeed, unless a political system is adopted that genuinely protects the rights of all Bosnians, the international community would be reneging on its responsibility to protect if it were to give up executive powers. Although Bosnian leaders believe they have democratic mandates and should be left alone to govern, the legitimacy of their mandates must be considered provisional as long as they fail to work on behalf of the entire electorate.

How, therefore, might it be possible to square the circle: to construct a political system that provides ethno-national security to all Bosnians wherever they live, but which does so without cementing ethno-national division? How also to achieve this at a time when both the economic and political climates are deteriorating?[28]

If, as discussed in Chapter 8, current trends continue, a return to hostilities cannot be ruled out. While it is easy to forecast future conflict, it is difficult to predict with any certainty how that might develop—and which community is likely to come out best, given the likely involvement of the neighbouring countries. As things stand, the Serb leadership appears to be in the strongest position and is, therefore, most conservative. It is closest to achieving ethno-national security for Serbs by virtue of the division into entities, the inadequacy of non-Serb returns and the fact that it dominates Republika Srpska. While Serb leaders may want more autonomy, they can continue to use the Dayton Peace Agreement to shield Serbs from the threat of Bosniak domination and to block any initiatives that limit their room for manoeuvre. If, however, there were to be a return to hostilities, Serbs would have most to lose, thanks to Republika Srpska's vulnerable geography, lack of international sympathy as a result of the scale of war-time ethnic cleansing and the relative weakness of Serbia.

The Bosniak leadership knows it has numbers on its side. Bosniaks dominate the Federation and would be in a position to dominate the whole of Bosnia if the country were not divided into entities. Their leaders believe that Bosniaks were the injured party in the war and that this injustice, which is manifested in the existence of Republika Srpska, should be put right. They most wish to see change and generally feel the Bosniak position would be improved in the event of new hostilities. However, they would almost certainly be dependent upon Croat and, above all, Croatian support to achieve major change.

The Croat leadership is currently in the weakest position and Croats are generally most disenchanted with the peace process, even though predominantly Croat areas are often the most prosperous. Croat political weakness is a reflection of the dwindling proportion of Croats in Bosnia and the importance of the size of a community in the political system. The marginalisation and ongoing exodus of Croats is the ultimate confirmation to Serbs that Republika Srpska must remain for Serbs to stay in Bosnia. The Croat position is, however, changing in the wake of Croatia's membership of the European Union. Indeed, the Croat leadership's hand may become the strongest, since Bosnia's Croats are also EU citizens and Croatia will be in a position to influence international policy on their behalf. It will be exceptionally difficult for the European Union to uphold policies that appear to leave Croats as second-class citizens.

The stakes in Bosnia's endgame are extremely high. Segregation has not yet run its course. Seeking to achieve ethno-national security in geographic terms leads to conflict, as self-determination for one of the country's peoples will inevitably come at the expense of the other two. Since today's entity boundaries were created by force, they would also have to be defended by force to evolve into genuine ethno-national borders. They are, however, indefensible. As a result, further population transfers would be required before stable ethno-national frontiers might eventually be created, possibly even involving the Bosniak population of Sandžak, which is currently divided between Serbia and Montenegro. The choice facing the various ethno-national elites, therefore, is between making compromises to ensure that no people ends up losing out, on the one hand, and risking the future of their peoples in Bosnia, on the other.

With such high stakes, there has to be interest in an alternative arrangement that provides Croats and Serbs with ethno-national security within Bosnia, and gives Bosniaks a Bosnian state, if such a settlement can be designed. This is not, however, a question to which much international time and thought has been devoted since the Dayton negotiations. So how might Bosnia be reconfigured to move beyond zero-sum politics, creating a win-win situation for all parties and ultimately for the country to evolve into a functioning democracy?

The starting point has to be the building blocks of the state, whether Bosnia should be a country of citizens or of ethno-national groups. Given the salience of ethno-national identity and the strong likelihood that most Croats and Serbs would prefer to live in Croatia and Serbia respectively, the only realistic option is the latter, irrespective of the instincts of Western diplomats and officials. Moreover, specific references to group rights feature prominently in the existing constitutions in the concept of constituent peoples, and ethno-national representation is integral to most key institutions. The issue is not how to remove ethno-national identity from Bosnian society, but how to neutralise its impact by making it explicit, while also accommodating Bosnians who do not identify with the three constituent peoples. That will require changing the way in which ethno-national representation is built into the system by overturning the incentives: to reward ethno-national collaboration instead of conflict and thereby enable different peoples to live together, even if they do not necessarily appreciate one another.

Arguably the most contentious matter in the break-up of the former Yugoslavia was the issue of sovereignty: whether it was fundamentally geographic or ethno-national. As discussed in Chapter 4, Serb representatives argued that it lay in the ethno-national group. This position was, however, rejected by the Badinter Commission, which determined that republican borders would become international frontiers and that Serbs would be entitled to the rights of a minority in Bosnia (and Croatia).[29] The concept of sovereignty within the nation nevertheless remains popular and powerful, and could provide mechanisms to balance different interests. Indeed, the Serb position regarding sovereignty was rooted in Yugoslav legal tradition and the concept of constituent peoples. Constituent peoples were in effect sovereign peoples around whom the country and its republics were built. This explains Serb anger at the Badinter Commission's opinion, and at the Croatian parliament's earlier decision to strip Serbs of their status as a constituent people in Croatia, demoting them to a national minority as soon as the HDZ took office in 1990.[30] Indeed, the ensuing campaigns to carve out Serb territory in both Croatia and Bosnia may even be interpreted as a response to this change in Serb status.

When the Constitutional Court ruled that all three of Bosnia's peoples were constituent throughout the country, it was effectively saying that they were all sovereign and that sovereignty was shared. If developed, the concept of shared sovereignty could be harnessed to establish formal relationships with the neighbouring states and to construct an internal balance among Bosnia's constituent peoples that makes it impossible for one community to dominate the others, building ethno-national security into the settlement.

At present, Croatia and Serbia are both guarantors of the Dayton settlement; the Federation is permitted to form a special relationship with Croatia; and Republika Srpska has done so with Serbia. There would, however, be many benefits both for the region and for Bosnia to forming deeper and more formal relations with both Croatia and Serbia. Since Croats and Serbs are sovereign in Bosnia, most have or are entitled to Croatian and Serbian citizenship, and most would wish to live in Croatia or Serbia, a better arrangement for the entire region could be that of a double confederation. This would also correspond to the arrangement envisaged in the 1994 Washington Agreement to end the Bosniak-Croat War, which established the Federation as a proto-state for the whole of Bosnia, together with a confederation with Croatia.[31]

There are many advantages to a double confederation. In the first instance, the relationships with Croatia and Serbia would become genuinely transparent, unlike today's 'special relationships'.[32] Secondly, it would become possible for people, goods and ideas to move freely within one linguistic and cultural space, making Bosnia a bridge rather than a battleground between Croatia and Serbia. Perhaps most importantly, it would allow Croats and Serbs the desired union with Croatia and Serbia. Such an arrangement is currently unacceptable from a Bosniak perspective, but could have advantages if Bosnia's integrity could be guaranteed and the country's internal structure redesigned.

A double confederation would only be possible if the neighbouring countries behaved responsibly. Here the European Union could play a useful role by imposing strict conditionality on Croatia and Serbia. In the 1990s, such conditionality would have had minimal effect. Today, however, it is in the interest of both Croatia and Serbia to see a stable Bosnia. Moreover, a confederal relationship can be presented by all sides as a victory. It would mean rebuilding the positive links that existed twenty-five years ago, enabling the three countries to combine resources and harmonise procedures in key areas; creating a more fluid population and therefore changing ethno-national composition; and obliging Bosnia, Croatia and Serbia jointly to address controversial issues from the past.

Creating a double confederation would only be acceptable to Bosniaks if accompanied by major internal restructuring, including the dissolution of Republika Srpska. Such a move, which is opposed by all Serb political parties, would only be possible within the framework of a political system that could guarantee ethno-national security without partition. Constructing such a system is difficult because of the legacy of the past twenty-five years: the flawed multi-party democracy established in 1990; the war and ethnic cleansing; the shortcomings of both the Dayton Peace Agreement and its implementation; and the re-introduction of an equally flawed ethno-democracy. No amount of system design will reverse the effects of ethnic cleansing or reconstruct Bosnia as it was before the war. It is, nevertheless, possible to devise systems for balancing the interests of the country's peoples to overcome the institutionalised discrimination faced by so many Bosnians, so that it becomes possible for every Bosnian citizen—or, for that matter, every Croatian or Serbian citizen, if Bosnia were to become part of a double confederation—to make a home anywhere in the country.

Although the legacy of the past twenty-five years limits the options available to system designers, the failure of Bosnia's democracy may ultimately prove useful in fostering reconciliation. As things stand, each people has its own narrative of the past and explanation for how and why Bosnia disintegrated, invariably placing most of the blame at the door of one or both of the country's other peoples. There is, however, a more neutral interpretation that is more historically accurate and has the potential to help rebuild relations between communities. According to this view, Bosnia disintegrated because conflict was imported from elsewhere in the former Yugoslavia, and the multi-party system put in place in Bosnia in 1990 was flawed and became a catalyst for conflict rather than a framework for managing differences. If, therefore, a system can be designed and agreed that builds in ethno-national security, it can also help set in train a genuine reconciliation process.

The shortcomings of Bosnia's consociational democracy have been discussed in Chapter 7.[33] Even political scientists who advocate consociationalism—grand coalitions involving representatives of all peoples, the need for consensus in decision-making and proportional representation—recognise it will not work in the absence of over-arching loyalties to the state and a tradition of elite accommodation. In a society as divided as Bosnia today, consociationalism is not appropriate. An alternative approach to finding accommodation in divided societies, often associated with the writing of Donald L. Horowitz,[34] seeks to shift the focus of politics away from ethno-national identity towards other, less volatile issues. This is achieved by using institutions, and, in particular, the electoral system, to foster inter-ethnic co-operation and 'make moderation pay'. It is often referred to as 'centripetalism', since the objective is to make the focus of political competition centripetal rather than centrifugal, that is, to bring people together.

The fundamental flaw in Bosnia's electoral system is that candidates need only seek votes from one ethno-national group to win office. Bosniaks can be elected without receiving a single vote cast by a Serb or a Croat, and vice versa. Given the lack of ethno-national security, the prime factor motivating the electoral decisions of most Bosnians is fear of the prospect of rule by the two constituent peoples to which they do not belong. Understandably, therefore, almost everybody votes for candidates and parties promising the most robust defence against the perceived threat. But since those parties are themselves the greatest threat to the two other peoples, the consequence is a vicious cycle of fear and insecurity.

The logical outcome of the existing system is conflict, because the incentives reward extremist positions. Having been elected by the votes of a single community, an ethno-national party will only represent what it deems the interests of its people. The experience of both fifteen months of democracy before the war and the peace process to date demonstrates that these parties view every issue in zero-sum terms and are unable to make compromises. Bosnian politicians pursue the most uncompromising tactics because they have learned that the way to get ahead in the existing system is to defend the interests of their own community as aggressively as possible. If, however, the logic of the system were changed, it is possible that the same individuals would adopt very different positions. Indeed, politicians behaved very differently before 1990 in response to a different set of incentives.

Although there are no examples of centripetal democracies to draw inspiration from, the elements of such a system can be put together from electoral practice in various countries and adapted to the Bosnian context. A system involving multiple proportional voting would build in ethno-national security; prevent the tyranny of the majority; provide incentives for conciliation by obliging politicians to seek support from different peoples; give Bosnians a chance to vote on issues, not simply according to their ethno-national identity; facilitate stable and efficient government; and, with time, build a pluralistic party structure.[35]

The surest way to oblige politicians to seek votes from outside their own community is by dividing the electorate into Bosniak, Croat and Serb electoral rolls[36] and using multiple voting. Electors would vote as Bosniaks, Croats and Serbs and cast separate ballots to choose their Bosniak, Croat and Serb political representatives. In addition, Others could vote directly for their own representatives to ensure that they, too, have political representation.[37]

To ensure equitable ethno-national representation, it would be necessary to add several features. Firstly, the ethno-national results have either to be set in advance or to reflect exactly the proportion of each community in the electorate. The ethno-national results might, therefore, reflect the ethno-national breakdown at the time of the 1991 census, pre-agreed figures designed to ensure a particular ethno-national balance, or, most realistically, turnout on the day. If voting is compulsory[38] and simple proportional representation is used, the ethno-national results would match the changing ethno-national composition of the country or region. Secondly, each community must have the same influence on who is elected in the other communities. This is possible by 'weighting' the votes of each community.[39] Thirdly, a minimal threshold of support needs to be set from a candidate's own community to ensure that 'straw men', that is, individuals who do not genuinely represent their own people, are not elected. And fourthly, decision-making in the legislatures has to be on the basis of super-majorities, requiring a majority of Bosniak, Croat and Serb deputies. Under this system, there is no need for additional chambers to protect vital national interests, such as the House of Peoples.[40]

Every element of this system has its roots in earlier Bosnian or Habsburg democratic practice. Separate ethno-national electoral rolls and ethno-nationally designated seats were used by Habsburg legislators who, already in the late nineteenth and early twentieth centuries, had to address very similar issues to those facing Bosnia today. They did this on the basis of accords among peoples living on the same territory. The first such solution was the so-called Moravian Compromise of 1905 between Czechs and Germans.[41] This was followed soon afterwards by similar sovereignty-sharing 'compromises' in Bukovina, among four peoples, and Galicia, between two.[42] As a result of the First World War and the dissolution of Austria-Hungary, however, it is impossible to assess the success or durability of these settlements.

The concept of ethno-nationally designated seats already exists in Bosnia at several levels of government, including the presidency and the Houses of Peoples at state and Federation levels. It was used in the first post-war elections to Mostar's city council (with seats divided three ways among Bosniaks, Croats and Others) as well as the six Mostar municipal councils that then existed (with seats divided on the basis of the 1991 census). Both the ethno-national composition of the proposed 1878 Bosnian parliament and the actual 1910 Bosnian parliament were also predetermined.[43] Ethno-national predetermination of election results is therefore a familiar concept in Bosnia. Moreover, multiple voting was used at the presidential level in the 1990 elections in which seven members—two Bosniaks, two Croats, two Serbs and one Other—were elected.[44] The difference between the 1990 system and the one proposed here is that the former gave Bosniaks a greater say in the selection of Croats and Serbs, while the latter ensures each community an identical say.[45]

If Bosnia were to become a parliamentary democracy in which the key offices of state, such as those of the president and prime minister, were appointed by the legislature, there would be no impediment for any citizen, Bosniak, Croat, Serb or Other, to obtaining any office. In this way, the system would, unlike at present, be in line with the European Convention on Human Rights.

Though complex, the system outlined above is fair in ethno-national terms and considerably simpler and cheaper than the existing system. This approach does not necessarily appeal to Westerners, who may wish to see Bosnia emerge into a classical Western liberal democracy in which the population shares a Bosnian identity. However, that approach has already failed. The proposed system creates a dependency relationship between the

CHANGING THE LOGIC OF BOSNIAN POLITICS

elected and the entire electorate, holding politicians accountable and obliging them to take the views of different communities into consideration if they wish to get ahead. The incentives are designed to foster moderate behaviour. This, in turn, opens up possibilities for moving beyond identity politics, for responsible discussion and analysis of the past, including eventually the creation of a truth and reconciliation (or at least recognition) process, as well as the development of constructive and progressive positions in currently sensitive areas such as education. By recreating a tolerant environment, it also reopens the possibility for mixed marriages and more fluid social and demographic conditions.

Sceptics will inevitably question the capacity of such a system to change the logic of Bosnian politics. It is, therefore, important to trial such a system. Moreover, two places in the country are ideally suited to it: Brčko and Mostar. Brčko remains under a supervisory regime, albeit suspended, and Mostar is unable to agree an electoral system, let alone govern itself effectively. Such a system could therefore be tested in these two places before being rolled out elsewhere. The extent of segregation at the local level today poses problems for the introduction of such a system, given that it is premised on multi-ethnicity, but these problems can be overcome.

The potentially transformative structural reforms proposed here have been presented, above all, to generate discussion on better ways to manage the Bosnian Question. The most important element is the electoral system, which has the potential to change the logic of Bosnian politics. For this reason, it will also be resisted by the existing political elite, which benefits from the current system. Bosnia's unravelling may need to continue before such solutions appear desirable. However, if such a package were ever to be embraced by either the international community or public opinion in Bosnia and then adopted by the Bosnian parliament with the necessary two-thirds majority, it should, ideally, also be ratified by a referendum among every ethno-national group to give it the popular credibility and support that the current settlement has always lacked. Before that can happen, a major public debate will have to take place.

10

CONCLUSION

'Deep-rooted conflict demands deep-rooted conflict management. A doctor who treats a patient's symptoms may bring short-term relief of suffering. But a doctor who treats and cures the underlying illness that caused the symptoms brings a long-term solution to the patient's problems. In conflict management there needs to be a shift of focus, beyond the surface approach of treating symptoms, to a deeper level where underlying illnesses are directly addressed.'

David Bloomfield and Ben Reilly[1]

Treating symptoms

Two decades after the Dayton Peace Agreement came into force, Bosnia is not at war. However, the absence of war is not peace. Bosnia has not moved on from its experience of conflict. The issue of relations among Bosniaks, Croats and Serbs dominates political discourse. Many of the same politicians are still active and continue to use provocative, insensitive and irresponsible rhetoric. The reality is institutionalised discrimination at a local level throughout the country against anyone who is not from the majority community and, increasingly, anyone who is not linked to the ruling political party. Political processes are deadlocked. The country is in a state of political, social and economic paralysis. As the international

CONCLUSION

community has reduced its presence and involvement in the country, conditions have deteriorated steadily, irredentist agendas have resurfaced and the outlook is increasingly negative. The optimism of the immediate post-war period has been replaced by a fatalistic pessimism.

Perhaps none of this should be a surprise. Peace processes often prove disappointing and countries afflicted by ethno-national conflict frequently slip back into war. But Bosnia is different from most countries emerging from ethno-national war. It has received substantial international support over the past twenty years and benefits from both financial aid and the presence of a peacekeeping force. It is not just in Europe but surrounded by the European Union and NATO. Moreover, it has been offered the prospect of eventual membership in both organisations. And despite growing divisions, the country's communities retain powerful, enduring and generally constructive links. Bosnia could and should be in a much better position. Indeed, even today it remains possible to turn the peace process around, though the challenge becomes harder as time passes.

Bosnia has been in crisis ever since Yugoslavia began disintegrating in the late 1980s. Despite its many shortcomings, the Yugoslav Federation had provided a framework in which Bosnians of every ethno-national origin were able to live together and, within the ideological parameters of that state, to prosper. As the most ethno-nationally mixed of Yugoslavia's republics, Bosnia had most to lose from the country's disintegration, but could not immunise itself against this prospect. Conflict was generally imported from elsewhere in the Yugoslav Federation, from Belgrade and Zagreb in particular, despite the wishes of the vast majority of the population. Insufficient time and thought were given to designing and building an appropriate political system in the wake of the demise of communism. Bosnia's fate was more or less sealed in the 1990 elections. As soon as the results came in, processes were set in train whose logical conclusion was the ethno-national division of society and large-scale population transfers.

The international community played little role in Yugoslavia's disintegration. However, the complexity, severity and scale of the fallout from the Yugoslav conflict were such that it could not be dealt with internally. International intervention was required to mitigate its consequences, to bring fighting to an end and to guide the subsequent peace process. The European Community rapidly established an institution—the EC Peace Conference on Yugoslavia—to deal with the whole of Yugoslavia and address the causes of the conflict. In the absence of coercive powers, however, EC mediators had limited options and were unable to address the substance of the Yugoslav crisis in an effective and comprehensive way. In practice, they focussed their energies on the most belligerent parties, pleading with them to be reasonable, determining their minimal positions and seeking to persuade others to accept them. Amid escalating violence, they tried to head off war by mediating Bosnia's division into as yet undefined ethno-national territories—to no avail. As war engulfed Bosnia, the focus of international efforts shifted to the delivery of humanitarian aid.

The International Conference on the Former Yugoslavia that replaced the EC Peace Conference on Yugoslavia also aspired to address all issues emerging from Yugoslavia's dissolution, but ended up focussing on Bosnia. It nevertheless developed as good a blueprint for peace as could have been drawn up after a year of fighting in the absence of international appetite for coercive intervention. Had Washington backed the Vance-Owen Plan and been willing to commit the number of peacekeepers it subsequently deployed to oversee implementation of the Dayton Peace Agreement, the fighting would likely have ended some two years earlier. The Vance-Owen Plan would also almost certainly have been easier to implement, with a better chance of delivering long-term stability, as it built multi-ethnicity into the settlement. However, until the international community was prepared to intervene with force, the fighting continued.

The Dayton Peace Agreement may not have been as impressive or coherent a document as the Vance-Owen Plan, but it was a peace accord as opposed to a proposal and it ended more than three-and-a-half years of fighting. As such, it was a major achievement. Despite many flaws, it also set in train a process that held out the possibility of a better future for all Bosnians. No matter how grim today's situation may appear, it is incomparably better than it would have

CONCLUSION

been had the Dayton talks not succeeded in ending the war. The peace process has, nevertheless, failed and only by recognising this will it become possible to chart a different course and head off the growing danger of a return to violence.

Failure was not pre-ordained, but the result of treating symptoms rather than addressing the underlying illness. The symptoms included physical destruction, a moribund economy and the humanitarian needs of an impoverished population. The underlying illness was and remains the country's political system, that is, its ethno-democracy. The massive reconstruction programme helped alleviate the symptoms so that physically the country looks better; the economy experienced many years of growth until the international financial crisis reached Bosnia in 2009; and the immediate humanitarian needs of the population were largely met. However, the injection of vast resources as if Bosnia had experienced a natural disaster, combined with failure to reform the political system, had the effect of reinforcing the power bases of the ethno-national parties, enabling them to develop and finance patronage networks, thereby aggravating the underlying illness.

Since the peace accord required broad consensus to function and there was little trust among the parties, extensive international involvement was built into the settlement. This meant in practice that Bosnia's evolution was highly dependent on international policy. This, in turn, depended on the level of risk the international community was willing to take and on the desired outcomes: whether the aim was to put things right or to give Bosnians the time and space to find their own solutions.

Political revitalisation was critical to Bosnia's longer-term prospects. However, there has been none. While competitive elections are fundamental to democracy, the assumption that elections are of themselves positive, and that it is possible to learn democracy via repeated ballots, is false. Indeed, a poorly designed electoral system in a multi-ethnic state can have extremely negative, long-term consequences. Bosnia's September 1996 elections were supposed to create the institutions necessary to take the peace process forward. Instead, they cemented ethno-national division; provided 'pseudo-democratic legitimisation of extreme nationalist power structures', as OSCE Chairman-in-Office Flavio Cotti had warned; and entrenched an insidious political system, undermining prospects for multi-ethnicity, reconciliation and lasting peace. Moreover, the flawed 1996 polls cast a long dark shadow across the entire peace process, making the task of creating a self-sustaining settlement more difficult than it had been at the outset.

The international community changed course in 1997 as it became clear that the peace process had stalled, that the country risked returning to war and that greater engagement was necessary to improve the prospect of lasting peace. This new direction manifested itself in a more forceful military posture, which, in turn, opened up opportunities for civilian implementation of the peace accord. The peacekeeping force, which has not suffered a single casualty to hostile fire, began systematically arresting war-crimes suspects, supporting refugee return and intervening in support of the high representative. And the high representative, whose mandate was reinterpreted to augment his authority with the Bonn Powers, became the driving force behind peace implementation.

The OHR started operating on an ever-wider range of fronts to take the peace process forward. On the one hand, it sought to take advantage of political opportunities, such as the power struggle in Republika Srpska. On the other, it sought to address specific obstacles to peace implementation, establishing where problems lay and developing policies to deal with them. In this way, the mission became a well-intentioned effort to do what was best for Bosnia, its peoples and, in particular, the greatest victims of the war. Although the Bonn Powers were originally envisaged to break procedural deadlocks and to deal with specific and concrete threats to peace implementation, they evolved into the primary tool for advancing reforms. In this way, the emphasis of high representative decisions shifted from return-related matters to rule-of-law issues, state- and institution-building measures, and later to decisions seeking to promote European standards of accountability, professionalism and transparency in the political, legal, security, administrative, educational and corporate spheres.

Although no one considered the Dayton settlement to be an optimal solution for Bosnia, successive high representatives feared opening it up. Instead, they focussed their energies on overcoming obstructionism, on the one hand, and on reforms aimed at turning Bosnia into a functional state, on the other. This reached its zenith during Lord Ashdown's mandate. Double-hatted as high representative and EU special representative, Lord Ashdown pressured the Republika Srpska authorities to co-operate with the ICTY by removing large numbers of officials from their posts. And he set up processes that led to the adoption of comprehensive reforms in the fields of intelligence, tax collection and defence, with a view to preparing Bosnia for Euro-Atlantic integration.

By becoming the driver of reforms, the international community became an actor rather than an observer, with the high representative the most important decision-maker in the country. As a result, high representatives had a tendency to present a narrative of success that may have overstated the extent of the progress. The OHR and successive high representatives did not seek to distort reality. Rather, they were obliged both to balance the competing concerns and outlooks of all PIC members and also to spearhead efforts to transform Bosnia from an ethno-nationally divided, dysfunctional and war-torn wreck of a country into a genuine candidate for membership in the European Union and NATO. They were operating in uncharted territory and forced to be innovative, albeit within the structures of the peace accord. Given the scale and complexity of the reforms, they could not expect immediate results. Nevertheless, with the exception of police restructuring, the major internationally supervised, institution-building projects had largely run their course by 2006; the limits of what could be achieved by decree had essentially been reached; and the period during which the use of executive powers could be justified as emergency measures had expired.

Post-conflict to pre-conflict

As long as the OHR maintained a firm hand on the peace process and drove through reforms, it was possible to make it appear as if the country was making progress. Moreover, there had been a number of breakthroughs and genuine achievements, such as defence reform, over the years. However, the scale of the international involvement and the pressure brought to bear on almost every matter were so enormous that they masked the true state of affairs. Since the international community's overriding aim had been to develop self-sustaining institutions capable of taking Bosnia from the 'era of Dayton' to the 'era of Brussels', the ultimate test of the peace process was the ability of those institutions to function in the absence of international intervention. When they were put to the test in the course of 2006 and 2007, they were found wanting.

The test came soon after Lord Ashdown stepped down at the end of January 2006 to be succeeded by Schwarz-Schilling as the fifth high representative and second EU special representative. Schwarz-Schilling came into office committed to overseeing a transfer to local ownership of the peace process. This was to be realised by closing the OHR and restructuring the international presence in favour of a reinforced EU mission headed by the EU special representative to support Bosnia's further recovery and guide it towards eventual membership of the European Union. As the political climate deteriorated and it became clear that this policy was failing, Schwarz-Schilling changed course and persuaded the PIC to keep the OHR open. In addition, before stepping down as high representative, Schwarz-Schilling sought to set in motion a constitutional reform process. He hoped to establish a formal link between constitutional reform and transition from an OHR-driven process to an EUSR operation. This was necessary, he believed, to ensure the success of transition, whenever that might come. In the event, however, the process never went beyond a handful of exploratory meetings.

Both the powers of the high representative and Bosnia's constitutional settlement had been analysed in a report published by the Council of Europe's Venice Commission in March 2005. This document acknowledged that the use of the Bonn Powers had been beneficial for Bosnia and its citizens in the aftermath of war, but argued that the justification for using the Bonn Powers 'becomes more questionable over time'. It also drew specific attention to the weakness of the state government in comparison with the entities. And it concluded that it was 'unthinkable that Bosnia can make real progress with the present constitutional arrangements', drawing a

CONCLUSION

link between the gradual phasing out of the executive powers of the high representative and a parallel process of constitutional reform.

Although the recommendations contained in the Venice Commission's report were purely advisory, they set the scene for nine months of discreet talks on constitutional reforms aimed at equipping Bosnia for EU accession, involving the country's eight most important political parties. Discussions were constructive, despite differences in outlook and objective among participants. The atmosphere deteriorated, however, as a potential agreement on constitutional amendments began to emerge, and ultimately it was not possible to muster sufficient votes for the so-called April Package to be adopted. This failure had a lasting significance for it exposed the depth of feeling on Bosnia's state structure and the difficulty of amending the Dayton Peace Agreement using the mechanisms for change contained within it. Moreover, the acrimonious debate around the April Package unleashed ill feeling that coloured the political atmosphere in the run-up to the October 2006 elections.

Although Schwarz-Schilling succeeded in keeping the OHR open, he failed to alter the direction of international policy towards Bosnia. Transition from an OHR armed with the Bonn Powers into an EUSR mission equipped with an advisory mandate was not tied to constitutional reform. Policy-making was not driven by conditions on the ground, but by fatigue with Bosnia, particularly when growing commitments in Afghanistan and Iraq sapped international resolve. Moreover, the PIC was increasingly divided: Russia was pressing for immediate OHR closure; most EU countries were resigned to transition, with the European institutions, France, Germany and Italy determined to hasten that process, and the United Kingdom most sceptical; Canada and Japan were ambivalent; Turkey was wary of any move to give up the Bonn Powers; and the United States was concerned by the gravity of the situation yet unable to provide fresh momentum.

The key question was whether the 'pull of Brussels' was strong enough to replace the 'push of Dayton' as both the driver of reform and the glue holding Bosnia together. Despite Brussels' success in assisting reform processes in eight formerly communist Central and

Eastern European countries that joined the European Union in 2004, this was asking a huge amount. Indeed, even had international strategy towards Bosnia succeeded in creating genuinely self-sustaining institutions, OHR closure would have been fraught and complex, given the institution's deep involvement in Bosnian life for more than a decade.

From the December 1997 Bonn Peace Implementation Conference, the high representative had been the lynchpin of both the international community in Bosnia and the Bosnian political system, able to prevent paralysis by overriding domestic institutions. By pushing through policies that the domestic authorities would never have agreed among themselves, the OHR was able to take the peace process forward. But even after more than a decade of intrusive international intervention and investment on an unprecedented scale—and despite the carrot of eventual accession to the European Union and NATO—the results in terms of a self-sustaining settlement were modest. Bosnia's reality did not correspond to the rhetoric of progress and Euro-Atlantic integration. The fundamental cleavages, fears and mindsets that had initially paralysed Bosnian society between the 1990 elections and the outbreak of war continued to plague political life.

While opinion polls have indicated for many years widespread support among all Bosnians for closer relations with and eventual membership of the European Union, the European Union has had a credibility problem among the Bosnian population. This was the result of its record during the Wars of Yugoslav Dissolution; an ongoing perception of weakness as a result of its apparent belief in and focus on 'soft' as opposed to 'hard' power; and its own debate over internal reform to cope with enlargement and how that has impacted on future enlargement policy. Moreover, the EU accession process is a mechanism aimed at preparing countries for membership of the European Union, not a tool for managing ethno-national conflict.

In the absence of consensus in the PIC, the OHR was paralysed by its own Steering Board and increasingly passive in the face of challenges to the Dayton settlement. The international community's unilateral retreat left a vacuum in which unfulfilled agendas returned to the forefront of Bosnian politics. Whereas once the OHR had set the parameters of acceptable behaviour in public life with the threat of impositions or removals, it now only intervened on the extremely rare occasions when the PIC Steering Board agreed no other course of action was possible. This greatly reduced the prospect of anyone holding political office being sanctioned. And it enabled political parties to revert to type and to focus their energies on dominating the public sector so as to foster, maintain and control networks of patronage at a time of declining resources.

Bosnia signed a Stabilisation and Association Agreement (SAA) with the European Union, putting the relationship onto a contractual footing, in June 2008. This was supposed to herald a new era, to help build political consensus within the country and focus minds on European integration. However, it failed to have the desired impact. If anything, the downward trajectory that the country had been on since 2006 accelerated after the SAA signing, and has continued accelerating ever since.

The SAA was only signed after principles for police restructuring, which had been presented as non-negotiable for more than three years, were abandoned. The argument for dropping this condition was that it was more important to bring Bosnia into a wider reform process than to insist indefinitely on restructuring in one area at the expense of all others, since it would, in any case, have to be revisited at a later stage. While the logic was sound, the mutually exclusive positions exposed in police reform negotiations proved a harbinger of the fate of other reform processes. Indeed, even after the SAA had been ratified by all EU member states, it could not be brought into force as Bosnia had failed to comply with or even to make 'credible effort' towards implementing the European Court of Human Rights' Sejdić-Finci ruling. Though this became the focus of EU efforts in Bosnia, it was not possible to agree a compromise solution. The importance placed on implementation of the Sejdić-Finci ruling, and the time spent on it, did not preclude progress in other areas. Yet there was no progress. In the face of political resistance, the European Union shelved Bosnia's European Partnership document, the paper setting out short-term and medium-term reform priorities, criteria and conditions, preferring to support whatever the country's elites agreed among themselves. Meanwhile, unemployment jumped, foreign investment slumped and debt soared. The country remained locked in its downward spiral, lurching from crisis to crisis, which eventually, in February 2014, tipped over into violence.

The rioting that affected most cities in the Federation did not degenerate into inter-ethnic conflict, though several leaders tried to present it as such. Moreover, as long as the international community retains a Chapter VII peace-enforcement mandate in Bosnia, it should be in a position to deal with any contingency that might arise. If the mandate were terminated, however, the consequences would inevitably be destabilising. In the November 2014 annual vote in the UN Security Council on extending EUFOR's mandate, Russia abstained, putting the European Union and the United States on notice that it might decide to bring the EUFOR mandate to an end. Even though Bosnia has had a single army since the beginning of 2006, the country joined NATO's Partnership for Peace at the end of that year, and little heavy weaponry remains, the possibility of a return to hostilities cannot be ruled out.

Talk of a return to war has grown in direct proportion to the discrepancy between the rhetoric of international policy-makers and Bosnia's reality. The urging and occasional pleading of international officials hoping to persuade Bosnian political leaders to see reason, build consensus and focus on their country's European future have failed to have any impact. Bosnia's trajectory since 2006 is a consequence of the shift in international strategy to local ownership. The Dayton process has appeared to be coming to an end with decision-making increasingly in the hands of domestic authorities, even though the issues that had led to war have not been resolved. In these circumstances, Bosnian leaders behave as if they are approaching the endgame, jockeying for position in preparation for the day when the Dayton settlement is opened up.

Changing incentives

It is currently almost impossible to be optimistic about Bosnia's future. Bosnian political leaders may agree declarations on their country's EU orientation or even satisfy the five objectives set for

CONCLUSION

OHR closure. However, the country will remain mired in zero-sum politics. Unless this self-destructive calculus can be broken, Bosnia will remain paralysed. And only when the international community is able to recognise the extent of its failure will it be possible to address the systemic nature of the country's malaise.

International officials continue to insist that the Dayton Peace Agreement must not be violated and repeat the mantra that there is no alternative to Bosnia's Euro-Atlantic path. At the same time, however, they are aware that Bosnia will not be able to make genuine progress towards Euro-Atlantic integration unless it transforms its governing structures. Despite this, the international community has no appetite for constitutional reform and would prefer to put it off in the hope that progress can be made via reforms in other areas. The assumption underlying international policy remains that the prospect of Euro-Atlantic integration has the capacity to transform Bosnia, despite a decade of evidence to the contrary.

Reluctance to open up the Dayton settlement is understandable given the results of earlier attempts at reform, including the April Package, the Prud and Butmir processes, and endless rounds of negotiations about how to implement the Sejdić-Finci ruling, as well as prevailing attitudes to reform among Bosnia's political elites. Just as the focus of the Dayton talks was on the map, Bosnia's rival ethno-national leaders think of constitutional reform, above all, in terms of different ways to carve up their country. Each has well-rehearsed and mutually exclusive positions on how this should be done. The Bosniak leadership will aim for the maximum degree of integration and, ideally, the abolition of entities; the Croat leadership will seek what they view as the best formula for protecting the interests of the country's dwindling Croat community, and, ideally, the creation of a third entity; and the Republika Srpska leadership will seek the maximum degree of autonomy and, ideally, internationally sanctioned secession. It is a recipe for paralysis at best and renewed conflict at worst.

Given these diametrically opposed visions for the country, the prospects of positive change coming from within are minimal. If current trends continue, Bosnia will almost certainly remain paralysed, the economy will continue to decline and society will decay, with inevitable knock-on effects for the security environment. Moreover, if there were a return to hostilities, the stakes would be extremely high. The process of ethno-national segregation has not yet run its course. Self-determination for one of the country's peoples would inevitably be at the expense of the other two. Since today's entity boundaries were created by force, they would also have to be defended by force. They are, however, indefensible and further population transfers would be required before stable ethnonational frontiers could be created.

The positions of the rival ethno-national leaderships on constitutional reform are a manifestation of the underlying illness in Bosnia, namely its political system. In terms of attitudes and outlook, the war never ended. Political elites pursue the same goals they did during the war; they deploy public resources to this end; and every issue is viewed in zero-sum terms. Expecting sustainable solutions from the structures that cause the problem was naïve twenty years ago and is irresponsible today. Progress has only been made when these structures have been bypassed or overridden. Indeed, only after representatives of Croatia and Serbia replaced the Bosnian Croat and Bosnian Serb leaderships as the key negotiators was it possible to conclude the Dayton Peace Agreement itself. And the reforms that have given Bosnia the semblance of a functioning state—from common vehicle licence plates to a common currency and a single army—were either imposed or driven through by the OHR.

Despite international reluctance to recognise failure in Bosnia, it will soon be impossible to ignore the gravity of the situation. When that day arrives, the international community will have little choice but to begin addressing the shortcomings of the peace process, which will require major revision of the Dayton settlement. This, in turn, will involve re-opening the many points of contention that formed the historical, political, economic and intellectual backdrop to the war: self-determination; statehood; sovereignty; definitions of 'nation'; and the institutions of representative democracy and the mandates they confer. In this way, Bosnia's internal structure, the relative merits of partition as opposed to reintegration and, with it, the formal division of Bosnia, including the secession of parts of the country, will be up for discussion.

CONCLUSION

Opening a debate on Bosnia's future presents both a risk and an opportunity. There have always been better ways of managing the Bosnian Question than the Dayton settlement, but getting to them requires a paradigm shift. Although the legacy of the past twenty-five years limits the options available to system designers, the failure of Bosnia's democracy may ultimately prove useful in fostering reconciliation. Bosnians are currently divided in their interpretations of the past, divisions that make it difficult to move on. A more historically accurate interpretation of the disintegration than the competing ethno-national narratives would put the emphasis on how conflict was imported from elsewhere, and, above all, on the systemic flaws in the multi-party system established in 1990 that served as a catalyst for conflict rather than a framework for managing differences. The paradigm shift, therefore, requires examining how democracy can be effective in a multi-ethnic state and designing a system that is tailored to Bosnia's needs. It also requires re-examining Bosnia's relationship with its neighbours and developing mechanisms whereby the neighbouring countries are integrated into the Bosnian settlement in a more constructive manner. And it requires developing new Euro-Atlantic mechanisms to support and drive through systemic change.

The issue of ethno-national security for all Bosnia's peoples and citizens will have to be addressed. This requires moving beyond consociational structures and, in particular, addressing the consequences of the country's ethno-democracy, that is the contradiction between the *demos* and the *ethnos*. The challenge is and always has been to transform politics from a zero-sum into a positive-sum process. To create positive-sum outcomes, it is necessary to change the incentives in the political system, starting with the electoral system, so as to foster inter-ethnic co-operation and make moderation pay.

It is possible to design a better system for balancing the interests of Bosniaks, Croats and Serbs both in Bosnia and the wider region. But the impetus for such a redesign will not come from within. The vested interests of the country's ethno-national elites in the current system are too great. They are its primary beneficiaries and will block reforms that undermine their control over society. The impetus for change must come from without. And it will be necessary to take on the vested interests to push through reform. The international community will therefore have to take the lead and to manage the process. This task could and should have been carried out much earlier, when international resources were greater and attention keener. But even now, it remains possible to turn Bosnia around and resurrect the peace process. And even if the odds against success are high, it is imperative that a creative and determined attempt is made in order to forestall further tragedy.

NOTES

1. INTRODUCTION

1. Peter Harris is a South African human rights lawyer and executive chairman of Resolve Group Management Consultancy. Ben Reilly is dean of the Sir Walter Murdoch School of Public Policy and International Affairs at Murdoch University in Western Australia. The quotation is from *Democracy and Deep-Rooted Conflict: Options for Negotiators* (Stockholm: International IDEA, 1998), p. 389.

2. BOSNIAN QUESTION

1. Marko Attila Hoare is a reader at Kingston University in London and author, among other books, of *The History of Bosnia: From the Middle Ages to the Present Day* (London: Saqi Books, 2007, from which this quotation is taken, p. 44.
2. The Ottoman conquest of the territory corresponding to today's Bosnia took place over more than two centuries, beginning with attacks on the Bosnian Kingdom in 1384 and culminating in the capture of Bihać in 1592. Several good histories of Bosnia have been published since the outbreak of hostilities, including Robert J. Donia and John V.A. Fine's *Bosnia-Hercegovina: A Tradition Betrayed* (London: Hurst, 1994) and Noel Malcolm's *Bosnia: a short history* (London: Pan Macmillan, 1994). This chapter draws on both of those works and especially on Hoare, op. cit., *History of Bosnia*.
3. From the Congress of Berlin to annexation, France, Germany, Italy, the Ottoman Empire, Russia and the United Kingdom had consulates in Sarajevo monitoring Austria-Hungary's administration of Bosnia.
4. According to the 1910 census, 43 per cent of the population was Serb, 32 per cent Muslim and 24 per cent Croat.

5. The Yugoslav idea was born in Croatia in the 1830s with the Illyrian movement, whose name was derived from Illyricum, the Roman province whose territory roughly corresponded to what became Yugoslavia. The Illyrianists believed in the ethno-national, linguistic and cultural unity of all South Slavs.
6. Figures reproduced from Hoare, op. cit., p. 107.
7. Slovenia was divided between Germany, Hungary and Italy. Italy, which already possessed Istria, grabbed much of Dalmatia and created a Montenegrin protectorate. Parts of Croatia, including Baranja, Međimurje and a strip of Slavonia went to Hungary, as did much of Vojvodina. The German-inhabited region of Vojvodina, the Banat, became self-governing under German administration. Bulgaria acquired Macedonia as well as a corner of Serbia. Albania, itself an Italian protectorate, swallowed Kosovo.
8. Zemaljsko antifašističko vijeće narodnog oslobođenja Bosne i Hercegovine.
9. Antifašističko vijeće narodnog oslobođenja Jugoslavije.
10. The books are Kočović's *Žrtve drugog svetskog rata u Jugoslaviji* or *Victims of the Second World War in Yugoslavia* (London: Naša reč, 1985, in Serbo-Croatian) and Žerjavić's *Yugoslavia: Manipulations with the Number of Second World War Victims* (Zagreb: Croatian Information Centre, 1993).
11. Of this 85,000, Žerjavić calculates that 12,000 were Croats and Muslims, 13,000 Jews, 10,000 Roma and the remaining 50,000 Serbs. Žerjavić calculated the approximate numbers who were handed over by the British and executed as between 45,000 and 50,000 Croats and Muslims, 1,500 Serbs and Montenegrins and 8,000 Slovenes.
12. In addition to the six republics—Bosnia, Croatia, Macedonia, Montenegro, Serbia and Slovenia—Vojvodina became an autonomous province and Kosmet an autonomous region within Serbia, in recognition of the large non-Serb populations living there. Kosmet was renamed Kosovo and became an autonomous province in 1968. Unlike republics, autonomous regions did not have the right to secede.
13. The issue of autonomy for predominantly Serb regions of Croatia was considered but deemed unnecessary. Had autonomy been granted to these regions, then by extension the same status would probably have been accorded to the predominantly Muslim Sandžak, divided between Serbia and Montenegro, and, in time, to the predominantly Albanian regions of Macedonia.
14. The communists moved against Croat, Jewish, Muslim and Serb cultural associations that had been recreated at the end of the Second World War, forcing them to close and founding a joint association. In

addition, they put prominent representatives of each community on trial: Archbishop Alojzije Stepinac in Croatia (sentenced to sixteen years' hard labour); royalist leader Draža Mihailović in Serbia (executed in 1946); and groups of young Muslim activists in 1946 (who received relatively short prison sentences) and in 1949 (four of whom were executed). Moreover, the communists banned various items of clothing traditionally worn by Muslim women, including the hijab, veil and burka.

15. Figures from Hoare, op. cit., p. 331.
16. The most prominent Muslim politician was Džemal Bijedić, who became Yugoslavia's prime minister in 1971 and remained in that post until his death in a plane crash in 1977.

3. DISINTEGRATION

1. Steven L. Burg is Adlai Stevenson professor of politics and director of the Center for German and European Studies at Brandeis University. Paul S. Shoup is professor emeritus of politics in the Department of Government and Foreign Affairs at the University of Virginia. They are joint authors of *The War in Bosnia-Herzegovina: Ethnic Conflict and International Intervention* (Armonk, NY and London: M.E. Sharpe, 1999) from which this quotation is taken, p. 62.
2. The system by which the Communist Party controlled appointments to all key positions.
3. This account of Yugoslavia's disintegration is largely drawn from my earlier book *Yugoslavia's Bloody Collapse: Causes, Course and Consequences* (London: Hurst, 1995). Burg and Shoup, op. cit., is the primary source for developments within Bosnia.
4. Economic data come from David A. Dyker's *Yugoslavia: Socialism, Development and Debt* (London: Routledge, 1990).
5. The Greater Serbian agenda grew out of the thinking and writing of Dobrica Ćosić, one of Serbia's most distinguished novelists. Ćosić, a former partisan who was purged by Tito in 1968 for nationalism, was the most prominent member of the Serbian Academy of Sciences and Arts, which drafted in 1985 a memorandum claiming that an anti-Serb bias had been engrained in the Yugoslav Communist Party during the interwar period with a policy of 'strong Yugoslavia, weak Serbia'. The draft memorandum also alleged that Albanians were committing genocide against Serbs in Kosovo.
6. This trend was reversed in the 1991 census, with the percentage of self-declared 'Yugoslavs' falling.

7. The situation of many people originally from elsewhere in the former Yugoslavia later emerged as a major issue after some 18,000 were 'erased' from official databases, losing their rights in Slovene society.
8. According to the 1981 census, 75.1 per cent of Croatia's population was Croat and 11.6 per cent was Serb.
9. The HDZ polled 41.5 per cent; two multi-ethnic former communist parties together polled 34.5 per cent; and the multi-ethnic Koalicija narodnog sporazuma (Coalition of National Agreement, or KNS) 15 per cent of the vote. This translated into 69 per cent, 23.5 per cent and 4 per cent of parliamentary seats respectively.
10. Serbian media labelled all leading Croats Ustašas, including Ivica Račan, the leader of the SDP, even though the Ustašas interned his parents and most of Croatia's Serbs voted for his party.
11. The day that the Croatian parliament appointed Franjo Tuđman president, it also revoked legislation protecting the rights of minorities. The constitutional amendment requiring a two-thirds majority for any change to laws concerning minorities was repealed on the basis of a simple majority.
12. One of Tuđman's first moves was to offer Jovan Rašković, founder and then leader of the Serb ethno-national party in Croatia, the Srpska demokratska stranka (Serb Democratic Party, or SDS), one of five vice-presidential posts in his government. On advice from Belgrade, Rašković rejected the offer.
13. The Constitutional Court was at the time headed by Kasim Trnka who was to become a prominent member of the SDA.
14. According to the April 1991 census, 43.6 per cent of the 4,354,911 population declared themselves Muslim, 31.3 per cent Serb, 17.3 per cent Croat and 5.2 per cent Yugoslav. 2.2 per cent did not belong to any of these categories. Of the 110 deputies elected to the Chamber of Municipalities, 43 were from the SDA, 38 from the SDS, 23 from the HDZ and just 5 from the non-nationalist parties.
15. Izetbegović obtained the second-largest number of votes behind Fikret Abdić, also of the SDA and former head of Agrokomerc. Abdić stepped aside to allow Izetbegović as head of the party to be president. The other individuals elected to the presidency were two Serbs, Biljana Plavšić and Nikola Koljević of the SDS; two Croats, Stjepan Kljuić and Franjo Boras of the HDZ; and one 'Other', Ejup Ganić of the SDA, a Muslim from Serbia's Sandžak who presented himself as a 'Yugoslav'.
16. While the JNA disarmed the territorial defence forces of Croatia and Bosnia, it was not so successful in the case of Slovenia. Slovene JNA

officers alerted Slovenia's new authorities to the plans so that they could take counter-measures. In this way, Slovenia retained some 40 per cent of its territorial army's weapons.

17. This was achieved through an illegal loan from Serbia's main bank to the Serbian government. In effect, the bank printed whatever money Milošević felt he needed to get elected, effectively stealing 18 billion dinars, or $1.7 billion at prevailing exchange rates, from the rest of the country. This move ended the Marković reform programme and triggered a return to inflation as soon as the size of the 'loan' became clear. Milošević had already stopped transferring customs and excise receipts to the federal treasury, imposed tariffs on 'imports' from Slovenia and Croatia and begun 'nationalising' the assets of Slovene and Croatian companies in Serbia.

18. 93.2 per cent of the Slovene electorate turned out to vote in the referendum. Of these, 94.6 per cent, that is, 88.2 per cent of the total electorate, voted for independence.

19. The name was derived from the former military frontier or *vojna krajina* that the Habsburgs created to defend their territories from the Ottomans in the sixteenth century and which remained in place until 1881. The term came to mean any Serb-held territory in Croatia even though some of it had never been part of the military frontier. The self-proclaimed Serb mini-state in Croatia called itself the Republika Srpska Krajina (Republic of Serb Krajina, or RSK).

20. Prospects of compromise were severely undermined when Milošević replaced Rašković with Milan Babić at the head of the SDS in September 1990. At the time, Rašković was abroad seeking financial and moral support among the Serb diaspora.

21. On 3 June 1991, Izetbegović and Kiro Gligorov, his Macedonian counterpart, presented the rest of the Yugoslav Federation with their own compromise model for Yugoslavia in a last-ditch attempt to stave off disintegration.

22. The referendum was formally presented as a choice between a confederation and a federation. In the poll, 84 per cent of the Croatian electorate voted, of whom 93 per cent, 78.1 per cent of the total electorate, supported the proposal 'that the Republic of Croatia, as a sovereign and independent state, which guarantees cultural autonomy and all civic rights to Serbs and members of other nationalities in Croatia, can enter into a union of sovereign states with other republics'. 92 per cent rejected remaining within a federal Yugoslavia.

23. The *troika* consisted of the foreign minister of the country holding the

European Community's six-month rotating presidency, the foreign minister of the country that had previously held the presidency and the foreign minister of the country that would next hold the presidency.

4. WAR AND PEACE

1. James Gow is professor of international peace and security and co-director of the War Crimes Research Group at King's College London as well as author of numerous books on both the former Yugoslavia and international security, including *Triumph of the Lack of Will: International Diplomacy and the Yugoslav War* (London: Hurst, 1997), from which this quotation is taken, pp. 66–7.
2. In total, eight Slovene and thirty-nine JNA troops died, and 111 Slovene and 163 JNA troops were wounded, while more than 2,500 JNA conscripts were taken prisoner. In addition, two Austrian photographers, eight foreign truck drivers and two Slovene civilians were also killed.
3. The title of the most comprehensive examination of the West's involvement in Yugoslavia's disintegration, Josip Glaurdić's *The Hour of Europe: Western Powers and the Breakup of Yugoslavia* (New Haven: Yale University Press, 2011) by Josip Glaurdić, is inspired by this comment. Poos' exact words, as he set off from Luxembourg for Belgrade on 28 June 1991, were: 'This is the hour of Europe. It is not the hour of the Americans.' In addition to Glaurdić's book, this account of the Wars of Yugoslav Dissolution and peace-making efforts draws on my own, *Yugoslavia's Bloody Collapse* (London: Hurst, 1995); Stephen L. Burg and Paul S. Shoup's *The War in Bosnia-Herzegovina* (Armonk, NY and London: M.E. Sharpe, 1999); Richard Caplan's *Europe and the Recognition of New States in Yugoslavia* (Cambridge: Cambridge University Press, 2005); Derek Chollet, *The Road to the Dayton Accords: A Study of American Statecraft* (New York and London: Palgrave Macmillan, 2005); and James Gow, op. cit..
4. The decision to move against Slovenia was taken in haste by the JNA High Command and the intervention was poorly planned. Although the JNA would probably have been able to assert control over Slovenia, any plans to make an example of Slovenia were overruled by Serbia.
5. The Commission's detractors often referred to it as the 'Banditer Commission'.
6. A CIA document leaked in November 1990 warned that the 'Yugoslav' experiment had failed and that the country would break apart violently within eighteen months.
7. EC drafters took Italy's German-speaking minority in the Alto Adige or Southern Tyrol as their model.

8. Montenegro also rejected it under pressure from Serbia after initially accepting.
9. A frustrated Marković leaked a transcript of a telephone conversation between Milošević and Karadžić in September 1991 to illustrate the former's complicity.
10. This was in answer to Lord Carrington's question as to whether the Socialist Federal Republic of Yugoslavia continued to exist after some republics had seceded, as Serbia and Montenegro argued, or whether all the republics were equal successors.
11. This was in answer to Lord Carrington's question as to whether the Serb population of Croatia and Bosnia, as one of the constituent peoples of Yugoslavia, had the right to self-determination.
12. This was in answer to Lord Carrington's question as to whether the internal boundaries between Croatia and Serbia and between Bosnia and Serbia should be regarded as frontiers in terms of public international law. Of all the Badinter Commission's opinions, this was the most controversial, since it involved selective citation of Article 5 of Yugoslavia's 1974 Constitution.
13. Germany subsequently announced on 20 December 1991 that it would recognise Slovenia and Croatia three days later, but that it would only implement this decision on 15 January 1992.
14. Caplan, op. cit., p. 97.
15. Caplan, op. cit., p. 98.
16. In the referendum, which took place on 10 November 1991, 98 per cent of voters in an estimated 85 per cent turnout backed the creation of such a republic if Bosnia sought to break away from Yugoslavia.
17. In this session Karadžić warned that moves towards independence were leading the republic 'into a hell in which the Muslims will perhaps perish'.
18. Landmark verdicts at the ICTY in 2001 included convictions for rape, torture and sexual enslavement. It was the first time that an international tribunal had brought charges solely for crimes of sexual violence against women.
19. The Croat leadership's vision had been far more Bosnian in the wake of the 1990 elections, when the HDZ had been dominated by Croats such as Stjepan Kljuić who lived as a minority among Muslims and Serbs in Central Bosnia. Kljuić's ousting at Zagreb's behest in February 1992 and his replacement by Mate Boban from Western Herzegovina, where Croats formed a greater proportion of the population than in Croatia itself, represented a sea change in vision.

20. The Commission of Experts was created by UN Security Council Resolution 780 of 6 October 1992 and five members were appointed to it on 26 October.
21. Lord Owen published an edited volume of documents entitled *Bosnia-Herzegovina: The Vance/Owen Peace Plan* (Liverpool: Liverpool University Press, 2013) twenty years after he originally unveiled the Plan, providing extensive detail of the reasoning behind it.
22. Under the Owen-Stoltenberg Plan, which was also known as the Union of the Republics of Bosnia, a tripartite territorial division, complete with tunnels and flyovers to ensure ethno-national contiguity, was envisaged, with Sarajevo and Mostar under UN and EU administration respectively. The share of territory awarded to the Muslim republic, eventually 33.6 per cent, was too small to persuade Izetbegović to agree.
23. Under the Contact Group Plan, which was negotiated by representatives of France, Germany, Russia, the United Kingdom and the United States, a two-way territorial division was envisaged between the newly created Federation, which would have 51 per cent of territory, and Republika Srpska, which would have 49 per cent. Sarajevo was to be under UN administration. No agreement could be reached on the boundary.
24. The UN Security Council declared Srebrenica a 'safe area' on 16 April 1993, and extended this status to Bihać, Goražde, Sarajevo, Tuzla and Žepa as well in Security Council Resolution 824 of 6 May 1993.
25. Three US diplomats working on Yugoslav matters resigned in protest and frustration at US inaction in the face of ethnic cleansing during the Bush administration.
26. This offensive involved capturing Maslenica Bridge, Peruća Dam and Zemunik Airport, all of which were supposed to have been handed over under the Sarajevo Accord.
27. This offensive, called Operation Flash (*Bljesak*), involved recapturing the parts of Western Slavonia under Serb control.
28. Figures for the number of Serbs who fled vary. The cited figure is that of the United Nations whose peacekeepers and representatives were present at the time. The real figure is probably lower since the RSK had been haemorrhaging people for many years.
29. According to the Croatian Helsinki Committee, 677 Serb civilians were killed in Operation Storm, many of whom had chosen to stay put.
30. Talks were taking place in Switzerland on the eve of the Croatian government offensive. Despite the military build-up and immediate threat, RSK leaders could not be persuaded to accept a settlement that involved reintegration into Croatia.

31. The hostage-taking was in response to two days of NATO air strikes against ammunition dumps, aimed at pressuring the VRS into halting its offensive against the Goražde safe area.
32. Before Milošević made this concession on the eighteenth day of the talks, the plan had been for Sarajevo to have a special status much like Washington D.C. in the United States.

5. ELECTIONS AT ANY PRICE

1. Derek Chollet is assistant secretary of defense for international security affairs in the US Department of Defense and author of *The Road to the Dayton Accords: A Study of American Statecraft* (New York and London: Palgrave Macmillan, 2005), from which this quotation is taken, p. 194.
2. In his memoir *To End a War* (New York: Random House, 1998), Holbrooke describes how Izetbegović complained that the name Republika Srpska 'is like the Nazi name' (p. 130). Later (p. 135), he writes: 'We underestimated the value to Pale of retaining their blood-soaked name. We may also have underestimated the strength of our negotiating hand...'
3. Neither the Bosnian Croat leadership nor the Bosnian Serb leadership initialled the Dayton Peace Agreement in Dayton, though both did sign in Paris on 14 December 1995.
4. The programme, eventually worth about $500 million in equipment and training, involved Brunei, Egypt, Jordan, Malaysia, Qatar, Saudi Arabia, Turkey and the United Arab Emirates as well as Germany and the United States and lasted from 1996 until 2002.
5. Izetbegović's discussions with Momčilo Krajišnik, speaker of the Republika Srpska National Assembly, on this matter is covered in James Gow's *Triumph of the Lack of Will* (London: Hurst, 1997), p. 256. Ivo Komšić, a Croat member of the wartime presidency, published a joint declaration signed on 16 September 1993 by Izetbegović and Krajišnik specifically including provision for a referendum, which can be found in the documentation section of his wartime diary, *The Survived Country– Dividing Bosnia and Herzegovina: Who, When, Where* (Sarajevo: Synopsis, 2013), p. 461.
6. The number of Serbs who left the Sarajevo suburbs at that time was substantially greater than 60,000, possibly as many as 100,000, but many were already displaced.
7. The suburbs were Grbavica, Hadići, Ilijaš, Ilidža and Vogošća.
8. This was the case in the first four suburbs to be handed over. In Grbavica, which was handed over on 19 March 1996, the process was more orderly.

9. To this day, there is no official translation of Bosnia's constitution.
10. At the time when the Federation constitution was being drafted, however, it was viewed as a possible basis for a three-way solution in Bosnia and therefore as the constitution of the entire country, into which Serbs, too, would be incorporated.
11. The number and contours of the cantons, though not all their names, were determined in May 1996 after the final territorial division agreed in Dayton. The Federation's ten cantons are Una-Sana, whose seat is Bihać; Posavina, whose seat is Orašje; Tuzla, whose seat is Tuzla; Zenica-Doboj, whose seat is Zenica; Bosnia-Podrinje, whose seat is Goražde; Central Bosnia, whose seat is Travnik; Herzegovina-Neretva, whose seat is Mostar; West Herzegovina, whose seat is Široki Brijeg; Sarajevo, whose seat is Sarajevo; and Canton 10, whose seat is Livno.
12. At the time, the final name of what became Herzegovina-Neretva Canton had not been decided. Canton names were supposed not to have any ethno-national connotations and to be named after the governing city or regional geographic features.
13. The PIC consisted of the following countries: Albania, Austria, Belgium, Bosnia, Bulgaria, Canada, China (resigned 2000), Croatia, Czech Republic, Denmark, Egypt, Federal Republic of Yugoslavia (Serbia and Montenegro), Finland, Former Yugoslav Republic of Macedonia, France, Germany, Greece, Hungary, Ireland, Italy, Japan, Jordan, Luxembourg, Malaysia, Morocco, Netherlands, Norway, Oman, Pakistan, Poland, Portugal, Romania, Russia, Saudi Arabia, Slovakia, Slovenia, Spain, Sweden, Switzerland, Turkey, Ukraine, United Kingdom and United States. The PIC's other members were the Office of the High Representative, Brčko Arbitration Panel (dissolved 1999 after making its Final Award), Council of Europe, European Bank for Reconstruction and Development, European Commission, International Committee of the Red Cross, ICTY, IMF, NATO, OSCE, UN, UN High Commission for Human Rights, UN High Commission for Refugees, UN Transitional Administration of Eastern Slavonia (disbanded 1998) and the World Bank. In addition, the following countries and organisations were or became PIC observers: Australia, Central Bank of Bosnia, Estonia, European Investment Bank, Holy See, Human Rights Ombudsman in Bosnia, Iceland, International Federation of Red Cross and Red Crescent Societies, International Mediator for Bosnia, International Organization for Migration, Latvia, Liechtenstein, Lithuania, New Zealand, South Africa and the special co-ordinator of the Stability Pact for South

Eastern Europe. The London Peace Implementation Conference also established a PIC Steering Board to work under the chairmanship of the high representative as the executive arm of the PIC. The original Steering Board members were Canada, France, Germany, Italy, Japan, Russia, the United Kingdom, the United States, the presidency of the European Union, the European Commission, and the Organisation of the Islamic Conference (renamed Organisation of Islamic Cooperation in 2011), represented by Turkey. The Netherlands joined as an observer with the right to speak in 2003 in recognition of the scale of its contribution to the peace process. Spain joined the Steering Board in 2007 after agreeing to take responsibility for the OHR's archive and legacy after the organisation's closure.

14. According to the religious communities, 3,290 religious buildings had been damaged or destroyed during the war. According to the Islamic community, 614 mosques of a pre-war total of 1,144 had been destroyed and 307 damaged, in addition to 557 *mesdzids* (small mosques), 954 *mektebs* (schools for Koranic readers), fifteen *Tekkes* (Dervish lodges), ninety *turbes* (Islamic shrines) and 1,425 other community buildings. According to the Catholic Church, 269 Catholic religious buildings had been totally destroyed and 731 damaged. According to the Serbian Orthodox Church, 125 church buildings and sixty-six other religious objects had been destroyed, and 172 churches and fifty other objects damaged.

15. More than 2,000 kilometres of roads, seventy bridges and half the electricity network had been destroyed during the war. But even before the war, Bosnia's infrastructure was in a poor condition as a result of under-investment during the later years of communist rule.

16. A Greek-sponsored initiative called the Royaumont process was created to 'guide implementation of the Paris/Dayton Peace Agreement, at the same time incorporating it into a wider perspective covering the whole region'. It had a secretariat but few, if any, achievements.

17. According to Chollet, op. cit., p. 195, the high representative's mandate was deliberately limited by the US drafters of the Dayton Peace Agreement when it became clear that the post would go to a European.

18. So cynical did US policy appear at the time that OSCE employees nicknamed their organisation the 'Organisation for Securing Clinton's Election'.

19. At the 1991 census, 34.8 per cent of the population was Bosniak, 33.8 per cent Croat and 19 per cent Serb.

20. The OSCE had been the CSCE, the Conference on Security and

Co-operation in Europe, from its creation in 1973 until 1995. The Bosnian mission was its first field operation.

21. The OSCE appeared so out of its depth to its own staff that a group started bringing out a spoof mission magazine entitled *Mission Impossible*.

22. Figures are taken from the 'Constituent Peoples' Decision of the Constitutional Court of Bosnia and Herzegovina' (U-5/98), and were originally calculated by the International Management Group and the UNHCR.

23. Annex 3, Article IV stated that: 'A citizen who no longer lives in the municipality in which he or she resided in 1991 shall, as a general rule, be expected to vote in person or by absentee ballot, in that municipality,' and continues, 'Such a citizen may, however, apply... to cast his or her ballot elsewhere.' It went on to point out that: 'By Election Day, the return of refugees should already be underway, thus allowing many to participate in person...'

24. The registration was carefully calculated so that the numbers of Serbs in each municipality would be just enough to ensure a majority, with, for example, 31,278 registered in Brčko and 19,746 in Srebrenica. On the day of the election, refugees were bussed in from the Federal Republic of Yugoslavia to these municipalities, fed and looked after for the day. It was often the first time they had been there.

25. Proportional representation is actually a good way to ensure that minority views are represented, since each party receives a corresponding proportion of parliamentary seats to its share of the vote. But in the absence of other safeguards for minority communities or incentives to cross the ethno-national divide and reward moderation, that representation will only be formal.

26. For instance, Dodik was a friend of Sejfudin Tokić, both of whom had been members of Ante Marković's SRSJ, and the two men met up twice during the war, once in Italy and once in Hungary.

27. Holbrooke's role in persuading Karadžić to leave the political scene has generated enormous speculation about a deal between the United States and Karadžić, by which Karadžić was to be left at liberty in return for stepping down. Since being captured and extradited to The Hague for trial at the ICTY, Karadžić's defence has argued that such an agreement existed and that therefore Karadžić should be set free. The most comprehensive write-up of this alleged agreement appeared in Matjaž Klemenčič, 'The International Community and the FRY/ Belligerents, 1989–1997', in Charles Ingrao and Thomas A. Emmert

(eds), *Confronting the Yugoslav Controversies* (West Lafayette, IN: Purdue University Press, 2010). According to this account, Holbrooke's associate Christopher Hill drafted a memorandum that was signed by Bosnian Serb officials Aleksa Buha, Momčilo Krajišnik and Biljana Plavšić and Serbian officials Slobodan Milošević and Milan Milutinović, in addition to Karadžić; see p. 189.

28. Details of the 1996 elections come from 'Elections in Bosnia and Herzegovina' (Sarajevo: ICG Bosnia Project Report 16, 22 September 1996) and the 30 October 1996 addendum to it that I wrote together with colleagues. The report includes full analysis of the improbably high turnout, calculated to have been at least 105 per cent of the electorate.

29. Attempts by the ethno-national parties and especially the SDS to pack municipalities were largely successful. Nevertheless, in five municipalities, four in the Federation and one in Republika Srpska, ballots cast by absentee voters created situations where representatives of cleansed populations had majorities on the councils. These were Bosniak-controlled Bosanski Petrovac, where displaced Serbs won a majority of seats; Croat-controlled Drvar and Bosansko Grahovo, where displaced Serbs won a majority of seats; Croat-controlled Žepče, where displaced Bosniaks won a majority of seats; Croat-controlled Glamoč, where displaced Bosniaks and displaced Serbs together won a majority of seats; and Serb-controlled Srebrenica, where displaced Bosniaks won a majority of seats.

30. Full details of the 1997 municipal elections can be found in 'Beyond Ballot Boxes: Municipal Elections in Bosnia and Herzegovina' (Sarajevo: ICG Bosnia Project Report 26, 10 September 1997) and the 14 October 1997 extended press release 'ICG Analysis of 1997 Municipal Election Results', which I wrote together with colleagues.

6. OVERRIDING 'DEMOCRACY' TO IMPLEMENT DAYTON

1. Robert M. Hayden is professor of anthropology, law and public and international affairs at the University of Pittsburgh as well as director of its Center for Russian and East European Studies. He is author of *Blueprints for a House Divided: The Constitutional Logic of the Yugoslav Conflicts* (Ann Arbor, MI: University of Michigan Press, 1999), from which this quotation is taken, p. 10.

2. Debates and divisions in the Clinton administration are described in Ivo H. Daalder's *Getting to Dayton: The Making of America's Bosnia Policy* (Washington D.C.: Brookings Institution, 2000).

3. In the event, the additional police officers failed to materialise in the desired numbers, though the IPTF did grow to just over 2,000.

4. The Arbitral Tribunal had been established in accordance with Annex 2, Article V of the Dayton Peace Agreement. It comprised one arbitrator from each entity and a third arbitrator and presiding officer who was appointed by the president of the International Court of Justice, as the entities were unable to agree on a mutually acceptable candidate. The Arbitral Tribunal operated according to the rules of the UN Commission on International Trade Law and Roberts B. Owen, a US lawyer, was the presiding officer.

5. According to the Sintra communiqué: 'The Steering Board is concerned that the media has not done enough to promote freedom of expression and reconciliation. It declared that the High Representative has the right to curtail or suspend any media network or programme whose output is in persistent and blatant contravention of either the spirit or letter of the Peace Agreement.'

6. In the wake of SFOR's takeover of Banja Luka, SRT had compared the peacekeeping force to the Nazi SS in a video clip.

7. In the weeks leading to the elections, which Plavšić had called, SRT broadcast out of its Banja Luka studios with reporting that was probably as partisan, though less crude, on behalf of Plavšić as it had earlier been on behalf of Karadžić and Krajišnik.

8. Although Dodik required Bosniak and Croat support to form a government, all his ministers were Serbs.

9. The relevant section of the Bonn Peace Implementation Conference conclusions read as follows:

   'The Council welcomes the High Representative's intention to use his final authority in theatre regarding interpretation of the Agreement on the Civilian Implementation of the Peace Settlement in order to facilitate the resolution of difficulties by making binding decisions, as he judges necessary, on the following issues:

   a) timing, location and chairmanship of meetings of the common institutions;

   b) interim measures to take effect when parties are unable to reach agreement, which will remain in force until the Presidency or Council of Ministers has adopted a decision consistent with the Peace Agreement on the issue concerned;

   c) other measures to ensure implementation of the Peace Agreement throughout Bosnia and Herzegovina and its Entities, as well as the smooth running of the common institutions. Such measures may include actions against persons holding public office or officials who are absent from meetings without good case or who are found by the High Representative to be in violation of legal commitments made under the Peace Agreement or the terms for its implementation.'

10. The specific reference was the following: 'The Council confirmed that there is no alternative to the Peace Agreement as the foundation for the political and economic development of Bosnia and Herzegovina, its two multi-ethnic Entities and three constituent peoples (along with Others) and for sustainable peace in the entire region.'

11. The difficulty inherent in internationals taking decisions about matters such as passport design was immediately apparent. The first batch of new passports had to be pulped because it was printed with a mistake in the local language.

12. Four of the seven original banknotes, which were issued in June and July 1998, contained errors in the Cyrillic legends. The number five on the Bosnian five-mark note did not appear in Cyrillic at all. The most likely explanation is that the French printer was not used to working with Cyrillic. The Republika Srpska authorities initially refused to distribute the notes, but then relented with the result that the erroneous notes entered into circulation.

13. The anthem that was selected on the basis of the work of a commission and enacted by the high representative in June 1999 had no words. A parliamentary commission eventually agreed a text on the basis of a competition in February 2009. However, the parliament rejected that text in a July 2012 vote. A decade after the anthem's adoption, internet commentators posted back-to-back recordings of the Bosnian anthem and that of Faber College, the fictional Pennsylvania college that featured in National Lampoon's 1978 film *Animal House* on YouTube, alleging they were too similar for coincidence.

14. Of its 1998 budget of 442 million Bosnian marks, 76 million or 17 per cent came from foreign grants and credits.

15. The SRS was the party of indicted war criminal Vojislav Šešelj.

16. The SDS's strong showing was in part a consequence of the banning of the SRS, much of whose support it picked up. The SDS may also have benefitted from a call from Holbrooke for it to be banned.

17. Jelavić was subsequently found guilty by the State Court of abuse of office, embezzlement and lack of commitment in office in November 2005. He was sentenced *in absentia* to ten years in prison, having moved to Croatia after getting word of the likely verdict. Jelavić appealed the verdict from Croatia and the Court of Appeal for the State Court

annulled the ruling against him and called for a new trial. Jelavić has not returned to Bosnia to face trial.

18. Despite carrying out a comprehensive audit, the provisional administrator failed to present any hard evidence of alleged fraud on the part of the Bosnian Croat political elite.

19. All figures come from the UNHCR, many of which are also cited in Florian Bieber's *Post-War Bosnia: Ethnicity, Inequality and Public Sector Governance* (Basingstoke and New York: Palgrave Macmillan, 2006), p. 112.

20. After the RRTF's closure, responsibility for its work was given to the Ministry for Refugees and Human Rights.

21. The individuals were Pero Raguž, the mayor of Stolac, and Drago Tokmačije, deputy mayor of Drvar, who were dismissed in March and April 1998 respectively.

22. The RRTF drew up a Property Law Implementation Plan to drive through implementation of the new legislation to ensure that returnees received their properties back, despite resistance from the local authorities.

23. The Dayton Peace Agreement specified in Annex 2, Article V.1 ('Arbitration for the Brčko Area') that: 'The Parties agree to binding arbitration of the disputed portion of the Inter-entity Boundary Line in the Brčko area indicated on the map attached at the Appendix.' However, in the rush to wrap up the Dayton talks, no map was attached. As a result, the area of arbitration was itself controversial.

24. The first supervisor was Robert W. Farrand, a US ambassador, who served in this capacity between March 1997 and June 2000. He has been followed by seven other US officials: Gary L. Matthews (between June 2000 and October 2001); Henry Lee Clarke (between April 2001 and December 2003); Susan R. Johnson (between January 2004 and September 2006); Raffi Gregorian (between September 2006 and August 2010); Roderick W. Moore (between September 2010 and September 2013); Tamir G. Waser (between October 2013 and August 2014); David M. Robinson (between September 2014 and August 2015); and Bruce G. Berton (since September 2015).

25. The Arbitral Award was rejected by the Republika Srpska National Assembly and has never been formally recognised.

26. If nobody is elected, a simple majority vote is held, and in the event of a third round, there is a run-off between the two most popular candidates.

27. The decision can be found on the OHR's website; see 'Constituent

Peoples' Decision of the BiH Constitutional Court', www.ohr.int/ohr-dept/legal/const/default.asp?content_id=5853 (last accessed October 2015).

28. The decision covered many more issues, including the role of the Serbian Orthodox Church in Republika Srpska, and the existence and use of official languages. It is analysed particularly well in Bieber, op. cit., pp. 121–133.

29. Members of the commissions represented all constituent peoples and Others in equal numbers. They were proposed by the entity parliaments and appointed by the high representative. All political parties were represented apart from the HDZ, which was boycotting all institutions as a result of its dispute with the international community over the OSCE's imposition of changes to the way in which delegates to the Federation's House of Peoples were selected.

30. Among the provisions of greatest concern was one granting citizens the right to call referendums. Another amendment labelled Bosnian, the name most Bosniaks call the language they speak, 'Bosniak'.

31. The prime ministers of each entity were also able to nominate one Other as a minister from the quota of the largest constituent people, that is from the Serb quota in Republika Srpska and from the Bosniak quota in the Federation.

32. The definition was as follows: exercise of the rights of constituent peoples to be adequately represented in legislative, executive and judicial bodies; identity of one constituent people; constitutional amendments; organisation of public authorities; equal rights of constituent peoples in the process of decision-making; education, religion, language, promotion of culture, tradition and cultural heritage; territorial organisation; public information system; and other issues treated as being of vital national interest if so claimed by two thirds of one of the caucuses of the constituent peoples in the House of Peoples or Council of Peoples.

33. The changes required further legislation to establish mechanisms to ensure effective implementation, which did not materialise. Although High Representative Petritsch was eager to take this process forward, his successor Lord Ashdown dropped it in favour of his own programme of 'Justice and Jobs'.

34. The full title of the ICTY, which was created by Resolution 827 of the UN Security Council, was the International Tribunal for the Prosecution of Persons Responsible for Serious Violations of International Humanitarian Law Committed in the Territory of the Former Yugoslavia since 1991.

35. The case was prepared and filed by Francis Boyle, a University of Illinois international law professor, who served as a pro bono legal adviser to Izetbegović.

36. Joint criminal enterprise is a controversial legal doctrine used to prosecute political and military leaders for war crimes committed during the Wars of Yugoslav Dissolution, whereby each member of an organised group may be individually held responsible for crimes committed by the group in the context of a common plan.

37. The last ICTY indictee to be extradited to The Hague was Goran Hadžić, a Croatian Serb leader indicted in 2004, who was extradited from Serbia in July 2011. His trial began in October 2012. He was diagnosed with terminal brain cancer in November 2014 and provisionally released on humanitarian grounds in April 2015.

38. They were sentenced to twenty-eight, twenty and twelve years respectively.

39. General Krstić was sentenced to forty-six years in prison, reduced to thirty-five on appeal. In June 2010, Colonel Ljubiša Beara and Lieutenant-Colonel Vujadin Popović were convicted of genocide, among other crimes, for their role in the Srebrenica massacre and sentenced to life imprisonment. While elements of their conviction were overturned on appeal in January 2014, the genocide convictions and life sentences were upheld.

40. Article 2 of the 1948 UN Convention on the Prevention and Punishment of the Crime of Genocide defines genocide as 'any of the following acts committed with intent to destroy, in whole or in part, a national, ethnical, racial or religious group, as such: killing members of the group; causing serious bodily or mental harm to members of the group; deliberately inflicting on the group conditions of life, calculated to bring about its physical destruction in whole or in part; imposing measures intended to prevent births within the group; [and] forcibly transferring children of the group to another group'.

41. Of the 161 indictments, 124 relate to events in Bosnia. The remainder relate to events in Croatia, Kosovo and Macedonia.

42. Anniversary of both the 1389 Battle of Kosovo and the 1914 Sarajevo assassination.

43. The genocide charge related specifically to Bosnia.

44. Šešelj was provisionally released from the ICTY in November 2014 on humanitarian grounds before a verdict was issued, as a result of deteriorating health following diagnosis of metastatic cancer.

45. Others allegedly part of this joint criminal enterprise included Blagoje

Adžić, Milan Babić, Radmilo Bogdanović, Veljko Kadijević, Radovan Karadžić, Ratko Mladić, Franko Simatović (a Croat), Jovica Stanišić and Dragan Vasiljković.

46. In prison in Sweden, Plavšić reverted to her earlier unrepentant position. In her memoir, *Svedočim* (Banja Luka: Trioprint, 2005), she wrote that she had only pleaded guilty to save the Serb people from the burden of collective guilt. She was released from prison on 27 October 2009 after serving two thirds of her sentence.

47. Krajišnik was released from prison on 1 September 2013 after serving two thirds of his sentence.

48. The other co-defendants were Valentin Čorić, Milivoj Petković, Slobodan Praljak, Berislav Pušić and Bruno Stojić.

49. In addition, one indictee committed suicide when surrounded by SFOR troops with no possibility of escape.

50. The ICTY-related removals and other measures had an almost immediate impact. Whereas the Republika Srpska authorities had hitherto failed to hand over any indictees, they suddenly developed the capacity to track down and arrest war-crimes suspects. In November 2004, Republika Srpska police acted upon a warrant from the Sarajevo Cantonal Court and arrested eight individuals indicted for war crimes. In January 2005, they apprehended the first ICTY indictee, Savo Todorović, who had run a detention camp near Foča during the war. Todorović's arrest and handover were followed by six more in the following three months.

51. In June 2013, the ICTY announced that it expected to complete its work in 2016.

52. Though the figure of 16,000 has been formally cited by the State Prosecutor's Office, the likely number is considerably lower.

53. The Council of Ministers adopted a National War Crimes Strategy in December 2008. According to this Strategy, the most complex cases will be processed at the state level, while less complex cases may be transferred to lower-level courts.

54. 'War crimes in BiH: Criminal procedures in Bosnia and Herzegovina 1992–2006. Indictments, appeals, verdicts' (Sarajevo: ABA/CEELI and Association of Prosecutors BiH, 2006) provides details of fifty-four processes that took place between 1992 and 2006 in the Federation, Brčko District and Republika Srpska.

55. At the time, ICTY indictees Goran Hadžić, Karadžić and Mladić were all at liberty, albeit lying low, in Serbia.

56. A version of the Supreme Defence Council records was used at the

ICJ proceedings, but some portions had been redacted in the interests of Serbian national security.

57. The ICMP was established at the initiative of US President Bill Clinton in 1996 at the G7 summit in Lyon, France, to confront the issue of persons missing as a result of the Wars of Yugoslav Dissolution.

58. DNA evidence revealed that the body of one man was found in eleven parts, in four separate secondary mass graves, two of which were more than 50km from the other two.

59. The ICMP has developed a DNA database in the former Yugoslavia by taking blood samples from close to 90,000 relatives of nearly 30,000 missing persons and more than 26,700 bone samples taken from mortal remains exhumed from mass graves. The DNA techniques involved have subsequently been used to identify victims in the wake of other tragedies including the 2004 Asian tsunami and 2005's Hurricane Katrina.

60. See 'Peace-brokering amid ethnic cleansing' in Chapter 4 for more details of the RDC's findings in *The Book of the Dead*.

61. If established, RECOM aims, among other things, to produce a definitive list of the dead and missing along with a list of camps and other detention sites used between 1 January 1991 and 31 December 2001 in the former Yugoslavia.

62. The UN IPTF's vetting became controversial after the closure of the mission at the end of 2002. In the course of vetting police officers, the UN IPTF withheld certification from several hundred. These decertified police officers lost their employment, with no right of appeal against the UN IPTF's decision. Only the UN Security Council could create an appeals process, which it was not prepared to do. A compromise brokered by the OHR in 2007 enabled decertified police officers to apply for entry-level vacancies.

63. The Brussels PIC declaration explicitly listed a series of institutions, including a professional civil service, a state treasury, a court of first instance, public corporations and the regulatory bodies and structures necessary for a common market.

64. Eventual solutions brokered by the OHR involved entity-based associations formally linked at the state level in line with other Dayton structures. It did not, however, recognise the separate entity structures that Republika Srpska's political leaders had argued for based on the UK precedent of separate international teams from England, Northern Ireland, Scotland and Wales.

65. The eight ministries were Civil Affairs, Foreign Affairs, Foreign Trade

and Economic Relations, Finance and Treasury, Human Rights and Refugees, Justice, Security, and Transport and Communications.

66. The structure of the Defence Ministry differed from that of the eight existing ministries in that there were two deputy ministers in addition to the minister, not one, so that all three constituent peoples were represented at the top of the Ministry.

67. The first governor of Bosnia's Central Bank was the New Zealander Peter Nicholl. He remained Central Bank governor beyond his six-year term by becoming a Bosnian citizen, before relinquishing the post at the end of 2004.

68. A standby arrangement is an IMF financing programme that makes short-term assistance available to countries experiencing temporary or cyclical balance-of-payments deficits.

69. Establishment of the Central Bank is described in 'Reshaping International Priorities in Bosnia and Herzegovina—Part II: International Power in Bosnia' (Sarajevo: European Stability Initiative, 1 March 2000).

70. Media reform is examined in Nidžara Ahmetašević, 'Intervening in the Media Sector: Media Anarchy in post-war Bosnia and Herzegovina' (Graz: Working Paper No. 6, University of Graz Centre for Southeast European Studies, December 2012).

71. The medium that benefitted most from international and especially US largesse was *Nezavisne novine* (The Independent), a Banja Luka-based daily founded in 1996 by Željko Kopanja with some initial capital from Milorad Dodik. *Nezavisne novine* adopted a country-wide approach to newsgathering, in contrast to most publications in Bosnia, and uncovered many abuses of power under the SDS regime. Indeed, its investigative reporting nearly cost Kopanja his life after a bomb was placed under his car in October 2000. Since Dodik's return to power in February 2006, most observers consider *Nezavisne novine* to have become close to authority and to have lost its independence.

72. The Open Broadcast Network operated under international supervision between September 1996 and 2000, and received roughly $20 million in donations. The station was sold to Ivan Ćaleta, a Croatian entrepreneur, who sold it to its current owner, the German commercial broadcaster RTL, in 2004. The other large-scale media project, the Swiss-funded Free Elections Radio Network, operated between 1996 and 2001. In 2001, it was subsumed into the public broadcasting system (PBS).

73. Article III.1 (h), concerning the responsibilities of the institutions of

Bosnia, states that: 'The following matters are the responsibility of the institutions of Bosnia and Herzegovina... Establishment and operation of common and international communications facilities.'

74. The new structure provided for three broadcasters, one providing state-wide services, the other two serving the entities, each with its own responsibility for content and financial management. Three separate boards of governors were to be appointed by their respective parliaments that would together comprise the PBS board of governors. Three separate and complementary licences would be issued by the CRA. A joint legal entity, the corporation, would be established by the three broadcasters, accountable to the PBS board of governors and responsible for property management, technical resources, advertising, international representation, foreign programme rights, and harmonising systems, policies and procedures across the three broadcasters. There would also be a single and uniform subscription system, where all income (including advertising revenues) would go into a single account.

75. I am grateful to Daniel Lindvall for much of the information and analysis on police reform that comes from his doctoral dissertation, 'The Limits of the European Vision in Bosnia and Herzegovina: An Analysis of the Police Reform Negotiations' (Stockholm: Södertörn Doctoral Dissertations, 2009).

76. In the entity Laws on Internal Affairs that the high representative eventually imposed in both entities, ethno-national representation was set according to the 1991 census.

77. The State Border Service officially changed its name to the State Border Police in July 2007.

78. Customs revenue collection and tax avoidance were catalogued by the EU's Customs and Financial Assistance Office (CAFAO) in a series of reports implicating political leaders in both entities.

79. Initially, the three councils together had a total of seventeen national members, including six from the Federation, six from Republika Srpska, and five from the state level, as well as eight international members, two of whom served as president and vice president. The proportion of internationals was set to decline over time until the HJPCs became purely domestic institutions.

80. All figures are reproduced from Alexander Mayer-Rieckh, 'Vetting to prevent future abuses: reforming the police, courts and prosecutor's offices in Bosnia and Herzegovina', in Alexander Mayer-Rieckh and Pablo de Greiff (eds), *Justice As Prevention: Vetting Public Employees in Transitional Societies* (New York: International Center for Transitional Justice, 2007).

81. According to the HJPC, the ethno-national composition of the judiciary in Republika Srpska changed from 2.3 per cent Bosniaks, 3.7 per cent Croats, 2.8 per cent Others and 91.2 per cent Serbs, to 22.8 per cent Bosniaks, 8.1 per cent Croats, 3.5 per cent Others and 65.6 per cent Serbs. In the Federation, the composition changed from 64.8 per cent Bosniaks, 23.1 per cent Croats, 2.8 per cent Others, and 9.6 per cent Serbs, to 56.5 per cent Bosniaks, 21.9 per cent Croats, 2.5 per cent Others and 19.1 per cent Serbs.

82. The Criminal Procedure Code was, in many ways, a legal revolution, since it introduced aspects of an adversarial procedure into a country that had previously used an accusatorial procedure. This created a hybrid legal system with both European and Anglo-Saxon elements, similar to that used at the ICTY. Police and prosecutors became responsible for conducting investigations, in contrast to the previous system in which judges performed this role. Prosecutors and defence lawyers were to make their case through the introduction of evidence, examination, and cross-examination of witnesses, in contrast to the previous system, where judges led the questioning. Another new feature was the introduction of plea-bargaining.

83. The State Court comprises three divisions: criminal, administrative and appellate. The criminal division is further subdivided into three sections: war crimes; organised crime, economic crime and corruption; and general crime.

84. The international presence was originally scheduled to remain until the end of December 2009.

85. The last international judges left the State Court at the end of December 2012. See 'Transitioning' in Chapter 8 for more on the end of their mandates.

86. Lord Ashdown greatly improved the international community's co-ordination mechanisms and succeeded in channelling international efforts more effectively than his predecessors.

87. The political preconditions were adopting an Election Law and providing election financing; adopting a Civil Service Law; establishing a permanent secretariat in the presidency; adopting rules and procedures for the Parliamentary Assembly; adopting a single passport and central registration mechanism; implementing the Law on the State Border Service and ensuring funding; and allocating funding for the Constitutional Court. The economic preconditions were abolishing the payment bureaux; establishing a state treasury; removing trade barriers between the entities; establishing a single Bosnian National

Institute for Standards; adopting laws on competition and consumer protection; implementing FDI legislation and adopting restitution legislation. The democratic preconditions were implementing property laws; creating the conditions for sustainable return; implementing decisions of the human rights institutions; approving and implementing the Law on the Judicial Service; and implementing public broadcasting reforms.

88. The outstanding issues were implementation of the Law on the State Border Service and ensuing funding; implementation of decisions of the human rights institutions; and implementation of public broadcasting reforms.

89. Political issues covered more effective governance; more effective public administration; effective judiciary; effective human rights provisions; and complying with existing conditionality. Economic issues covered reliable statistics; budget legislation; and budget practice. Technical requirements covered European integration; developing a single economic space; consistent trade policy; customs and taxation reform; integrated energy market; public broadcasting; tackling crime and especially organised crime; and managing asylum and migration.

90. European Partnerships were drawn up with all countries aspiring to EU membership in the wake of agreement on 'The Thessaloniki agenda for the Western Balkans' in June 2003.

91. On p. 362 of *To End a War*, op. cit., Richard Holbrooke wrote: 'The most serious flaw in the Dayton Peace Accords was that it left two opposing armies in one country, one for Serbs and one for the Croat-Muslim Federation... creating a single army or disarming BiH was not possible.'

92. Revelations about the Orao sales led to five resignations, including by the Republika Srpska defence minister and chief of staff.

93. In the wake of NATO's Istanbul Summit in June 2004 and Bosnia's failure to be invited to join the Partnership for Peace, High Representative Lord Ashdown removed fifty-nine officials from office in Republika Srpska in an attempt to oblige the political leadership of that entity to co-operate with the ICTY.

94. The relevant section of Lord Ashdown's memoir, *Swords And Ploughshares: Bringing Peace to the 21st Century* (London: Orion, 2007), is on p. 249, a copy of which Republika Srpska Prime Minister Dodik placed on display under glass in his office. Lord Ashdown wrote: 'I rang Chris Patten in late October and asked him if he would weigh in as Commissioner and say that these reforms were required if BiH

wanted to join Europe. As always he agreed, and we drafted a letter for him to send to the presidents along those lines...' The reference was not specifically to police reform, but to Lord Ashdown's entire 'Justice and Jobs' programme.

7. RHETORIC AND REALITY

1. Tihomir Loza is deputy director of Transitions Online, a news service covering former communist countries in transition, including Bosnia. The quotation comes from an afterword he wrote for Christophe Solioz's *Turning Points in Post-War Bosnia* (Baden-Baden: Nomos, 2007), p. 154.
2. Petritsch used them sixty-two times and Lord Ashdown ninety-one times.
3. Only 157 occasions were recorded on the OHR website.
4. Under Schwarz-Schilling, between February 2006 and July 2007, the Bonn Powers were used on sixty-seven occasions. Under Miroslav Lajčák, between July 2007 and March 2009, they were used thirty-two times. And under Valentin Inzko, between April 2009 and January 2014, they were used eighty-two times. This was a total of 958 times between December 1997 and September 2014. Of these, fifty-six related to lifting bans on individuals who had been removed, one under Petritsch, thirty-eight under Ashdown, seventeen under Schwarz-Schilling, and forty-six under Inzko, including one decision lifting fifty-eight bans.
5. At the top of the section discussing his time in Bosnia, 'The Savage War of Peace—Bosnia 2002–2003', on p. 232 of Lord Ashdown's memoir, *Swords and Ploughshares* (London: Orion, 2004), he placed the vulgar Bosnian phrase '*Lako je tudžim kurcem gloginje mlatiti*'. He translated it as 'It is easy to beat thorn bushes with other people's pricks', explaining that a Bosnian friend had said it to him when he had asked why politicians left him to make their decisions. He frequently repeated the line when making 'soft' impositions.
6. The report is discussed in more detail in 'Revisiting the Bosnian Question', Chapter 9.
7. In its assessment of the OHR, the Venice Commission acknowledged that use of the Bonn Powers had been beneficial for Bosnia and its citizens in the aftermath of war. However, it made clear that: 'This practice does not correspond to democratic principles when exercised without due process and the possibility of judicial control.' Moreover, it argued that the use of the Bonn Powers 'becomes more questionable over time' and called for a 'progressive phasing out of these powers and for the establishment of an advisory panel of independent lawyers for

the decisions directly affecting the rights of individuals pending the end of the practice'.

8. The other two were Paul Williams of the Public International Law and Policy Group, a Washington-based non-governmental organisation providing pro bono legal assistance to developing countries in conflict, and Bruce Hitchner, chairman of the Dayton Peace Accords Project at Tufts University, Boston, MA.

9. Together with Jason Crosby, Don Hays published an account of the process entitled 'From Dayton to Brussels: Constitutional Preparations for Bosnia's EU Accession' (Washington D.C.: USIP Special Report No. 175, October 2006).

10. Entity voting in practice meant the capacity of legislators from one entity to block legislation.

11. High turnover of key positions is common in many countries in the wake of a change of government, and in the case of Dodik and Republika Srpska, the OHR turned a blind eye, since Dodik had been the international favourite and, above all, was not the SDS. Dodik's party, the SNSD, had the same acronym as in 1996, but its name changed in 2001 following a merger, from Stranka nezavisnih socijaldemokrata to Savez nezavisnih socijaldemokrata, that is from the Party of Independent Social Democrats to the Alliance of Independent Social Democrats.

12. The Montenegrin referendum took place on 21 May 2006 under the supervision of Miroslav Lajčák, then special envoy of Javier Solana, the European Union's High Representative for the Common Foreign and Security Policy. For the results of the referendum to be approved by the European Union, the pro-independence campaign needed to obtain more than 55 per cent of the vote. The campaign scraped over this threshold, with 55.5 per cent of the vote, and the Montenegrin parliament formally declared independence on 3 June.

13. Since voters in the Federation are able to vote for either the Bosniak or the Croat member of the presidency (but not both) and there are many more Bosniaks in the Federation than Croats, it had theoretically always been possible for Bosniaks to select a favoured Croat candidate. Since most Bosniaks had voted for one of the Bosniak candidates in earlier ballots, this had not happened previously. As it became clear, however, that Silajdžić would easily win the contest for the Bosniak member of the presidency, many Bosniaks and especially SDP voters decided to use their votes to elect the Croat member. Because of a split in the votes of Croat electors between the candidates of the HDZ BiH

and the HDZ 1990, Komšić was able to win the largest number of votes and therefore become the Croat member of the presidency.

14. See Michael Mann, *The Dark Side of Democracy: Explaining Ethnic Cleansing* (Cambridge: Cambridge University Press, 2005). The thesis that ethnic cleansing is a phenomenon of modern-day democratisation in particular multi-ethnic settings, and not the work of primitive evil-doers, has greatly influenced this section and other chapters about balancing the interests of different peoples living together.

15. In addition to the five general elections, with votes for the presidency, state parliament, entity parliaments and cantonal assemblies (in 1996, 1998, 2000, 2002 and 2006), the following ballots had also taken place since the Dayton Peace Agreement: the Mostar municipal election in June 1996; an extraordinary election to the Republika Srpska National Assembly in November 1997; and municipal elections in 1997, 2000 and 2004. There have subsequently been general elections in 2010 and 2014, municipal elections in 2008 and 2012, and an extraordinary election for the Republika Srpska president in November 2007.

16. The changes imposed in the wake of the Constitutional Court ruling are discussed in 'Building multi-ethnicity', Chapter 6.

17. After Mill argued that democracy functions best in mono-ethnic societies, Lord Acton replied that if this were indeed the case, one consequence would be bloodletting and migration on an unprecedented scale. In a foretaste of late twentieth and early twenty-first century debates among political scientists, he therefore suggested it was more important to secure liberal protections than to link ethno-national identity to democracy.

18. John Stuart Mill, *Considerations on Representative Government* (London: Parker, Son and Bourn, 1861), p. 289.

19. Consociationalism and its shortcomings are discussed further in 'Revisiting the Bosnian Question', Chapter 9.

20. The creation of the party system in 1990 is discussed in 'Democratic dawn', Chapter 3.

21. The only comprehensive examination of the 1990 elections is Suad Arnautović, *Izbori u Bosni i Hercegovini '90: analiza izbornog procesa* (Sarajevo: Promocult, 1996).

22. In practice, voters did not use all seven ballots despite being entitled to do so. Instead, they tended to vote for members of the presidency from their own community and possibly one or two more. This was, in part, the result of a campaign by the HDZ, SDA and SDS to persuade their followers not to 'interfere' in the affairs of other communities

and, where each party had nominated a candidate, only to cast ballots for their own ethno-national representatives as well as for the Other.

23. Much writing about Karadžić has stressed the fact that he was an outsider in Sarajevo; that he came from Montenegro; that his father had been a Četnik in the Second World War who was imprisoned for nationalism by the communists; and that he had been brought up on tales of Serb legends. While all of this is no doubt true, it also forms part of an *ex post facto* attempt to explain how he emerged as the Serb leader who oversaw appalling crimes. In 1998, I helped make a documentary on Karadžić called *The World's Most Wanted Man* for Frontline. The most revealing element of this documentary was not the extent of Karadžić's evil, but actually his charm, wit and ostensible humanity. Moreover, it seems that most who met him during his years hiding in the open as an alternative medical practitioner came away with similar impressions.

24. See 'Recognition and recrimination', Chapter 4.

25. See 'Democratic dawn', Chapter 3.

26. The support given to Dodik's SNSD over many years, for example, helped the party to develop effective tactics for winning elections, but failed to persuade it to draw up a programme geared towards reconciliation.

8. WHITHER BOSNIA?

1. Chris Patten is chancellor of the University of Oxford. The quotation comes from a speech he made in 2002 in London at a conference on organised crime in the Balkans, when he was European external relations commissioner.

2. For more on the ICJ ruling, see 'Justice', Chapter 6.

3. Russia's dissenting position was registered in a footnote to the communiqué.

4. Schwarz-Schilling's imposition is discussed in 'Justice', Chapter 6.

5. The conflict between the OHR and Republika Srpska in the wake of this imposition is examined in Philippe Leroux-Martin, *Diplomatic Counterinsurgency: Lessons from Bosnia and Herzegovina* (New York: Cambridge University Press, 2014).

6. Lajčák's imposition changed the necessary quorum for decision-making in the Council of Ministers in such a way that decisions could in future be made by the majority of those present and voting, stipulating that a 'simple majority' would only require one representative from each constituent people instead of two.

7. The changes were to cover two issues: 'entity voting' and the quorum required to hold a session of the House of Representatives. Under the new rules of procedure, at least one third of the votes of representatives present from each entity were required for decisions to be made. According to the existing rules of procedure, one third of representatives elected from each entity had to be present. In the House of Representatives, the quorum was to become a majority of all members, that is, twenty-two of the forty-two delegates. The additional requirement that at least ten delegates from the Federation and five from Republika Srpska had to be present was to be dropped so that a small minority would no longer be able to prevent the House of Representatives from holding a session by not showing up.

8. The Serb walkout is described in 'Recognition and recrimination', Chapter 4.

9. Lajčák clearly felt let down, a point he made emphatically when he stepped down as high representative to become Slovakia's foreign minister in February 2009.

10. The six institutions were the Agency for Forensic Examination; Institute for Education and Professional Upgrading; Agency for Police Support; Independent Board; Citizens' Complaint Board; and Police Officials Complaint Board.

11. Instead of a simple majority vote, as originally proposed by the OHR, decisions in the House of Representatives would be adopted by a majority, including one third of the votes from each entity. If this did not occur, members of the collegium could try to negotiate such a majority in the next three days. If the collegium failed to do that, decisions would be adopted by a majority of the deputies present at a session, on condition that more than two thirds of deputies from each entity had not voted against it.

12. This implied a revision of the original decision. These revisions were intended to prevent abuses, such as the deliberate calling of sessions when delegates were absent, and to establish timelines to regulate acceptable absences when all delegates from one entity might be absent.

13. Although the leaders of all six parties in the governing coalition signed the Mostar Agreement and the Action Plan, the SDA broke ranks when the cosmetic nature of police reform became clear in terms of the legislation, and its deputies voted against adoption of the laws.

14. The Law on the Directorate for Co-ordination of Police Bodies and Agencies to Support the Police Structure of Bosnia established four police bodies: the Directorate for Co-ordination of Police Bodies; the

Agency for Forensic Examination; the Agency of Advanced Training of Personnel; and the Agency for Police Support. However, the Directorate was only competent to co-ordinate the state bodies, SBP and SIPA. Moreover, the state, entity and cantonal police already had their own agencies for forensic examination, training and police support, whose abolition was not foreseen in the new Law.

15. Daniel Lindvall, doctoral thesis, 'The Limits of the European Vision in Bosnia and Herzegovina: An Analysis of the Police Reform Negotiations' (Stockholm: Södertörn Doctoral Dissertations, 2009), p. 180.

16. The work of the Badinter Commission is discussed in 'Self-determination, legitimacy and hostilities' and 'Recognition and recrimination', Chapter 4.

17. The Appeal of Milorad Bilbija et al, Decision No. AP-953/05 of 8 July 2006, concerning appeals by Milorad Bilbija and Dragan Kalinić who were removed by the high representative in June 2004.

18. Bosnia's presidency would address to the high representative, as chair of the Steering Board of the Peace Implementation Council, all matters in the Constitutional Court ruling that ought to be considered by the international authorities.

19. In the intervening period, EUFOR's presence has continued to decline, falling in September 2012 to 600 soldiers, backed up by over-the-horizon forces.

20. This replaced the Mission Implementation Plan, originally introduced during Lord Ashdown's tenure as high representative, which had comprised forty-seven reform targets.

21. Reporting has, nevertheless, remained restrained in comparison with the reporting in the months leading up to and during the war, and in the first two years of the peace process.

22. In March 2008, average net earnings in Republika Srpska (731 Bosnian marks or €374) overtook average net earnings in the Federation (723 Bosnian marks or €370).

23. This 2006 sale was by public tender. However, Telekom Srbija offered close to €200 million more than the second highest bidder, Telekom Austria.

24. Under this direct sale, Zarubezhneft paid €125.8 million for a 75 per cent share of the refinery at Bosanski Brod, a 66.75 per cent share in the Modriča refinery, and a 70 per cent share in Banja Luka-based Petrol. Zarubezhneft also pledged to repay the debts of these three companies, amounting to more than €72 million, and to invest between

€600 and €700 million in the modernisation of Republika Srpska's oil industry.

25. For more on these conclusions, see the next section, 'Transitioning'.

26. Areas such as border control, immigration and asylum, import and export of arms and responsibilities over international and inter-entity criminal law enforcement.

27. Areas such as the procurement and provision of identity documents.

28. Reforms in the fields of defence, intelligence, the ITA and the HJPC leading to formal transfers of competencies are described in 'Institution-building' and 'Euro-Atlantic integration', Chapter 6. The reform of electricity transmission took place between 2002 and 2006. In 2004, a state regulatory commission became operational. The Bosnian electricity network was unified in 2006 into a state-level Transmission Company (Transco), based in Banja Luka, which is monitored by an independent system operator at the state level based in Sarajevo. Despite formal agreement on the restructuring, however, Transco has not functioned well, due in part to a prolonged boycott of management board meetings by members from Republika Srpska. Soon after returning to power, Dodik proposed restructuring Transco in such a way that operational areas follow, but do not cross, the inter-entity boundary line.

29. This was also the approach followed in the case of Bulgaria and Romania, which joined the European Union in 2007, and Croatia, which joined in 2013.

30. A National Fiscal Council was created and agreement reached on a permanent ITA co-efficient, thereby formally meeting the criteria for fiscal sustainability. Likewise, a National War Crimes Strategy, a National Justice Sector Strategy, and a Law on Aliens and Asylum were adopted, thereby formally meeting the criteria for entrenchment of the rule of law.

31. The original Prud communiqué stated only that the three leaders had agreed to amend the constitution and had discussed four areas: compliance with the European Convention on Human Rights; state competencies; improving the effectiveness of state institutions; and territorial organisation. They subsequently added several 'basic principles': that Bosnia was a sovereign state; that it was a democratic, social and secular state founded on the rule of law and with legislative, executive and judicial powers; and that it was a decentralised state, with three levels of government, each of which exercised legislative, executive and judicial authority. In relation to the three tiers of

government, they specified that the middle level should consist of four units, but each had his own contradictory explanations of how this would be done. Čović interpreted this as providing the basis for a Croat entity; Tihić as the basis for four economic regions crossing the inter-entity boundary line; and Dodik as having no impact on Republika Srpska, but opening up the possibility of splitting the Federation into two entities and turning the country into a confederal structure.

32. After spending five days in custody, Čović was released on appeal and the sentence eventually quashed.

33. Having been convicted of lack of commitment in office by the State Court, Ivanić was freed on appeal and acquitted by its Appeal Court in July 2010.

34. Branković was subsequently acquitted in October 2010.

35. In total, 73.8 per cent of Bosnians believed their country was heading in the wrong direction, compared with 8.8 per cent who believed it was heading in the right direction. Bosniaks were most pessimistic, with 77.3 per cent believing that the country was heading in the wrong direction and 5.2 per cent in the right direction. Serbs were next most pessimistic, with 71.3 per cent believing the country was heading in the wrong direction and 7.3 per cent in the right direction. Croats were most optimistic, but even so 69.3 per cent believed the country was heading in the wrong direction, with 11.2 per cent believing it was heading in the right direction.

36. In addition to calling for a reassessment of sixty-eight competencies allegedly transferred from the entity to the state (considered in 'Zero-sum politics and ever-rising tension', above), the conclusions, which entered into force on 16 June, asserted, among other things, that the high representative's powers were unconstitutional.

37. In addition to Brussels, Republika Srpska already had representational offices in Belgrade, Jerusalem, Moscow and Stuttgart. Since then, three more have been opened in Vienna (in March 2012), Washington D.C. (in October 2013) and Thessaloniki (in December 2013).

38. The extent of Republika Srpska's lobbying in the United States, including details of all money spent, is in the public domain because of US legislation on disclosure. Similar data are not collected in the European Union.

39. For more on the creation of the State Court and State Prosecutor's Office and the international component of these institutions, see 'Institution-building', Chapter 6.

40. The police officials were Herzegovina-Neretva Cantonal Police

NOTES pp. [205-210]

Commissioner Himzo Đonko and SIPA officer Radoslav Jovičić. Jovičić's ban was subsequently lifted and he became Republika Srpska's interior minister in February 2013.

41. This was the first constitutional amendment to have been adopted.
42. The group included Swedish Foreign Minister and first High Representative Carl Bildt, Slovak Foreign Minister and sixth High Representative Miroslav Lajčák, Director-General for External and Politico-Military Affairs at the Council of the European Union Robert Cooper, EU Commissioner for Enlargement Olli Rehn and Deputy US Secretary of State James Steinberg.
43. A deputy of one of the senior officials summed up the talks at a conference by reworking a well-known Winston Churchill quotation on the Battle of Britain, saying: 'Never have so many, so senior officials offered so much and got nothing.'
44. Two thirds of the loan was earmarked for the Federation and one third for Republika Srpska. In return, the Federation was expected to cut its 2009 budget by €207 million and Republika Srpska €73 million. The state government and Brčko District were also expected to reduce spending by €20 and €5 million respectively. There was a three-year grace period before it was necessary to begin servicing the debt.
45. See 'Justice', Chapter 6, for more on the ICTY's completion strategy.
46. Paragraph 39 of the EU Council conclusions of 8 December 2009 stipulated that: 'The Council stresses that it will not be in a position to consider an application for membership by Bosnia and Herzegovina until the transition of the OHR to a reinforced EU presence has been decided.'
47. For most of the peace process, the European Union's contribution to the OHR budget was 53 per cent; that of the United States 22 per cent; Japan 10 per cent; Russia 4 per cent; Canada 3.03 per cent; the Organisation of Islamic Cooperation (OIC) 2.5 per cent; and others 5.57 per cent. In practice, however, the EU contribution was greater, as Russia unilaterally reduced its own contribution and other smaller contributors failed to make regular payments. In 2015–16, the European Union's contribution was 54.37 per cent; that of the United States 22 per cent; Japan 10 per cent; Canada 3.03 per cent; the OIS 2.5 per cent; Russia 1.2 per cent; and others 6.9 per cent.
48. To hasten agreement on state and defence property, the OHR prepared an inventory of state property between August and December 2009 that was presented to the entity, state and Brčko governments to serve as a basis for discussion.

313

49. For more on the Constitutional Court ruling and the reforms emerging from it, see 'Building multi-ethnicity', Chapter 6.
50. The Other was a Montenegrin.
51. Federation President Borjana Krišto refused to make appointments to the Federation Constitutional Court after her preferred candidate for one position was rejected. The Federation Constitutional Court was hamstrung without the full contingent of judges until January 2015 and the Vital National Interest Panel was unable to sit.
52. In the Dayton Peace Agreement, the Convention was referred to by its original name, the European Convention for the Protection of Human Rights and Fundamental Freedoms.
53. In a similar, September 2008 case that the European Court of Human Rights is yet to rule on, Ilijaz Pilav, a Bosniak from Republika Srpska, argued that he, too, faced discrimination, as he was not able to stand for election to the presidency, since only a Serb could be elected from Republika Srpska.
54. The judgement and background is explained in Lucy Claridge, 'Discrimination and political participation in Bosnia and Herzegovina: Sejdic and Finci v. Bosnia and Herzegovina' (London: Minority Rights Group International, 12 March 2010). Minority Rights Group International represented Finci.
55. For details of Bosnia's Council of Europe admission and post-accession programme, see 'Euro-Atlantic integration', Chapter 6.
56. This ruling is discussed in 'Building multi-ethnicity', Chapter 6.
57. The declaration concluded that: 'Parliament resolutely rejects the entity [Republika Srpska] challenging the State Court and Prosecutors, which were established by the Constitution and laws of Bosnia as an indispensable part of an independent and impartial judicial system, and cannot be denied by a single entity.' It also condemned attacks from Republika Srpska on state institutions, including, in particular, OSA-OBA, the Intelligence and Security Agency, and SIPA, the State Investigation and Protection Agency, and affirmed support for the work of these bodies in protecting the constitutional order and combatting organised crime, corruption, terrorism and war crimes.
58. The post had been vacant for fourteen months.
59. France had been the last to ratify it on 10 February 2011.
60. Set out in the EU Council conclusions on Bosnia of 21 March 2011.
61. The EUSR mandate is set out of 18 July 2011 in the decision appointing Peter Sørensen as EU special representative.
62. The Schengen Area comprises twenty-six countries, twenty-two of which are EU member states.

63. Details of the visa liberalisation process are covered in 'Bosnian Visa Breakthrough May 2009–September 2009: Detailed Scorecard of Bosnia and Herzegovina's results in meeting the EU Schengen White List Conditions' (Berlin/Brussels/Sarajevo: European Stability Initiative, 16 October 2009).
64. 'The HDZs' refers to both parties of the old HDZ after their split: the HDZ BiH and the HDZ 1990.
65. Outgoing Federation Finance Minister and Deputy Prime Minister Vjekoslav Bevanda of the HDZ BiH also sought the opinion of the Federation Constitutional Court.
66. Most PIC members wanted Inzko to intervene as discreetly as possible and ruled out a more comprehensive intervention that would have sought to address the lacunae in the legislation that had allowed the situation to develop. Russia was opposed to any intervention.
67. The HDZ BiH had learned that the Federation Constitutional Court would likely rule against the appeal. Bevanda also withdrew his request for an opinion.
68. For more on the HNS, see 'Promoting "moderates"', Chapter 6.
69. The election of the president and vice presidents of Republika Srpska in 2010 also failed to reflect Croat opinion. Emil Vlajki, a controversial academic who had at times declared himself to be both Jewish and Yugoslav and was best known for extreme Serb positions, was elected as Croat vice president of Republika Srpska, primarily on the basis of Serb votes.
70. The issue is examined in Dmitriy Kovtun, Alexis Mayer Cirkel, Zuzana Murgasova, Dustin Smith and Suchanan Tambunlertchai, 'Boosting Job Growth in the Western Balkans' (Washington D.C.: IMF Working Paper, 28 January 2014).
71. For more on the European Partnership, see 'Euro-Atlantic integration', Chapter 6.
72. EU policy in Bosnia is examined in Kurt Bassuener and Bodo Weber, 'House of Cards: the EU's 'reinforced presence' in Bosnia and Herzegovina' (Sarajevo and Berlin: Democratization Policy Council Policy Paper, 1 May 2013).
73. P. 6 of the 2011 progress report stated: 'The lack of agreement between stakeholders in the country regarding the projects to be financed under the IPA 2011 national programme delayed the completion of the programming exercise in 2011. The difficulties encountered during the programming exercise demonstrate the need to urgently address the issue of coordination on EU matters within the country's

institutions at every level. Strengthening coordination mechanisms on the programming of future EU financial assistance and on other EU matters, is an issue to be addressed as a matter of urgency.'

74. The Zemaljski muzej reopened in September 2015 after an agreement in principle was signed between various levels of government to finance it and other national cultural institutions. In effect, predominantly Bosniak authorities committed to funding these institutions from the next financial year.

75. The Constitutional Court had ruled that identity numbers had to use the official names of municipalities as adopted in Republika Srpska's Law on Territorial Organisation. In May 2009 amendments to this legislation, the names of certain municipalities were changed, including, for example, removing the prefix Bosanski/a in front of Brod and Gradiška.

76. The dilemma facing Bosnian voters at the ballot box is examined in Asim Mujkić and John Hulsey, 'Explaining the Success of Nationalist Parties in Bosnia and Herzegovina', *Politička Misao*, vol. 47, no. 2 (2010), pp. 143–58. The prospects for change in the October 2014 elections are discussed in Valery Perry, 'Is Substantial Political Reform in Bosnia and Herzegovina Possible through the Ballot Box in October 2014?' (Sarajevo: Democratization Policy Council Policy Note, New Series #7, September 2014).

77. As a member of both the European Union and NATO, Croatia is now in a position to exert great influence over international policy towards Bosnia, despite effectively being a party to the conflict. Since both organisations work on the basis of consensus, Croatia could even obstruct decision-making in other areas if its positions are not adopted. Indeed, Cyprus, Greece and Slovenia have used their influence in recent years as members of either the European Union or NATO or both to assert themselves at the expense of Turkey, Macedonia and Croatia respectively. Zagreb will almost certainly seek to alter the Dayton settlement to the advantage of the Bosnian Croats, who also form part of the Croatian electorate. The open question is whether Croatia will seek reform of the entire settlement or the creation of a third, Croat entity.

78. For more on the establishment of the supervisory regime, see 'Changing course' and 'Building multi-ethnicity', Chapter 6.

79. When Lady Ashton met with Dodik in Banja Luka in May 2011, she was seated and photographed in front of the map of Republika Srpska in which Brčko was presented as an integral part of Republika Srpska.

80. Having rejected sections of various PIC communiqués over the years, Russia rejected the May 2014 communiqué in its entirety.
81. The Bosniak caucus of the Republika Srpska Council of Peoples argued that a mixture of new legislation and property taxation would eventually lead to the expropriation of land belonging to Bosniaks who had been expelled from Republika Srpska.
82. A non-governmental organisation called Prvi mart (First of March), founded to encourage and help Bosniaks and Croats register to vote in Republika Srpska, complained that it faced systematic obstruction and intimidation.
83. The most notorious example was the construction of a Serbian Orthodox church in Budak, a hamlet without an Orthodox community, in the vicinity of the Srebrenica-Potočari Memorial Foundation and Cemetery.
84. After the ECtHR ruled in July 2013 that the State Court had applied the wrong criminal code in relation to two cases (Abduladhim Maktouf and Goran Damjanović), the Constitutional Court controversially decided that all people convicted in this way needed to be retried, thereby making possible their release from custody. In this way, twenty convicts who had been found guilty were freed before the loophole was closed in January 2015. This included General Novak Djukić, sentenced to twenty years for ordering an artillery strike on Tuzla that killed seventy-one people, who absconded to Serbia.
85. The United Nations Development Programme attempted to measure social inclusion in Bosnia in 2007 and found that just over half of the population did not have a normal standard of living, was not covered by health insurance, had inadequate access to education, could not participate in society and lacked access to services.
86. The Constitutional Court ruled in July 2012 that the legislation fell outside the competence of the entity legislature and was therefore unconstitutional, and that the competence to regulate such matters fell within the exclusive jurisdiction of the state parliament.
87. The protest failed to achieve its aims, but the children have not returned to learning under the curriculum of Republika Srpska.
88. The six points were taxes on jobs; barriers to jobs; business climate; enterprises; corruption; and social protection.
89. Under Annex 4, Article VI of the Dayton Peace Agreement, Bosnia's Constitutional Court was to have nine members, three of whom were to be selected by the president of the European Court of Human Rights. The Bosnian parliament was entitled to change by law the

method of selection of these judges five years after their initial appointment, but no such legislation has been passed to date.

90. The two perpetrators were convicted and sentenced to forty-five and fifteen years in prison respectively.

91. On 4 September 2015, High Representative Inzko took the unprecedented step of submitting a special report to UN Secretary-General Ban Ki-moon informing him and the UN Security Council that Republika Srpska was 'in clear breach' of the Dayton Peace Agreement and in particular of Annex 4 ('Constitution of Bosnia') and Annex 10 ('Civilian Implementation of the Peace Settlement').

92. In the event that the EUFOR mandate is not extended, it may be possible for a NATO-led force to take over. Although NATO only has a modest physical presence in Bosnia and is focussing on defence reform, it has, nevertheless, retained the Chapter VII peace-enforcement mandate it had under Annex 1 of the Dayton Peace Agreement.

93. According to a UNDP-commissioned poll that appeared in the media in November 2013, close to two thirds of people in Bosnia believed that there would be no new armed conflict in the Balkans, and a little over one third believed that there would. In terms of attitudes to a potential war, 13.5 per cent of Bosniaks, 12.6 per cent of Croats and 1.5 per cent of Serbs said that they would be willing to fight.

94. This is discussed in 'Changing course', Chapter 6.

95. The SDA's analysis of Dayton implementation and the consequences of premature OHR closure can be found on the party's web site at www.sda.ba, last accessed 7 December 2015.

96. For discussion of the events of 1995, see 'Getting to Dayton', Chapter 4.

97. Since 2007, there has also been a United World College in Mostar, the 12th United World College in the world. This school offers English-language education to students from all ethno-national backgrounds throughout Bosnia and beyond. Some 60 per cent of pupils are Bosnians. The remaining 40 per cent come from elsewhere in the former Yugoslavia and the rest of the world.

98. In November 2010, the Constitutional Court ruled that two aspects of the state Election Law enshrined in the Mostar City Statute violated international standards and Bosnia's constitution, and tasked the state parliament with making amendments to the Election Law by December 2011. Specifically, the Constitutional Court found the difference between the weights of votes in the city's six constituencies could not be justified and that voters in the former central zone were disadvantaged, as they were only able to elect councillors from a

city-wide list. After the parliament failed to meet the deadline, the Constitutional Court made an additional ruling, deleting the offending articles. In the absence of these articles, the Central Election Committee decided in May 2012 that it could not organise elections in Mostar.

99. For more on Mostar and the peace process there, see 'Civilian deployment', Chapter 5.

100. In addition to the Sejdić-Finci ruling, the ECtHR has several similar cases pending against Bosnia. Moreover, it ruled against Bosnia in July 2014 in the case of Azra Zornić who had complained that she was unable to run for the presidency because she declared her identity as a citizen without ethno-national affiliation.

9. CHANGING THE LOGIC OF BOSNIAN POLITICS

1. According to opinion polling carried out by PRISM Research in 2013 for the USAID 'Constitutional Reform in BiH: Engaging Civil Society' Project, 88 per cent of the population supported attempts at constitutional reform, representing 98.5 per cent of Croats in the Federation, 91.5 per cent of Bosniaks in the Federation and 79.5 per cent of Serbs in Republika Srpska. The figures are cited in Raluca Raduta, 'Constitutional and Governance Reforms in Bosnia and Herzegovina: Does Public Opinion Matter?' (Sarajevo: Democratization Policy Council Policy Note, New Series # 08, January 2015).

2. In addition to returning to Republika Srpska, Serbs have, for example, returned to the Federation in the municipalities of Bosanski Petrovac, Bosansko Grahovo and Drvar, where they form the majority. In addition to returning to the Federation, Bosniaks have returned to Republika Srpska to the municipality of Srebrenica, as well as to other areas in which they are concentrated, including Janja near Bijeljina, Kozarac near Prijedor and Kozluk near Zvornik.

3. Members of the Bosniak diaspora expelled from areas that now form part of Republika Srpska have been buying properties in Sarajevo in preparation for eventual return upon retirement.

4. The Constitutional Court ruled in March 2006 that the entities needed to change their anthems, flags and coats of arms because they were discriminatory.

5. The fact that there are thirteen ministers of education (one in each canton, one in each entity and one in Brčko) has made education reform especially challenging.

6. For details of schooling in Brčko, see 'Building multi-ethnicity', Chapter 6.

7. In November 2014, the Federation Supreme Court ruled that the practice of 'organising school systems based on ethnic background and implementing curriculums on ethnic principles, which divide children', such as 'two schools under one roof', was discriminatory. It therefore ordered schools to implement 'common integrated multicultural education facilities'. To date, however, there has been no change.

8. When travelling abroad for international conferences, Bosnia's rival ethno-national leaders often go out together in the evening.

9. In *Then They Started Shooting: Children of the Bosnian War and the Adults They Became* (Cambridge, MA and London: Harvard University Press, 2005), child psychiatrist Lynne Jones traced the attitudes of Bosniak and Serb schoolchildren in Goražde and Foča, respectively, and found that, without contact with peers from other communities, their views hardened over time.

10. Determining precise levels of total international spending in Bosnia is complex. Reconstruction aid forms only one element. Arguably, the most important and largest element has been the international military presence. This expenditure is, however, calculated in different ways by the different troop contributors, with some countries calculating the entire cost of deployment and others just the marginal costs, namely the additional spending generated by the deployment. A 2007 Norwegian-funded study by a Bosnian think-tank, the Independent Bureau for Humanitarian Issues, entitled 'Reconstruction Survey in Bosnia and Herzegovina 2007' estimated total international spending on Bosnia-related issues, including the sums spent on Bosnian refugees abroad, the cost of the international military presence and all forms of aid, at between $46 and $53 billion.

11. The World Bank made clear in a report early in the peace process that the Dayton structures would cost Bosnia a great deal in terms of economic efficiency. For details, see William Fox and Christine Wallich, 'Fiscal Federalism in Bosnia-Herzegovina' (Washington D.C.: World Bank Policy Research Working Paper 1714, January 1997).

12. The structure and work of the Constitutional Court as well as its decision on the constituency of peoples are discussed in 'Building multi-ethnicity', Chapter 6.

13. Mandić was jailed for five years in 2006 for abuse of office and fraud at a bank he formerly managed. A year later, he was acquitted of war crimes.

14. The following section draws extensively on a doctoral thesis by Roland Kostić entitled 'Ambivalent Peace: External Peacebuilding, Threatened

Identity and Reconciliation in Bosnia and Herzegovina' (Uppsala: Uppsala University, 2007). Kostić's point of departure is political theory on social and ethno-national identity.

15. The concept of the societal security dilemma was developed by the so-called Copenhagen School in the early 1990s. The Copenhagen School has redefined the concept of security, placing special emphasis upon its societal aspects, namely the securitisation of ethno-national identity. The key work is Barry Buzan, Ole Wæver and Jaap de Wilde, *Security: A New Framework for Analysis* (Boulder, OH: Lynne Rienner, 1997).

16. See 'Dark side of democracy', Chapter 7.

17. The opinion polling was financed by the Swedish foreign ministry and carried out by the PULS agency in summer 2005.

18. Predominantly Bosniak political parties believed threats to Bosniak group existence to be great, even though they also considered the actual importance of group identity to be low. This was in contrast to wider Bosniak opinion, which considered the importance of group identity to be high. Both Croat and Serb political parties and wider Croat and Serb opinion considered the importance of group identity to be high.

19. For details of the Constitutional Court ruling, see 'Building multi-ethnicity', Chapter 6.

20. The only party with a negative view of external security-building was the extremist and by then minor Srpska radikalna stranka (Serb Radical Party, or SRS).

21. The exception was Dodik's SNSD, then in opposition and viewed as one of the more moderate parties, which held a positive view of the ICTY's impact on reconciliation. Given the change in the SNSD's outlook since returning to government in February 2006 and the comments of Dodik himself, it is safe to assume that the SNSD's position today would be akin to that of the other Serb political parties in 2005.

22. Again, the position of the SNSD has since aligned with other Serb political parties.

23. Discussed in 'Limits of liberal peace-building', Chapter 7.

24. The Venice Commission suggested that the panel should be composed of international experts, given the confidential nature of its work. Despite this proposed structure, no such body was formed.

25. The Treaty on the Final Settlement with Respect to Germany was signed on 12 September 1990, paving the way for German unification on 3 October 1990. Under the terms of the Treaty, France, the Soviet

Union, the United Kingdom and the United States renounced all authority, and Germany became fully sovereign on 15 March 1991, just under forty-six years after the end of the Second World War.

26. 'The Responsibility to Protect', Report of the International Commission on Intervention and State Sovereignty (Ottawa: International Development Research Centre, December 2001).

27. Paragraphs 138 and 139 of the World Summit's outcome document state the following:

138. Each individual State has the responsibility to protect its populations from genocide, war crimes, ethnic cleansing and crimes against humanity. This responsibility entails the prevention of such crimes, including their incitement, through appropriate and necessary means. We accept that responsibility and will act in accordance with it. The international community should, as appropriate, encourage and help States to exercise this responsibility and support the United Nations in establishing an early warning capability.

139. The international community, through the United Nations, also has the responsibility to use appropriate diplomatic, humanitarian and other peaceful means, in accordance with Chapters VI and VIII of the Charter, to help protect populations from genocide, war crimes, ethnic cleansing and crimes against humanity. In this context, we are prepared to take collective action, in a timely and decisive manner, through the Security Council, in accordance with the Charter, including Chapter VII, on a case-by-case basis and in cooperation with relevant regional organizations as appropriate, should peaceful means be inadequate and national authorities are manifestly failing to protect their populations from genocide, war crimes, ethnic cleansing and crimes against humanity. We stress the need for the General Assembly to continue consideration of the responsibility to protect populations from genocide, war crimes, ethnic cleansing and crimes against humanity and its implications, bearing in mind the principles of the Charter and international law. We also intend to commit ourselves, as necessary and appropriate, to helping States build capacity to protect their populations from genocide, war crimes, ethnic cleansing and crimes against humanity and to assisting those which are under stress before crises and conflicts break out.

28. In its 'Opinion on the Constitutional Situation in Bosnia and Herzegovina and the Powers of the High Representative', the Venice

Commission concluded that 'it is desirable for the citizens at some stage to decide to have an entirely new constitution based on their own wishes and drafted during a period without ethnic strife.'

29. Discussed in 'Self-determination, legitimacy and hostilities' and 'Recognition and recrimination', Chapter 4.
30. Discussed in 'Democratic dawn', Chapter 3.
31. The 1994 Washington Agreement is discussed in 'Getting to Dayton', Chapter 4.
32. High representatives from Petritsch to Schwarz-Schilling felt obliged to intervene to influence or amend agreements between Republika Srpska and Serbia.
33. See 'Dark side of democracy', Chapter 7.
34. Horowitz's seminal work is *Ethnic Groups in Conflict* (Berkley: University of California Press, 1985).
35. Most elements of the system, together with a discussion of the drawbacks and merits of different electoral systems, were originally presented in 'Changing the Logic of Bosnian Politics: ICG Discussion Paper on Electoral Reform' (Sarajevo: ICG Bosnia Project Report 32, 10 March 1998), which I wrote.
36. Ethno-national electoral rolls exist or have existed in many countries at different times, such as Cyprus and Fiji. In addition, they were becoming the system of choice in Austria-Hungary in the early twentieth century.
37. This represents a major improvement for this group, since they have minimal political representation at present.
38. Voting is compulsory in many countries, including multinational states such as Belgium, where the relative size of each community is an important factor in politics.
39. If, for the sake of example, 50 per cent of the electorate is Bosniak, 40 per cent Serb and 10 per cent Croat, the legislature would have the same proportion of Bosniak, Serb and Croat deputies, that is 50 per cent Bosniak, 40 per cent Serb and 10 per cent Croat. However, ballots cast by Croats would be multiplied by a coefficient of 5 to give Croats an equal say in the selection of Bosniak and Serb deputies, and ballots cast by Serbs would be multiplied by a coefficient of 1.25 to give Serbs an equal say in the selection of Bosniak and Croat deputies.
40. The Venice Commission's report also proposed abolishing the House of Peoples and putting the vital-national-interest veto into the House of Representatives, to 'streamline procedures and facilitate the adoption of legislation without endangering the legitimate interests of any people'.

41. The Moravian Compromise established two voting lists, one German and one Czech, in which Moravians were able to choose to which they wanted to belong. The provincial assembly allotted a set number of seats for each of its chambers, which divided the Germans and Czechs roughly 40:60. This was somewhat advantageous for the Germans, since the actual ratio by population was closer to 35:65, but the compromise also locked in a Czech majority.

42. The literature on the Habsburgs' experiments with electoral systems in multi-ethnic provinces in the early twentieth century is largely in German and Czech. The only literature in English is Peter Mirejovsky's doctoral thesis, 'In Search of a Bohemian Compromise: Czech-German Negotiations 1908–1914' (Toronto: University of Toronto, 1982).

43. Discussed in 'Ethno-national identities and rivalries', Chapter 2.

44. Discussed in 'Democratic dawn', Chapter 3.

45. The proposed system would only work if electors were to vote in all categories, which did not happen in the 1990 election to the presidency. One way to ensure that people vote in all categories would be to consider ballots that left categories blank to have been spoiled.

10. CONCLUSION

1. David Bloomfield is former chief executive of the Glencree Centre for Peace and Reconciliation in the Republic of Ireland. Ben Reilly is dean of the Sir Walter Murdoch School of Public Policy and International Affairs at Murdoch University in Western Australia. The quotation is from *Democracy and Deep-Rooted Conflict: Options for Negotiators* (Stockholm: International IDEA, 1998), p. 21.

BIBLIOGRAPHICAL NOTE

On the eve of Yugoslavia's disintegration, there was hardly a book in print about Bosnia in any Western language. In the intervening quarter century, several hundred have been published, making the Bosnian conflict one of the most written about. Given the quantity of publications, the quality has inevitably been mixed. There are, nevertheless, many that provide insight into Bosnia's history, disintegration into war and peace process. This note is not a comprehensive list of books and articles, but rather a review of relevant literature, both on Bosnia and on divided societies, that has contributed to my understanding of events, as well as details of key documents of enduring significance to the peace process. It is designed both to provide information on the sources I have used and to help anyone seeking more information on specific areas. All titles contribute to a better understanding of the conflict, if only, in some instances, to explain the attitudes of key players towards it.

The absence of a good history of Bosnia in the early years of the war persuaded many observers that the conflict was a manifestation of ancient hatreds. While superficially compelling, these arguments could not stand up to academic scrutiny. The publication of two good histories of Bosnia in 1994–*Bosnia and Hercegovina: A Tradition Betrayed* (London: Hurst, 1994) by Robert J. Donia and John V.A. Fine Jr and *Bosnia: A Short History* (London: Macmillan, 1994) by Noel Malcolm–discredited the ancient-hatreds thesis. Marko Attila Hoare's *The History of Bosnia: From the Middle Ages to the Present Day* (London: Saqi Books, 2007) is an excellent addition to the literature, and the account of Bosnia's history that I have looked to in particular.

BIBLIOGRAPHICAL NOTE

Ivo Banac's *The National Question in Yugoslavia: Origins, History, Politics* (Ithaca, NY: Cornell University Press, 1984) is the starting point for understanding relations among the peoples of the former Yugoslavia. Aleksa Djilas' *The Contested Country: Yugoslav Unity and Communist Revolution, 1919–1953* (Cambridge, MA: Harvard University Press, 1991) examines national policy from the creation of the first Yugoslavia through its destruction and the Second World War to the formation of the second Yugoslavia. In *The Yugoslav Experiment, 1948–1974* (London: Hurst, 1977), Dennison Ivan Rusinow analyses the evolution of Tito's Yugoslavia. David A. Dyker's *Yugoslavia: Socialism, Development and Debt* (London: Routledge, 1990) examines Yugoslavia's economic failings.

On sections relating to Yugoslavia's disintegration, I generally relied on my own book, *Yugoslavia's Bloody Collapse: Causes, Course and Consequences* (London: Hurst, 1995). There are, in addition, several other informative publications, including Susan L. Woodward's *Balkan Tragedy: Chaos and Dissolution after the Cold War* (Washington D.C.: Brookings Institution, 1995) and Laura Silber and Allan Little's *The Death of Yugoslavia* (London: Penguin/BBC Books, 1995). Moreover, Sabrina P. Ramet succinctly summarises and analyses many of the competing theses about Yugoslavia's disintegration in *Thinking about Yugoslavia: Scholarly Debates about the Yugoslav Breakup and the Wars in Bosnia and Kosovo* (Cambridge and New York: Cambridge University Press, 2005). Mark Thompson's *Forging War: The Media in Serbia, Croatia and Bosnia-Hercegovina* (Avon: The Bath Press, 1994) considers the role of media. Josip Glaurdić's *The Hour of Europe: Western Powers and the Breakup of Yugoslavia* (New Haven, CT: Yale University Press, 2011) is the most up-to-date account of Yugoslavia's disintegration and the international diplomacy surrounding it that ends with the beginning of the Bosnian War.

James Gow's *Triumph of the Lack of Will: International Diplomacy and the Yugoslav War* (London: Hurst, 1997) examines the international diplomacy around the Wars of Yugoslav Dissolution and was completed soon after the Dayton Peace Agreement came into force. Gow argues that a critical opportunity for peace was missed in 1993 when Washington failed to support the Vance-Owen Plan. This is also the lament of EU negotiator Lord David Owen in

BIBLIOGRAPHICAL NOTE

Balkan Odyssey (San Diego, New York and London: Harvest Book, 1995). And twenty years after the Vance-Owen Plan was rejected, Lord Owen returned to this theme in an edited volume of documents entitled *Bosnia-Herzegovina: The Vance/Owen Peace Plan* (Liverpool: Liverpool University Press, 2013). In retrospect, it does seem that Bosnia's prospects would have been considerably better had the Vance-Owen Plan received the diplomatic support that it required in 1993. Brendan Simms' *Unfinest Hour: Britain and the Destruction of Bosnia* (London: Penguin, 2001) is an indictment of British policy towards the former Yugoslavia in the first half of the 1990s. Ivo Komšić, one of the Croat members of Bosnia's wartime presidency, published his wartime diary, *The Survived Country–Dividing Bosnia and Herzegovina: Who, When, Where* (Sarajevo: Synopsis, 2013). This provides some insight into the Bosnian government's thinking and useful details of the 1994 Washington Agreement that ended the war between Bosniaks and Croats.

The most complete account of Bosnia's disintegration and war is *The War in Bosnia-Herzegovina: Ethnic Conflict and International Intervention* (Armonk, NY, and London: M.E. Sharpe, 1999) by Stephen L. Burg and Paul S. Shoup. Peter Radan's *The Break-up of Yugoslavia and International Law* (London and New York, NY: Routledge, 2002) is a critical analysis of the work of the Badinter Commission. Richard Caplan's *Europe and the Recognition of New States in Yugoslavia* (Cambridge: Cambridge University Press, 2005) addresses one of the great controversies of the Wars of Yugoslav Dissolution, namely the impact of international recognition of Slovenia and Croatia on Bosnia. Charles Ingrao and Thomas A. Emmert's edited *Confronting the Yugoslav Controversies* (West Lafayette, IN: Purdue University Press, 2nd ed., 2012) is a composite work of many historians and social scientists from South Eastern Europe and the West that examines eleven controversial issues emerging out of Yugoslavia's disintegration, including the role of the international community.

Several UN commanders penned accounts of their time in Bosnia, some to justify the policies they adopted, others to vent frustration at not being able to do more. General Lewis MacKenzie, the Canadian who was first to command the United Nations Protection

327

Force (UNPROFOR) in Sarajevo, gave his side of the story in *Peacekeeper: The Road to Sarajevo* (Vancouver: Douglas and McIntyre, 1993). General Philippe Morillon, a French UNPROFOR commander whose actions helped create the United Nations safe-haven policy, published his memoirs soon after leaving Bosnia in *Croire et oser: Chronique de Sarajevo* (Paris: Grasset, 1993). General Sir Michael Rose, the first British commander of UNPROFOR, presented his account of events in *Fighting For Peace: Bosnia 1994* (London: Harvill, 1998). General Francis Briquemont, a Belgian UNPROFOR commander, let off steam in *Do something, General! Chronique de Bosnie-Herzégovine, 12 juillet 1993–24 janvier 1994* (Brussels: Labot, 1998). Colonel Bob Stewart, the British commander in Central Bosnia between October 1992 and May 1993, during the most intensive Bosniak-Croat fighting, provided his perspective in *Broken Lives: A Personal View of the Bosnian Conflict* (London: HarperCollins, 1994). French General Jean Cot, who commanded UNPROFOR between July 1993 and March 1994, penned *Demain la Bosnie* (Paris: L'Harmattan, 1999).

The difficulties faced by UNPROFOR are examined in *With No Peace to Keep: UN Peacekeeping and the War in the former Yugoslavia* (London: Media East West, 1996), a collection of essays edited by Ben Cohen and George Stamkoski. David Rieff examines the shortcomings of the United Nations mission in Bosnia in *Slaughterhouse: Bosnia and the Failure of the West* (London: Simon and Schuster, 1995). Marko Attila Hoare's *How Bosnia Armed* (London: Saqi Books, 2004) is an in-depth analysis of the war from the perspective of the Bosnian government and Bosnian Army. And Tim Ripley's *Operation Deliberate Force: The UN and NATO Campaign in Bosnia 1995* (Lancaster: CDISS, 1999) examines the 1995 air campaign that paved the way for the Dayton peace talks.

Tone Bringa's *Being Muslim the Bosnian Way: Identity and Community in a Central Bosnian Village* (Princeton and London: Princeton University Press, 1995) is an examination of Bosniak identity by an anthropologist who lived in a Bosnian village during the 1980s. *The Bridge Betrayed: Religion and Genocide in Bosnia* (Berkeley, Los Angeles and London: University of California Press, 1996) by Michael Sells analyses the role and abuse of religion in the conflict. *Genocide in Bosnia: the Policy of "Ethnic Cleansing"* (College Station, TX: Texas A&M University Press, 1995) by Norman Cigar examines the ideological preparation for ethnic cleansing.

The July 1995 Srebrenica genocide is dissected both by Pulitzer Prize-winning journalist David Rohde in *Endgame: The Betrayal and Fall of Srebrenica, Europe's Worst Massacre Since World War II* (New York: Farrar, Straus and Giroux, 1997) and by Jan Willem Honig and Norbet Both, in *Srebrenica: Record of a War Crime* (London: Penguin, 1996). Chuck Sudetic, a former reporter with *The New York Times*, draws on the experience of his wife's brother-in-law's family, who were from Srebrenica, to write *Blood and Vengeance: One Family's Story of the War in Bosnia* (New York: W.W. Norton, 1998). And Emir Suljagić, today Bosnia's deputy defence minister, provides a first-hand account of life in Srebrenica during the war and the genocide in *Postcards from the Grave* (London: Saqi Books, 2005).

After the fall of Srebrenica, the United States took over the mediation role from the European Union and United Nations. Richard Holbrooke describes the events leading to the Dayton Peace Agreement in *To End a War* (New York: Random House, 1998). Ivo H. Daalder, director of European Affairs at the National Security Council co-ordinating US policy on Bosnia during 1995 and 1996, examines the debates in the Clinton administration in *Getting to Dayton: The Making of America's Bosnia Policy* (Washington D.C.: Brookings Institution, 2000). And Derek Chollet provides an engaging and exhaustive account of the process leading to the Dayton talks as well as of the talks themselves in *The Road to the Dayton Accords: A Study of American Statecraft* (New York and London: Palgrave Macmillan, 2005).

The first, third and fourth high representatives, Carl Bildt, Wolfgang Petritsch and Lord Paddy Ashdown published books about Bosnia: *Peace Journey: The Struggle for Peace in Bosnia* (London: Orion, 1999), *Bosna i Hercegovina od Daytona do Evrope* (Sarajevo: Svjetlost, 2002) and *Swords And Ploughshares: Bringing Peace to the 21ˢᵗ Century* (London: Orion, 2007) respectively. All three accounts provide insight into the authors' outlooks as well as the challenges they faced, with Lord Ashdown's the most revealing. Indeed, Milorad Dodik, then Republika Srpska prime minister, placed a copy of Lord

Ashdown's memoir under glass in his office to draw visitors' attention to p. 249. Lord Ashdown had candidly written that he had at times asked European External Relations Commissioner Chris Patten to say that certain reforms were required if Bosnia wished to join Europe and that Patten had obliged.

The first academic study of the peace process to be published was David Chandler's aptly named *Faking Democracy After Dayton* (London: Pluto Press, 1999). Chandler focuses on the early elections and is hostile to the very concept of international intervention. In *Blueprints for a House Divided: The Constitutional Logic of the Yugoslav Conflicts* (Ann Arbor, MI: University of Michigan Press, 1999), Robert M. Hayden is extremely sceptical about the prospects of the peace process on the basis of a comprehensive analysis of the peace accord. Moreover, the case he presents holds up well sixteen years later. Sumatra Bose's *Bosnia after Dayton: Nationalist Partition and International Intervention* (London: Hurst, 2002) covers the first five years of the peace process in detail and includes interesting insight on the consequences of partition based on the experience of India. Roberto Belloni's *State Building and International Intervention in Bosnia* (London and New York: Routledge, 2007) covers the first decade of the peace process, arguing that long-term transformation requires the active involvement and empowerment of civil society. Florian Bieber's *Post-War Bosnia: Ethnicity, Inequality and Public Sector Governance* (Basingstoke and New York: Palgrave Macmillan, 2005) also covers much of the first decade of the peace process and offers probably the most comprehensive account published to date. Ed Vulliamy's *The War is Dead, Long Live the War: Bosnia: The Reckoning* (London: Bodley Head, 2012) is an important book, though it does not provide much detail of the peace process. One of the journalists who entered Serb-run detention camps in August 1992, Vulliamy returned twenty years later to investigate the fate, outlook and prospects of people he had got to know, including camp survivors, during the war. The result is extremely sobering.

The debate over local ownership started in earnest with publication of 'Lessons from Bosnia and Herzegovina: Travails of the European Raj', by Gerald Knaus and Felix Martin in the *Journal of Democracy*, vol. 14, no. 3 (2003), pp. 60–74. This article is extremely critical of the OHR's operations in Bosnia and the executive power wielded by the high representative. *Ownership Process in Bosnia and Herzegovina: Contributions on the International Dimensions of Democratization in the Balkans* (Baden-Baden: Nomos, 2003), which was edited by Christophe Solioz, Svebor Dizdarevic and Wolfgang Petritsch, is far more positive about the impact of international intervention. And Solioz's *Turning Points in Post-War Bosnia: Ownership Process and European Integration* (Baden-Baden: Nomos, 2007) heralds a European future for Bosnia. Philippe Leroux-Martin's *Diplomatic Counterinsurgency: Lessons from Bosnia and Herzegovina* (New York: Cambridge University Press, 2013) examines the conflict between the OHR and Republika Srpska in 2007 after Miroslav Lajčák attempted to streamline decision-making procedures in state institutions. And Sofía Sebastián-Aparicio's *Post-War Statebuilding and Constitutional Reform: Beyond Dayton in Bosnia* (London: Palgrave Macmillan, 2014) analyses attempts to reform the Dayton settlement between 2006 and 2012.

Three books specifically cover international supervision in Brčko, two of which were written by former OHR employees, including Robert W. Farrand, the first supervisor. In *Reconstruction and Peace Building in the Balkans: The Brcko Experience* (London, Boulder, New York, Toronto and Plymouth: Rowman and Littlefield, 2011), Farrand lays out the challenges he faced and explains how he addressed them during the three years he spent in Brčko. Matthew Parish's *A Free City in the Balkans: Reconstructing a Divided Society in Bosnia* (London: I.B. Tauris, 2009) is a more insightful book that includes discussion of the complexities of post-war governance in multi-ethnic states. The book is critical of international intervention, though the analysis is undermined by gratuitous comments about former colleagues and the OHR in general. Adam Moore's *Peacebuilding in Practice: Local Experience in Two Bosnian Towns* (Ithaca, NY, and London: Cornell University Press, 2013) covers the peace process in Mostar as well as in Brčko.

Justice reform in Bosnia and war-crimes trials, both at the International Criminal Tribunal for the former Yugoslavia (ICTY) in The Hague and in Bosnian courts, have been key elements of the peace process. Andy Aitchison's *Making the Transition: International Intervention, State-Building and Criminal Justice Reform in Bosnia and Herzegovina* (Cambridge, Antwerp and Portland, OR: Intersentia, 2011) describes international efforts to reform Bosnia's judiciary and analyses their impact. 'War Crimes in BiH: Criminal Procedures in Bosnia and Herzegovina 1992–2006. Indictments, Appeals, Verdicts' (Sarajevo: ABA/CEELI and Association of Prosecutors BiH, 2006) provides details of fifty-four processes that took place between 1992 and 2006 in the Federation, Brčko District and Republika Srpska. In *The Key to My Neighbor's House: Seeking Justice in Bosnia and Rwanda*, (New York: Picador, 2001), Elizabeth Neuffer, a *Boston Globe* journalist who was to die in Iraq, provides an analysis of the potential significance of the ICTY to both the Bosnian peace process and more generally to countries recovering from conflict. Former *Le Monde* journalist and 2000–6 ICTY spokesperson Florence Hartmann penned a revealing and damning assessment of the obstacles placed in the way of the ICTY in *Paix et Châtiment, Les Guerres secrètes de la politique et de la justice internationales* (Paris: Flammarion, 2007). Publication got her in trouble with her former employer, which indicted her for disclosing confidential information, found her guilty of contempt of court, fined her and, several years later, imprisoned her for five days. Lara J. Nettelfield's *Courting Democracy in Bosnia and Herzegovina: The Hague Tribunal's Impact in a Postwar State* (New York: Cambridge University Press, 2010) is a more generous assessment of the ICTY's impact and legacy.

Lara J. Nettelfield and Sarah E. Wagner's *Srebrenica in the Aftermath of Genocide* (New York: Cambridge University Press, 2013) examines the consequences of genocide in Srebrenica and efforts to rebuild. In *Then They Started Shooting: Growing Up in Wartime Bosnia* (Cambridge, MA: Harvard University Press, 2005), child psychiatrist Lynne Jones traces the attitudes of Bosniak and Serb schoolchildren in Goražde and Foča, respectively, over the years. She found them to be extremely resilient given their wartime experience, but that, in the absence of contact with peers from other communities, their views hardened with time. Christian Jennings' *Bosnia's Million Bones, Solving the World's Greatest Forensic Puzzle* (London: Palgrave Macmillan, 2012) is about the search for the missing in Bosnia. It is also a lively history of the International Commission on Missing Persons, the international agency founded in Bosnia to address this issue in 1996 that became an international organisation in its own right in 2015.

In addition to published sources, I benefitted greatly from two doctoral dissertations: Daniel Lindvall's 'The Limits of the European Vision in Bosnia and Herzegovina: An Analysis of the Police Reform Negotiations' (Stockholm: Södertörn Doctoral Dissertations, 2009) and Roland Kostić's 'Ambivalent Peace: External Peacebuilding, Threatened Identity and Reconciliation in Bosnia and Herzegovina' (Uppsala: Uppsala University, 2007). The former was my primary source in relation to police reform. The latter examines external peace-building in Bosnia via political theory on social and ethno-national identity and includes the results of particularly insightful opinion polling.

The websites of all international organisations involved in the peace process and especially the OHR's website contain a vast amount of relevant data. The OHR's website is especially informative and includes the text of the Dayton Peace Agreement in English. There are, in addition, two documents of enduring significance for the peace process. These are the Constitutional Court's 2000 decision on the constituency of peoples (U-5/98) and the Council of Europe Venice Commission's 2005 'Opinion on the Constitutional Situation in Bosnia and Herzegovina and the Powers of the High Representative' (Venice: European Commission for Democracy through Law, 11 March 2005). Various think-tanks have written on Bosnia over the years. I made extensive use of International Crisis Group reports, though primarily from the period when I worked for the organisation in the 1990s. I also systematically consulted European Stability Initiative reports, a handful of which I had also contributed to. For the second decade of the peace process, Democratization Policy Council reporting is thorough, informative and insightful. The online archives of both the Institute for War and Peace Reporting and the Balkan Investigative Reporting Network provide an invaluable research tool.

The writing of Arend Lijphart is critical to an understanding of consociationalism and its limitations that is especially relevant in

BIBLIOGRAPHICAL NOTE

relation to Bosnia. This includes, in particular, *Democracy in Plural Societies: A Comparative Exploration* (New Haven, CT: Yale University Press, 1977) and *Patterns of Democracy: Government Forms & Performance in Thirty-Six Countries* (New Haven, CT: Yale University Press, 1999). An alternative approach to finding accommodation in divided societies that seeks to shift the focus of politics away from ethno-national identity, often referred to as centripetalism, is associated, in particular, with the writing of Donald L. Horowitz. His most celebrated book in this field is *Ethnic Groups in Conflict* (Berkeley, CA: University of California Press, 1985). The writing of the so-called Copenhagen School—Barry Buzan, Ole Wæver and Jaap de Wilde—on the societal security dilemma in, for example, *Security: A New Framework for Analysis* (Boulder, ON: Lynne Rienner, 1998) has also influenced my outlook. And Michael Mann's *The Dark Side of Democracy: Explaining Ethnic Cleansing* (Cambridge and New York: Cambridge University Press, 2005) helped me to understand the potential dangers of democratisation, or rather of poorly designed multi-party systems, in particular multi-ethnic settings such as Bosnia.

In attempting to develop alternative models for Bosnia's constitutional and electoral architecture, I drew inspiration from the following works: Peter Harris and Ben Reilly's edited *Democracy and Deep-Rooted Conflict: Options for Negotiators* (Stockholm: International IDEA, 1998); Andrew Reynolds, Ben Reily and Andrew Ellis' edited *Electoral System Design: The New International IDEA Handbook* (Stockholm: International IDEA, 2005); Andrew Reynolds and Ben Reilly's *Electoral Systems and Conflict in Divided Societies* (Washington D.C.: National Academy Press, 1999); and Ben Reilly's *Democracy in Divided Societies: Electoral Engineering for Conflict Management* (Cambridge and New York: Cambridge University Press, 2001).

INDEX

INDEX

INDEX

INDEX

Bond, Clifford, 195

Bonn, 13, 14, 113, 114, 294n9

Bonn Peace Implementation Conference, 13, 14, 113, 114, 294n9

Bonn Powers, 13, 14, 113, 143, 148, 153, 156, 167, 169, 170, 184, 186–188, 191, 192, 201, 202, 204, 205, 208, 215, 228, 247, 248, 250, 254, 255, 270, 273, 305n4, 305n7 (introduction) 113 (phasing out) 186 (use) 169, 170, 305n4 (Venice Commission assessment) 305n7

Boras, Franjo, 284n15

Border control, 311n25

Borders, 56, 59, 70, 143, 150, 258, 259 (Bosnia's) 70, 150 (ethno-national) 258 (redrawing of) 56, 59

Borovo Selo, 48, 49

Borrowing, 217

Bosanski Brod, 310n24, 316n75

Bosanski Petrovac, 319n2

Bosansko Grahovo, 293n29, 319n2

Bosnia, xvii-xxvi, 1–34, 37, 41, 43, 44, 48, 51, 53, 54, 56–60, 62–71, 73, 75, 76, 78–86, 92–94, 96–100, 103–109, 113, 114, 120, 123, 124, 126, 128, 131, 132, 135–143, 145, 150, 152–157, 160–168, 170–174, 176–191, 193, 195, 197–206, 209, 210, 213, 215–220, 222, 223, 225, 228–239, 241, 242, 244, 247–250, 253, 255, 257–281, 282n12, 284n16, 287n11, 287n12, 287n16, 290n9, 290n10, 290n13, 291n13, 295n10, 296n17, 293n41, 293n43, 301n67, 305n5, 305n7, 310n18, 314n57, 316n77, 318n92, 318n97, 319n100 (annexation in 1908) 20, 21 (Council of Europe membership) 154, 155 (Croat

banovina) 25 (Cutileiro Plan) 65 (dead in Second World War) 29 (economy) 93, 207, 224 (elections, 1990) 4, 5, 16, 33, 41–44, 57, 172, 180–182, 229, 249, 264, 267, 274 (elections, 1996) xx, xxi, 9, 12, 13, 91, 97–106, 109, 113, 114, 146, 177, 269, 270, 273 (elections, 1998) xxi, 117 (elections, 2000) 117, 118, 120 (elections, 2002) 115, 117, 121, 128, 129, 176 (elections, 2006) 167, 170, 171, 174, 176–179, 183, 194, 198, 218 (elections, 2010) 207, 213, 214, 217, 218, 223 (elections, 2014) 228, 233 (ethno-national composition/mix) 5, 31, 43 (EU membership) 14, 153, 191, 209, 215, 233, 274 (EU membership application) 209 (international recognition) 7, 16, 60 (Kingdom of Serbs, Croats and Slovenes) 23 (mayoral elections, 2004) 119 (municipal elections, 1997) 105, 106, 149 (municipal elections, 2000) 117 (municipal elections, 2004) 117 (municipal elections, 2008) 194 (outbreak of war) 66 (Partnership-for-Peace membership) 160 (reconstruction) xxii, 93 (referendum) 60 (relationship with the European Union) 11, 92, 96, 154, 189, 203, 209, 213, 225, 233, 275 (Second World War) 25–29 (trajectory) xix, 229, 230, 234, 275, 276 (wartime destruction) 93

Bosniak, xviii, xxvi, 17, 83, 89, 111, 170, 171, 177, 195, 198, 207, 210, 211, 223, 226, 232, 233, 236, 239, 252, 257, 263, 277 (caucus of Republika Srpska Council of Peoples), 210, 211 (children) 233

INDEX

16, 22, 85, 249, 252, 253, 265, 279
Bosnian Serb Assembly, 63
Bosnians, xvii, xviii, xxi, xxiv, xxv, 3–5, 9, 13, 14, 17, 42, 67, 81, 101, 114, 128, 141, 153, 165, 176, 188, 191, 201–203, 207, 210, 217, 228, 229, 242, 244–247, 250, 251, 255, 256, 261, 262, 267–269, 274, 279, 312n35, 318n97
Bosnia-Podrinje Canton, 290n11
Boundaries, 258, 278, 287n12 (entity) 278
Boutros-Ghali, Boutros, 70
Boyle, Francis, 298n35
Bread queue massacre, 70
Branković, Nedžad, 200, 312n34
Bratunac, 139
Brčko, 10, 32, 76, 78, 83, 85, 105, 110, 111, 121–126, 160, 205, 206, 230, 231, 237, 239, 244, 265, 292n24, 296n23, 313n48, 316n79 (2004 elections) 124 (Arbitral Award) 123, 231, 296n25 (Arbitral Tribunal) 110, 123, 230, 231, 294n4 (arbitration) 78 (Arbitration Panel) 290n13 (condominium) 123, 124 (constitutional amendment) 205 (corridor) 76 (corruption) 231 (criminal code) 217 (decision-making) 125 (District) 124, 160, 169, 205, 206, 217, 299n54, 313n44 (District Assembly) 124, 125, 126 (District Statute) 125, 126 (economy) 231 (education reform) 124, 125 (electoral system) 125 (electricity/power supply) 205, 206, 230 (ethno-national composition) 123 (executive authority) 124 (executive order) 205, 206 (Final Award) 193,

205, 206 (impositions) 126, 205 (interim award) 110 (interim rulings) 123 (map) 296n23, 316n79 (minority returns) 123, 124 (multi-ethnic administration) 121, 123, 124 (multi-ethnicity) 239 (police restructuring) 124 (ruling) 123 (supervision/supervisor) 100, 121, 124–126, 205, 206, 296n24 (supervisory authority) 124 (tax administration) 160 (vital-interest mechanisms) 125
Bremen, 94
Brioni, 52, 53 (Accord) 52 (resolutions) 53
Britain, 70, 109
British, 28, 52, 109, 282n11(Army) 28 (forces) 28 (foreign minister) 52 (special forces) 109
Broadcaster/s, 146, 147 (Croatia) 147 (entity) 147 (Federation) 147 (multi-ethnic) 146, 147 (Serbia) 147 (state) 147
Broadcasting, 146, 147 (code of practice) 146 (memorandum of understanding on future of) 147
Brod, 316n75
Brotherhood and unity, 25, 27
Brunei, 289n4
Brussels, xxii, 11, 93, 142, 153, 161, 163, 166, 174, 184, 185, 187, 191, 192, 202, 203, 205, 208, 215, 228, 248, 255, 272, 273, 312n37 ('era of') 161, 166, 272 ('pull of') xxii, 153, 184, 187, 191, 192, 248, 273
Budak, 317n83
Budimir, Živko, 220, 222
Budget, 199, 220, 225, 226 (Bosnia) 199 (cuts) 226 (Federation) 220 (Republika Srpska) 199 (support) 225
Bugojno (terrorism), 235

INDEX

INDEX

INDEX

INDEX

INDEX

INDEX

INDEX

80, 93, 104, 156, 289n2, 292n27, 295n16

Holiday Inn, 66

Holy See, 290n13

Horowitz, Donald L., xxi, xxv, 261

Horvat, Branko, 39

Hostilities, xxiii, xxv, 6, 7, 9, 13, 18, 28, 46, 52, 53, 56, 57, 61, 66, 68, 69, 73, 82, 85, 95, 96, 107, 108, 157, 184, 236, 237, 255-257, 276, 278 (Bosnia) 7, 66, 68, 69 (Croatia) 46, 61 (cessation of) 82 (end of) 9, 18, 85, 95, 96, 157 (new) 257 (outbreak of) 255 (possibility of renewed) xxiii, xxv, 107, 237 (resumption of) 184 (return to) 236, 256, 257, 276, 278 (Second World War) 28 (Slovenia) 6, 53

Hotel Ero, 95

House of Peoples, 88, 90, 101, 118, 119, 128, 129, 175, 176, 211-213, 219, 220, 222, 263, 264, 297n29, 297n32 (composition) 90, 101 (change to selection of delegates in Federation) 118, 119, 297n29 (Federation) 88, 90, 118, 119, 128, 129, 212, 219, 220, 222, 297n29, 297n32 (quorum) 90 (Serb caucus of Federation) 211

House of Representatives, 90, 98, 104, 129, 172, 175, 234, 309n7, 309n11 (April Package rejection) 172 (composition) 90 (elections) 98 (Federation) 98, 129 (quorum) 309n7 (speaker) 234

Housing/housing stock, 9, 93, 96

Hrvatska demokratska zajednica, see HDZ

Hrvatska narodna zajednica, see HNZ

Hrvatski narodni sabor, see HNS

Hrvatska seljačka stranka, see HSS

Hrvatska stranka prava, see HSP

Hrvatsko vijeće odbrane, see HVO

HSP, 219-222

HSS, 23-25 (killing of deputies in Belgrade parliament) 24

Human rights, 11, 55, 59, 77, 87, 89, 91, 92, 100, 127, 140, 149, 154, 155, 250, 251, 256, 303n87, 304n88 (constitutional guarantees in Republika Srpska) 87 (group) 250 (individual) 250 (institutions) 304n87, 304n88 (international instruments for protection of) 127 (legislation) 251

Human Rights and Refugees Ministry, 301n65

Human Rights Chamber, 11, 91, 138, 139, 145

Human rights court (in Federation), 89

Human Rights Ombudsman, 11, 91, 290n13

Humanitarian, 9, 69, 70, 73, 93, 102, 115, 116, 256, 268, 269 (aid) xx, 9, 69, 70, 93, 102, 115, 268 (effort) 73 (intervention) 256 (needs) 116, 269

Hungarian, 26, 40, 62 (minority in Slovenia) 40 (population) 62 (rule) 26

Hungary, 282n7, 290n13, 292n26

Hungarians, 53, 61

Hunting clubs, 237

Hurd, Douglas, 73

Hurricane Katrina, 300n59

HVO, 68, 69, 75, 82, 157, 159

Hyperinflation, 145

Iceland, 290n13

ICJ, 68, 131, 137, 140, 185, 194, 294n4, 300n56 (Bosnia versus Serbia and Montenegro genocide case) 137, 140, 185, 194

INDEX

INDEX

INDEX

Inzko, Valentin, 200–202, 204, 205, 207–210, 214–216, 220, 228, 232, 250, 305n4, 315n66, 318n91 (Brčko impositions) 205 (Dodik challenge) 201 (impositions) 208, 220 (mandate of international judges and prosecutors) 204 (removals) 204 (Republika Srpska National Assembly conclusions) 204 (special report to UN Secretary-General Ban Ki-moon) 318n91 (suspension of CEC decision) 220 (temporary financing in Federation) 220 (use of Bonn Powers) 305n4
IPA, 225, 226
IPTF, 11, 91, 110, 116, 124, 142, 148–150, 154, 294n3, 300n62 (mandate) 148 (police vetting) 142, 149
Iraq, 50, 55, 157, 172, 235, 273 (invasion of Kuwait) 50, 55 (US invasion) 157
Ireland, 290n13
Irredentist agendas, xix, 267
Islam (conversion to), 18
Islamic, 15, 18, 82, 235, 291n14 (community) 235, 291n14 (countries) 82 (fighters) 235 (law) 18 (terrorism) 235
Islamic Declaration, 41
Islamic State, 235
Istanbul Summit, 162
Istria, 26, 282n7
ITA, 160, 175, 193, 311n30 (co-efficient) 311n30 (permanent co-efficient methodology) 193
Italian, 26, 40, 99 (EU presidency) 99 (minority in Slovenia) 40 (rule) 26
Italy, 24, 25, 28, 54, 201, 202, 209, 273, 281n3, 282n7, 286n7, 290n13, 291n13, 292n26

Ivanić, Mladen, 118, 200, 312n34
Izetbegović, Alija, xvii, 41, 43, 58, 60, 62, 63, 74, 77–80, 84, 126, 133, 213, 252, 284n15, 285n21, 288n22, 289n2, 289n5, 298n35 (appeal for deployment of UN peacekeepers) 62 (early career) 41 (ICTY investigation) 133
Izetbegović, Bakir, 213, 218, 234

Jajce, 28
Japan, 201, 273, 290n13, 291n13, 313n47 (OHR budget contribution) 313n47
Janja, 319n2
Jasenovac, 29
Jelavić, Ante, 120, 295n17, 296n17
Jerusalem, 312n37
Jew/s, 18, 19, 29, 141, 212, 282n11 (dead in Second World War) 29
Jewish community/cultural associations, 21, 282n14
JMO, 23–25
JNA, 44–53, 57, 58, 61–63, 68, 284n16, 286n4 (Bosnia) 62, 63, 68 (Brioni Accord) 52 (Croatia) 47–49, 58, 61 (Kosovo) 46 (Serbian alliance) 45 (Slovenia) 51, 53, 286n4
Johnson, Ralph R., 203
Johnson, Susan R., 296n24
Joint Commission on Security and Defence, 158
Joint criminal enterprise, 131, 133–135, 298n36, 298n45
Joint List, see ZL
Joint Staff, 158, 159
Jordan, 289n4, 290n13
Journalism schools, 146
Jović, Borisav, 47–49
Jovičić, Radoslav, 313n40
JRZ, 24
Judicial reform/s, 136, 142, 145, 151, 155, 156, 215 (vetting) 142

INDEX

INDEX

INDEX

INDEX

INDEX

127 (Council of Peoples) 129, 130, 210–212, 297n32, 317n81 (defence minister resignation) 304n92 (dissolution) 260 (economy) 196 (ethno-national composition in 1991) 101 (ethno-national composition of government) 129 (extradition) 87 (extraordinary 1997 elections) 112 (government) 130, 203, 214, 221 (government building) 199, 203 (independence referendum) 177 (Interior Ministry) 148 (international support) 114, 115 (Law on Holidays) 234 (leaders/ leadership) 94, 202, 206, 226, 277, 300n64, 304n93 (media) 112 (military intelligence service) 157 (municipal government) 87 (national bank) 87 (Official Gazette) 206 (oil industry) 197, 311n24 (parliament) 87 (police) 149, 164, 299n50 (power struggle) 105, 110, 117 (president) 87, 315n69 (prime minister) 87 (Prosecutor's Office) 208 (representational offices) 312n37 (representatives) 163 (secession) 232, 237, 238, 277 (Senate) 87 (sovereignty) 87, 197, 198 (special parallel relationship with Serbia) 90 (Srebrenica apology) 139 (Srebrenica Commission) 138 (Supreme Court) 87, 129 (tax administration) 160 (UN Security Council reports) 203 (US lobbying) 203 ('vital-interest' mechanism) 101 (vice president) 87, 315n69 (vulnerable geography) 83, 237, 257 (western half) 109
Republika Srpska Constitutional Court, 87, 129, 211, 130

(rulebook) 211 (Vital National Interest Panel) 130, 211
Republika Srpska Krajina, see RSK
Republika Srpska National Assembly, 72, 87, 90, 98, 104, 111–113, 117, 128–130, 163, 178, 188, 196, 202, 204, 205, 211, 214, 216, 234, 236, 296n25 (1996 elections) (conclusions) 196, 202, 204, 205, 216 (dissolution) 111 (referendum legislation) 214, 215, 236
Research and Documentation Centre, 67, 140
Responsibility to prevent, 256
Responsibility to Protect, 255, 256
Responsibility to react, 256
Responsibility to rebuild, 256
Restitution legislation, 304n87
Return and Reconstruction Task Force, 122, 296n20, 296n22
Returnees, 122, 123, 195, 226, 235 (Bosniak) 195, 226 (Srebrenica) 195
Return/s, 92, 97, 114, 121–123, 148, 170, 242, 243, 257, 270 (data) 243 (minority) 122, 123 (failure of) 242 (non-Serb) 257 (process) 114, 242 (refugee) 148, 270 (refugees and displaced) 92, 97, 121
Rhetoric, xviii, 2, 33, 47, 70, 71, 165, 170, 171, 176, 177, 179–183, 193–195, 203, 214, 218, 229, 237, 242, 244, 266, 274, 276 (Dodik) 170, 176, 183, 195, 203, 214, 237
Riga Summit, 159
Riots, 227, 233, 276 (Belgrade, 9 March 1991) 45, 47, 57 (Mostar, Sarajevo, Tuzla and Zenica, February 2014) 227, 233
Road Map for Bosnia, 154, 155, 163
Robinson, David M., 296n24
Roma, 29, 212, 282n11 (dead in Second World War) 29

INDEX

INDEX

INDEX

INDEX

INDEX